Cyberlaw for Global E-Business:
Finance, Payments, and Dispute Resolution

Takashi Kubota
Waseda University, Japan

Information Science REFERENCE

INFORMATION SCIENCE REFERENCE
Hershey · New York

Acquisitions Editor:	Kristin Klinger
Development Editor:	Kristin Roth
Senior Managing Editor:	Jennifer Neidig
Managing Editor:	Sara Reed
Copy Editor:	Joy Langel
Typesetter:	Jeff Ash
Cover Design:	Lisa Tosheff
Printed at:	Yurchak Printing Inc.

Published in the United States of America by
Information Science Reference (an imprint of IGI Global)
701 E. Chocolate Avenue, Suite 200
Hershey PA 17033
Tel: 717-533-8845
Fax: 717-533-8661
E-mail: cust@igi-global.com
Web site: http://www.igi-global.com

and in the United Kingdom by
Information Science Reference (an imprint of IGI Global)
3 Henrietta Street
Covent Garden
London WC2E 8LU
Tel: 44 20 7240 0856
Fax: 44 20 7379 0609
Web site: http://www.eurospanonline.com

Copyright © 2008 by IGI Global. All rights reserved. No part of this publication may be reproduced, stored or distributed in any form or by any means, electronic or mechanical, including photocopying, without written permission from the publisher.

Product or company names used in this set are for identification purposes only. Inclusion of the names of the products or companies does not indicate a claim of ownership by IGI Global of the trademark or registered trademark.

Library of Congress Cataloging-in-Publication Data

Cyberlaw for global E-business : finance, payment, and dispute resolution / Takashi Kubota, editor.

  p. cm.

  Summary: "This book examines cyberlaw discussions on topics such as cybercrime and risk management, electronic trading systems of securities, digital currency regulation, jurisdiction and consumer protection in cross-border markets, and international bank transfers. An invaluable resource for business experts, lawyers, scholars, and researchers, it provides comprehensive research from a global perspective on the legal and financial implications of e-business"--Provided by publisher.

  Includes bibliographical references and index.

  ISBN-13: 978-1-59904-828-4 (hardcover)

  ISBN-13: 978-1-59904-830-7 (ebook)

  1. Electronic commerce--Law and legislation. 2. Computer crimes. 3. Electronic trading of securities--Law and legislation. 4. Electronic commerce--Law and legislation--Japan. I. Kubota, Takashi.

  K1005C93 2008

  343.09'944--dc22

                                2007023535

British Cataloguing in Publication Data
A Cataloguing in Publication record for this book is available from the British Library.

All work contributed to this book set is new, previously-unpublished material. The views expressed in this book are those of the authors, but not necessarily of the publisher.

Table of Contents

Foreword xi

Preface xiii

Acknowledgment xxii

Section I
E-Finance

Chapter I
Cybercrime, Cybersecurity, and Financial Institutions Worldwide / *Pauline C. Reich* 1

Chapter II
Enhancing Cyber Risk Management with the Framework of ERM and Basel II /
Junji Hiwatashi 34

Chapter III
IT Development and the Separation of Banking and Commerce: Comparative Perspectives
of the U.S. and Japan / *Takashi Kubota* 53

Chapter IV
Laws and Regulations on Proprietary Trading System (PTS) in Japan:
Japanese Alternative Trading System (ATS) /
Motoaki Tazawa 67

Chapter V
The Holding and Transfer of Interests in Securities in England and Japan Compared
with the Holding and Transfer of Funds / *Tomonori Fujiike* 88

Section II
E-Payment

Chapter VI
Global Trends of Payment Systems and the Next-Generation RTGS Project in Japan /
Masaashi Nakajima 109

Chapter VII
Technical and Legal Concerns about Global Card Payments / *Fernando Barrio* 128

Chapter VIII
The Regulation of New Forms of Electronic Fund Transfers in Japan Focusing on
Electronic Money / *Takashi Nakazaki* 142

Chapter IX
Commodity Based Digital Currency: A Legal Analysis / *Evelyn Lim Meow Hoong* 168

Chapter X
Mistakes in Remittance to Account / *Masao Yanaga* 182

Section III
E-Contracts and Dispute Resolution

Chapter XI
Doing International Business Online for the Small and Medium Enterprise / *Sam Edwards* 195

Chapter XII
Consumer Protection in Cross-Border E-Commerce Markets / *Shino Uenuma* 210

Chapter XIII
Cyber Contract and Indian Law / *Jibitesh Mishra and Biswajit Tripathy* 227

Chapter XIV
E-Commerce and Dispute Resolution: Jurisdiction and Applicable Law in a Dispute
Arising from a Computer Information Transaction / *Naoshi Takasugi* 239

Chapter XV
Cross-Border Court Jurisdiction and Economic Law Application in Electronic
Commerce / *Takeshi Kawana* 255

Compilation of References 272

About the Contributors 287

Index 291

Detailed Table of Contents

Foreword xi

Preface xiii

Acknowledgment xxii

Section I
E-Finance

Chapter I
Cybercrime, Cybersecurity, and Financial Institutions Worldwide / *Pauline C. Reich* 1

While the benefits of the Internet and other forms of computer networks are streamlining financial institutions, the same institutions are often among the first institutions to be affected by Cybercrime and Cybersecurity issues due to the financial incentives as well as their strategic place in each nation's infrastructure and economy. We must look not only at the efficiency, but also at the negative aspects of the use of technology by financial institutions. Consumers as well as businesses must be well informed about conducting transactions in the safest manner possible. The nature of the Internet is cross-border, and thus Cybercrime and Internet Security issues involving financial institutions should be made known by international organizations, regional organizations, and when there have been cross-border law enforcement collaborations in investigations, extraditions, and so forth. At present, due to the fact that law is generally written at the national (or even state level, as is the case of Identity Theft law in the U.S.), there is a need for reporting of cross-border cases in the literature if such data can be obtained from law enforcement officials by scholars.

Chapter II
Enhancing Cyber Risk Management with the Framework of ERM and Basel II /
Junji Hiwatashi 34

How is it possible to enhance efficiency of management and to control cyber risk at the same time so that sustainable growth is achieved? Possible solutions were found in ERM and Basel II. First, a newly introduced ERM is a tool not only for defense against loss but also for a formidable weapon to seek sustainable returns. Appropriate coordination and cooperation in implementing risk management on a firm-wide basis encourages firms to identify, analyze, measure and control all material risks such as cyber risk, and to provide a sound base to make strategic decision on the balance of risk and return, or risk adjusted return on equity. Second, in Basel II, operational risk such as cyber risk is explicitly introduced. The author proposes a practical framework based on ERM and Basel II. It consists of policies and structure, and five steps. This framework is based on the practices of financial institutions but could be applied and expanded to firms in general.

Chapter III
IT Development and the Separation of Banking and Commerce: Comparative Perspectives
of the U.S. and Japan / *Takashi Kubota* 53

Unlike the UK, Germany, France, and some major countries that permit entries from banking to commerce and vice versa ("two-way" regulation), the United States and Japan have maintained a policy of separating banking and commerce out of concern that the mixing of the two activities would result in the misallocation of credits, anti-competitive effects, exposure of deposit insurance, and taxpayers to greater risks from commerce and additional supervisory burdens on banking and antitrust regulators. However, this separation is now being reconsidered both in the U.S. and Japan. With IT development, linking online banking and Internet commerce may increase profitability through operating synergies between the two firms and reduce average costs and information costs. Future changes in the financial environment may produce other synergies and the degree of separation should be suitable for such business development. This chapter introduces current laws and discussions in both countries and considers the future of the separation policy in Japan.

Chapter IV
Laws and Regulations on Proprietary Trading System (PTS) in Japan /
Motoaki Tazawa 67

In order to improve convenience for investors through competition among stock exchanges, operation of Proprietary Trading Systems (PTS) was authorized as a form of securities business under the Securities and Exchange Act. The Japanese PTS is equivalent to ATS (Alternative Trading System) ECNs (Electronic Communications Network) in the United States and MTF (Multilateral Trading Facilities) under MiFID in the EU. In 1998, ATS ECNs had already started in the United States and Japan's PTS followed the U.S. model. Telecommunication and information technologies and computer technologies made PTS possible, and PTS make the border between the market and brokers ambiguous. Traditional regulations on broker-dealers and stock exchanges will inevitably be reviewed and regulations on securities markets will have to be reformed.

Chapter V
The Holding and Transfer of Interests in Securities in England and Japan Compared
with the Holding and Transfer of Funds / *Tomonori Fujiike* 88

This chapter compares account-based securities settlement systems with payment systems in which funds are transferred through bank accounts in England and Japan and examines a desirable securities system to harmonize the relevant countries' jurisprudence considering U.S. securities system and relevant international trends. It argues that there should be two broad areas of similarity in both systems;

compartmentalization of a legal relationship between related parties and the method of transfer of securities and funds. It also argues, however, that, due to the differences in the legal nature of both financial assets, there are some differences between both systems in order to response intermediary risk. The purpose of this chapter is not only to propose that similar legal issues in both systems should be resolved in the same ways as much as possible, but also to distinguish issues which could be resolved in commercial law from issues which should be resolved in the field of regulations by financial authorities in securities system.

Section II
E-Payment

Chapter VI
Global Trends of Payment Systems and the Next-Generation RTGS Project in Japan:
Japanese Alternative Trading System (ATS) /
Masaashi Nakajima 109

This chapter investigates the evolutionary process of the payment system against the background of structural changes. At the early stage, most payment systems were Designated-Time Net Settlement (DTNS) systems. Then, Real-Time Gross Settlement (RTGS) systems were introduced, which had the merit of reducing settlement risks. This first trend was followed by the deployment of Hybrid systems and Integrated systems. The Bank of Japan (BOJ) is proceeding with the Next-Generation RTGS (RTGS-XG) project. This project is regarded as a typical enhancement of payment systems following the global trend. The features and benefits of the RTGS-XG are closely analyzed.

Chapter VII
Technical and Legal Concerns about Global Card Payments / *Fernando Barrio* 128

Well into the first decade of the twenty-first century, it is fair to say that card payments are the cyberspace payment method by definition and, therefore, in order not to deter the development of commercial transactions carried out by electronic means, they should be accepted globally in the same or similar manner, which also means that the technology and rules applicable to them should be the same or closely harmonized. However, as this chapter tries to explain, while there are some characteristics that have made cards' acceptance truly global in scope, there have been historical, economic, and regulatory forces that resulted in different jurisdictions favoring the use of different technologies and different legal architectures for the deployment and control of cards as a means of payment, which may both obstruct the possibility of extending the benefits derived from the use of card payments and avoid the extension of the negative features associated with their utilization.

Chapter VIII
The Regulation of New Forms of Electronic Fund Transfers in Japan Focusing on
Electronic Money / *Takashi Nakazaki* 142

In this chapter, after surveying existing Japanese public laws that regulate the transfer of funds via the Internet, and focusing on electronic money in particular, It will be discussed how these existing regulations may apply to new electronic payment methods that may not have been accounted for when these regulations were established, whether the regulations are sufficient to both provide convenience to the user and protect their safety, and whether these regulations are desirable as business conditions for developing electronic money. Through these discussions, certain objectives will be developed, which should be taken into account when developing regulations in Japan on the transfer of funds via the Internet. Also, this chapter discusses anti-money laundering regulations applicable to transfers of funds on the Internet, focusing on electronic money, and will examine how Japanese money laundering regulations may apply to cross-border transfers of funds using overseas electronic money services. Through this examination, the chapter will attempt to suggest desirable money laundering regulations on domestic electronic money in the near future. Furthermore, this chapter discusses real money trade and point-rewarded programs in view of function of payment or transferring funds electronically in extended research sections, and closes by predicting future research directions.

Chapter IX
Commodity Based Digital Currency: A Legal Analysis / *Evelyn Lim Meow Hoong* 168

Financial innovations bring new challenges and new risks besides advantages to the world of finance in cyberspace and in the real world. These innovations evolve alongside the development of cyberspace creating more e-business opportunities. One such innovation is digital currency. As cyberspace develops, this financial innovation allows more and more players into a formerly closed market of providing a medium of intrinsic purchasing power which was generally supplied by a nation's central bank in the form of money. What then, is the legal status of this digital currency in a nation?

Chapter X
Mistakes in Remittance to Account / *Masao Yanaga* 182

Some courts have recently ruled in Japan with regard to mistakes in remittance to account. While the Supreme Court held that the recipient has become a depositor of a savings deposit as much as the remitted amount of the receiving bank as a result of a remittance, and the recipient obtains a bank deposit in the amount equivalent to the transferred amount, even where there was no legal relationship which could be used as a legal basis for the remittance between the person who requested the remittance and the recipient, it held that the person who made a demand for repayment of a bank deposit while knowing that there was a remittance to account made into its bank account by error, and received the repayment shall be guilty of fraud. In addition, some lower courts held that it is fair and equitable to interpret that the receiving bank must directly refund to the originator with regard to the originator's claim to refund, as much as the amount of the erroneous remittance as unjustified enrichment. Thus, the position of Japanese courts is still in disarray in respect to the legal consequences of mistakes in remittance to account.

Section III
E-Contracts and Dispute Resolution

Chapter XI
Doing International Business Online for the Small and Medium Enterprise / *Sam Edwards* 195

This chapter addresses the primary difficulties that small and medium enterprises face when doing business online with international partners. The guidance provided in this chapter is primarily for owners of small and medium enterprises rather than legal for professionals. The two main problems inhibiting online transactions are a lack of trust between the parties and the risk inherent in the exchange. This chapter analyzes ways to address these problems. Many of the practical suggestions in this chapter are inspired not by million dollar deals but by playground transactions between children. Often the simple solutions are the best ones.

Chapter XII
Consumer Protection in Cross-Border E-Commerce Markets / *Shino Uenuma.* 210

Due to the development of the Internet, global e-commerce markets are growing greatly. From the viewpoint of consumers, cross-border transactions involve some difficulties in obtaining redress from problematic businesses. In e-commerce markets, consumers have also experienced other kinds of difficulty. To increase consumer protection in global e-commerce markets, various attempts have been made by the private and public sectors. This chapter gives an overview of current attempts, and considers the possibility of future methods to achieve effective consumer protection in cross-border e-commerce markets.

Chapter XIII
Cyber Contract and Indian Law / *Jibitesh Mishra and Biswajit Tripathy* 227

The usage of cyber contracts has increased exponentially in the recent times. However, the framework for this has not been clearly defined. The jurisdiction is also a major issue. In this chapter, we have revisited various types of electronic contacts, the cyber contract in the Indian content, and made an effort to find a uniform framework for this.

Chapter XIV
E-Commerce and Dispute Resolution: Jurisdiction and Applicable Law in a Dispute
Arising from a Computer Information Transaction / *Naoshi Takasugi* 239

When a dispute arises from e-commerce involving parties located in different nations, the parties immediately face conflict-of-laws issues such as judicial jurisdiction, applicable law, and extra-territorial effects of judgments. Taking into consideration that there is no unified conflicts law rules in the global level and, if any, the conflicts rules are usually based on the traditional international transactions, this chapter tries to discuss the dispute resolution systems suitable for e-commerce, especially for computer information transactions. As the result of the discussion, it becomes clear that further enhancement of a worldwide dispute resolution system suitable for e-commerce is desirable. In establishing a new system, the 1999 Guidelines for Consumer Protection in the context of electronic commerce, approved by the OECD, gives much inspiration. It is essential to balance between small-middle sized business entities and consumers, and between freedom and regulation.

Chapter XV
Cross-Border Court Jurisdiction and Economic Law Application in Electronic
Commerce / *Takeshi Kawana* 255

The purpose of this chapter is to examine international jurisdiction and choice of law for e-commerce involving economic legal issues. International jurisdiction and choice of law will be determined under private legal principles, but as e-commerce involves economic law as a law to ensure national economic stability, the court may consider economic law with both private and public legal functions. At that time there may be some conflict of law involving state economic policy, and it must be considered how to coordinate the conflict and create a universal legal structure for non-territorial cyberspace. This chapter will propose three layers of legal structure for e-commerce: the private law layer, the economic law layer, and the criminal law layer, all of which have perspectives for borderless cyberspace.

Compilation of References 272

About the Contributors 287

Index 291

Foreword

This book is about cyberlaw for global e-business, focusing especially on e-finance, e-payments, e-contracts, and dispute resolution. The development of e-business in recent years has led to a variety of legal issues concerning e-contracts, e-payments, dispute resolution, the field of e-finance, and in some cases intellectual property rights and taxes. However, national cyberlaw has proven too under-developed to deal with these issues that arise in e-business. In order to further develop the rules for global e-business a global approach based on each nation's experience in the international exchange of knowledge and know-how is needed.

Adopting this kind of global approach, this book discusses 15 of the latest topics regarding cyber laws, topics not only of present relevant, but also of future importance. With an array of talented contributors, ranging from leading lawyers, scholars, and policy-making authority officials from Japan, to distinguished lawyers, scholars, and experts from the United States, the United Kingdom, India, and Malaysia, this book offers an unprecedented in-depth analysis of cyberlaw issues arising in e-business, resulting in a unique collection of academic yet practical papers.

Three features make this book unique. Firstly, because this book utilizes the work of numerous experts who have been deeply involved in e-commerce policy making in Japan (one of the world's largest e-commerce markets second to America), this work will not only contribute to the limited English publications in this field, but will also provide insight to the state of affairs in Japan, a topic whose English publication is scarce. Secondly, besides experts from major developed nations like the U.S., the UK, and Japan, contributors also include specialists from India, Malaysia, and other emerging nations that have had success with policies promoting e-commerce, providing for a piece that offers a wide range of perspectives in this field. Finally, because the contributors, both scholars and business people, have actual experience with e-commerce, the analysis in this book is both theoretical and practical in perspective, making it a "useful book" for practitioners such as lawyers and specialists in the IT industry.

Although the topics covered are both diverse in region and reality, all are essential points when considering issues that arise in e-business. Section I: cybercrime, cyber risk management, Basel II, separation of banking and commerce, and PTS will deal with issues at the root of systems and infrastructure. Section II: paperless securities payment systems, global trends of funds payment systems, global card payments, new forms of electronic money, and commodity-based digital currency will deal with issues concerning new payment and currencies that accompany e-business. Section III: mistakes in remittance to account, doing international business online for small and medium enterprises, global consumer protection, cyber contracts, applicable law and dispute resolution, and economic law applications deals with law, practice, and theory involved in global contracts and dispute resolution. Reading through these sections, the reader can gain an understanding as to the problems and state of affairs of local attempts towards global developments in cyberspace and e-business, as well as gain insight as to what global measures can be taken in regards to these issues.

Of the book's contributors, Professor Takashi Kubota, Professor Masao Yanaga, and Professor Motoaki Tazawa are fellow researchers with whom I have been working for several years on the Group for International Finance of the "Transparency of Japanese Law Project," a Ministry of Education, Culture, Sports, Science, and Technology (MEXT) Specified Field Research Project. My other colleagues Koji Kinoshita (Professor, Doshisha University, Japan), Noritaka Yamashita (Associate Professor, Osaka University, Japan), Tetsuro Morishita (Associate Professor, Sophia University, Japan), and Mami Shimomura (Professor, Osaka University, Japan) screened submitted papers as reviewers. Therefore, as the title of this book suggests, this work is the first published product of the joint research conducted by members of the Group for International Finance of the "Transparency of Japanese Law Project." We are constantly looking to further develop research about financial law in the global society, so responses from readers are warmly invited.

Yoshiaki Nomura
Osaka University, Japan
November 2007

Yoshiaki Nomura is a professor and former dean at Osaka School of International Public Policy, Osaka University, Japan. He obtained a LLM at Harvard (1986) and a LLB at Osaka University (1976). His specialties include international business law, international private law, international civil litigation, international economic law, and negotiation.

Preface

Though Internet business is dramatically growing, the legal response to it is inadequate and trails behind actual development. Textbooks and reference books on laws give detailed explanations regarding older models of online business but do not handle new issues very well. On the other hand, it is difficult for business people and lawyers involved in the Internet business to solve problems newly arising from the Internet based only on conventional knowledge. Even for business people and researchers who are not directly engaged in legal matters, it is indispensable to understand trends of legal issues to some extent for business planning or researching social impacts of such issues. Also, it is clear that many government officials and consultants involved in making laws related to Internet business must understand the latest legal issues.

In this book, experts and lawyers well versed in Internet business explain the latest topics, starting from the basic concepts in an easily understood way. This book focuses on fields that are very fundamental and that involving many legal issues including e-finance, e-payment, e-commerce, and dispute resolution. Legal issues related to Internet business are diverse and naturally involve intellectual property rights, antimonopoly laws, tax laws, and other regulations, detailed analysis of which, however, exceeds the limited space of this book. Yet, knowledge and concepts you will obtain from this book will be a resource to help you analyze those issues on your own. Most of the writers of this book are Japanese and many Japanese cases are cited, which may provide many cases interesting to readers from other nations, as few results of legal study in those fields in Japan have been published in English.

A. DEVELOPMENT OF THE CYBER LAWS

A variety of international and domestic standards have been created to deal with global development of Internet business. The United Nations Commission on International Trade Law (UNCITRAL) adopted the UNCITRAL Model Law on Electronic Commerce in 1996, which stipulates basic rules concerning electronic commerce, and the UNCXITRAL Model Law on Electronic Signatures in 2001, which provides rules on legal effectiveness of electronic signatures, and is used as a model that member nations can refer to when establishing domestic laws. The United States (U.S.), the European Union (EU), and Asian nations, have regarded e-commerce promotion as an important national policy while competing with each other. The U.S., where e-commerce is most developed, was active in legislation from the start, adopting in 1999 the Uniform Electronic Transaction Act (UETA) and the United Computer Information Transaction Act (UCITA), advising each state to establish relevant laws, and establishing the Electronic Signatures in Global and National Commerce Act (E-Sign Act). The EU issued EU directives regarding e-commerce and e-signature about the same time as the U.S. to unify e-commerce legislation in the EU territory.

Preparation of legislation is also being promoted in many Asian nations, including Singapore, Malaysia, South Korea, and Japan. For example, for consumer protection, the Organization for Economic Cooperation and Development (OECD) Guidelines for Consumer Protection in the Context of Electronic Commerce (1999) and the OECD Guidelines for Protecting Consumers from Fraudulent and Deceptive Commercial Practices Across Borders (2003), both stipulated by the OECD, are observed among the member nations. Efforts continue to establish international standards for intellectual property rights and international taxation concerning to e-commerce. Methods for handling e-commerce and Internet business have also been kept in mind in drawing up conventional international standards, such as for general rules of contracts, financial regulations, and dispute resolution.

Still, such efforts have been inadequate, and preparation of legislation always lags behind the diverse development of Internet business. To cope with elements that do not have adequately-prepared legislation, online business specialists and lawyers should attempt original interpretation of laws, prepare contracts coping with risks, or prompt the government to draw up fresh legislation.

An actual example that has already been resolved is cited. For online shopping, it is more efficient to prepare a system selling through account settlement independently than to seek assistance from a bank. However, in Japan, creating such a system has been considered difficult until recently because banks exclusively handle account settlement business. As a result of urging by online businesses, the Financial Services Agency deregulated account settlement, and since 1999 it has become easy for online businesses to obtain licenses related to Internet banking business. As for controversial issues about banks' demand to be allowed to enter into commerce, as a result of commercial businesses being allowed entry to banking, please refer to Chapter III of this book, in which situations in Japan, the U.S., and Europe are compared.

There are also problems that have begun to see clues to resolution but are yet to be resolved. In such an instance, in 2007, the Japanese Ministry of Economy, Trade and Industry (METI) started considering drawing up rules on a point-accumulation service system operated by a variety of businesses including discount stores, shopping malls, and airlines, as perks for their customers. METI believes that approximately one trillion yen worth of points have been issued in Japan, but such rules as to stipulate how to deal with points in case the company that issued the points has gone bankrupt, and how to protect consumers and personal information, have not been established and requires serious and urgent attention.

On the other hand, there are unresolved problems yet for which no solutions are in sight. One example is regulation of real money trade (RMT), exchange of virtual currency earned in online games for actual currency, such as dollars and yen. Though RMT is against the rules in many online games, many traders who exchange game currency for legal tender exist. There are many criminal groups gaining profits by earning game currency in China and other areas, with a market on a scale of over 15 billion yen. Existing laws, including criminal rules and taxation rules, are applicable to real space but not to virtual space. Thus RMT, which is not under control of established legislation, has gone underground and become a hotbed of fraud and money laundering. If the market scale continues to expand, the RMT problems may be big trouble for consumer protection and financial policy. Under those circumstances, an online game entitled Second Life appeared in the U.S. and about 10 million people have taken part in it. Exchanging game currency to real currency is officially approved under the rules of the game, which draws attention to the game as an attempt to pull RMT out of the underground. Development of Second Life may influence future decisions on policy regarding whether RMT should be made illegal or legal by regulations. Meanwhile, continuous deliberation is necessary regarding how to apply existing laws, which have been established to suit to real space, to virtual space.

Those points and game currency can be regarded as a form derived from cyber cash, which used to be discussed as electronic money. Many other forms of electronic money keep popping up everywhere in the globe, and extensive study on such money is required. Therefore, some chapters (VII through IX) in the second section elaborate on developing forms of electronic money while money laundering is covered in Chapter I.

B. STRUCTURE OF THE BOOK

Each of the three sections are explained very briefly. The detailed summary will be shown subsequently.

E-Finance

E-finance means e-business with wholesale or large value financial transactions except funds payment systems that are dealt with as e-payments. The legal concern is how to secure the stability and soundness of the rapidly growing market. E-finance includes not only the online activities of banks, securities firms, insurance companies, and others, but also the paperless transactions of securities. Without adequate supervision or standard rules, a huge systemic risk may arise.

The most important topics now in the global e-finance laws include: cybercrimes (Chapter I), cyber risk management (Chapter II), lifting the separation of banking and commerce (Chapter III), and electronic securities trading (Chapters IV and V). Cyberspace is now a hotbed of frauds, larceny, and money laundering. It is an urgent issue of criminal law study to shed light on its mechanism and to hammer out countermeasures. Financial institutions have risk management issues about how to cope with cyber risks while conforming to standards of the exchange rate mechanism (ERM) and Basel II. Further, there are some moves to revise the separation of banks from commerce in accordance with development of e-commerce, which is an issue for bank laws in Japan and the U.S., among other nations. As securities exchange has also been computerized, regulations on the alternative trading system (ATS) and international paperless account settlement are actively debated. The first section focuses on those latest issues.

E-Payments

E-payment means e-business with retail or small value financial transactions, but this book also covers large-value funds payment systems. E-payment is an element essential for almost all the online businesses, and it is indispensable for success in business to fully understand the latest legal issues regarding e-payment. The legal concerns are from both sides: consumer protection and the industry development or systemic risk perspectives. Traditional means include online credit cards, debit cards, e-money, and bank transfer. New types of money have emerged such as "point mileage banks" not run by banks and without supervision. Point mileage banks deal with points, not money. Thus we need to consider how to regulate it: the same as banks or as other ordinary business. On the other hand, the existing bank transfer system is not always consumer-friendly. Japanese banks did not care about the deposits stolen through the ATM network (Only recently Japan adopted the U.S. style $50 rule). The Japanese government is currently considering credit card payments, with adequate technical support like e-scott offered by SONY International, to be more effective measures against Internet auction fraud.

This section includes the most important recent topics: wholesale funds payment systems (Chapter VI), global card payments (Chapter VII), new types of e-money (Chapter VIII), commodity based digital currency (Chapter IX), bank transfer by errors (Chapter X). Large account settlement systems between banks are now facing big changes. Studying the moves of the changes is important for financial management of online business. Meanwhile, technical and legal issues of account settlement of credit cards, which plays a vital role in cyberspace, should be examined. Various types of e-money and commodity-based money, such as e-gold, have been developed all over the world, and how to comprehend them in terms of law is important both in the practical and academic phase. In addition, legal analysis of erroneous money transfers is a major issue for bank business rules. The second section focuses on those latest issues.

E-Contracts and Dispute Resolution

Internet business always entails electronic contract conclusion and cannot avoid being involved in dispute settlement in cyberspace. Different from regular contracts written on paper, contracts sealed in cyberspace are usually regulated under special legislation drawn up by each nation. While information on such legislation of the U.S., European and Asian nations are relatively easy to obtain, that of India and other newly-emerging nations is actually hard to get. Also in cyberspace, there are many cases in which it is unclear which country's law should be applied, or which country's courts should have jurisdiction, even if existing international private laws and international court jurisdiction rules are applied. Though many legal debates have taken place, the number of documents that sorted out those debates straightforwardly is not necessarily large.

This section includes useful guidance of most important topics as follows: doing international business online for the small and medium enterprise (Chapter XI), consumer protection in the cross-border e-commerce market (Chapter XII), cyber contracts and Indian law (Chapter XIII), e-commerce and private international law and jurisdiction (Chapter XIV), and cross-border court jurisdiction and economic law application in e-commerce (Chapter XV). Internet business is a field in which small and medium sized companies have more entries than large companies. Guidance about specific legal issues involved in launching an international online business for mid and small-sized companies is essential. Meanwhile, it is a little surprising that it has been unclear what kind of relief measures are available for consumers caught in trouble related to international Internet business. In this book, the most progressive experts offer specific advice regarding the matter. Also, e-contract laws of India, which is said to be an IT power but whose whole picture has not been unveiled compared to that of developed nations, is explained. In addition, international private laws and jurisdiction, and how much control regulations of a nation can have in cyberspace are logically discussed.

C. SECTION I: E-FINANCE

Chapter I: Cybercrime, Cybersecurity, and Financial Institutions Worldwide

While the benefits of the Internet and other forms of computer networks are streamlining financial institutions, the same institutions are often among the first institutions to be affected by cybercrime and cybersecurity issues due to the financial incentives as well as their strategic place in each nation's infrastructure and economy. We must look not only at the efficiency, but also at the negative aspects of the use of technology by financial institutions. Consumers as well as business must be well informed about conducting transactions in the safest manner possible. The nature of the Internet is cross-border, and thus cybercrime and Internet Security issues involving financial institutions should be made known by international organizations, regional organizations and when there have been cross-border law enforcement collaborations in investigations, extraditions, and so forth. At present, due to the fact that law is generally written at the national (or even state level, as is the case of Identity Theft law in the U.S.), there is a need for reporting of cross-border cases in the literature if such data can be obtained from law enforcement officials by scholars.

Chapter II: Enhancing Cyber Risk Management with the Framework of ERM and Basel II

Information technology (IT) has been rapidly developed to provide financial services with customers by the Internet. This service is available for 24 hours a day, 7 days a week beyond the boundary. On the other hand, technology-oriented financial services may face various cyber risks such as disruption caused by natural disaster and terrorist attack, impersonation and other events stemming from unauthorized access, and theft or alternation of data. Once these events occur, they could affect not only companies such as financial institutions but also their stakeholders such as customers and financial stability. These events lead to indirect effects such as lawsuits and bad reputation losing sound customer base immediately. Thus, it is critical to enhance cyber risk management in advance before nightmare in order to enjoy the benefits of IT. This chapter introduces the practical methods of enhancing cyber risk management efficiently and effectively with the framework of enterprise risk management (ERM) and Basel Accord II (Basel II). It aims to learn how to enhance cyber risk management as well as efficiency so that sustainable growth is achieved with the balance between risk and return or risk-adjusted return on equity.

Chapter III: IT Development and the Separation of Banking and Commerce: Comparative Perspectives of the U.S. and Japan

Unlike the UK, Germany, France, and some major countries that permit entries from banking to commerce and vice versa ("two-way" regulation), the United States and Japan have maintained a policy of separating banking and commerce out of concern that the mixing of the two activities would result in the misallocation of credits, anti-competitive effects, exposure of the deposit insurance and taxpayers to greater risks from commerce, and additional supervisory burdens on banking and antitrust regulators. However, this separation is now being reconsidered both in the U.S. and Japan. With IT development, linking online banking and Internet commerce may increase profitability through operating synergies between the two firms, and reduce average costs and information costs. Future changes in the financial environment may produce other synergies and the degree of separation should be suitable for such business development. This chapter introduces current laws and discussions in both countries and considers the future of the separation policy in Japan.

Chapter IV: Laws and Regulations on Proprietary Trading System (PTS) in Japan

In order to improve convenience of investors through competition among stock exchanges, operation of proprietary trading system (PTS) was authorized as one of the securities businesses under the Securities and Exchange Act. The Japanese PTS is equal to ATS (alternative trading system), ECN (electronic communications network) of the United States and MTF (multilateral trading facilities) of MiFID of EU. In 1998, ATS and ECN already started in the United States and PTS of Japan followed the U.S. model. Telecommunication and information technologies and computer technologies realized PTS and PTS is making the border between the market and brokers ambiguous. Traditional regulations on broker-dealers and stock exchanges will be inevitably reviewed and the regulations on securities markets will be unable to avoid reform.

Chapter V: The Holding and Transfer of Interests in Securities in England and Japan Compared with the Holding and Transfer of Funds

The purpose of this chapter is to compare indirectly held securities systems with funds transfers systems in order to examine whether the similar related risks and legal issues can be solved in the same way in the field of private commercial law. Under the indirectly held securities system, securities certificates are "immobilized" or "dematerialized," so that transfers of interests in securities are implemented through the adjustment of balances in relevant accounts instead of through the physical delivery of certificates. Such a system appears similar to the system relating to the holding and transfer of funds through bank accounts although interests in securities have been regarded as proprietary rights whereas monetary deposits amount to mere personal rights enforceable against banks. In addition, this chapter aims, in comparing the legal systems of relevant countries, to harmonize the relevant in order to avoid the inconsistency of laws in cross-border securities transactions. In comparing national legal systems, Japanese law and English law (including applicable EU law) will be mainly considered. Furthermore, as the need arises, consideration will be given to U.S. securities systems and relevant international trends.

D. SECTION II: E-PAYMENT

Chapter VI: Global Trends of Payment Systems and the Next-Generation RTGS Project in Japan

This chapter investigates the evolutionary process of the payment system with the background of the structural changes. At the early stage, most of the payment systems were the Designated-Time Net Settlement (DTNS) systems. Then, the Real-Time Gross Settlement (RTGS) systems were introduced, which had the merit of reducing the settlement risks. This first trend was followed by the deployment of the Hybrid Systems and the Integrated Systems. The Bank of Japan (BOJ) proceeds with the Next-Generation RTGS (RTGS-XG) project. This project is regarded as a typical enhancement of payment system following the global trend. The features and benefits of the RTGS-XG are closely analyzed.

Chapter VII: Technical and Legal Concerns about Global Card Payments

Well into the first decade of the 21st century, it is fair to say that card payments are the cyberspace payment methods per antonomasia and, therefore, in order to not imply a deterrence to the development of commercial transactions carried out by electronic means, they should be accepted globally in the same or similar manner, which also means that the technology and rules applicable to them should be the same or closely harmonized. However, as this chapter tries to explain, while there are some characteristics that have made cards' acceptance truly global in scope, there have been historical, economic, and regulatory forces that resulted in different jurisdictions favoring the use of different technologies and different legal architectures for the deployment and control of cards as a mean of payment, which may both confabulate with the possibility of extending the benefits derived from the use of card payments and avoid the extension of the negative features associated with their utilization.

Chapter VIII: The Regulation of New Forms of Electronic Fund Transfers in Japan Focusing on Electronic Money

In this chapter, after surveying existing Japanese public laws that regulate the transfer of funds via the Internet, and focusing on Electronic Money in particular, how these existing regulations may apply to new electronic payment methods that may not have been accounted for when these regulations were established will be discussed, whether the regulations are sufficient to both a provide convenience to the user and protect their safety, and whether these regulations are desirable as business conditions for developing Electronic Money. Through these discussions, certain objectives which should be taken into account when developing regulations in Japan on the transfer of funds via the internet will be developed. Also, this chapter discusses anti-money laundering regulations applicable to transfers of funds on the Internet, focusing on Electronic Money, and will examine how Japanese money laundering regulations may apply to cross-border transfers of funds using overseas Electronic Money services. Through this examination, this chapter will attempt to suggest desirable money laundering regulations on domestic Electronic Money in the near future. Furthermore, this chapter discusses real money trade and point-rewarded program in viewpoint of function of payment or transferring funds electronically in the extended research sections, and predicts the future research directions at the end of this chapter.

Chapter IX: Commodity Based Digital Currency: A Legal Analysis

Financial innovations bring new challenges and new risks besides advantages to the world of finance in cyberspace and in the real world. These innovations evolve alongside the development of cyberspace creating more e-business opportunities. One such innovation is the digital currency. As cyberspace develops, this financial innovation allows more and more players into a formerly closed market of providing intrinsic purchasing power medium which was generally supplied by a nation's central bank in the form of money. What is then this digital currency legal status in a nation?

Chapter X: Mistake in Remittance to Account

Some courts have recently ruled in Japan with regard to mistake in remittance to account. While the Supreme Court held that the recipient has become a depositor of a savings deposit as much as the remitted amount of the receiving bank as a result of a remittance, and the recipient obtains a bank deposit in the amount equivalent to the transferred amount even where there was no legal relationship which could be used as a legal basis for the remittance between the person who requested the remittance and the recipient, it held that the person who made a demand for repayment of a bank deposit while knowing that there was a remittance to account made into its bank account by error and received the repayment shall be guilty of fraud. In addition, some lower courts held that it is fair and equitable to interpret that the receiving bank must directly refund to the originator with regard to the originator's claim to refund as much as the amount of the erroneous remittance as unjustified enrichment. Thus, the position of Japanese courts is still in disarray in respect with the legal consequence of mistake in remittance to account.

E. SECTION III: E-CONTRACTS AND DISPUTE RESOLUTION

Chapter XI: Doing International Business Online for the Small and Medium Enterprise

This chapter is designed to address the primary difficulties small and medium enterprises face when doing business online with international partners. The guidance provided in this chapter is primarily for owners of small and medium enterprises rather than legal professionals. The two main problems inhibiting online transactions are a lack of trust between the parties and the risk inherent in the transaction. This chapter analyzes ways to address these problems. Many of the practical suggestions in this chapter are inspired not by million dollar deals but by playground transactions between children. Often the simple solutions are the best ones.

Chapter XII: Consumer Protection in Cross-Border E-Commerce Markets

Due to the development of the Internet, global e-commerce markets are largely growing. From the view point of consumers, cross-border transactions involve some difficulties to get redress against problematic businesses. In e-commerce markets, consumers have also experienced another kind of difficulties. To increase consumer protections in global e-commerce markets, various attempts have been made by private sectors and public sectors. This chapter overviews current attempts, and considers possibility of future methods to realize effective consumer protections in cross-border e-commerce markets.

Chapter XIII: Cyber Contract and Indian Law

The usage of cyber contracts has increased exponentially in the recent times. However, the framework for this has not been clearly defined. The jurisdiction is also a major issue. In this chapter, the electronic contacts of various types and the cyber contract in the Indian content have been revisited and an effort to find out a uniform framework for this has been made.

Chapter XIV: E-Commerce and Dispute Resolution: Jurisdiction and Applicable Law in a Dispute Arising from a Computer Information Transaction

When a dispute arises from e-commerce involving parties located in different nations, the parties immediately face conflict-of-laws issues such as judicial jurisdiction, applicable law, and extra-territorial effects of judgments. Taking into consideration that there is no unified conflicts law rules in the global level and, if any, the conflicts rules are usually based on the traditional international transactions, this chapter tries to discuss the dispute resolution systems suitable for e-commerce, especially for computer information transactions. As the result of the discussion, it becomes clear that further enhancement of worldwide dispute resolution system suitable for e-commerce is desirable. In establishing a new system, the 1999 Guidelines for Consumer Protection in the Context of Electronic Commerce approved by OECD gives us much inspiration. It is essential to balance between small-middle sized business entities and consumers and between freedom and regulation.

Chapter XV: Cross-Border Court Jurisdiction and Economic Law Application in Electronic Commerce

The purpose of this chapter is examining international jurisdiction and choice of law at e-commerce involving economic legal issues. International jurisdiction and choice of law will be determined under the private legal principles, but as e-commerce involves economic law as a law to ensure national economic stability, the court may consider economic law with both private and public legal functions. At that time there may be some conflict of law involving state economic policy, and then it must be considered how to coordinate the conflict and create universal legal structure according to the non-territorial cyberspace. This chapter will propose the three layers of legal structure for e-commerce; private law layer, economic law layer, and criminal law layer, all of which have the viewpoints for the borderless cyberspace.

The research of this book was partially supported by the Japanese Ministry of Education, Science, Sports, and Culture, Grant-in-Aid for 609, 16090101, 2004-2009.

Takashi Kubota
Waseda University, Japan
November 2007

Acknowledgment

With thanks to those who have contributed much to the writing of this book:

1. Institutions:

- United Nations Committee for International Trade Law (UNCITRAL)
- Bank for International Settlements (BIS)
- Committee on International Monetary Law of the International Law Association (MOCOMILA)
- Euroclear
- The Society for Worldwide Interbank Financial Telecommunication (SWIFT)
- U.S. Federal Reserve System
- U.S. Federal Trade Commission (FTC)
- Bank Negara Malaysia
- Bank of Japan (BOJ)
- Japanese Bankers Association (Zenginkyo)
- Japanese Financial Services Agency (FSA)
- Japanese Ministry of Economy, Trade and Industry (METI)
- Next Generation Electronic Commerce Promotion Council of Japan (ECOM)
- IGI Global

2. Persons:

- Kent Anderson, Senior Lecturer, Australian National University, Australia
- Diego Devos, Deputy General Counsel, Legal Service, BIS, Switzerland
- Ignacio Gomez-Sancha, Attorney, Iberoclear, Spain
- Pamela Gonzalez de Cordova, Attorney, Loyens Winandy, Belgium
- Kazuo Iwasaki, Professor Emeritus, Nagoya University, Japan
- Noboru Kashiwagi, Professor Emeritus, University of Tokyo, Japan
- Yutaka Kurihara, Professor, Aichi University, Japan
- Ki-su Lee, Professor Emeritus, Korea University, Korea
- Kenji Sasaki, President, Sasaki International Academy, Japan
- Toshio Sawada, Vice-Chairman, ICC International Court of Arbitration, Japan
- Toshiko Sawada, Executive Director, EC Network, Japan
- Kazuaki Sono, Professor Emeritus, Hokkaido University, Japan

Section I
E–Finance

Chapter I
Cybercrime, Cybersecurity, and Financial Institutions Worldwide

Pauline C. Reich
Waseda University, Japan

ABSTRACT

While the benefits of the Internet and other forms of computer networks are streamlining financial institutions, the same institutions are often among the first institutions to be affected by Cybercrime and Cybersecurity issues due to the financial incentives as well as their strategic place in each nation's infrastructure and economy. We must look not only at the efficiency, but also at the negative aspects of the use of technology by financial institutions. Consumers as well as businesses must be well informed about conducting transactions in the safest manner possible. The nature of the Internet is cross-border, and thus Cybercrime and Internet Security issues involving financial institutions should be made known by international organizations, regional organizations, and when there have been cross-border law enforcement collaborations in investigations, extraditions, and so forth. At present, due to the fact that law is generally written at the national (or even state level, as is the case of Identity Theft law in the U.S.), there is a need for reporting of cross-border cases in the literature if such data can be obtained from law enforcement officials by scholars.

INTRODUCTION

These days, financial institutions in developed and many developing countries worldwide have adopted use of the Internet and computers in their transactions. Unfortunately, criminal elements are often one step ahead of legitimate businesses and consumers in finding ways to commit cybercrimes.

According to a recent report from London:

There is an issue of under reporting across the UK. A U.S. survey identified the global cost of e-crime as £1 trillion annually. Lloyds of London estimated that the 'I Love You' virus cost the global economy $10 billion. A recent report by the DTI/PricewaterhouseCoopers (PWC) indicated that 84% of large UK businesses had *a malicious security incident last year and that 21% of respondents to a Government survey felt 'at risk' to e-crime whereas only 16% worried more about a burglary.*

It is widely recognized that e-crime is the most rapidly expanding form of criminality, encompassing both new criminal offences in relation to computers (viruses and hacking, etc.) and 'old' crimes (fraud, harassment, etc.), committed using digital or computer technology.

The Met [London Metropolitan Police] is currently conducting a review of its approach to e-crime. A review of all MPS high-tech assets and external relationships has been conduced to identify areas for improvement or where gaps exist that require addressing.

The report identified digital forensics as the area most in need of investment in the near future. With increasing utilisation of digital technology, the demand for associated forensic services is likely to increase by 30-40% over 2006/2007. There is a need to plan for future demand, in order to prioritize expenditure on the increasing costs of outsourcing. (OUT-LAW, 2007b[1])

Definitions of Cybercrime and Cybersecurity

There is no exact definition of "Cybercrime." It varies from country to country. It may be called "computer crime" or be referred to by other titles in the legislation. Some countries are able to use existing laws to apply to crimes against computers and networks, for example, through the adoption of amendments to their Criminal Laws. Other countries have adopted completely new laws to address the acts we may consider cybercrimes, for example, the Republic of Korea, and also apply parts of traditional laws. Still other countries have no laws to address such acts that are considered crimes elsewhere.

Since there are no consistent definitions of the terms "Cybercrime" or "Cybersecurity," the same actions may be characterized in various terms, for example, "computer crime," "computer intrusion," "Internet security," "network intrusion," and so forth, in laws and policies of various nations and international organizations.

Despite the lack of consistent definitions, here are a few definitions from various places:

Computer crimes—also called:

1. **Computer-related crime:** The use of a computer is integral to committing the offense; examples are offenses such as computer-related forgery (where false data are put forward as authentic) and computer-related fraud (the fraudulent interference with or manipulation of data to cause property loss)
2. **Computer crime:** A general label for offenses in which a computer is the object or the offense or the tool for its commission
3. **Internet crime:** Crimes in which the use of the Internet is a key feature and includes content-related offenses such as possession of child pornography, or in some countries, the dissemination of hate or racist material
4. **E-crime:** A general label for offenses committed using an electronic data storage or communications device (Australian Institute of Criminology, 2005[2])

Cybercrime is defined both in statutes adopted by countries and economies, and at times at state or commonwealth levels, but not in the Council of Europe Convention on Cybercrime, which, as has been pointed out by commentators, has a broader meaning at the international level. It is then:

an umbrella term to refer to an array of criminal activity including offenses against computer data and systems, computer-related offenses, content offenses, and copyright offenses. This wide definition of Cybercrime overlaps in part with general offense categories that need not be ICT-dependent, such as white-collar crime and economic crime. (Australian Institute of Criminology, 2005[3]).

As if these terms are not confusing enough to absorb, there is also the label of "high tech crime" used in places such as the United Kingdom and Australia. Agencies in both countries "deal with crimes that rely on the use of ICT, or which target ICT equipment, data, and services. Their focus is on the complex networking capacity of ICT, which creates a previously unimaginable platform for committing and investigating criminal activity." According to the same crime brief, "the distinction between the use of ICT as either the object or as a tool of offending... has been adopted by Statistics Canada (2002)..." This two part division of high tech crime has been used for the analysis of such crimes in Australia (Australian Institute of Criminology, 2005[4]).

For some additional definitions, the reader may want to consult Wikipedia[5] and laws from their own and other jurisdictions, and those who are more ambitious may wish to read some law journal articles and books discussing the lack of consistent or universal definitions (Brenner, Susan W., 1998[6]).

Cybersecurity—also called "Internet security," may also include DDOS, cyberterrorism, attacks on critical information infrastructure, cyberwar.

A simple definition:

Cybersecurity—Ensuring the safety and security of networked information systems. (Weismann, Miriam F. Miquelon, 2006[7]).

Surveys Assessing the Extent of Cybercrime and Cybersecurity Issues

Several annual surveys conducted by organizations in the United States and Australia indicate the extent of Cybercrime's effects on financial institutions in those countries:

FBI/CSI Annual Survey 2005

The FBI 2005 Cyber Crime Survey[8], which included responses from over 2000 organizations in four states, found that 20% of organizations surveyed reported sustaining 20 or more computer security attacks in 2004. Virus problems were reported by 83% of organizations; spyware problems were reported by 79%. More than 20% said they had experienced port scans or data sabotage.

The survey defines a "computer security incident" as "any real or suspected adverse event in relation to the security of computer systems of computer networks." Of the organizations surveyed, 13.8% were in the financial and banking industries. According to one comment in the survey, "Larger organizations are a bigger target for attackers, but they also have larger IT budgets and more standardization."[9] Thus, financial institutions should be in the forefront when it comes to acquisition of the latest technology to prevent such attacks, however security professionals often say that the cybercriminals are one step ahead of the latest innovations due to the high stakes of committing crimes against financial institutions.

The security technologies reportedly used by the organizations surveyed in the annual FBI/CSI survey were:

- **Antivirus software:** 98.2%
- **Firewalls:** 90.7%
- **Antispam software:** 76.2%
- **Antispyware software:** 75.0%
- **Limits on which users can install software:** 52.8%
- **Access control lists (server based):** 48.9%
- **Physical security:** 47.8%
- **Periodic required password changes:** 46.9%
- **VPNS:** 46.3%
- **Password complexity requirements:** 46.3%

- **Encrypted login:** 31.9%
- **Encrypted files (for transfer):** 31.6%
- **Website content filtering:** 24.5%
- **Intrusion prevention/detection system:** 23.0%
- **Encrypted files (for storage):** 22.2%
- **Smartcards (card, PCMCIA, USB, etc.):** 6.7%
- **Biometrics:** 4.4%
- **Other:** 2.3%[10]

Looking at reported financial fraud, the total amount for all surveyed organizations was $3,152,500, with an average loss of $16,966. 75.1% of 1762 organizations that responded incurred financial losses due to computer security incidents.[11]

Organizations that had experienced computer security incidents within the 12 months preceding the survey took the following actions:

- 72.9% installed security updates on their networks
- 62.0% installed additional computer security software
- 38.9% did not report incident(s) to anyone outside the organization
- 28.1% strengthened corporate security policies
- 21.6% installed additional computer security hardware
- 19.4% attempted to identify the perpetrator of the computer security incident
- 11.5% attempted to contact the organization's Internet Service Provider
- 9.1% reported computer security incidents to law enforcement
- 8.5% engaged an outside security investigator
- 7.1% other
- 2.0 reported the computer security incident to a lawyer in order to seek a civil remedy[12]

Those who did not report the incident(s) to law enforcement agencies did not do so because:

- 49.5% said that there was no criminal activity involved
- 48.4% said that the incident was too small to report
- 23.1% did not think law enforcement was interested in such incidents
- 23.1% did not think law enforcement could help
- 9.1% other
- 5.3% not sure
- 3.6% general fear of engaging law enforcement and what it would involve
- 1.2% thought a competitor might take advantage if they knew[13]

Attacks came from 36 different countries, according to the survey. Thirty-six percent were alleged to be from the United States and twenty-four percent from the People's Republic of China, however masking software often makes it unclear where an attack actually originates.[14]

2006 Australian Computer Crime and Security Survey

Among the key findings of a similar type of annual survey relevant to this chapter indicated:

The greatest sources of financial loss for 2006 were due to theft or breach of proprietary or confidential information (over $2 million on average); computer facilitated financial fraud (over $100,000 average)...[15]

Of 389 organizations surveyed, 6% were financial institutions.[16]

Security technologies used in 2006 were:

- **Anti-spam filters:** 90%
- **Anti-virus software:** 98%
- **Digital IDs, certificates:** 47%

- **Virtual private network:** 86%
- **Encrypted login/sessions:** 46%
- **Encrypted files:** 43%
- **IDS:** 44%
- **Firewalls:** 98%
- **File integrity assessment tools:** 17%
- **Biometrics:** 5%
- **Smart cards, one time tokens:** 24%
- **Reusable passwords:** 54%
- **Access control:** 90%
- **Other:** 5%[17]

When electronic attacks harmed the confidentiality, integrity, or availability of network data or systems in the 12 months prior to the survey, the suspected motives for 2006 were:

- **Indiscriminate (attacker found and exploited vulnerability randomly):** 38%
- **To use system resources to conduct further attacks with anonymity:** 26%
- **To demonstrate attacker skill:** 27%
- **Unsolicited malicious damage:** 55%
- **Personal grievance:** 13%
- **Foreign government political advantage:** 0%
- **Other political interests, for example, "hacktivism":** 6%
- **Competitor commercial advantage, for example, industrial espionage/sabotage:** 3%
- **To utilize system resources for personal purposes:** 31%
- **Illicit financial gain:** 20%
- **Unknown:** 3%[18]

The following types of electronic attack, computer crime, and computer access misuse and abuse were detected in the 12 months prior to the 2006 survey:

- Insider abuse of Internet access, e-mail, or computer system resources 62%
- Unauthorized access to information by an insider (abuse of privileges) 8%
- **System penetration by outsider:** 7%
- **Laptop theft:** 58%
- **Theft of handheld computers:** 9%
- **Theft of other computer hardware or devices:** 20%
- **Trojan or rootkit malware infection (non-self-propagating malware):** 21%
- **Virus or worm infection:** 64%
- **Interception of communications (voice or data):** 1%
- **Degradation of network performance associated with heavy network scanning:** 17%
- **Denial of service attack:** 18%
- **Sabotage of data or networks:** 5%
- **Telecommunications fraud:** 4%
- **Theft/unauthorized use of staff or customers' online access credentials (i.e., ID theft):** 6%
- **Computer facilitated financial fraud:** 6%
- **Unauthorized privileged access:** 15%
- **Theft or breach of proprietary or confidential information:** 14%[19]

Of course, this survey was not specifically aimed at eliciting data from financial institutions; the results give a perspective on types of security issues in general affecting Australia's Internet users.

Symantec Australia Survey of Users in Australia and New Zealand

Symantec announced on October 24, 2006 that "more than 50% of Australian and New Zealand PC users consider the Internet fundamental to their daily lives, but 80% of them remain unaware of online threats." The survey "canvassed 28,660 Symantec users in Australia and New Zealand to determine their attitudes toward Internet security."

Some of the key findings were:

- More than 60% of respondents divulge their personal information monthly to gain access to online services but more than half of them are uncomfortable doing so.
- Less than 15% of respondents were confident they could recognize a fraudulent Web site.

.... Home users are a prime target for attackers seeking financial gains and online threats are constantly evolving....[20]

THE COUNCIL OF EUROPE CONVENTION ON CYBERCRIME

The nature of the Internet is cross-border, while the nature of laws applicable to financial institutions tends to be addressed to crime at the national, state, or local level. As a result, adopted laws may not be effective in combating Cybercrime, which may involve cross-border fraud or new forms of crimes not contemplated when the laws were adopted.

The Council of Europe Cybercrime Convention[21] entered into force on July 2, 2004. As of September 27, 2006, 15 countries had ratified it, and 43 countries had signed it. Most of the countries are EU members, however, the United States ratification became effective on September 22, 2006. Japan signed the Convention and South Africa has also signed it, but neither of the latter two countries has yet ratified it.

The Council of Europe Cybercrime Convention has the potential of harmonizing Cybercrime laws worldwide if and when countries have modified their national laws in order to be able to meet the standards outlined in the convention.

Despite the aim of harmonization, the convention does not define "Cybercrime." As explained by Professor Henrik W. K. Kaspersen, who chaired the Council of Europe drafting committee that developed the Recommendation of 1995 and the Cybercrime Convention of 2001:

Cybercrime is a term of 'hype' and not a legal definition. The term may include any crime that has been committed by means of electronic equipment or in an electronic environment. When I follow the categorization of the substantive-law chapter of the Cybercrime Convention (Arts. 2-9), cybercrime is any crime directed against computer systems and networks and their information content (cybercrime in a narrow sense); it also includes computer-related crimes like fraud and forgery in the broadest sense committed by electronic means, offences concerning a violation of intellectual-property rights on protected works in an electronic form, and content-related offenses, in particular criminal content. The procedural part of the Cybercrime Convention brings under the heading of cybercrime also those crimes for the investigation of which electronic evidence has to be collected and safe-guarded from computer systems or networks. One of the common elements of these crimes is that they may be committed wholly or partially on the territory of different states because of the perpetrator's use of international global communication networks. (Kaspersen, Henrik W.K., 2006[22]).

While not a legal definition, the above explanation is valuable for understanding both Cybercrime and Cybersecurity as interpreted in various terms used in legislation adopted or under consideration worldwide.

The value of the Convention is that can be used as a model for national legislation, even by countries that have not and will not ratify it. This is useful if combined with Multilateral Legal Assistance Treaties (MLATs) that enable extradition if both countries are "on the same page" with their legislation, however, as seen in the case of the "Love Bug" virus which arose in the Philippines and was spread to computers worldwide, if the country from which Cybercrime is sent does not have legislation in place, then the cybercriminal cannot be extradited to be tried under the laws of the country where the victim has been damaged (Purugganan, Abraham A., 1998[23]). This is called the "dual criminality" principle[24].

FINANCIAL INSTITUTIONS AFFECTED BY VARIOUS FORMS OF CYBERCRIME

Banks

Online Banking

United States

More than 35 million American households bank online, though the growth rate slowed to about 10% in 2005 from more than 300% 10 years ago, according to industry newsletter, the *Online Banking Report*. A poll by the American Bankers Association shows that "only one-fourth of people go to the Internet most often for their banking needs, as opposed to branches or automated teller machines. Online transactions are projected to account for 44% of all self-service banking, including ATMs and touch-tone phone systems, by 2010, compared to 10% at the beginning of this decade, according to the Tower Group, a financial services advisory firm (Smitherman, Laura, 2006[25]).

The Federal Financial Institutions Examination Council (FFIEC)[26] issued stricter guidance for Internet banking in October 2005, basically ordering banks to require more than a simple user name and password (Zeller, Tom Jr., 2006[27]). The guidance supersedes the August 8, 2001 FFIEC agency guidance entitled *Authentication in an Electronic Banking Environment*. The new guidance is called *Authentication in an Internet Banking Environment*.[28] Financial institutions were required to have implemented such dual factor authentication by December 31, 2006.

The Guidance notes that, since 2001, "there have been significant legal and technological changes with respect to the protection of customer information; increasing incidents of fraud, including identity theft; and the introduction of improved authentication technologies." It addresses "why financial institutions regulated by the agencies should conduct risk-based assessments, evaluate customer awareness programs, and develop security measures to reliably authenticate customers remotely accessing their Internet-based financial services." It applies to both retail and commercial banks, and does not endorse any particular technology; financial institutions are advised to use the guidance when evaluating and implementing authentication systems and practices whether provided internally or by a service provider. It notes that "Although this guidance is focused on the risks and risk management techniques associated with the Internet delivery channel, the principles are applicable to all forms of electronic banking activities."[29]

The key points of the guidance are that the five agencies consider single-factor authentication, used as the only control mechanism, to be inadequate for "high-risk transactions involving access to customer information or to the movement of funds to other parties. Financial institutions offering Internet-based products and services to their customers should use effective methods to authenticate the identity of customers using those products and services. The authentication techniques employed by the financial institution should be appropriate to the risks associated with those products and services. Account fraud and identity theft are frequently the result of single-factor (e.g., ID/password) authentication exploitation. Where risk assessments indicate that the use of single-factor authentication is inadequate, financial institutions should implement multifactor authentication, layered security, or other controls reasonably calculated to mitigate those risks."[30] Based on the *FFIEC Information Technology Examination Handbook, Information*

Security Booklet[31] (December 2002), financial institutions are advised to periodically ensure that their information security program:

- Identifies and assesses the risks associated with Internet-based products and services
- Identifies risk mitigation actions, including appropriate authentication strength
- Measures and evaluates customer awareness efforts
- Adjusts, as appropriate, their information security program in light of any relevant changes in technology, the sensitivity of customer information, and internal or external threats to information
- Implements appropriate risk mitigation strategies

CUSTOMER AUTHENTICATION TECHNIQUES AND METHODS

Methods used by financial institutions include: customer passwords, personal identification numbers (PINS), digital certificates using a public key infrastructure (PKI), physical devices such as smart cards, one-time passwords (OTPs), USB plug-ins or other types of "tokens," transaction profile scripts, biometric identification, and so forth.[32]

ATMs

Scenario: ATM Theft in Japan

At an ordinary-looking ATM, a false card slot is affixed over the original card slot. The false slot holds an additional card reader used to copy card information. We see an ordinary monitor and pamphlet holder at the ATM station. The pamphlet holder houses a hidden micro-camera. The hidden camera is angled to view the monitor and the keypad and to transmit wireless photos of them up to 200 meters away. The camera hidden in the pamphlet box includes its own battery and transmission antenna (Sasaki, Shigeru, 2006[33]).

Authentication Methods Applied in the Real World

Banks in many countries are now implementing new forms of authentication.

Biometrics

At a recent conference held in Singapore at which the author was a participant, a representative from Fujitsu Laboratories Ltd. Research Center for Image Processing and Biometrics Technologies discussed Palm Secure, palm vein authentication which had been developed by that lab. It works when the customer places the palm of his/her hand over a sensor. The sensor emits a near-infrared light. The near-infrared image of the palm vein pattern is captured. The scanning data is stored as a template.

There are also contact types of biometrics, for example, a vein on the back of the hand or the finger.[34]

Sources of the data presented were:

- Back hand vein www.veid.net
- Hand Geometry: University of Buffalo/Center for Unified Biometrics and Sensors
- Facial Recognition: Applied Optics, February 2005
- Signature/Voice: www.hitachi.com, August 2005 (Shigeru, Sasaki, 2006[35])

Law Adopted in One Jurisdiction and Case Study from Another

Republic of Korea

The Electronic Financial Transaction Act was promulgated on April 28, 2004, and became effective on January 1, 2007. It "(1) regulates business enterprises engaged in electronic financial transactions, (2) governs transactions conducted by electronic machines such as computers, ATM machines and telephones, and so forth, and (3) provides the basic entry level operation requirements for engaging in electronic financial transactions" (Shin and Kim, 2006[36]). One of the problems noted in Korea is that "non-financial enterprises (e.g., telecom companies) and unqualified smaller companies have been performing electronic financial services without being subject to any regulation" (Shin and Kim, 2006[37]). The main purposes of the EFT Act are to:

1. Protect users by placing stricter responsibility on financial institutions or service providers for "electronic financial accidents"
2. Protect the credit of users by holding financial institutions or service providers liable "in the case of willful misconduct or negligence of an assistant provider."
3. Make users feel legally secure by introducing basic legislation for electronic financial transactions
4. Increase user safety and the security of electronic financial transaction systems by imposing on service providers "the duty to meet certain security control and compliance requirements" (Shin and Kim, 2006[38])

An enforcement decree was expected in September 2006, and following its issuance, the Financial Supervisory Commission was to issue detailed supervisory guidelines (Shin and Kim, 2006[39]).

United Kingdom

In the UK, fraudsters have been using "increasingly advanced" devices to tamper with bank cash machines, allowing them to copy, or "skim" card details from customers. Cash machine fraud totaled 65.8 million British pounds in 2005, according to industry organization Apacs (Cronin, Jon, 2006[40]). Some banks are responding using new technological means. For example, Alliance & Leicester "is introducing new double identity check measures which will come into force when customers access their accounts." When customers log in, the bank first identifies the customer's computer. Then the bank confirms to the customer that it is genuinely the bank by showing "a unique image or phrase previously chosen by the customer." (Cronin, Jon, 2006[41]).

Lloyds Bank TSB has announced plans to improve security for customers using its cash machines. In the process known as "skimming," which involves criminals placing devices into the card entry slot of a cash machine to copy a customer's card details, a hidden camera overlooking the cash machine key pad simultaneously records the customer's PIN number. The combination of the two acts enables criminals to produce counterfeit cards which can then be used to withdraw cash. In order to reduce the risk of ATM fraud, Lloyds TSB is attaching anti-skimming devices to its ATMs throughout Britain. This system blocks the recording of customers' card details by scrambling each card's magnetic stripe details as they are copied by a skimming device (Cronin, Jon, 2006[42]).

Online Securities Firms

United States

For three months this year, overseas hackers broke into customer accounts on two online stock brokerages, TD Ameritrade Holding Corp. and E-Trade Financial Corp., in a "pump and dump" stock trading scheme that is estimated to have led to at least $22 million in losses. The attacks were launched by identity thieves in Eastern Europe and Asia who primarily used keylogging software delivered via Trojan horses or other malware to steal users' confidential information as they logged onto public computers or their own infected machines. They then logged into existing customer accounts, or created dummy accounts, to buy shares in seldom traded stocks, driving prices up so that they could sell their own previously purchased shares for a profit. TD Ameritrade announced on October 24, 2006 that it had spent $4 million to compensate customers who suffered losses after their accounts had been broken into. E-Trade confirmed on October 18, 2006 that it had spent $18 million to compensate its customers. The FBI, U.S. Securities and Exchange Commission, and the National Association of Securities Dealers were reportedly working together to investigate the fraud. It was unknown whether E-Trade's losses would be covered by insurance, but TD Ameritrade's CFO expressed confidence that the company could obtain restitution if it could prove the fraud was from the same source. No data had been stolen from TD Ameritrade's databases nor had its servers been breached during the incident, however its security measures had been circumvented. It has a dedicated security team using special software to monitor for anomalous activity such as users logging in from unusual IP addresses and large withdrawals of money. E-Trade uses antifraud software that monitors accounts for unusual behavior and also offers optional tokens that generate six-digit codes that change every 60 seconds and users must enter with their user names and passwords when logging in. The CTO of a security vendor noted that the software used by E-Trade to monitor whether users are logging in from their usual IP address can be tricked by skillful hackers, and that tokens are ineffective against identity thieves who use names and Social Security numbers to create new bank or stock trading accounts (Lai, Eric, 2006[43]).

This type of case is not new. In 2005, *Business Week* reported that the SEC had posted a warning on its Web site with tips for safeguarding online trading accounts, and was handling many such cases. Online brokerage accounts were being looted by hackers who were exploiting the weaknesses of investors' computers rather than the online brokerages' systems. As of 2005, *Business Week* reported that there was no more than $20 million stolen in one year, however consumers had $1.7 trillion worth of assets with online brokerages at the time, according to the Tower Group, a financial research and consulting group (Borrus, Amy, 2005[44]).

As is the case with online banking, the real cost of such security lapses is the loss of public confidence in doing transactions via the Internet (Borrus, Amy, 2005[45]).

Investment fraud can also arise from an offering that "uses false or fraudulent claims to solicit investments or loans, or that provides for the purchase, use, or trade of forged or counterfeit securities (U.S. Department of Justice, 2003[46]).

Home computer users are the vulnerable ones. An October 2004 survey by America Online and the National Cyber Security Alliance found that 84% of American computer users keep sensitive personal information, including financial data, on their home PCs.

The criminals use hacking or phishing to obtain customers' information, combined with identity theft and securities fraud in "complex scams executed by gangs. Generally, it's two or three people working together," according to an FBI expert. "The usual profile is people with graduate degrees in finance or banking." The FBI, Secret Service, and private security firms believe that most online stock thieves are based in Eastern Europe (U.S. Department of Justice, 2003[47]).

According to the SEC, this is how the computer fraudsters operate:

a. Crooks use a virus or key-logging program to hack into your PC to get account details and passwords.
b. Once into your account, they sell some or all of your stocks over a few days.
c. They direct your broker to move the cash, usually to a bank account opened in your name.
d. Associates pull out money as cash and wire it to a hard-to-trace offshore account (U.S. Department of Justice, 2003[48]).

Credit Card Companies

Credit or debit card fraud is the unauthorized use of a credit or debit card to fraudulently obtain money or property. Credit/debit card numbers can be stolen from unsecured Web sites, or can be obtained through identity theft schemes (U.S. Department of Justice, 2003[49]).

Case Study

United States

In November 2006, the United States Federal Trade Commission and Guidance Software, Inc., a vendor of computer products, settled a complaint filed by the Federal agency alleging that the company had not utilized reasonable security measures to protect sensitive computer data. Specifically, the company's lax security efforts had enabled hackers to access sensitive credit card data of its customers, and thereby contradicted promises made on its Web site. The agency announced on November 16, 2006 that it would require the company to implement a comprehensive cybersecurity plan and have independent security audits every other year for 10 years.

The facts of the case were that in December 2005, the company had informed its customers that hackers had broken into a company database and stolen about 3,800 credit card numbers, apparently through a SQL injection attack. Security researchers had, however, identified SQL injection attacks as far back as 2000 and researchers had published multiple articles on how to protect against SQL injection attacks by 2005.

In addition, although the company made claims about data security on its Web site, it stored credit card information in clear, readable text that was easy to access from outside the company. The FTC also alleged the company had failed to assess the vulnerability of its network to commonly known or reasonably foreseeable Web-based attacks such as SQL injection attacks, thus failing to implement "simple, low-cost and readily available defenses." This was the FTC's fourteenth case challenging faulty data-security practices by companies that handle sensitive consumer information.[50]

Case Study

United States

In November 2006, the FBI planned to announce the arrest of at least 16 individuals in connection with a global Cybercrime investigation of a series of phishing attacks against a "major financial institution" that occurred between August and October 2004. Agents conducted investigations in the U.S. and abroad to identify a ring of identity thieves who were acquiring and trading stolen credit and debit card numbers through an online forum. The investigation targeted both hackers, who compromised about 50 servers in order to launch the phishing attacks, and those who sought to acquire the stolen financial data. Three arrests were made in the U.S. and eleven were made in Poland. Additional arrests were expected to be made in Romania.[51]

Case Study

Australia

Computer-Facilitated Compromise of Financial Data

Australian High Tech Crime Centre

In August 2005, a report was received by the above center stating that a server belonging to an Australian payment gateway had been unlawfully accessed and that about 46,000 credit card records might have been exposed to compromise. As a result of the fast action of the hosting company, the server was immediately taken off-line and the hard drive and logs were forwarded to the AHTCC.

Once the potentially compromised credit card numbers had been disseminated to all the relevant banks and credit card provider, the logs were examined. The examination, with information received from the hosting company enabled the police to identify an IP address in Melbourne and a potential suspect. The compromised server hard drive was also analyzed and numerous pieces of evidence linking the IP address to the unauthorized access were discovered. No evidence was found indicating that the offender had accessed the credit card database.

Following further investigation, a search warrant was executed for the offender's premises in September 2005. A number of computer items were seized and the offender was arrested and interviewed. During the interview, the offender admitted to having gained access to the compromised server for the purpose of testing his skills and getting recognition from the hacking community. He stated that he had not done it for any monetary gain and that he had not known of any credit card database.

In February 2006, the offender pled guilty to two charges of Unauthorized Modification of Data to Cause Impairment. In handing down the decision, the magistrate stated that she viewed the offense as very serious because it undermined people's confidence in the e-commerce system. The offender was convicted and fined $2,000 and ordered to pay $3,000 in compensation to the hosting company.[52]

E-Money, E-Payments

Online Auctions/Retail and Phony Escrow Services

In this type of fraud, there is misrepresentation of a product advertised for sale through an Internet auction site or the non-delivery of products purchased through an Internet auction site (U.S. Department of Justice, 2003[53]).

In an effort to persuade a wary Internet auction participant to buy, the fraudster will propose the use of a third-party escrow service to facilitate the exchange of money and service. The victim is unaware that the fraudster has spoofed a legitimate escrow service. The victim sends payment or merchandise to the phony escrow service and receives nothing in return (U.S. Department of Justice, 2003[54]).

Online Gambling

United States

On September 29, 2006, the United States Congress passed the Unlawful Internet Gambling Enforcement Act of 2006,[55] legislation "designed to prohibit U.S. banks and credit card companies from processing payments for illegal online gambling. Financial services companies and the U.S. Chamber of Commerce had expressed concerns about the compliance burdens that would be imposed, such as tracking and blocking potentially millions of transactions." The legislation will be enforced by regulations to be written by the Federal Reserve and the U.S. Treasury Department (Edwards, Greg, 2006[56]).

As one lawyer noted, it is easy to enact laws prohibiting Internet gambling, but much harder to enforce them (Waddell, David, 2006a[57]). The response to this view from a legislator (Bill First): "Although we can't monitor every online gambler or regulate offshore gambling, we can police the financial institutions that disregard our laws." The Act restricts electronic fund transfers and use of credit cards in connection with such wagers—players can no longer make wagers or collect winnings using electronic fund transfers, credit or debit cards, or other online payment systems. The Act requires the U.S. Treasury Department to issue regulations that would prohibit approving a transaction between a U.S.-based customer account and an Internet gambling merchant. Financial institutions would be required to follow these regulations and would be subject to fines or penalties if they fail to comply" (Waddell, David, 2006b[58]).

The legislation was 10 years in the making. Many had expressed concerns that alternative means, including electronic money, would arise to take the place of the traditional means of paying for gambling and recouping gambling winnings. There were also calls for legalization of gambling (Weinberg, Joel, 2006[59]), since it is such a popular pastime for Americans (this author is not one of them, however, nor do I drink beer or watch football or baseball on television!).

OTHER FORMS OF CYBERCRIME REPORTED TO BE DIRECTED AT FINANCIAL INSTITUTIONS

Identity Theft

According to the U.S. Department of Justice, "Identity theft occurs when someone appropriates another's personal information without their knowledge to commit theft or fraud. Identity theft is a vehicle for perpetrating other types of fraud schemes. Typically, the victim is led to believe they are divulging sensitive personal information to a legitimate business, sometimes as a response to an e-mail solicitation to update billing or membership information, or as an application to a fraudulent Internet job posting (Weinberg, Joel, 2006[60]).

According to Javelin Strategy & Research of Pleasanton, California, "identity theft in all of its forms last year caused an estimated $56.6 billion in losses, with 1 in 25 people affected by it" (Lai, Eric, 2006[61]). Of course, identity theft can be committed by means other than cybercrime, and it is cybercrime that is one focus of this chapter.

Some notorious cases arising in the past few years in the United States were those involving Lexis/Nexis databases and a credit card clearing company.

Identity theft has become a major issue in the United States, and data stolen from databases, for example, the Lexis/Nexis and ChoicePoint thefts in 2004 have made consumers quite anxious. The Lexis/Nexis database was a hacking job, while the ChoicePoint theft involved fraudulent representation that the thief needed to buy lists of personal information for business purposes. Unfortunately, to date effective Federal legislation about identity theft has not been passed. Some states have, however, adopted such legislation, for example, the state of California[62].

Phishing

Definition: This is a scheme in which perpetrators use spoofed (phony) Web sites in an attempt to dupe a victim into divulging sensitive information such as passwords, credit card and bank account numbers. The victim, usually via e-mail, is provided with a hyperlink that directs him/her to a fraudster's Web site. This fraudulent Web site's name closely resembles the true name of the legitimate business. The victim arrives at the company's legitimate Web site and is convinced by the site's content that he/she is in fact at the company's legitimate Web site and is tricked into divulging sensitive personal information. Spoofing and phishing are done to further perpetrate other schemes, including identity theft and auction fraud (U.S. Department of Justice, 2003[63]).

Examples

United States: Credit Unions

The Credit Union National Association reported that a string of phishing scams enticed members with cash rewards in exchange for answering a customer satisfaction survey. The scams were aimed at credit unions and credit union organizations. A link in the e-mailed scam took victims to well-crafted Web sites that mimic an organization with proper images and layout. The sites typically include surveys inquiring about the quality of service or online banking services of the organization. At the bottom of the page is a request for account information in order to deposit a $20 reward.[64]

Keylogging Software

Scenario

A consumer receives an e-mail notice that an expensive item had been charged to his credit card account. An Internet link included in the message is supposed to enable him to dispute the charge. Instead, the site "silently installed a password-stealing program that transmitted all of his personal and financial information." The data is stolen by an Internet fraud ring using Web-based software to manage large numbers of illegally commandeered computers. The data of the one consumer, and that of thousands of other victims, is sent to a Web site hosted by a Russian Internet Service Provider. That site is "currently the home base for a network of sites designed to break into computers through a security hole in Microsoft's Internet Explorer Web browser. The data thieves use the IE flaw to install programs known as 'keyloggers' on computers that visited the specially coded Web pages. The keyloggers then copy the victims' stored passwords and computer keystrokes and upload that information to the database... The central database feeds the stolen data back to Web sites running the hacking software, where hackers can sort it by any number of variables, such as financial institution or country of origin ..." (Krebs, Brian, 2006[65]).

Symantec and other security experts found earlier versions of the same software installed on two other Web sites, "one of which is still active and has harvested password information from nearly 30,000 victims, the bulk of whom reside in the United States and Brazil... More than half of the viruses, worms and other malicious computer code that Symantec now tracks are designed not to harm host machines but to surreptitiously gather data from them" (Krebs, Brian, 2006[66]).

According to a security incident handler at the SANS Internet Storm Center, which monitors hacking trends, a recent estimate was that nearly 10 million U.S. households own a computer that is infected with some kind of keystroke logging program. Although not every PC user whose keystrokes are logged has experienced financial losses, the same source estimates that organized crime groups have access to roughly $24 million in bank assets from accounts of the owners of the infected machines (Krebs, Brian, 2006[67]).

Brazil

In February 2006, Brazilian Federal police arrested 55 people in the northern city of Campina Grande and surrounding states (of whom at least nine were minors) for "seeding" the computers of "unwitting" victims with keyloggers that "recorded their typing whenever they visited their banks online. The tiny programs then sent the stolen user names and passwords back to members of the gang." According to news reports, the fraud ring had stolen about U.S. $4.7 million from 200 different accounts at six banks since it began operations in May 2005 (Zeller, Tom Jr., 2006[68]).

According to the general manager of Brazil's Computer Emergency Response Team, "These Trojans are very selective... They monitor the Web access the victims make, and start recording information only when the user enters the sites of interest to the fraudster" (Zeller, Tom Jr., 2006[69]).

French Bank Accounts

A ring similar to the Brazilian one was broken up by Russian authorities in the same month. It used keylogger Trojans "planted in e-mail messages and hidden in Web sites to draw over U.S. $1.1 million from personal bank accounts in France"(Zeller, Tom Jr., 2006[70]).

Spoofing

This is a technique by which a fraudster pretends to be someone else's e-mail or Web site. This is typically done by copying the Web content of a legitimate Web site to the fraudster's newly created fraudulent Web site (U.S. Department of Justice, 2003[71]).

Trojan Horses

Case Study

Sweden

According to an Out-Law report, the Swedish bank Nordia was hit by what the Internet Security firm McAfee has characterized as the "biggest Internet fraud in history." As much as 600,000 British pounds was stolen over a 3-month period from 250 customer accounts, as reported in the Swedish press.

E-mails were sent to the bank's customers asking them to download a piece of software which they were told was a piece of anti-spam software. In fact, it was actually software which was activated when customers tried to log onto the Internet banking site for Nordia. It recorded their log-in details and asked them to log-in again due to a "fictional error." Their second log-in attempt was then recorded, giving hackers enough information to access their accounts. The report notes that "Most Internet banks only ask for a portion of an access code at login to prevent one-off spying attempts from gaining the whole code, but the fake error messages ensured that the Nordia hackers were given access to enough information to access an account." The police informed Computer Sweden that the information was sent to servers in the United States and to Russia, from where money was taken from the users' accounts.

About 250 customers were stated to have been targeted over a 15-month period, and the criminals escaped notice by only transferring small amounts of funds from the targeted amounts and doing so gradually. The software was written especially to target the Nordia system. It was a modification of a more general Trojan application, called "Haxware."

The bank refunded the stolen money to each of the customers. A bank spokesperson stated that most of those affected were not running anti-virus applications.[72]

Botnets

Definition: "A botnet—also known as a 'zombie network' or 'zombie army'—is a collection of Internet-connected PCs that have been compromised by infection from malicious software." That compromise means they can be controlled remotely by a malicious outsider, often without the PC owner's knowledge. Computers not protected by adequate antivirus and firewall software are at greatest risk of being added to a botnet.

Armies of zombie PCs are used by cybercriminals for sending spam or viruses or committing denial-of-service attacks. Capacity on botnets is rented out to criminal gangs or individuals for as little as $10 for a couple of hours by their creator—often a very commercially motivated virus writer.

A zombie army was used in a high profile distributed denial of service attack against Akamai Technologies in 2006, affecting the Web sites of some of its big-name tech clients.[73] In June 2006, police in London, working in cooperation with Finnish law enforcement authorities, arrested three suspected virus writers in connection with an "international conspiracy to infect computers using viruses attached to unsolicited commercial e-mail," (SPAM). "The viruses ran in the background on an infected computer without the knowledge of the computer's owner, allowing the criminals behind the virus to access any private and commercial data stored on the computer."(Espiner, Tom, 2006[74]).

Hijacked computers have become one of the most serious security problems on the Internet. "Malicious remote-control code turns a computer into a zombie via security holes in software, a worm, or a Trojan horse. It then runs silently in the background, letting an attacker send commands to the system, unbeknownst to its owner.... Criminals make money by networking their zombies into a 'botnet'. They put these networks to work mounting denial-of-service attacks against online businesses in extortion schemes; hosting faked Web sites [see "phishing" discussion] used in phishing schemes; and relaying spam. Attackers also often load adware and spyware onto compromised systems, earning a kickback from the makers of these programs or reselling the private data of their victims."[75]

Spyware

Japan

The number of arrests for Cybercrime in 2005 rose by 51.9% from 2004, to a total of 3,161 cases. One of the reported crimes committed by using spyware software was when a perpetrator obtained information about the bank account of a company that paid its bills online, and wound up stealing $10,000 from the corporation.[76]

Online Money Laundering

A recent warning by Panda Software informed the public of the phenomenon of "mules" used for online money laundering. These are persons who participate in money laundering operations. Such participation is rewarded with commissions and is the financial incentive to convince the mules to handle third party money, depositing it into their personal bank accounts for further transfer to various accounts. The press release states: "The increase in cyber-crime has led criminals into an aggressive recruitment drive for mules on the Internet. Their preference is for normal users who are not related to any type of organized crime. This is because, in the event of an investigation, the prime target of the authorities is the person laundering the money, and therefore the more distant the link between the mule and the criminals, the more difficult it will be to trace the latter." Panda Software indicated that, while monitoring spammed e-mail traffic and malicious Web sites, it has observed the online activities related to money laundering and was therefore advising users to steer clear of such schemes. "Laundering money for cyber-crooks can have very serious consequences for users. Bear in mind that the mule is, to all intents and purposes, a scapegoat. They are laundering the profits of Internet crime, and this is a jailable offense." (Oiaga, Marius, 2006[77]).

Another report indicates that "electronic transfers are the preferred method of moving money between accounts. Scam artists use anonymous e-mail accounts and pre-paid cell phones, called burners, which they discard often."(deLeon, Joseph M., 2006[78]).

Insider Threats

The IBM Global Business Security Index Report summarized trends in security for 2005. One of the trends noted was insider attacks. It forecasted that "as software becomes more secure, computer users will continue to be the weak link for companies and organizations. Criminals will focus their efforts on convincing end users to execute the attack instead of trying to find vulnerabilities in software."[79]

Security Measures

The author recently asked the Chief Information Officer of a bank in Japan what was the greatest Cybercrime problem in banking at this time. Instead of the expected responses outlined elsewhere in this chapter, his response was "insider threats." These threats range from the intentional ones generated inside their companies' firewalls, as well as negligence caused by employees, contractors, and visitors to an office logging on to the corporate network without heeding company security policies. One New York bank ordered a software agent installed on each computer, which checks that each PC, laptop or other device is in compliance with security policies. It "runs all new anti-virus definitions, disallows instant messaging applications, checks for the most recent operating system patches, and makes sure that the personal firewall is configured properly....It allows IT folks... visibility into all the endpoints connecting into the network, whether they are remote or in the office....and gives them the confidence of knowing exactly what is connected to the network and the ability to remediate it instantly."(Paul, Lauren Gibbons, 2006[80]).

Terrorism, Cyberterrorism and Financial Institutions

In November 2006, a jihadist Web site warned that attacks would be launched against online stock trading and banking Web sites, but the U.S. Department of Homeland Security indicated that there was no information to corroborate the threat. The threat was one of a denial of service attack but a government official noted that many financial services Web sites are "well-fortified to withstand such an attack even if it came" (Hall, Mimi, 2006[81]).

EMERGING PRIVACY ISSUES

Case Study

Belgium-U.S. and Swift

Recently, a controversy has surfaced about a secret transfer deal between the U.S. Treasury and the Belgium-based Society for Worldwide Interbank Financial Telecommunication (SWIFT). A Belgian commission stated in September 2006, that SWIFT had "breached rules on storing data and had failed to honor commitments to inform clients or Belgian authorities about what data had been transferred." SWIFT and the U.S. authorities said that the records were subpoenaed as part of "targeted investigations into suspected terrorist activity." SWIFT's response was that it had done its best to comply with the European data privacy principles of "proportionality, purpose, and oversight" and had only transmitted a "limited subset" of the data. It has stated that it supports demands for the U.S. and EU authorities to "work together to develop an improved framework to reconcile data privacy protections."[82]

United Kingdom

It has been reported that the UK government is considering allowing banks to share data on up to 40 million bank accounts without the account holders' permission. The accounts were opened before banks routinely asked permission to share account data with credit reference agencies, mostly those opened before the late 1990s. The proposal conflicts with existing data protection legislation and is phrased in one of four government options being considered as "circumventing existing data protection legislation." [83]

Also in November 2006, the British Bankers' Association was reported to have agreed to government data sharing proposals on suspected financial criminals, but said they wanted the public sector to share its data with them. The banks also expressed doubts about whether the plans would actually help to catch criminals.

The association represents 240 banks from 60 countries.[84]

PRESENT NEEDS OF LAW AND LAW ENFORCEMENT

The present needs of the legal community (prosecutors, judges, law enforcement) are for the adoption of legislation to address cybercrime and cybersecurity issues. From country to country, there are different types of laws, with different names, definitions of what constitutes a cybercrime, and coverage. The Council of Europe Convention on Cybercrime provides a model of what national-level laws should cover and enables cross-border collaboration. On the other hand, in some countries concerns have been expressed about overbreadth in laws allowing excessive government control over and intrusion into private information, for example, financial records and account data.

While, for example, money laundering by criminal and terrorist elements should be addressed, excessive regulation in some countries affects the interests and privacy rights of innocent citizens whose data are being investigated without any suspision of wrongdoing. A more moderate approach needs to be considered for adoption in those jurisdictions (Harold, Kristin, 2006[85]).

There are also needs for attorneys, judges, prosecutors, and police to receive continuous up-to-date training about Cybercrime issues and modifications to criminal procedures needed to address investigations and prosecutions of Cybercrime when there are digital records which become electronic evidence. There are in too many countries insufficient funds and resources to train police and other law-related personnel. Perhaps secured online training in the local languages in developed and developing countries would be the best way to ensure that all are on the "same page," so to speak.

As for law enforcement personnel, another important area is computer forensics and many countries have been asking for such training for their police. Judges also need to have knowledge of this area to ensure that due process rights have been protected when police search computers seized during an investigation.

FUTURE NEEDS OF LAW AND LAW ENFORCEMENT

A major problem is that the strategies of cybercriminals are constantly changing. This year's problems may not be as problematic next year, as the criminals change their methods and use of technology. Thus, cases must be analyzed and reported on an annual basis, whether by police agencies or the private sector. Secured communications in-country and internationally are also important when there are patterns observed in Cybercrime activities.

There is also a need for communication between the law-related professions and the technology/security community, but this may create a delicate balance because some security professionals do not wish to collaborate with the police, but only to monitor network attacks in a more generalized manner. The question of degree of collaboration will need to be resolved.

Interdisciplinary dialogues between law and IT/security professionals are really needed and will continue to be needed. As technology changes so frequently, there is a need to educate one another on a regular basis. Many law professionals are not familiar with technology *per se*, and IT/security professionals likewise may not know the legal provisions and procedures related to Cybercrime. Interdisciplinary dialogues, as have recently appeared in IEEE publications (Dempsey, James X. and Rubinstein, Ira, 2006[86]), for example, are useful and important to both communities and should increase.

Finally, there is a present need that will continue into the future to have trained Information Security and IT law professionals in all countries worldwide. There is currently a shortage of such professionals in most places. Today's students should be informed and encouraged to enter such emerging fields as IT law, computer forensics, and Information Security as early as possible. New curricula, for example in the law faculties and law schools worldwide, are needed to train law professionals, preferably in interdisciplinary settings in which there are students from other fields, for example, Business, Computer Science, and Public Policy. In addition, governments and the private sector, particularly the financial institutions that may be most affected by Cybercrime and Cybersecurity issues, must fund programs for undergraduate, graduate, and professional school students, as well as retraining for existing employees and professionals.

CONCLUSION

While the benefits of the Internet and computer networks, as well as computers and other forms of technology, are streamlining financial institutions, the same institutions are often among the first institutions to be affected by Cybercrime and Cybsecurity issues due to the financial incentives as well as their strategic place in each nation's infrastructure and economy. We must look not only at efficiency, but also at the negative aspects of the use of technology by financial institutions. Consumers and businesses must be well informed about conducting transactions in the safest manner possible.

Each of the discussions of a Cybercrime or Internet Security issue in this chapter makes reference only to single-nation data. Very few, if any, cross-border Cybercrime or Internet Security cases have been discussed in the literature, except, perhaps, for money laundering or cyberterrorism issues. The nature of the Internet is cross-border, and thus Cybercrime and Internet Security issues involving financial institutions should be made known by international organizations, regional organizations, and when there have been cross-border law enforcement collaborations in investigations, extraditions, and so forth. At present, due to the fact that law is generally written at the national (or even state level, as is the case of Identity Theft law in the U.S.), there is a need for reporting of cross-border cases in the literature if such data can be obtained from law enforcement officials by scholars.

Future Research Directions

There is an ongoing need for monitoring of forms of cybercrime arising in countries and across borders, that is, arrests, convictions, and the adoption of adequate laws to prosecute cybercrime defined in national law. Additionally, there is a need for funding for such research, for example, in the form of research institutes, in which scholars can track forms of crimes, cases that come to the courts, and assist legislators in drafting laws. Furthermore, there is a need for collaboration between the law professions and Information Technology professionals, and those involved in policy making.

Furthermore, lawyers, judges, police, and legislators need up-to-date information on how cybercrimes occur and how cross-border issues can be addressed by law. Since the Internet and other forms of technology are changing daily, as are the crimes using them or operating against their use, it is necessary to have constant research to maintain control over cybercrimes that could be threats to such areas as financial transactions, e-commerce, e-government, and so forth.

REFERENCES

Associated Press. (2006, September 28). *Belgian premier says SWIFT secretly supplied U.S. with bank data.* Retrieved September 30, 2006, from http://www.siliconvalley.com/mld/siliconvalley/news/editorial/15630604.htm?template

AusCERT. (2006). *Australian computer crime and security survey, 20.* Retrieved from http://www.auscert.org/au/render.html?it=2001

Australian Institute of Criminology. (2005, January). *High tech crime brief, concepts and terms, new crimes and old crimes committed in new ways.* Retrieved from http://www.aic.gov.au

Borrus, A. (2005, November 14). Invasion of the stock hackers. *BUSINESS WEEK, 38,* 40.

Brenner, S. W. (1998). Cybercrime law and policy in the United States. In P. C. Reich (Ed.), *Cybercrime and security.* Oceana, a division of Oxford University Press.

Computerworld. (2006, October 24). *New symantec survey reveals security doubts shape Internet behavior.* Retrieved November 8, 2006, from http://www.computerworld.com.au/index.php/id;1356571409;fp;;fpid;;pf;1

Council of Europe. (2001, November 23). Convention on Cybercrime (CETS 185). Budapest. Retrieved from http://conventions.coe.int/Treaty/en/Treaties/Html/185.htm

Cronin, J. (2006, March 15). Taking on Britain's banking fraudsters. *BBC News.* Retrieved November 8, 2006, from http://news.bbc.co.uk/2/hi/business/4808830.stm

CUISPA IT Security Cooperative. (2006). *Announcements.* Retrieved October 10, 2006, from http://www.cuispa.or/announcement.php?12

De Leon, J. M. (2006, November 29). Anatomy of a scam. *The Frederick News-Post.* Retrieved December 1, 2006, from http://www.fredericknewspost.com\sections/printer_friendly.htm?storyid=54393&secti

Dempsey, J., & Rubinstein, I. (2006, May/June). Lawyers and techologies: Joined at the hip? *IEEE Security and Privacy* (pp. 15-19).

Edwards, G. (2006, October 3). *U.S. banking group sees protections in Internet gambling bill.* Retrieved October 3, 2006, from http://www.smh.com.au/news/breaking-news/us-banking-group-sees-protections-in-int...

Entrust, Inc. (2006, August). *Understanding the FFIEC guidance on authentication: What you should know as the deadline approaches.* Retrieved from www.knowledgestorm.com/shared/write/collateral/WTP/12962_29300_28879_Understanding_FFIEC_Guidance.pdf?kis=1296244&KSC=1261869603

Espiner, T. (2006, June 27). *Police arrest suspected bot herders.* Retrieved December 6, 2006, from http://news.com.com/2102-7348_3-6088552.html?tag=st.util.print

FBI/CSI. (2005). *2005 Computer crime survey.* Retrieved December 6, 2006, from http://www.digitalriver.com.v2.0-ing.operations/naievigi/site/media/pdf/FBICCS2005.pdf

FFIEC. (2006). Retrieved November 1, 2006, from www.ffiec.gov/pdf/authentication_guidance.pdf (hereinafter "Guidance")

Gross, G. (2006). *Security vendor settles charges after getting hacked.* Retrieved November 20, 2006, from http://www.computerworld.com/action/article.do?command=viewArticleBasic&tax...

Hall, M. (2006, November 30). U.S. warns that terrorists are calling for cyberattack on banks, brokerages. *USA Today.* Retrieved from http://infragard.net/library/us_warns.htm

Harold, K. (2006, September 6). Bill makes threat of 'Big Brother watching' very real, experts warn. *Ottawa Business Journal.* Retrieved from http://www.ottawabusinessjournal.com/329658445911597.php

Internet Gambling Enforcement Act of 2006. Retrieved from http:www.rules.house.gov/109_2[nd]/text/hr/49543.portscr.pdf <accessed 12/6/06>, www.playwinningpoker.com/online/poker/legal/uigea <accessed 12/6/06>

Kaspersen, H. W. K. (2006). Jurisdiction in the cybercrime convention. In Brenner & Koops

(Eds.), *Cybercrime and jurisdiction: A global survey*. The Hague: T.M.C. Asser Press.

Krazit, T. (2006). *FBI nabs phishers in US, Poland; Next stop: Romania*. Retrieved December 6, 2006, from http://networks.silicon.com/webwatch/0,39024876,39163835,00.htm

Krebs, B. (2006, March 16). Hacking made easy. *Washington Post*. Retrieved October 15, 2006, from http://www.washingtonpost.com/wp-dyn/content/article/2006/03/16/AR20060316009...

Lai, E. (2006). Identity thieves hit customers at TD Ameritrade, E-Trade. *Computerworld*. Retrieved November 20, 2006, from http://www.computerworld.com/action/article.do?command=printArticleBasic&art...

Lomas, N. (2006). *Security from A to Z: Botnet*. Retrieved December 6, 2006, from http://news.com.com/2102-7355_3-6138435.html?tag=st.util.print

Mostrous, A., & Cobain, I. (2006). CIA's secret UK bank trawl may be illegal. *The Guardian*, Retrieved August 21, 2006, from http://www.guardian.co.uk/terrorism/story/0,,1854813,00.html

Oiaga, M. (2006). *Panda software warns of online money laundering schemes*. Retrieved October 15, 2006, from http://news.softpedia.com/news/Panda-Software-Warns-of-Online-Money-Laundering...

OUT-LAW News. (2006, November 1). *UK banks agree to data sharing, warn on outcomes*. Retrieved November 20, 2006, from http://out-law.com/default.aspx?page=7438

OUT-LAW News. (2007, January). *Bank hit by 'biggest ever' hack*. Retrieved February 28, 2007, from http://out-law.com/deafult.aspx?page=7629

OUT-LAW News. (2007, January). *London Police can't cope with cybercrime*. 1/30/07, 2007 Archives, OUT-Law_COM.htm

Paul, L. G. (2006, August 7). Bank thwarts threats from within. *eWeek*. Retrieved September 19, 2006, from http://www.eweek.com/article2/0,1895,1997957,00.asp

Physorg.com. (2006). *FBI survey finds cybercrime rising*. Retrieved November 30, 2006, from http://www.physorg.com/printnews.php?newsid=10166

Physorg.com. *Fingerprint advances will fight cybercrime*. Retrieved November 30, 2006, from http://www.physorg.com/printnews.php?newsid=11171

Physorg.com. *More targeted cyber attacks likely in 2006*. Retrieved November 30, 2006, from http://www.physorg.com/printnews.php?newsid=10148

Purugganan, A. A. (1998). Philippine cybersecurity update: Laws, cases and other legal issues. In P. C. Reich (Ed.), *Cybercrime and security*. Oceana Publications: Oxford University Press.

Sasaki, S. (2006). *Keynote speech*. Conference for the Asian IT Standardization (CAIST), Singapore, November 2, 2006 (author's file).

Security Breach Information Law, SB 1386. Ch. 915 (California). Retrieved from http://info.sen.ca.gov/pub/01-02/bill/sb_1351-1400/sb_1386_bill_200220926_chaptered.html

Shin & Kim (2006). *Legal update: Recent developments in the Korean legal environment*. Summer 2006 (pp. 7-8).

Smitherman, L. (2006). Online banking won't be so easy anymore. *Nashua Telegraph*. Retrieved October 12, 2006, from http://www.nashuatelegraph.com/apps/pbcs.dll/article?Date=20061010&Category=B

The Register. (2006, October 16). UK.gov may allow data sharing on 40 million bank accounts. Retrieved November 20, 2006, from http://www.theregister.co.uk/2006/10/16/uk_bank_data_

sharing_proposals/ Consultation paper at http://reporting.dti.gov.uk/cgi-bin/rr.cgi.http://www.dti.gov.uk/files/file34513.pdf

United Press International. (2006). *Japan police struggle against cybercrime*. Retrieved November 30, 2006, from http://www.physorg.com/printnews.php?newsid=11178

U.S. Department of Justice. (2003). *Operation cyber sweep, Justice Department announced 'operation cyber sweep' targeting online economic fraud*. Retrieved November 20, 2003, from http://www.fbi.gov/dojpressrel/pressrel03/cyber112003.htm and http://www.fbi.gov/cyber/cysweep1.htm

Waddell, D. (2006, June 7). *Internet wagering becomes a felony in Washington state*. Retrieved December 6, 2006, from http://info.detnews.com/casino/newdetails.cfm?column=waddell&myrec=251

Waddell, D. (2006, October 11). *Congress passes Unlawful Internet Gambling Enforcement Act of 2006*. Retrieved December 6, 2006, from http://info.detnews.com/casino/newdetails.cfm?column=waddell&myrec=262

Weinberg, J. (2006). *Everyone's a winner: Regulation, not prohibiting, Internet gambling*. 35 S.W. U.L. Rev.293, 2006.

Weismann, M. F. Miquelon (2006). International cybercrime: Recent developments in the law. In R. D. Clifford (Ed.), *Cybercrime: The investigation, prosecution and defense of a computer-related crime* (2nd ed.). NC: Carolina Academic Press.

ZDnet. (2006). *Zombies try to blend in with the crowd*. Retrieved November 29, 2006, from http://news.zdnet.com/2102-1009_22-6127304.html

ZDNETINDIA. (2006). *'Logic bomb' backfires on insider hacker*. Retrieved December 14, 2006, from http://www.zdnetindia.com/print.html?iElementId=164631

Zeller, T., Jr. (2006, February 27). Cyberthieves silently copy your passwords as you type. *The New York Times*. Retrieved June 29, 2006, from http://www.nytimes.com/2006/02/27/technology/27hack.html?ei=5088&en=b794....

ADDITIONAL READING

America Online and the National Cyber Security Alliance, *AOL/NCSA Online Safety Study*, 12/05, pdf.

Ackerman, E. (2006, September 29). PayPal agrees to settle lawsuits; Firm to give users better information. *San Jose Mercury News*, (CALIFORNIA).

Akron Beacon Journal (Ohio), "*Don't Buy Into Fraud at Auction Web Sites*," 8/6/04, p. D1.

Akron Beacon Journal (Ohio), "*PayPal to Fine Users Who Violate Policy*," 9/14/04, p. D2.

Allen, P. (2006, April 1). Add another bolt to the cyber door; Financial institutions are searching for multifactor authentication strategies as regulators push more security mandates. *Wall Street & Technology*, p. 28.

Amato-McCoy, D. M. (2006, July 1). Closing the door on criminals: Regulations and increased incidents of fraud are forcing banks to rethink their siloed detection initiatives. *Bank Systems and Technology*. Retrieved from http://banktech.com (p. 31).

Anti-Phishing Working Group. (2006, October) *The crimeware landscape: Malware, phishing, identity theft and beyond*. Retrieved from http://www.antiphishing.org/reports/APWG_CrimewareReport.pdf

APACS (UK payments association). *Top tips for safe online banking and shopping*. Retrieved from www.cardwatch.org.uk and www.banksafeonline.org.uk

Barnett, L. (2006). eBay urged to get tough on fraudsters. *Press Association Newsfile.*

BBC NEWS. (2006, October 20). *European phishing gangs targeted.* Retrieved from http://news.bbc.co.uk/2/hi/technology/4825072.stm

BBC NEWS. (2006). *Internet crime to hit homes hard.* Retrieved from http://news.bbc.co.uk/1/hi/technology/5377334.stm

BBC NEWS. (2006). *Some shops lacking chip and pin.* Retrieved from http://news.bbc.co.uk/2/hi/business/4705774.stm

Ballard, M. (2006, January 20). Banks make it easy for scammers. *Channel Register.* Retrieved from http://www.channelregister.co.uk/2006/01/20/fat_lazy_banks/

Better Business Bureau. (2005, January 26). *New research shows that identity theft is more paper than online.* Retrieved from http://www.bbb.org/alerts/article.asp?ID=565

Beveridge, J. (2006, June 20). Frauds flex plastic muscle. *Herald Sun* (p. 56).

Brenner, S. W., & Koops, B. (2006). *Cybercrime and jurisdiction: A global survey.* T.M.C. Asser Press: The Hague.

Brenner, S. W. (2001). Is there such a thing as 'virtual crime'? *California Criminal Law Review, 1*(4). Retrieved from http://www.boalt.org/bjcl/v4/v4brenner.htm

Bednarz, A. (2005, June 13). Online businesses face credit card security deadline. *Network World* (p. 79).

Berger, Andrew K. (2007, February 22). Is that really you? ID theft and authentication, Part I. *E-Commerce Times.* Retrieved from http://www.technewsworld.com/rsstory/55888.html

Berger, A. K. (2007, February 25). New Layers of Defense: ID Theft and Authentication, Part 2. *E-Commerce Times.* Retrieved from http://www.technewsworld.com/rsstory/55945.html

Boone, R. (2006, May 14). Junk e-mail: When in doubt, don't respond. *The Olympian* (Olympia, Washington), Business and Financial News.

BS Banking Bureau (2001). *RBI unveils Net banking norms.* Retrieved from http://www.rediff.com/money/2001/jun/21net.htm

Bruno-Britz, M. (2005, October 1). Online authentication is a two-way street; Zions, ING are among the banks starting to deploy mutual authentication technology. *Bank Systems & Technology* (p. 11).

Business Wire. (2004, March 13). PayPal alerts customers about possible deceptive e-mails. *Business Wire.*

Cassidy, M. (2004, March 3). eBay scammer mixes baby formula scheme. *San Jose Mercury News* (p. 1C).

Chabrow, E. (2005, March 21). Feds mull identity protection—House committee chairman says legislation to restrict the sale of Social Security numbers is likely in wake of ChoicePoint and LexisNexis breaches. *InformationWeek,* p. 67.

Clark, D. (2003, July 21). Gone 'phishing': New form of ID theft prompts warning. *National Journal's Technology Daily,* (P.M. Ed.).

Clarke, D. (2005, August 15). Fraudsters pose as anti-fraud group. *Investment News.*

Crain's Cleveland Business. (2006, October 2). identiCenter. 10/2/06 (p. 27).

Computer Weekly. (2006, June 28). *Finance firms face surge in security breaches.* Retrieved from http://www.computerweekly.com/Articles

Daily Yomiuri. (2006, April 15). Suspected heads of ATM data-theft group arrested (p. 2).

De Noma, M. (2006). *Testimony for the United States Senate Committee on banking, housing and urban affairs, combating child pornography by eliminating pornographers' access to the financial* payment system. http://www.icmec.org/en_x1/pdf/MikeDeNomaTestimony.pdf

Downing, R. W. (2005). Shoring up the weakest link: What lawmakers around the world need to consider in developing comprehensive laws to combat cybercrime. *Columbia Journal of Transnational Law, 43,* 705.

Electricnews.net. (2006, September 7). High tech crime forum to fight phishing. *The Register,* www.theregister.co.uk/2006/09/07/irish_phishing_forum/

Encarnacao, J. (2007, February 27). Thievery—Third of four parts—Banks shore up ID security: Thanks to government regulation, lenders lead retailers in assessing fraud risk. *The Patriot Ledger,* http://ledger.southofboston.com/articles/2007/02/27/news/news01.txt

Feig, N. (2006, September 1). The final countdown; As the FFIEC online banking authentication deadline looms, banks work through the confusion to select their solutions. *Bank Systems & Technology,* p. 11.

Feig, N. (2006, September 1). Keeping insiders out; A new BITS database of bank employees who have committed insider fraud aims to keep them from being rehired. *Bank Systems & Technology,* p. 21.

Garretson, C. (2006, April 3). Phishing steals spotlight at MIT spam conference. *Network World* (p. 10).

Garvey, M. J. (n.d.). Switch and bait: Scams target the smaller fry—with customers of large institutions wary, e-mail crooks turn to smaller banks. *Informationweek News,* p. 30.

Gaudin, S. (2006, July 21). *UBS trial aftermath: Even great security can't protect you from the insider.* Retrieved from http://www.financetech.com/news

Gayer, J. (2003, May). *Policing privacy: Law enforcement response to identity Theft.* Retrieved from www.calpirg.org/reports/policingprivacy2003.pdf

Gordon, S., & Ford, R. (2006, August). On the definition and classification of cybercrime. *Journal In Computer Virology, 2*(1).

Gross, G. (2006, August 24). *Investigator urges companies to report cybercrime.* Retrieved from http://www.computerworld.com/

Greenemeier, L. (2006, May 1). Growth can be risky business: Financial institutions are focused on selling, to the detriment of data security. *Bank Systems & Technology,* p. 23.

Greenemeier, L. (2006, March 1). Security: Banks benefit as authentication providers duke it out. *Bank Systems & Technology,* p. 12.

Greenemeier, L. (2005, November 14). Online businesses step up their authentication services—Worries are growing that online ID-theft threats will hinder electronic banking growth. *Information Week,* p. 32.

Hansard, S. (2006, June 26). SEC scrutinizes firms for vulnerability to hackers; Computer criminals have adopted more sophisticated techniques. *Investment News,* p. 1.

Hasch, M. (2006, August 17). PNC Bank customers defrauded on phony Katrina aid sites. *Pittsburgh Tribune.*

Heinricks, A. M. (2007, February 25). Computer dangers that lurk within. *Pittsburgh Tribune-Review.* Retrieved from http://pittsburghlive.com/x/pittsburghtrib/news/rss/s_494080.html

Higashi, N. (2005, March 6). Devices offer handy way for businesses to identify customers. *The Yomiuri Shimbun.*

Horwath, A. (2006, August 7). Banks introduce electronic password gadget to beat rise in internet fraud. *The Scotsman.* Retrieved from http://news.scotsman.com/scitech.cfm?id=1141612006

Investment News. (2006). *Editorial: Congress must combat identity theft* (p. 8).

IT Compliance Institute. (2006, November 6). *Prosecution watch—Police break up phishing gang in U.S., Poland.* Retrieved from http://www.itcinstitute.com/display.aspx?id=2589

Iron Port Systems, Inc. (2006, September) Malware trends: The attack of blended spyware crime. *The Web Security Report.* Retrieved from www.websecurityreport.com

Keizer, G., & Bruno-Britz, M. (2006, August 1). Deep sea phishing in Citi's waters; Phishing scheme circumvents two-factor authentication. *Bank Systems & Technology* (p. 15).

Kellermann, T. (2004, November). CISM, "Money laundering in cyberspace," The World Bank Financial Sector Working Paper.

Kendler, P. B. (2006). Security outlook. *Bank Systems & Technology* (p. 40).

Kopytoff, V. (2004, June 15). eBay settled PayPal fraud lawsuit. *The San Francisco Chronicle* (p. C3).

Kopytoff, V. (2002, July 13). New York wants PayPal's records on dealings with Net casinos. *The San Francisco Chronicle* (p. B1).

Langberg, M. (2006, August 28). Most identity theft not online, but hype is scaring away users, and could harm tech economy. *San Jose Mercury News.*

Lazarus, D. (2005, November 6). *Data theft bill a step backward.* Retrieved from http://www.sfgate.com/cgi-bin/article.cgi?file=/c/a/2005/11/06/BUGP0FJ17S1.DTL&t...

Lemos, R. (2005, December 7). Consumers improving security, but gaps remain. *Security Focus.* Retrieved from http://www.securityfocus.com/print/news/11361

Lemos, R. (2006, November 3). *FBI nabs suspected identity-theft ring.* Retrieved from http://www.securityfocus.com/print/brief/347

Leyden, J. (2006, November 3). FBI-led probe nets phishing gang. *The Register.* Retrieved from http://www.theregister.co.uk/2006/11/03/operation_cardkeeper_phishing_arrests/

Leyden, J. (2006, September 22). Online manuals enable ATM reprogramming scam. *The Register.* Retrieved from http://www.theregister.co.uk/2006/09/22/atm_reprogram_scam/

Leyden, J. (2006, October 25). ID theft cam hunt goes global. *The Register.* Retrieved from http://www.theregister.co.uk/2006/10/25/id_theft_scam_hunt/print.html

Loeb, M. (2004, August 11). MONEY: Internet auctions can be a rip-off; Be aware of con artists' tricks. *The Sun-Herald* (p. F3).

Marlin, S. (2005, June 20). Visa system targets credit-fraud rings—Now it's up to banks to work this latest weapon against ID theft into their systems. *InformationWeek* (p. 32).

Marlin, S. (2005, July 11). To catch an ID thief—Bank-sponsored identity theft assistance center will share information with the FTC to help catch identity thieves. *InformationWeek* (p. 64).

Marlin, S. (2005, October 24). Banks told to step up security against identity theft—Regulators give them until end of 2006 to add two-step protection. *InformationWeek* (p. 32).

McAfee Virtual Criminology Report (2006, December). *Organised crime and the Internet.* Retrieved from www.mcafee.com/us/local_content/white_papers/threat_center/wp_virtual_criminology_report_2007.pdf

McLaughlin, K. (2006, July 24). Voice phishers work harder to get your number. *Computer Reseller News* (p. 49).

McMillan, R. (2006). Malaysia government portal used by PayPal phishers. *Network World*. Retrieved from http://www.networkworld.com/news/2006/111806-malaysia-government-portal-used-by.html

Messmer, E. (2005, March 7). Financial firms bolster authentication. *Network World*.

Messmer, E. (2005, October 18). Advisory body calls for stronger authentication in Internet banking. *Network World*.

Messmer, E. (2006, September 6). Banks under gun to bolster online security: Federal guidance pushes industry to find safer ways to protect transactions. *Network World*.

Messmer, E. (2006, October 27). Tech presents legal system with 'tremendous curves'. *Computer World*. Retrieved from http://www.computerworld.com/action/article.do?command=viewArticleBasic&taxonomyName=cybercrime_hacking&articleId=82

Mitchell, L. (2000, October 16). E-cash aims to ease security-and-privacy-concerned shoppers. *InfoWorld* (p. 102).

Musgrove, M. (2004, March 16). PayPal warns its customers to safeguard personal data: Phony e-mails sent to try to get credit card numbers. *The Washington Post* (Final Edition).

National Cyber Security Alliance (2005, December 7). *One in four computer users hit by phishing each month, acccording to major in-home consumer safety study*. Retrieved from http://www.staysafeonline.org/news/press_dec07_2005.html

National Journal's Technology Daily. (2004, May 18). *Crime* (PM Edition).

National Security Alliance and Bank of America. (2006, May). *Online Fraud Report*.

Newsfactor Magazine Online (2006, May 26). House panel backs internet gambling limits. Retrieved from http://www.newsfactor.com/story.xhtml?story_id=123000036V46

New York State Information Security Breach and Notification Act. Retrieved from http://www.cscic.state.ny.us/security/securitybreach/

Nikkei Weekly (2005, May 9). *Smart ATM cards gaining popularity*.

PWC Advisory and CIO Magazine, *The Global State Of Information Security* 2006, pdf.

Parke et al. v. Cardsystems Solutions, Inc. CGC-05-442624. Retrieved from http://www.techfirm.com/cardsystems.pdf

Paul, Lauren Gibbons, *Bank thwarts threats from within*. Retrieved from http://www.eweek.com/article2\0,1895,1997957,00.asp

Productivity Software. (2005, May). *Travelex implements Norkom Software to service all operations*.

Pierson, G. (2007, February 28). *Securing your online ID: Beyond username and password*. Retrieved from http://www.technewsworld.com/rsstory/55998.html

Radcliff, D. (2002, January 14). Cybersleuthing solves the case: Computer forensic investigators use a variety of methods and tools to nab cybercriminals. *ComputerWorld*, p. 36.

Radcliff, D. (2002, January 14). Forensic detectives; cybercops; digital sleuths. Call them what you will, the emerging ranks of IT forensics professionals not only solve systems crimes—They can also add to the bottom line. *ComputerWorld* (p. 32).

Radcliff, D. (2005, April 11). Fighting back against phishing; In the past year, attacks have grown in volume and sophistication, but online merchants are on the offensive with consumer education and new authentication tools. *ComputerWorld*, p. 48.

Radcliff, D. (2006, May 22). Sport phishing morphs into cybercrime wave; Organized criminals unleash armies of botnets to steal confidential information. *Network World* (p. 40).

Radcliff, D. (2006, June 26). Online banks strengthen security: Financial firms tap multifactor authentication to give customers an added level of protection. *Network World* (p. 59).

Ramasastry, A. (2005, February 10). *Do banks have a legal duty to notify customers about specific computer viruses? A Miami suit raises the question.* Retrieved from http://writ.lp.findlaw.com/ramasastry/20050210.html

Ramasastry, A. (2005, July 13). *Do banks and other businesses have a duty to notify customers of computer security breaches? A recent California suit, and a possible federal law.* Retrieved from http://writ.lp.findlaw.com/ramasastry/20050713.html

Ramasastry, A. (2006, March 29). *Debit card debacles: Why consumers need to worry about the recent, massive wave of debit card fraud, and what legal and technological protections can prevent future harm.* Retrieved from http://writ.lp.findlaw.com/ramasastry/20060329.html

Ramasastry, A. (2006, July 7). *The Treasury Department's secret monitoring of international funds transfers: Why it is probably legal, at least in the United States.* Retrieved from http://writ.lp.findlaw.com/ramasastry/20060707.html

Ramasastry, A. (2006, October 10). *The new federal law banning payments for online gambling: Why it's the wrong choice.* Retrieved from http://writ.lp.findlaw.com/ramasastry/20061010.html

Ramstack, T. (2005, October 6). Giuliani offers strategy on identity theft. *The Washington Times.*

Reich, P. C. (Ed.). (1998-present, looseleaf). *Cybercrime and security, 3.* Oceana: Oxford University Press.

Roberts, S. (2005, November 28). Increased security needed to tackle phishing threat. *Business Insurance* (p. 11).

Seoul Metropolitan Police Agency. (n.d.). *Holes in Internet banking security.* Retrieved from http://www.cybercrime.go.kr/community/download.html?code=eng_news&filename=Holes_in_Internet_Banking_Security.pdf

Spicer, P. (2006, January 9). Identity thieves may target your affluent clients. *Investment News* (p. 28).

Spiller, K. (2005, Juanuary 5). eBay's PayPal appears in latest e-mail fraud. *The Telegraph.*

States News Service (2006, September 28.). Louisiana Attorney General reaches agreement with PayPal to protect consumers. *States News Service.*

Sturdevant, C. (2005, November 21). Reporting fraud should be easy: Simple, clear instructions will benefit all phish finders. *eWeek* (p. 51).

Sullivan, B. (2004, March 8). *PayPal fraud process scrutinized.* MSNBC.com

Sydney M. X. (2006, April 18). *Net to reveal accounts* (p. 11).

Tabb, L. (2006, May 1). Tony Soprano and my social security number. *Wall Street & Technology* (p. 54).

TECHWEB. (2006, March 20). *Visa warns software may store PINS.*

TECHWEB. (2006, March 8). *Researchers terminate sites selling trojans.*

TECHWEB. *TechEncyclopedia.* Retrieved from http://www.techweb.com/encyclopedia

The Economic Times (India). (2006, March 20). Brisk demand for anti-fraud software. *The Economic Times,*

Tobin, A. (2006, February 19). Growing anger over Ebay payment firm. *Sunday Times* (LONDON), P. 9.

U.S. Department of Justice. (2005, November 1). *Houston man pleads guilty to federal identity theft charges, says Justice Department*. Retrieved from http://www.usdoj.gov/criminal/cybercrime/hattenPlea.htm

U.S. Department of Justice. (2005, November 28). *Man pleads guilty to infecting thousands of computers using worm program then launching them in denial of service attacks*. Retrieved from http://www.usdoj.gov/criminal/cybercrime/clarkPlea.htm

U.S. Department of Justice. (2006, February 28). *Cleveland, Ohio man sentenced to prison for bank fraud and conspiracy*. Retrieved from http://www.usdoj.gov/criminal/cybercrime/flurySent.htm

U.S. Department of Justice. (2006, June 23). *Former Technology Manager Sentenced to a Year in Prison for Computer Hacking Offense; Jury Convicted Defendant for Placing Computer 'Time Bomb' On Employer's Network that Corrupted Over 57,000 Records*. http://www.usdoj.gov/criminal/cybercrime/sheaSent.htm

U.S. Department of Justice. *Six Defendants plead guilty in internet identity theft and credit card fraud conspiracy: Shadowcrew Organization was called 'one-stop online marketplace for identity theft'*. Retrieved from http://www.usdoj.gov/criminal/cybercrime/mantovaniPlea.htm

Valentine, L. (2006, May 1). Collaboration is job one. *Bank Systems & Technology*.

Voelker, M. P. (2006, September 1). Stay a step ahead of fraud: Perpetrators of fraud are changing tactics faster than traditional methods of detection can track. Predictive analytics, authentication and rules engines are helping companies detect and fight crime. *Intelligent Enterprise* (p. 39).

Vijayan, J. (2005, December 14). Card skimmers eyed in Sams Club data theft; An Alabama credit union official says the breach may affect thousands of customers. *ComputerWorld*.

Vijayan, J. (2006, March 10). Lack of candor heightens public concern about debit card fraud; Credit card firms remain mostly mum about thefts. *ComputerWorld*.

Vijayan, J. (2006, November 17). Retail breach forces banks to cancel cards; Data compromise in Michigan results in fraudulent credit, debit transactions. *ComputerWorld*.

Visa USA. Common frauds—Email frauds—Phishing. Retrieved from http://usa.visa.com/personal/security/protect_yourself/common_frauds/phishing...

Visa USA. *Online shopping protection*. Retrieved from http://usa.visa.com/personal/security/protect_yourself/common_frauds/online_shopping_prot...

Wall Street & Technology. (2006, November 1). *Mystery shopping for effective fraud prevention* (p. 14).

Wall Street & Technology. (2006, May 1). *Four keys to stronger online security* (p. 12).

Ward, M. (2006, July 18). Criminals exploit net phone calls. *BBC News*. Retrieved from http://news.bbc.co.uk/2/hi/technology/5187518.stm

Westby, J. (2003). *International guide to combatting cybercrime*. American Bar Association, Privacy and Computer Crime Committee. Section of Science and Technology Law. Chicago, Il.

Westby, J. (2004). *International guide to cyber security*. American Bar Association, Privacy and Computer Crime Committee. Section of Science and Technology Law. Chicago, Il.

Westby, J. (2005). *International guide to privacy*. American Bar Association, Privacy and Computer Crime Committee. Section of Science and Technology Law. Chicago, Il.

Young, T. (2006, December 15). *Cybercrime set to develop its own economy*. Retrieved from http://www.computing.co.uk/articles/print/2171083

Zetter, K. (2006, July 28). Confessions of a cyber-mule. *Wired News*. Retrieved from http://www.wired.com/news/technology/1,71479-0.html

NOTE: Where an Internet citation (URL) is not given for a source, it was found on LEXIS/NEXIS databases.

ENDNOTES

[1] OUT-LAW, "London Police can't cope with cybercrime," 1/30/07, 2007 Archives, OUT-Law_COM.htm

[2] Australian Institute of Criminology, High Tech Crime Brief, Concepts and Terms, New Crimes and Old Crimes Committed in New Ways, January 2005, http://www.aic.gov.au.

[3] *Id.*

[4] *Id.*

[5] *See* "Cybercrime" at http://en.wikipedia.org/wiki/Cybercrime

[6] *See, for example,* Susan Brenner, "Cybercrime Law and Policy in the United States," in Pauline C. Reich, Ed., CYBERCRIME AND SECURITY (Oceana, a division of Oxford University Press).

[7] Miriam F. Miquelon Weismann, "International Cybercrime: Recent Developments in the Law," in Ralph D. Clifford, Ed., CYBERCRIME: THE INVESTIGATION, PROSECUTION AND DEFENSE OF A COMPUTER-RELATED CRIME, 2ND Ed., Carolina Academic Press (North Carolina) p. 243.

[8] 2005 FBI Computer Crime Survey, http://www.digitalriver.com.v2.0-ing.operations/naievigi/site/media/pdf/FBICCS2005.pdf <accessed 12/6/06>

[9] Dr. Samuel Sander, Clemson University, Computer Engineering Department, *Id.,* page 4.

[10] *Id.,* page 5.

[11] *Id.,* page 5.

[12] *Id.,* page 11.

[13] *Id.,* page 12.

[14] "FBI survey finds cybercrime rising," http://www.physorg.com/printnews.php?newsid=10166 <accessed 11/30/06>

[15] AusCERT 2006 Australian Computer Crime and Security Survey, Executive Summary, page 4, http://www.auscert.org/au/render.html?it=2001

[16] *Id.,* page 5.

[17] *Id.,* page 8.

[18] AusCERT, 2006 Australian Computer Crime and Security Survey, page 20, http://www.auscert.org/au/render.html?it=2001

[19] *Id.,* page 21.

[20] "New Symantec Survey Reveals Security Doubts Shape Internet Behavior," Computerworld, October 24, 2006, http://www.computerworld.com.au/index.php/id;1356571409;fp;;fpid;;pf;1 <accessed 11/8/06>

[21] Council of Europe Convention on Cybercrime, Budapest, November 23, 2001 (CETS 185), http://conventions.coe.int/Treaty/en/Treaties/Html/185.htm

[22] Henrik W. K. Kaspersen, "Jurisdiction in the Cybercrime Convention," in Brenner and Koops, Editors, CYBERCRIME AND JURISDICTION: A Global Survey (2006), The Hague: T.M.C. Asser Press.

[23] *See* Abraham A. Purugganan, "Philippine Cybersecurity Update: Laws, Cases and other Legal Issues," in Pauline C. Reich, Editor, CYBERCRIME AND SECURITY, Oceana Publications, a division of Oxford University Press, 1998-present. For additional discussion of cross-border jurisdiction

over Cybercrime in countries worldwide, *see* Bert-Jaap Koops and Susan W. Brenner, Editors, CYBERCRIME AND JURISDICTION: A GLOBAL SURVEY, T.M.C. Asser Press, The Hague, 2006.

24 *See, for example,* Canada, Department of Justice, "Extradition Reform, Dual Criminality," http://www.hystuce,gc,ca.eb.bews.br.1998.extrart.htm/ and UNAFEI, Specific Problems that Arise in Cases Involving International Mutual Legal Assistance or Extradition," 114th International Training Course, Reports of the Seminar, Resource Material Series No. 57, www.unafei.or.jp/english/pdf/PDF_rms/no57/57-15.pdf

25 Laura Smitherman, "Online banking won't be so easy anymore," NASHUA TELEGRAPH, http://www.nashuatelegraph.com/apps/pbcs.dll/article?Date=20061010&Category=B <accessed 10/12/06>

26 This is a collaboration among the Board of Governors of the Federal Reserve System, the Federal Deposit Insurance Corporation, National Credit Union Administration, Office of the Comptroller of the Currency, and the Office of Thrift Supervision.

27 Tom Zeller Jr., "Cyberthieves Silently Copy Your Passwords as You Type," THE NEW YORK TIMES, February 27, 2006, http://www.nytimes.com/2006/02/27/technology/27hack.html?ei=5088&en=b794.... <accessed 6/29/06>

28 *See* www.ffiec.gov/pdf/authentication_guidance.pdf (hereinafter "Guidance") <accessed 11/1/06>

29 *Id.*

30 *Id.*

31 *Id. See also* FFIEC, Information Security IT EXAMINATION HANDBOOK, July 2006, http:// www.ffiec.gov/ffiecinfobase/htm_pages/infosec_book_frame.htm

32 Guidance and Appendix, and FDIC Study, "Putting an End to Account-Hijacking Identity Theft," (December 14, 2004) and the FDIC Study Supplement (June 17, 2005). For an overview of the various kinds of authentication methods and an explanation of each, *see* Entrust, Inc., "Understanding the FFIEC Guidance on Authentication: What you should know as the deadline approaches," August 2006, www.knowledgestorm.com/shared/write/collateral/WTP/12962_29300_28879_Understanding_FFIEC_Guidance.pdf?kis=1296244&KSC=1261869603

33 Shigeru Sasaki, Keynote Speech, Conference for the Asian IT Standardization (CAIST), Singapore, November 2, 2006.

34 *See, e.g.* "Fingerprint Advances Will Fight Cybercrime," Physorg.com, http://www.physorg.com/printnews.php?newsid=11171 <accessed 11/30/06>

35 Shigeru Sasaki, Keynote Speech, Conference for the Asian IT Standardization (CAIST), Singapore, November 2, 2006.

36 Shin and Kim, LEGAL UPDATE; Recent Developments in the Korean Legal Environment, Summer 2006, pp. 7-8.

37 *Id.*

38 *Id.*

39 *Id.*

40 Jon Cronin, "Taking on Britain's banking fraudsters," BBC News, March 15, 2006, http://news.bbc.co.uk/2/hi/business/4808830.stm <accessed 11/8/06>

41 *Id.*

42 *Id.*

43 Eric Lai, "Identity thieves hit customers at TD Ameritrade, E-Trade," COMPUTERWORLD, http://www.computerworld.com/action/article.do?command=printArticleBasic&art... <accessed 11/20/06>

44 Amy Borrus, "Invasion of the Stock Hackers," BUSINESS WEEK, November 14, 2005, pp. 38, 40.

45 *Id.*, p. 40.

46 U.S. Department of Justice, Operation Cyber Sweep, "Justice Department Announced

47 *Id.*
48 *Id.*
49 *Id.*
50 Grant Gross, "Security vendor settles charges after getting hacked," http://www.computerworld.com/action/article.do?command=viewArticleBasic&tax...<accessed 11/20/06>
51 Tom Krazit, "FBI nabs phishers in US, Poland; Next stop:Romania... " http://networks.silicon.com/webwatch/0,39024876,39163835,00.htm <accessed 12/6/06>
52 2006 Australian Computer Crime and Security Survey, p. 20.
53 U.S. Department of Justice, Operation Cyber Sweep, "Justice Department Announced 'Operation Cyber Sweep Targeting Online Economic Fraud, 11/20/03, http://www.fbi.gov/dojpressrel/pressrel03/cyber112003.htm and http://www.fbi.gov/cyber/cysweep1.htm
54 *Id.*
55 Internet Gambling Enforcement Act in http:www.rules.house.gov/109_2nd/text/hr/49543.portscr.pdf <accessed 12/6/06> The Anti-Gambling legislation is part of a comprehensive Port Security bill. For just the text of the Internet Gambling Enforcement Act of 2006, see, for example, www.playwinningpoker.com/online/poker/legal/uigea <accessed 12/6/06>.
56 Greg Edwards, "U.S. banking group sees protections in Internet gambling bill," http://www.smh.com.au/news/breaking-news/us-banking-group-sees-protections-in-int..." October 3, 2006, <accessed 10/3/06>
57 David Waddell, "Internet Wagering Becomes a Felony in Washington State," June 7, 2006, http://info.detnews.com/casino/newdetails.cfm?column=waddell&myrec=251 <accessed 12/6/06>
58 David Waddell, "Congress Passes Unlawful Internet Gambling Enforcement Act of 2006," October 11, 2006, http://info.detnews.com/casino/newdetails.cfm?column=waddell&myrec=262 <accessed 12/6/06>
59 *See, for example,* Joel Weinberg, "Everyone's a Winner: Regulation, Not Prohibiting, Internet Gambling," 35 Sw. U.L. Rev. 293 (2006)
60 *Id.*
61 Eric Lai, note 43, above.
62 Security Breach Information Law, SB 1386, Ch. 915) (California), http://info.sen.ca.gov/pub/01-02/bill/sb_1351-1400/sb_1386_bill_200220926_chaptered.html
63 U.S. Department of Justice, Operation Cyber Sweep, "Justice Department Announced 'Operation Cyber Sweep' Targeting Online Economic Fraud," 11/20/03, http://www.fbi.gov/dojpressrel/pressrel03/cyber112003.htm and http://www.fbi.gov/cyber/cysweep1.htm
64 In this operation, there were more than 125 investigations, over $100,000,000 in losses, more than 125,000 victims, 350 subjects, more than 125 arrests and convictions, the issuance of more than 90 search and seizure warrants, and over 70 indictments.
65 "Announcements," CUISPA IT Security Co-operative, http://www.cuispa.or/announcement.php?12 <accessed 10/10/06>
66 Brian Krebs, "Hacking Made Easy," WASHINGTON POST, March 16, 2006, http://www.washingtonpost.com/wp-dyn/content/article/2006/03/16/AR20060316009... <accessed 10/15/06>
66 *Id.*
67 *Id.*
68 Tom Zeller, Jr., note 4, *supra.*
69 *Id.* According to the same source, keylogger Trojans are "malicious bits of code that

can take advantage of vulnerabilities in unpatched, unprotected operating systems" and "are often hidden inside ordinary software downloads, e-mail attachments, or files shared over peer-to-peer networks. They can even be embedded in Web pages, taking advantage of Web browser features that allow sometimes powerful scripts and programs to run and install automatically." According to the Anti-Phishing Working Group, the number of Web sites known to be hiding this type of malicious code rose to more than 1,900 between November to December 2005. Antivirus company Symantec has reported that half the malicious software it tracks "is designed not to damage computers but to gather personal data."

[70] Id.

[71] U.S. Department of Justice, Operation Cyber Sweep, "Justice Department Announced 'Operation Cyber Sweep' Targeting Online Economic Fraud," 11/20/03, http://www.fbi.gov/dojpressrel/pressrel03/cyber112003.htm and http://www.fbi.gov/cyber/cysweep1.htm

[72] OUT-LAW News, "Bank hit by 'biggest ever' hack," 1/22/07, http://out-law.com/deafult.aspx?page=7629 <accessed 2/28/07>

[73] Natasha Lomas, "Security from A to Z: Botnet," http://news.com.com/2102-7355_3-6138435.html?tag=st.util.print <accessed 12/6/06>

[74] Tom Espiner, "Police arrest suspected bot herders," June 27, 2006, http://news.com.com/2102-7348_3-6088552.html?tag=st.util.print <accessed 12/6/06>

[75] "Zombies try to blend in with the crowd," ZD Net, 10/19/06, http://news.zdnet.com/2102-1009_22-6127304.html <accessed 11/29/06>

[76] United Press International, "Japan Police struggle against cybercrime," http://www.physorg.com/printnews.php?newsid=11178 <accessed 11/30/06>

[77] Marius Oiaga, "Panda Software Warns of Online Money Laundering Schemes," Softpedia, http://news.softpedia.com/news/Panda-Software-Warns-of-Online-Money-Laundering... <accessed 10/15/06>

[78] Joseph M. deLeon, "Anatomy of a scam," November 29, 2006, THE FREDERICK NEWS-POST, http://www.fredericknews-post.com\sections/printer_friendly.htm?storyid=54393&secti... <accessed 12/1/06>

[79] "More targeted cyber attacks likely in 2006," http://www.physorg.com/printnews.php?newsid=10148 <accessed 11/30/06>

[80] Lauren Gibbons Paul, "Bank Thwarts Threats from Within," eWeek, August 7, 2006, http://www.eweek.com/article2/0,1895, 1997957,00.asp <accessed 9/19/06>

[81] Mimi Hall, "U.S. Warns That Terrorists Are Calling for Cyberattack on Banks, Brokerages," USA Today, 11/30/06, http://infragard.net/library/us_warns.htm

[82] Associated Press, "Belgian premier says SWIFT secretly supplied U.S. with bank data," September 28, 2006, http://www.siliconvalley.com/mld/siliconvalley/news/editorial/15630604.htm?template <accessed 9/30/06>. *See also* Alexi Mostrous and Ian Cobain, "CIA's secret UK bank trawl may be illegal," August 21, 2006, The Guardian, http://www.guardian.co.uk/terrorism/story/0,,1854813,00.html <accessed 8/21/06>

[83] "U.K. gov may allow data sharing on 40 million bank accounts," October 16, 2006, http://www.theregister.co.uk/2006/10/16/uk_bank_data_sharing_proposals/ <accessed 11/20/06>. The consultation paper may be accessed at http://reporting.dti.gov.uk/cgi-bin/rr.cgi.http://www.dti.gov.uk/files/file34513.pdf

[84] OUT-LAW News, "UK banks agree to data sharing, warn on outcomes," 11/1/06, http://out-law.com/default.aspx?page=7438, <accessed 11/20/06>

[85] Kristin Harold, "Bill makes threat of 'Big Brother watching' very real, experts warn," 9/6/06, OTTAWA BUSINESS JOURNAL, http://www.ottawabusinessjournal.com/329658445911597.php

[86] James X. Dempsey and Ira Rubinstein, "Lawyers and Techologies: Joined at the Hip?" IEEE SECURITY AND PRIVACY, May/June 2006, http://www.computer.org/security, pages 15-19.

though this was reported to be much less than the 1998 levels (Naone, 2007). Phishing reports to APWG for May 2007 edged lower to 23,762, as phishing grew more targeted and narrowly focused on higher value brands. The password stealing crimeware URLs detected by APWG in May, also decreased more than 40% from April, to 3,088.

Chapter II
Enhancing Cyber Risk Management with the Framework of ERM and Basel II

Junji Hiwatashi
Bank of Japan, Japan

ABSTRACT

How is it possible to enhance efficiency of management and to control cyber risk at the same time so that sustainable growth is achieved? Possible solutions were found in ERM and Basel II. First, a newly introduced ERM is a tool not only for defense against loss but also for a formidable weapon to seek sustainable returns. Appropriate coordination and cooperation in implementing risk management on a firm-wide basis encourages firms to identify, analyze, measure and control all material risks such as cyber risk, and to provide a sound base to make strategic decision on the balance of risk and return, or risk adjusted return on equity. Second, in Basel II, operational risk such as cyber risk is explicitly introduced. The author proposes a practical framework based on ERM and Basel II. It consists of policies and structure, and five steps. This framework is based on the practices of financial institutions but could be applied and expanded to firms in general.

INTRODUCTION

Information technology (IT) has been rapidly developed to provide financial services with customers by the Internet. This service is available 24 hours a day, 7 days a week beyond the boundary. On the other hand, technology-oriented financial services may face various cyber risks such as disruption caused by natural disaster and terrorist attack, impersonation, and other events stemming from unauthorized access, and theft or alternation of data. Once these events occur, they could affect not only companies such as financial institutions but also their stakeholders such as customers and financial stability. These events lead to indirect effects such as lawsuits and bad reputation losing sound customer base immediately. Thus, it is critical to enhance cyber risk management in advance before the nightmare in order to enjoy the benefits of IT. This chapter introduces the practical methods of enhancing cyber risk management efficiently and effectively with the framework of Enterprise Risk Management (ERM) and Basel Accord II (Basel II). It aims to learn how to enhance cyber risk management effectively and efficiency so that sustainable growth is achieved with the balance between risk and return, or risk-adjusted return on equity.

LESSONS LEARNT FROM THE PAST

We are in the new age of information revolution. For example, owing to unprecedented IT development, we could tremendously save both the time and the cost of exchanging information. The current information revolution is said to be the fourth in the human history. Based on Drucker (1999), three revolutions are reviewed as follows: The first was writing 5,000 to 6,000 years ago in Mesopotamia. The second was the invention of written books first in China, perhaps as early as 1300 BC. The third was the innovation set off by Gutenberg in terms of printing press and movable type between 1450 and 1455. What was the impact? Before the third revolution, well trained and disciplined monks could protect their positions by showing their skills of copying books by hand, but by 1500, these monks became unemployed after this innovation of printing press (Drucker, 1990[2]). In the fourth revolution, computer networks are used for huge amounts of financial payments and settlements on a daily basis as well as exchanging information. For example, the Federal Reserve Board operates Fed-wire, a computerized network system of money transfer, in the United States. The Bank of Japan operates **BOJ-NET**, a computerized network system of money transfer, in Japan. SWIFT is used for cross border settlement among internationally active banks. It is recognized why critical cyber risk management is essential based on the following three lessons learnt from the past large events.

The Shadow of IT

The history of computer development is said to be that of security. Computer users are diversified from limited ones such as computer specialists in universities, research centers, big firms, and financial institutions to unlimited ones including their general staff and individuals. At first, computer system was developed to execute a huge number of transactions for payments of customers among financial institutions. These computer systems are called "closed network systems" in the sense that these transactions were accessed to computer and operation staff of financial institutions. In the closed system, the control methods of cyber risk were limited to those such as the entry and exit control of staff in main computer center. They used limited measures such as security video for monitoring and telecommunication protocol.

In the latter half of 1990s, open network systems such as the Internet, became very popular and used for financial services of individuals. On the other hand, it became easier to invade into computer network systems and get valuable information without permission. It is not rare to become victims of having privacy information stolen at the age of open network systems. For example, the privacy information such as names, addresses, and telephone numbers of users of an Internet connection service provider, was leaked twice, in June 2003 and January 2004. The event affected around 4.6 million users of this provider. Later, its operating company apologized to them for leaking these kinds of information and voluntarily sent a gift certificate of 500 yen or approximately U.S. $4 to each customer concerned. In May 2006, the Court in Osaka judged that its operating company had to pay 6,000 yen or U.S. $50 to the accusers of five members, asking the compensation for spiritual pain due to leaked privacy information. Inadequate cyber risk management such as defects of limited access control and regular compulsory password changes was responsible for the damages to customers.[3] It is reported that if other victims followed this suite, its operating company could pay around 30 billion yen or approximately U.S. $260 million.[4] Experts said that it was probably the first time for the Japanese court to order firms to impose the reparation related to leaking the information on individual persons in Japan. Given the law of observing privacy information of individual enacted in April 2005 in Japan, this event warns that firms could not survive without appropriately strengthening cyber risk management especially on privacy information in business. Thus, robust measures for cyber risk management are necessary to prevent these events.

The Lessons Learnt from September 11

Major operational disruptions could occur in the events of terrorism, climate changes, earthquakes, and severe pandemic flu. For example, the terrorist attack to the financial center in NY on September 11, 2001 (thereafter, September 11) caused material losses of talented staff of financial institutions, the damages stemming from their malfunction of settlement system in various NY financial markets, and the huge opportunity cost resulting from the suspended business of financial institutions. In the past, there were common understandings that IT staff was mainly responsible for the disruption of the computer system and that "contingent plan" should be ready for setting up the action plans after an emergency situation. This ad hoc solution was separated from day-to-day risk management. After September 11, senior management realized that they should take more initiatives in minimizing the impact of system disruption stemming from the terrorist attack and natural disaster in a strategic way. They recognized that a contingency plan should be more proactive and is upgraded into comprehensive business continuity plan (BCP), where priorities of recovering various business operations such as market related operations and wholesale transactions are clarified with the framework on targeted recovery time. Concrete policies and procedures of BCP are integrated into

Chart 1. Publication of authorities on business continuity planning

Contents	Writers (authorities)	Title of paper	Date
BCP at Financial Institutions	UK Financial Services Authority	FSA Working Paper on Business Continuity Management	April 2002
	Monetary Authority of Singapore	MAS Consultation Paper: Proposed Business Continuity Planning (BCP) Guidelines	January 2003
	Federal Reserve Board, Office of Comptroller of Currency, and the Securities and Exchange Commission	Interagency Paper on Sound Practices to Strengthen the Resilience of the U.S. Financial System	April 2003
	Bank of Japan	Business Continuity Planning at Financial Institutions	July 2003
BCP at authorities	UK Financial Services Authority	Business Continuity Management—A Staff Guide	November 2005
	Bank of Japan	Business Continuity Planning at the Bank of Japan	September 2003

(Source) The chart was made based on public information on the Web site (see the reference).

day-to-day risk management since BCP is vital for corporate survival and corporate brand.

System Troubles related to M&A Activities

Given very competitive financial markets, merger and acquisitions (M&A) are actively conducted in various industries such as financial ones. M&A used to be very active in U.S. banking and a limited number of banks held the majority of total banking assets. For example, the number of independent banking organizations in the United States decreased from 9,500 in 1989 to 6,800 in 1999. The share of total assets held by the 50 largest U.S. banking organizations increased from 55% in 1989 to 74% in 1999. This is especially true for the ten largest banks increasing from 26% to 49% during the same period (FRB, 2001[5]). Banking business becomes more and more dependent on computer systems. Managements of financial institutions desire to reduce the burden of computer investment by M&A. The same trend is found in Japanese financial industry.

In the past, since financial institutions had a lot of pressure to hurry up in pursuing the merit of M&A, it was not rare to see them pay little attention to enough preparation for the system integration of M&A. For example, in April 2002, major Japanese banks were merged into a mega bank and had serious system troubles such as delay in transfer of funds, dual withdraw of funds, and ATM malfunction due to the lack of its preparation. These troubles lost brand image of the mega bank with the order of business improvement from the regulatory authority, suffering from reputation risk.

EVOLUTION OF ENTERPRISE RISK MANAGEMENT

There are some misunderstandings among senior management of firms that risk management does not enhance corporate value and that resources allocation on risk management should be minimized, given intensive competition to survive and that so is the tax burden. These mindsets should be changed. The relationship between business and risk management is compared to that between an engine and a break of a car. It is said that Japanese users are very much satisfied with the break of a Porsch car. Since its break is very reliable, they can fully utilize its excellent engine to accelerate its speed in a satisfactory manner. In the same analogy, business staff may utilize its ability fully when good check and balance is built in so that professional advice of excellent risk management staff is used to enhance corporate value. This section delineates the evolution of ERM. Committee of Sponsoring Organizations of the Treadway Commission (COSO), a private-sector group, revised COSO framework and introduced ERM framework in 2004.

COSO Framework

COSO framework was introduced to solve the accounting problems in the United States. The false financial statements of companies had led to huge losses of their investors and debtors in the 1980s. In 1992, COSO, an independent private-sector group, set up for solving fraudulent financial reporting problems and issued the report on COSO framework to enhance internal control of companies. Internal control is the process for the board of directors, senior management, and other members of firms to implement. This process or framework is set for reasonable assurance to achieve the goals of (i) effectiveness and efficiency of business, (ii) reliability of financial statement, and (iii) compliance. It should be reminded that this improved risk management is only in terms of defense against loss.

Based on COSO framework, some guideline papers were issued by the **Basel Committee** for Bank Supervision (thereafter, the **Basel Committee**) and the inspection manual for financial institutions was issued by the Financial Service Agency, regulatory body in Japan. Unfortunately, it is not denied that some senior management of financial institutions used internal control as tools of setting up alibi to defend themselves rather than enhancing corporate value or satisfying their stakeholders. These attitudes might have delayed in solving non-performing loan problems.

ERM Framework

COSO announced a draft of ERM in 2003 and finalized it in 2004. The aims of ERM framework are as follows. First is to set up strategy to control risks which prevent from achieving goals. Second is to allocate management resources efficiently and effectively. Third is to enhance the integrity of financial accounting. The fourth is to observe regulations and rules.

What are the main differences from the original framework? First, the areas of contents are enlarged from internal control which mainly focuses on reducing or avoiding risks to ERM which mainly focuses on the balances between the nature of risks and their controls. Second, strategy and efficiency are as equally important as accountability of financial statement and compliance. ERM is a tool not only for defense against loss but also for a formidable weapon to control risks to obtain sustainable returns. Third, comprehensive structure, roles, and responsibilities are delineated clearly among the board of directors, senior management, business line managers, and so on. Appropriate coordination and cooperation in implementing risk management on a firm-wide basis encourages them to identify, analyze, measure, and control all material risks and to provide a sound base in order to make tactical decision based on risk-adjusted return or the balance between risk and return.

There are eight interrelated components in ERM. The effectiveness and efficiency of ERM

Chart 2. Eight components of enterprise risk management explained by COSO

Items	Contents
Internal Environment	The internal environment encompasses the tone of an organization and sets the basis for how risk is viewed and addressed by an entity's people, including risk management philosophy and risk appetite, integrity and ethical values, and the environment in which they operate.
Objective Setting	Objectives must exist before management can identify potential events affecting their achievement. Enterprise risk management ensures that management has in place a process to set objectives and that the chosen objectives support and align with the entity's mission and are consistent with its risk appetite.
Event Identification	Internal and external events affecting achievement of an entity's objectives must be identified, distinguishing between risks and opportunities. Opportunities are channeled back to management strategy or objective-setting processes.
Risk Assessment	Risks are analyzed, considering likelihood and impact, as a basis for determining how they should be managed. Risks are assessed on an inherent and a residual basis.
Risk Response	Management selects risk responses—avoiding, accepting, reducing, or sharing risk—developing a set of actions to align risks with the entity' risk tolerances and risk appetite.
Control Activities	Polices and procedures are established and implemented to help ensure the risk responses are effectively carried out.
Information And Communication	Relevant information is identified, captured, and communicated in a form and timeframe that enable people to carry out their responsibilities. Effective communication also occurs in a broadest sense, flowing down, across, and up the entity.
Monitoring	The entirety of enterprise risk management is monitored and modifications made as necessary. Monitoring is accomplished through ongoing management activities, separate evaluations, or both.

(Source) COSO (2004)

depends on whether these components actually exist and work appropriately. These components are stemmed from corporate management (see Chart 2).

BASEL II FRAMEWORK

The *Basel Committee* revised Basel Accord (Basel I) and announced "International Conversion of Capital Measurement and Capital Standards: a Revised Framework" (Basel II) in June 2004. Basel II (except for advanced approaches) started to implement at the end 2006. Those financial institutions which are allowed to use advanced approach will start Basel II at the end of 2007 so that enough preparation on robust data base is secured (FRB, 2006[6]).

The Background of Introducing Basel II

Basel I was announced in 1988 and introduced with some preparation periods to internationally active banks and other depository financial institutions in more than 100 countries. There are three reasons to review Basel I and to introduce Basel II. First, a simple capital formula of measuring credit risk has distorted their behaviors in terms of regulatory capital arbitrage in Basel I. Some banks reduced risk assets such as the size of lending assets and increased fee business of securitization and derivative transactions to save regulatory capital since risks were only captured based on risk assets. Given rapid developments of risk measurement and management tools, the *Basel Committee* allowed financial institutions to choose the methods of measuring adequate capital ratio so that financial institutions have incentives to develop their own risk management consistent with their business models and risk appetite (see Chart 4). Second, since Basel I was mainly focused on credit risk and market risk (especially trading), September 11 and other material cyber risk events forced financial authorities to cover operational risks such as cyber risk, explicitly in Basel II framework. Third, since the standard of its risk management methods has been established in both qualitative and quantitative ones, the concept of ERM is introduced in Basel II. This is the forward looking approach in the sense that even when financial institutions have enough capital, they could not survive without robust risk management, given rapidly changing environment.

Chart 3. Developments of Basel Accord I and II

	Events
1988	Basel I was announced.
1996	Basel I was revised with introduction of market risk mainly trading risk.
1998	Basel Committee started to review Basel I.
1999	Basel Committee announced first Consultation Paper.
2001	Basel Committee announced second Consultation Paper.
2003	Basel Committee announced third Consultation Paper.
2004	Basel Committee announced Basel II.
End-2006	Basel II (except for advanced approaches) was implemented.
End-2007	Advanced approach will be implemented.

(Source) The chart was made based on public information available in Basel (2004).

A Three Pillar-Approach

Basel I has an approach of only the first pillar in the sense that financial authorities are responsible for checking the minimum adequacy ratio of covering credit risk and market risk (mainly trading). However, the measurement of risks in Basel I turned to be inadequate and limited, given complicated business environment. For example, the risk weight of commercial lending assets is 8% across the board, meaning 8% of risk assets are regarded to be enough regulatory capital of lending regardless of the quality of borrowers. This formula could mislead financial institutions to tilt their portfolio toward high risk lending with high return since the risk is not fairly adjusted in regulatory capital framework. Thus, the first pillar needs to be strengthened to make the measurement more risk sensitive to reflect risk appetite and profile fairly in Basel II framework.

In addition to the first pillar, the second pillar and the third pillar are newly introduced in Basel II framework. Given rapid changes in external and internal environments, only the first pillar is not robust enough for financial system to be secured. The past non-performing problems in many countries revel that the roles of not only financial authorities but also financial institutions and market discipline should be collaborated in a supplemental way (see Chart 5). The analogies are found in various areas. For example, in engineering industry, there is an idea of "fail safe." An aircraft is designed to have alternative engines and hydraulically-operated machines. Once an engine or a hydraulically-operated machine fails to work, another back up engine or machine is ready to work properly in order to make an aircraft survive. Another analogy is "three arrows," which has an interesting episode in Japan. Motonari Mouri, a Japanese feudal lord (1497-1571) had three sons. He was said to warn them to be united by showing that one arrow could be easily broken but that three arrows, once united, could be hardly broken. In the West, Mayer Rothschild had five children sent to major European capitals to open branches in the family banking business. Five arrows were used as their emblem, implying the importance of unity[7].

CYBER RISK MANAGEMENT FRAMEWORK BASED ON ERM AND BASEL II

This section delineates a practical cyber risk management framework based on ERM and Basel II (see Chart 6). It consists of policies and structure, and five steps. These steps are (i) *event identification*, (ii) risk analysis, (iii) *risk mapping*, (iv) risk control, and (v) *capital management*. This framework is not the only solution. Different approaches may exist since each financial institution or firm faces different problems in different situations. However, readers may get some hints for their own frameworks since this is based on the practices of financial institutions (The Basel

Chart 4. Choices of measuring adequate capital ratio based on evolutional stages

Credit Risk	Operational Risk
The Standardized Approach	Basic Indicator Approach
Foundation Internal Ratings-Based Approach	The Standardized Approach
Advanced Internal Ratings-Based Approach	Advanced Measurement Approaches

(Source) The author made the chart based on public information available in Basel (2004)

Chart 5. Contents of a three pillar-approach

	Main Roles	Contents
The first pillar	Financial Authorities	Financial authorities are responsible for checking the minimum capital adequacy ratio of financial institutions. Financial institutions are allowed to choose the methods of measuring these risks based on the levels of risk management.
The second pillar	Financial Institutions	Financial institutions are responsible for holding adequate capital consistent with risk appetite and risk management. Financial authorities are responsible for checking its adequacy. While the risks covered in Pillar 1 are credit risk (excluding concentration risk), market risk (mainly trading), and operational risk, those in Pillar 2 include all the material risks such as credit risk (including concentration risk), market risk (in banking), and reputation risk.
The third pillar	Market (Market Discipline)	Financial institutions should disclose enough information on Basel II so that analysts, investors, and external rating agencies could assess the safety and soundness of financial institutions.

(Source) The author made the chart based on public information available in Basel (2004).

Committee, 2003[8]), and could be applied and expanded to firms in general.

Policies and Structure

The security policies of cyber risk management need to be documented to clarify the purposes and targets of implementing security measures in order to protect and enhance corporate value, shareholders' interest, and firms' brand. Since cyber risk management is an integral part of firm-wide management itself, the security policies should be approved by senior management or the board of directors, if necessary, and be familiar among all the employees concerned to implement concrete measures effectively and efficiently. More detail of the policies could be delineated in procedures given various business practices in different business lines. Internet-only banks have no brick and mortal branches. In addition, while all the transactions with customers are kept on bankbooks for verification in ordinal banking services in Japan, those in the Internet are not kept in physical records such as bankbooks. Given these environments, some depositors are still very cautious about the impacts of security troubles on their wealth management. Thus, it is critical to set up robust cyber risk management policies and procedures and to implement them on a firm-wide basis. These policies and procedures are consistent with various management issues such as goals and strategies of companies, risk appetite, philosophy on risk management, and policy on communication with stakeholders. Effective communication tools with stakeholders should be developed to enhance corporate value.

In corporate structure, cost effectiveness could be considered since each organization has limited resources with a different structure, given its nature of inherent risk and risk management style. At the same time, the effectiveness of risk control is also critical. For example, good check and balance with the segregation of duties is secured in ongoing monitoring on a daily basis and independent monitoring. Firms may need a firm-wide and independent risk management unit or risk management committee whose role is to take an initiative in coordinating, implementing, and monitoring the management of various risks including cyber risk, and reporting the present situations and challenges to senior management. In addition, control activities should be monitored by internal and external auditors (thereafter, auditors) independently from business line managers and risk managers. Through these processes, enterprise risk management is effectively monitored and modified made as necessary.

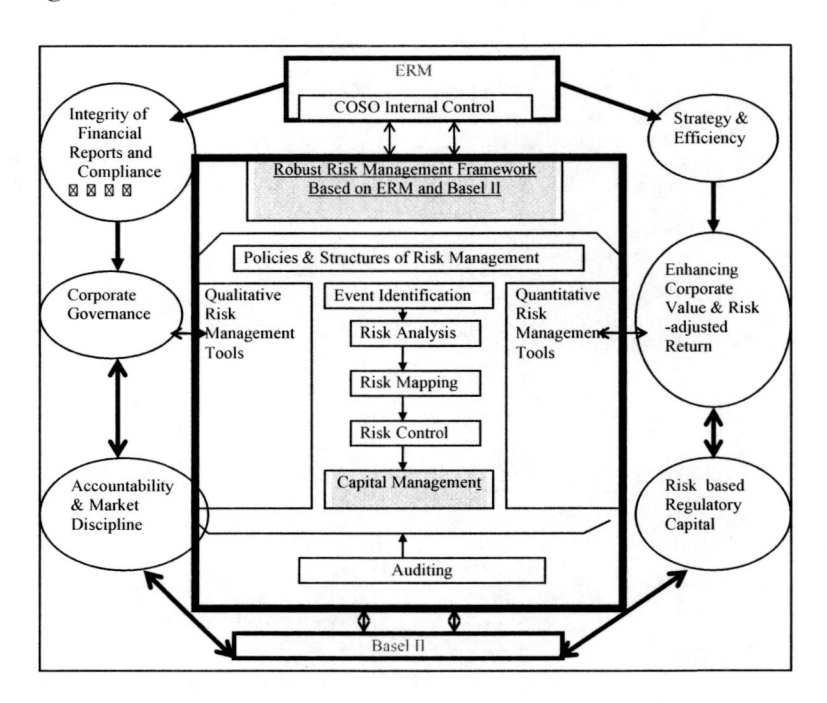

Chart 6. Risk Management Framework Based on ERM and Basel II

Five Steps of the Framework for Cyber Risk

Event Identification

We need to understand business requirements and the cyber risks we may face. For example, financial institutions are required to continue to operate for critical settlement business or resume its operation as soon as possible once it discontinues. Since huge amounts of transactions are paid and settled under financial network system on a daily basis, robust cyber risk management such as BCP enables financial institutions to enhance stakeholder's creditability and protect corporate brand and image. Thus, they should identify, for example, (i) what the critical business functions are, (ii) how interdependent business functions are, and (iii) what kinds of IT support they need in the case of disruption of commuter system.

Financial institutions are used to classify cyber risk by *causes of events* such as internal process, human, system, and external factors. However, it is found that identifying cyber risk by events is more practical and efficient. This is because events can be classified objectively and uniquely. On the other hand, *causes of events* are mixed in most of the cases. It is very difficult to classify cyber risk by causes of events objectively and uniquely. This lesson is learnt from insurance industry, where it has been using events or peril in identifying insurable risk such as car accidents and fraud for a long time. Insurance industry believes *event identification* is critical. These events related to cyber risk include (i) mistakes in inputting data, errors, and computer bugs in programming, (ii) small system troubles, (iii) major operational disruptions caused by terrorism, climate changes, earthquakes, and severe pandemic flu, (iv) crime, theft and alteration, impersonation, unauthorized access, and service interruptions, and (v) major system troubles such as those related to M&A activities.

Coordination among various business lines and risk management sections is needed in identifying potential events since this step could become a time consuming task. Therefore, it is useful to keep the criteria of these tasks on the same basis across the board as much as possible. For example, practical devises such as a worksheet could fit to financial institutions' own activities and risk management. It is necessary to set up robust database of both the past event data and potential one in order to measure operational risk based on events with "high frequency and low severity" and "low frequency and high severity" (see Chart 7).

Risk Analysis

It is useful to analyze causes of events by considering the various factors of how losses occur and how loss amount expands. This analysis on causes of events may enable financial institutions to understand the levels of exposures as well as that of risk management, and to implement effective risk control by taking the affect of risk management on risk measurement into account. Two approaches are explained as examples.

Self-Assessment (Scenario Analysis)

With collaboration of risk managers, business line managers make a self-assessment on frequency and severity by making scenario of possible events which could cause material losses or reputation risk. For example, after analyzing the causes of their events by classifying such factors as internal process, human, system, and external ones, their frequency and severity may be estimated. In the case of severity, the gross losses caused by events need to be analyzed and the losses that are later covered by insurance and collected by negotiation with customers for recovering losses need to be taken in to account. The process of expanding loss amounts through increases in expenses for lawyers and accountants, to deal with events and opportunity costs as indirect impact of occurring events also need to be analyzed. Auditors are required to review the appropriateness of self-assessment and conduct modifications if necessary.

Some financial institutions use *self-assessment* through the cycle of "Plan-Do-Check-Act." This assessment aims not only to review the robust risk management but also to increase the efficiency of operations with a collaboration and cooperation among business lines, risk management sections, and auditors. Once they identify potential events such as computer system troubles and analyze their causes such as weakness found in the assessment process, they conduct the risk management process (i) to *plan* measures, (ii) to *do* proactive safety and security procedures and educate security staff, (iii) to *check* the gap between the security targets and the realities, and (iv) to *act* based on remedies by review of risk management process. This firm-wide self-assessment is useful. For example, network system is spread on a firm-wide basis. While most of the sections enhance to safeguard the confidential information

Chart 7. Classification and sources of cyber risk data

	Events with "high frequency and low severity"	Events with "low frequency and high severity"
Sources of Events	Internal data	External data, scenario analysis, or dedicated data[9]
Examples of Events	Mistakes in inputting data, errors and computer bugs in programming, and small system troubles.	Major operational disruptions caused by terrorism, climate changes, earthquakes, severe pandemic flu, and major system troubles such as those related to M&A activities.

on customers, suppose that there exists a section which is less sensitive to protecting them from crime risk, theft and alteration, impersonation, unauthorized access, and service interruptions. Through that section, the confidential information could be leaked to the outside. Thus, the security standard should be set up and reviewed on a firm-wide base in the various processes such as self-assessment.

Value at Risk Method

In Basel II, if financial institutions wish to use advanced measurement approaches (AMA), they need to measure operational risks such as cyber risk to reflect day-to day risk management. Since those institutions which are allowed to use AMA are regarded as having a robust risk management, they need less regulatory capital than those institutions not allowed to use it since they have to satisfy the requirement of AMA. They may use their internal model such as *Value at Risk* (VaR[10]). VaR is measured based on business lines and risk categories with internal or external database as well as data created by scenario analysis reflecting dynamic changes of inherent risk and risk management levels.

Challenging issues in using VaR method of cyber risk are (i) establishing robust data base to avoid "garbage in garbage out" problem, (ii) developing sophisticated risk measurement models, (iii) balancing qualitative risk management and qualitative risk management, and (iv) how to estimate indirect loss appropriately. First, financial institutions tend to hasten to apply risk measurement into management tools but without consistent database, the result of risk measurement will not reflect reality and business line managers will not be persuaded by risk measurement. Second, the VaR depends on the assumptions of distribution functions, confident interval, the period of measurement, and quality of data. Stress test with changes in assumptions could provide senior management with wider views. Third, while risk measurement has strength in terms of enhancing efficiency and effectiveness of risk management, it has weakness in depending on the assumptions mentioned before. Thus, qualitative risk management initiated by business line managers on a daily basis continues to play an important role to cover the weakness of risk measurement. Fourth, cyber risk could bring about both direct loss and indirect loss. Direct loss is an actual loss or cash loss captured in ledger objectively. Indirect loss covers various aspects including expenses to deal with events and opportunity costs as indirect impact of occurring events and the impact of bad reputation stemming from cyber risk events. Especially in the case of cyber risk, indirect loss tends to be bigger than direct loss. Thus, it is important to estimate not only direct loss but also indirect loss appropriately. Auditors need to review its appropriateness.

Risk Mapping

Risk mapping is a tool to map the importance of various risks diversified in business lines. For example, this analysis is based on frequency and severity of events or risk scoring judged by risk managers and auditors. Frequency and severity could be classified in risk map or matrix with, say, 3 ×3 or 5 ×5. In the case of 3 ×3, we may find three ranges of frequency of possible events in terms of "once a year," "once a few or several years," and "once ten years" and three ranges of severity in terms of "small impact," "medium impact," and "large impact." We may delineate the whole picture of risk allocation among business lines and risk categories with a simple table before going into details and to enable them to decide the priority of risk control. The *risk mapping* is also called as heat map in the sense that heat means risk with red (danger), followed by yellow (caution), and green (safety). This used to be utilized in order to enhance internal control. For example, the results of auditing in business lines are scored across the board and reported to

Chart 8. Value at risk of cyber risk [11]

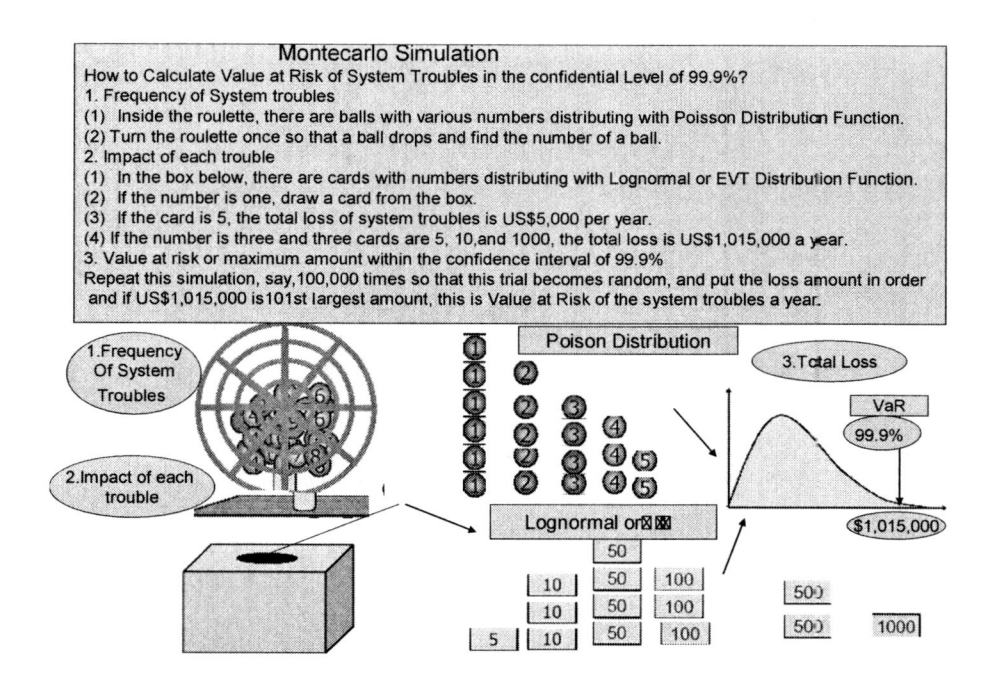

the board of directors with an overall picture so that even busy members of the board recognize where they should pay immediate attention in order to discuss controlling risk.

While a *risk mapping* is very useful, it is based on scoring with judgment, which tends to be subjective and might depend on the experiences and the ability of risk managers and auditors. Thus, with regard to the collaboration with quantitative risk management, it is possible to enhance *risk mapping* more objectively when financial institutions coordinate the results judged by risk managers and auditors with those of risk measurement.

Risk Control

Given limited management resources, it is useful to put priorities on risk control more objectively based on the *risk mapping* explained. Two kinds of risk control measures are explained as examples. One is a method of how to detect occurrence of events. In other words, this method seeks to reduce the frequency of occurring events. It is important to identify material factors causing events and to take related measures such as improving transaction flow so that internal process factors can be eliminated. Another method is how to detect expansion of losses stemming from events. This method aims to minimize or reduce the impact of losses once events occur. Effective measures based on the analysis of how to occur losses or how to expand losses may be taken.

The following is the case study of the latter, which is the *business continuity plan* (BCP) to minimize secondary impacts. The Business Continuity Institute (2005) defines it as "a holistic management process that identifies potential impacts that threaten an organization and provides a framework for building resilience and the capability for an effective response that safeguards the interests of its key stakeholders, reputation, brand, and value creating activities." But how is it possible to put appropriate priorities among various operations since most of staff members in financial institutions could insist that their own operations are indispensable to their individual customers? *Business continuity plan* should be an integral part of ERM in the sense that senior management needs to take responsibility for this plan and that all the participants in this activity understand it with clear priorities. In addition, industry-wide exercise as well as stand alone exercise of business continuity plan is desirable for the banking industry to enhance robust payment system. For example, the UK conducted the world largest simulation exercise of business continuity, in which over 3,000 people participated from 70 organizations. The exercise was designed to check how the UK financial industry was prepared for a simulated terrorist attack and was said to be a major success. According to KPMG (2005), four lessons were learnt. First, "a new automated damage assessment process was tested by the U.K. FSA. Particular attention needs to be given to the speed with which information can be collated in a fast moving event to avoid the picture being painted being out of date." Second, "it reinforced the need to continue to improve people-related responses within *business continuity plans* (e.g., staff welfare and communications, corporate verses individual responsibilities, reliance on key individuals)." Third, "more work is needed to identify supply chain interdependencies—no organization is an island." Fourth, "the analysis of participant feedback clearly shows that those organizations which invested time and effort in preparing for the exercise got most benefit from it."

Capital Management

It is ideal to prevent cyber risk from occurring or to reduce its damage to nil by perfectly controlling risk by all means. But for technical reasons and cost benefit aspects, these are almost unable to be realized. Therefore, it is critical to allocate *economic capital* to cyber risk as a buffer for future losses realized and to transfer it to the third party through insurance and ART (Alternative Risk Transfer), if any. An aggressive decision of mixing steps such as the risk control and the *capital management* rather than mixing them passively, need to be taken.

What is the practical merit of *capital management*? Capital is a buffer for rainy day. Since it has a cost, it is important to use it effectively and efficiently. Capital should be allocated based on the balance between risk (risk capital) and return. In the past, financial institutions evaluated business lines based on the return without considering the level of risks they faced. As a result, managements were misguided to put weight on risky business. But owing to effective *capital management*, in each business line such as e-banking, once credit risk, market risk, and operational risk such as cyber risk on the same basis such as VaR, are measured, the risk capital to business lines such as e-banking may be allocated. The business performance of e-banking based on risk-adjusted return on equity or risk capital could be easily compared with those of other business lines. This method gives a message to business line managers that risk management is as equally important as making profits.

In Chart 9, we assume that a financial institution has a traditional business A, where it collects funds in a deposit at branches and lend them to firms, and that it also operates an e-banking, where it collects funds in a deposit by the Internet and lends them to firms. E-banking has an advantage of reducing other costs such as human and office costs. Thus, e-banking provides higher interest rate with depositors than that of business A. Net margin is the difference between a revenue stemming from lending and all the costs of funding, other costs, and the expected loss stemming from credit and operational risks. The net margin of 0.6% in e-banking is higher than that of 0.4% in business A. Readers may misunderstand that e-banking is better than business A. However, the financial institutions need a buffer or risk capital against unexpected loss. When we consider risk-adjusted return on equity, e-banking, and business A show the same performance of 10%[12]. There are good incentives for business line managers to follow the advice from risk managers and auditors in order to enhance the ratio of risk-adjusted return on equity. If business line managers may reduce risk to desirable levels, risk-adjusted return on equity will improve in two ways. First, it reduces expected loss, leading to increase risk-adjusted return on equity. Second, it decreases unexpected loss, leading to increase risk-adjusted return on equity. It should be reminded that even when business line managers are not able to increase revenues but enhance risk management, they may improve risk-adjusted return on equity. Business line managers do not have to cheat in explaining to risk managers and auditors by pretending to follow their advices. They discuss with risk managers and audit staff how to enhance their risk-based performance, for example, by either reducing the level of risk taking or improving that of risk management. Through these processes, ERM is aimed to enhance efficiency and corporate value, and to satisfy stakeholder including all the employees.

Assumptions and explanations:

1. Business A lends U.S.$1 billion with funds from deposits at branches.
2. E-banking lends U.S. $1 billion with funds from the Internet.
3. Lending rates of Business A (2.5%) and E-banking (2.5%) are the same, while deposit rates of E-banking (0.6%) is higher than that of Business A (0.5%) due to lower other costs.
4. In credit risk, unexpected loss (UL) is 3 times larger than relative expected loss (EL) both in Business A and E-banking.
5. In operational risk, UL is 15 times larger than EL in e-banking, while UL is 10 times larger than EL in Business A. Market risk could be ignored for simplicity.
6. Since EL is observable and VaR equals to the total of EL and UL, the relationship between UL and EL could be derived both in credit and operational risks.

Chart 9. Risk-adjusted return on equity in business a and e-banking (Hypothetical Data)

	Revenue (Lending)	Costs	Funding	Others	Credit EL	Op EL
Business A	2.5%	2.1%	0.5%	0.5%	1.0%	0.1%
	25 million	21 million	5 million	5 million	10 million	1 million
E-banking	2.5%	1.9%	0.6%	0.1%	1.0%	0.2%
	25 million	19 million	6 million	1 million	10 million	2 million

the ratio relative to lending of U.S. $ 1billion

	Net Margin (A)	Credit UL (B)	Op UL (C)	Risk-adjusted Return on Equity D = (A)/((B) + (C))
Business A	0.4%	3.0%	1.0%	10%
	4 million	30 million	10 million	4million/40million
E-banking	0.6%	3.0%	3.0%	10%
	6 million	30 million	10 million	6million/60million

the amount relative to lending of U.S. $ 1billion

7. Net margin is the difference between the revenue and all the costs of funding costs, other costs (human and office costs), and EL of credit risk and Operational risk.
8. Risk-adjusted return on equity, which is the ratio of net margin relative to equity (risk capital), shows the efficiency of business based on the consideration of the balance between risk and return.

CONCLUSION

The practical methods were introduced to enhance cyber risk management efficiently and effectively with the framework of ERM and Basel II. Information technology has been rapidly developed to provide financial services with customers by the Internet. This service is available 24 hours a day, 7 days a week beyond the boundary. In addition, computer networks are used for huge amounts of financial payments and settlements on a daily basis. Thus, it is critical to enhance cyber risk management in advance before the nightmare in order to enjoy the benefits of IT. However, there are some misunderstandings spread among senior management that risk management does not enhance corporate value and that resources allocation on risk management should be minimized, given intensive competition to survive, and so is the tax burden. These mindsets should be changed. How is it possible to enhance efficiency and to control cyber risk at the same time so that sustainable growth is achieved?

Possible solutions were found in ERM and Basel II. First, a newly introduced ERM is a tool not only for defense against loss but also for a formidable weapon to control risks to seek sustainable returns. Appropriate coordination and cooperation in implementing risk management on a firm-wide basis encourages firms to identify, analyze, measure, and control all material risks such as cyber risk, and to provide a sound base to make strategic decision on the balance of risk and return, or risk adjusted return on equity.

The effective and efficient methods based on ERM are delineated to enhance cyber risk management. Second, in Basel II, operational risk such as cyber risk is explicitly introduced. The author proposes a practical framework based on ERM and Basel II. It consists of policies and structure, and five steps. These steps are (i) *event identification*, (ii) risk analysis, (iii) *risk mapping*, (iv) risk control, and (v) *capital management*. This framework is based on the practices of financial institutions but could be applied and expanded to firms in general. A Monte Carlo simulation technique may measure VaR of cyber risk so that capital is managed effectively and efficiently. Challenging issues in using qualitative risk management such as VaR as practical management tools are (i) establishing robust data base to avoid "garbage in garbage out" problem, (ii) developing sophisticated risk measurement models, (iii) balancing qualitative risk management and qualitative risk management, and (iv) how to estimate indirect loss appropriately. Based on this VaR extended from credit risk and market risk to operational risk such as cyber risk, limited resources of management could be used more effectively to enhance efficiency and to control cyber risk at the same time so that sustainable growth is achieved.

FUTURE RESEARCH DIRECTIONS

Future research directions in enhancing ERM are found in the following areas.

First, how should CEO of firms make a good and practical balance between qualitative risk management tools and qualitative risk management tools in achieving his or her goal as CEO? The former includes continuous self-assessment (CSA) and scenario analysis in analyzing possible events, their causes, and prevention measures. The latter includes calibration methods such as sensitivity analysis, VaR, and stress testing based on different assumptions. The former is easily accepted and understood by business line managers, but tends to be subjective in putting priorities in implementing ERM. The latter is very objective but its result depends on the assumptions of risk calibration methods and could face the issues of data quality. How to avoid garbage-in garbage-out problems in the process of robust data collection could be faced.

Second, how is the correlation of risk factors within the same risk category such as cyber risk and between/or among various risk categories such as credit risk and operational risk analyzed? For example, in the case of natural disaster, it may not be assumed that the earthquake in Tokyo could not occur at the same time of a hurricane in NY. On the other hand, if there is a weak risk control section in IT or poor communication among staff in system engineering, many system troubles and delay in system projects could be found in various business lines across the board at the same time. As for the correlation between or among various risks, it may not be assumed that credit risk could occur at the same time of the occurrence of operational risk. On the other hand, if there is a weakness in firm-wide risk management of a corporation, both credit and operational risks could occur at the same time reflecting weak risk management of senior staff wishing for higher returns. The co-relation within the same risk category and between/or among various risk categories could depend on whether causes are external or internal. Further studies on this issue are expected to enhance ERM.

Third, how is seamless and more risk-focused management established? It is important to coordinate BCP into comprehensive risk management. Some firms still think that BCP is the matter of the recovery of system and is separated from continuous risk management framework. However, there is a limit in responding to the problems after the events of disruption of system due to natural disasters and terrorism. In daily risk management, it is useful to discuss the possible events and their measures to prevent and minimize the impact of these events. As for risk-focused management, it is possible to reduce risk level and increase efficiency of operation at the same time when useful risk management framework is established and actually functions. The well balanced relationship between qualitative and qualitative risk management tools, which is mentioned in the first section of future research directions, could contribute to putting right priorities in achieving both goals of reducing risk level and increasing efficiency of operation at the same time.

REFERENCES

Bank of Japan. (2000). *The importance of information security for financial institutions and proposed countermeasures: With a focus on Internet-based financial services.* Retrieved February 25, 2007, from http://www.boj.or.jp/en/type/release/zuiji/kako02/data/fsk0004b.pdf

Bank of Japan. (2003). *Business continuity planning at financial institutions.* Retrieved February 25, 2007, from http://www.boj.or.jp/en/type/release/zuiji/kako03/fsk0307a.htm

Bank of Japan. (2003). *Business continuity planning at the Bank of Japan.* Retrieved February 25, 2007, from http://www.boj.or.jp/en/type/release/zuiji/kako03/sai0309a.htm

Basel Committee on Banking Supervision. (2003). *Sound practice for the management and supervision of operational risk.* Retrieved February 25, 2007, from http://www.bis.org/publ/bcbs96.htm

Basel Committee On Banking Supervision. (2004). *International convergence of the capital measurement and capital standards: A revised framework.* Retrieved February 25, 2007, from http://www.bis.org/publ/bcbs107.htm

Business Continuity Institute. (2005). *Good practice guidelines: A framework for business continuity management.* Retrieved February 25, 2007, from http://www.thebci.org/gpg.htm

Committee of Sponsoring Organizations of the Treadway Commission (COSO). (2004). *Enterprise risk management—Integrated framework—Executive summary*. Retrieved February 25, 2007, from http://www.coso.org/Publications/ERM/COSO_ERM_ExecutiveSummary.pdf

Drucker, P. F. (1999). *Management challenges for the 21st century*. New York: HarperCollins Publishers Inc.

Federal Reserve Board (FRB). (2001). *Supervision of large complex banking organizations*. Retrieved February 25, 2007, from http://www.federalreserve.gov/pubs/bulletin/2001/0201lead.pdf

Federal Reserve Board. (2003). *Interagency paper on sound practices to strengthen the resilience of the U.S. financial system*. Retrieved February 25, 2007, from http://www.federalreserve.gov/boarddocs/SRLETTERS/2003/sr0309.htm

Federal Reserve Board. (2006). *Notice of proposed rulemaking to implement Basel II risk-based capital requirements in the United States for large, internationally active banking organizations, Federal Reserve Release*. Retrieved February 25, 2007, from http://www.federalreserve.gov/boarddocs/press/bcreg/2006/20060330/default.htm

Federal Reserve Board. (2006b). *A U.S. perspective on Basel II implementation, Remarks by Governor Susan Schemidt Bies*. Retrieved February 25, 2007, from http://www.federalreserve.gov/boarddocs/speeches/2006/20061130/default.htm

Hiwatashi, J. (2004). Solutions on measuring operational risk. In V. Subbulakshmi (Ed.), *Operational risk —Measurement and management* (pp. 54-60). Punjagutta, Hyderabad: ICFAI University Press.

Hiwatashi, J., & Ashida, H. (2004). Operational risk management for central banks. In R. Pringle & N. Carver (Eds.), *New horizons in central bank risk management* (pp. 83-97). London: Central Banking Publications.

KPMG. (2005). *UK financial sector market-wide exercise 2005*. Retrieved February 25, 2007, from http://continuitycentral.com/news02493.htm which links the KPMG report.

Lam, J. (2003). *Enterprise risk management*. Hoboken, NJ: Wiley Finance.

Makino, T. (2006, February 20). *Operational risk management overview* (p. 29). Document presented at the Tokyo Round Table on Operational Risk sponsored by RMA. Retrieved March 10, 2006, from http://www.kriex.org/tokyoroundtable.asp

Monetary Authority of Singapore. (2003). MAS Consultation Paper: Proposed Business Continuity Planning (BCP) Guidelines. Retrieved February 25, 2007, from http://www.mas.gov.sg/masmcm/bin/pt1ConsultationPapers_Archive.htm

UK Financial Services Authority. (2002). *FSA Working Paper on Business Continuity Management*. Retrieved February 25, 2007, from http://www.fsa.gov.uk/Pages/Library/Communication/PR/2002/045.shtml

UK Financial Services Authority. (2005). *Business Continuity Management: A Staff Guide*. Retrieved on February 25, 2007, from http://www.fsa.gov.uk/pages/Information/pdf/incident.pdf

ADDITIONAL READING

Barton, T. L., Shenkir, W. G., & Walker, P. L. (2002). *Making enterprise risk management pay off*. Upper Saddle River, NJ: Financial Times/Prentice Hall.

Ferguson, R.W. Jr. (2004). Concerns and considerations for the practical implementation of the new Basel Accord. In R. Pringle & N. Carver (Eds.), *New horizons in central bank risk man-*

agement (pp. 195-205). London: Central Banking Publications.

Greenspan, A. (2004). International financial risk management. In R. Pringle & N. Carver (Eds.), *New horizons in central bank risk management* (pp. 33-40). London: Central Banking Publications.

Jorion, P. (2001). *Value at risk: The new benchmark for managing financial risk*. New York: McGraw Hill.

Olsson, C. (2002). *Risk management in emerging markets*. London: Financial Times/Prentice Hall.

ENDNOTES

[1] The author is a visiting lecturer of Saitama University and a director of the Financial System and Bank Examination Department at the Bank of Japan. The opinions in this chapter are the author's personal views and do not represent the Bank.

[2] See the details in Drucker (1999), pp. 102-103.

[3] See the detail in Asahi and Yomiuri newspapers dated May 20, 2006.

[4] The estimation was reported in Chugoku newspaper dated May 20, 2006.

[5] See more detail in FRB (2001) as reference.

[6] The Federal Reserve, the Office of the Comptroller of the Currency, the Office of Thrift Supervision and the Federal Deposit Insurance Corporation (the banking agencies) reached an agreement in July 2007 regarding the implementation of Basel II in the United States, leading to finalization of a rule implementing the advanced approaches for computing risk-based capital requirements of large banks. According to the announcement (http://federalreserve.gov/newsevents/press/bcreg/20070720a.htm), after the parallel run in 2008, Basel II will start in 2009 in the United States with the agreement on the periods of transitional floors, which provide for maximum cumulative reductions of 5 percent during the first year (2009), 10 percent in the second year (2010), and 15 percent in the third year (2011). After the end of second transition year period, the banking agencies will publish a study to determine if there are any material deficiencies by evaluating the new framework.

[7] See the details retrieved on August 21, 2006 retrieved from http://www.combustion.org.uk/newsletternov04/fivearrows.html.

[8] The Basel Committee (2003) issued "Sound Practice for the Management and Supervision of Operational Risk." This chapter aims for showing sound practice of operational risk including cyber risk through the process of Basel II. The framework of this chapter has been set up after the intensive discussion with risk managers and academic staff at home and abroad for several years. The author thinks that it is also basically consistent with the chapter (see the Principle 1-7).

[9] These data are set up based on the reference of peer groups' events of operational risk where similar financial institutions have experienced these events. For example, some financial institutions use external data of operational risk including cyber risk stemming from Operational Riskdata eXchange Association (ORE). Detailed information is available from http://www.orx.org.

[10] See Chart 8 to understand the practical method of its calibration.

[11] This visual explanation method of using roulette and box in explaining Montecarlo

Simulation is hinted by Makino (2006). The author thanks him for his permission in using his explanation method in this chapter, for better understanding of the readers.

[12] In this chapter, the focus is on how to enhance efficiency in terms of risk-adjusted return on equity. There is a methodology of calibrating corporate value with material data such as free cash flow and the weighted average of cost of capital (WACC).

Chapter III
IT Development and the Separation of Banking and Commerce:
Comparative Perspectives of the U.S. and Japan

Takashi Kubota
Waseda University, Japan

ABSTRACT

Unlike the UK, Germany, France, and some major countries that permit entries from banking to commerce and vice versa ("two-way" regulation), the United States and Japan have maintained a policy of separating banking and commerce out of concern that the mixing of the two activities would result in the misallocation of credits, anti-competitive effects, exposure of deposit insurance, and taxpayers to greater risks from commerce and additional supervisory burdens on banking and antitrust regulators. However, this separation is now being reconsidered both in the U.S. and Japan. With IT development, linking online banking and Internet commerce may increase profitability through operating synergies between the two firms and reduce average costs and information costs. Future changes in the financial environment may produce other synergies and the degree of separation should be suitable for such business development. This chapter introduces current laws and discussions in both countries and considers the future of the separation policy in Japan.

INTRODUCTION

The Separation Policy of Banking and Commerce

Unlike the U.K., Germany, France, and some major countries that allow entries from both banking to commerce and vice versa, the United States and Japan have maintained the policy of separating banking and commerce out of concern that the mixing of the two activities would result in bad effects as stated.

According to Brown (2002), "the U.S. has maintained this long-standing policy of separating banking and commerce out of concern that the mixing of banking and commercial activities would result in the misallocation of credit, extensive anti-competitive practices, and exposure of the federal safety net established for banking to a broad range of risks emanating from commercial sectors of the economy. Other concerns posed by the mixing of banking and commerce include overburdening the supervisory resources of the federal banking regulators, consumer privacy problems, and reduction of credit availability in local communities."

Japanese regulators have similar concerns. Although the indirect ties between main banks and commercial firms under the keiretsu control had been criticized by U.S. trade negotiators, Japanese law had long maintained the strict policy of separating banking from commerce until recently. This structural division between banking and commerce has been codified in the Banking Act[1] and the Antimonopoly Code.[2] As in the United States, Japan has maintained this separation policy out of concern that the mixing of banking and commercial activities would result in (1) the misallocation of credits, (2) anti-competitive effects, (3) exposure of the deposit insurance and taxpayers to greater risks from commerce, and (4) additional supervisory burdens by banking and antitrust regulators. The United States and Japan both learned from past economic crises (in 1929 in the U.S., in 1927 in Japan) before World War II and created the current system. As a result, banking is heavily regulated and separated from commerce, which is less regulated.

Lifting the Separation?

However, this separation is being reconsidered both in the U.S. and Japan. With IT development, linking online banking and Internet commerce may increase profitability through operating synergies between the two firms, and reduce average costs and information costs. Future changes in the financial environment may produce other synergies and the degree of separation should be suitable for such business development.

Compared with the strict separation in the U.S.[3] except for unitary thrifts, the Japanese government recently allowed "one-way" entry from commerce to banking with some requirements. Actually two recent reforms were introduced to allow commerce to enter into banking with fewer regulatory burdens. First, in August 2000, Japanese financial regulators allowed commercial companies to engage in "Internet" banking and the securities business with fewer requirements than a normal banking business. Second, in April 2006, commercial companies were allowed to become bank agencies by meeting some requirements. As a result, the current Japanese regulation of the separation of banking and commerce is called "one-way"[4] regulation, which means that commercial companies can start banking businesses but banks are restricted from starting commercial or non-banking businesses of their own and from holding many shares (details are shown later). Compared with Japanese regulation, the U.S. regulation is called "no-way"[5] regulation, which restricts both entries from banking and commerce. On the other hand, the regulations in the U.K., France, Germany, and other major E.U. countries are called "two-way"[6] regulation, which permits both entries from banking and commerce.[7] These trends can also be observed in the World Bank survey (Caprio, G., Levine, R.E., & Barth, J.R., 2001).

Some Japanese bankers insist that Japan should move to "two-way" regulation by permitting banks' subsidiaries or affiliates to engage in commercial business (e.g., real estate). Before illustrating the situations of both countries, let us observe why banks want to hold commercial shares.

Many promoters in the U.S. and Japan insist that a combination between commerce and banking may enhance profitability through operating synergies between the two firms. The emerged entity may reduce average costs by producing a wider array of complementary products. According to the FRBSF (1998), "as new technology has changed the way banks deliver their services, bank cost structures have come to look more like the cost structures of other non-bank information providers. Banks with excess data processing capacity, for example, would want to fill that capacity by offering services to other companies. Some national banks have leveraged their positions as providers of online banking to offer other Internet services to their customers. It is even easier to imagine that established Internet service providers would want to add banking services to their list of products."

However, one question can be raised. In the current financial situation, is there much room for producing synergies between banking and commerce? Banks can lend money, give advice, and send people to the commercial companies. In fact, even without a merger, banks have strongly controlled commercial companies under the "keiretsu" and "main bank" system in post-war Japan. Then, why do they need to own shares?

Why do They Want to Own?

As an answer, the FRBSF explains as follows: To reduce information costs, "banks would want to own firms (i.e., hold equity) in order to enhance their position as intermediaries. For example, by holding a large block of equity or by sitting on a company's board, a bank could provide a source of discipline to the management that would reassure less-informed investors. Liability to other creditors in the case of bankruptcy would tend to discourage banks from exercising control at the riskiest companies. But for many companies, this risk would be outweighed by the benefit the bank could provide by reducing financial constraints.

Another information-related reason for banks to hold equity is to reduce their exposure to moral hazard. If it is difficult for a lender to monitor a borrower's risks, limited liability borrowers will have incentives to increase the risk in their operations. Banks who anticipate this risk-shifting will either charge a higher price for the loan or demand more collateral. One way a firm can overcome this problem is to offer the bank an equity claim. The case of start-up ventures is a good illustration. By definition, start-ups have no track record on which to base an investment decision. Moreover, start-ups typically have little capital of their own and few tangible assets with which to collateralize a bank loan. If banks are to provide financing to these firms, they would need to take an equity claim."

However, at least in the Japanese context, these discussions are not very persuasive. By holding a large block of equity, banks' financial conditions may be riskier and much affected by market fluctuation. Observations by bank lenders are not usually less effective than those by equity shareholders due to the interlocking directorships within the keiretsu system, although it has weakened.

This chapter introduces current laws and discussions in the United States and Japan, and considers the future of the separation policy. It covers the U.S. situation first, the Japanese situation second, and considers the Japanese discussions third.

THE SITUATION OF THE SEPARATION IN THE U.S.

Let us observe the U.S. situation first by referring to FRBSF (1998).

Legislative History

In the U.S., banking and commerce have not always been separate. In the beginning of the 20th century, banks, including Chase Manhattan and Wells Fargo routinely took equity positions in commercial firms and sat on company boards. However, such relationships were criticized because banks could use their positions on multiple corporate boards to encourage collusion and because it may cause excessive concentration of economic power in their hands. From this antimonopoly perspective, the Clayton Act[8] was made in 1914 as an amendment to the Sherman Antitrust Act to prohibit interlocking directorates. In addition, after the stock market crash and subsequent bank failures in 1929, the Glass-Steagall Act[9] in 1933 and later the Bank Holding Company Act of 1956[10] reduced the scope of operations for banks and created a separation between banking and commerce.

But this separation has some exceptions. Bank holding companies can hold up to 5% of the voting stock and up to 25% of the voting and nonvoting stock in any firm. National banks can receive part or all of the interest payments on loans in the form of warrants or "equity kickers" and can own a 5% stake in a venture capital firm that owns up to 50% of any firm. In addition, "unitary thrifts"[11], thrift holding companies that own a single savings bank, have wide latitude to engage in commercial activities. Approximately one-quarter of the unitary thrifts now use their commercial powers to operate in real estate development. Commercial firms can purchase thrifts. In the 1980s, firms such as Ford Motor Company and Sears Roebuck bought thrifts. Wal-Mart tried to buy a thrift, but failed due to resistance from regional bankers. After this battle, the Gramm-Leach-Bliley Act of 1999[12] was introduced in 1999 and commercial firms were prohibited from buying thrifts. "No-way" regulation was maintained, but thrifts can still engage in other business to protect their privilege.

Regulators' Concerns

In the discussion of promulgating the Gramm-Leach-Bliley Act of 1999, the separation was actively debated and finally the separation was maintained because of regulators' strong concern.

According to FRBSF (1998), "The Depression-era legislation that separates banking and commerce was originally designed to check banks from exercising undue influence over the commercial sector. The same fears of uncompetitive practices persist." In addition, "deposit insurance is part of the federal safety net and can act as a form of subsidy to bank borrowing." "Given their current powers, banks, of course, have plenty of risk-taking opportunities to exploit the deposit insurance option." "A troubled commercial firm might have an incentive to shift bad assets to its banking affiliate (and exercise the deposit insurance option); or, a bank, in order to preserve its reputation, might have an incentive to bail out a struggling affiliate. In a worst case scenario, problems at a commercial affiliate could cause runs on the bank's deposits."

However, they do not deny the possibility of future reform. According to FRBSF (1998), "since the Glass-Steagall barriers are in place, it is difficult to say whether the gains from linking banking and commerce would be greater or less than the potential costs." "The potential benefits of linking banking and commerce are real and could grow in the future. If, someday, lawmakers choose to augment bank powers, they should proceed cautiously and with a mind to ensuring that the safety net does not extend beyond the banking sector." Even after the passage of the Gramm-Leach-Bliley Act of 1999, the separation of banking and commerce continues to be debated in the Congress. Some, including the ABA and Federal Reserve, argue that the failure to maintain a line of separation, especially in terms of ownership and control of banking organizations, would have potentially serious consequences, ranging from conflicts of interest to an unwarranted expansion of the financial safety net. Others argue that, if adequate safeguards are in place, the benefits from affiliations between banking and commerce can be realized without jeopardy to the federal safety net.

JAPANESE SITUATION

Legislative History

The first banking law in Japan was the 1872 National Bank Act. The first law concerning commercial banks was the 1890 Banking Act, which was modeled on the British banking system.[13]

At that time, there were two types of Japanese banks: big city banks, such as Mitsui Bank, Mitsubishi Bank, and Sumitomo Bank and small regional banks (Kaizuka, K., Kousai, Y., & Nonaka, I., Eds., 1996).[14] Big city banks had a wide variety of good customers but small regional banks had only a few borrower companies and were substantially linked to them. For example, 70% of Taiwan Bank's lending was to Suzuki Showten Corporation in the 1920s.[15]

When the performance of textile companies fell in the 1920s, such linked regional banks suffered from severe non-performing loan problems. In 1923, the Great Kanto Earthquake occurred and many banks and companies suffered losses. To rescue regional banks and to mitigate the losses, the central bank (the Bank of Japan) and the Japanese government bailed out the banks and compensated the losses very loosely, but this also produced a moral hazard.[16] In the National Diet, opposition parties strongly required the disclosure of poor bank performances, and a slip of the tongue[17] by the Minister of Finance triggered a run on regional banks. To cope with the banking crisis, the government strongly promoted mergers among regional banks and established the new Banking Law in 1927. The new law set minimum capital requirements. Out of the total of 1420 banks, 809 banks (57%) did not meet the requirement in 1927. From 1920 to 1932, the number of banks declined from 2001 to 625: In an average year, 19.6 banks were established, 43.5 banks failed, and 88.0 banks were merged.[18]

In the 1930s, Japanese companies obtained funds not so much by borrowing from banks (21.1%), but mainly by issuing stocks (31.0%) and raising the funds on their own (37.0%). During the war and early post-war period, they increased bank borrowing (1941-1944: 45.8%, 1946-1955: 31.7%) and the "keiretsu" system was created. According to Brown (2002), "In Japan, large banks are linked to large commercial firms through mutual control mechanisms that differ greatly from the traditional patterns of corporate affiliation and control found in the United States and Western Europe. Typically, a large Japanese bank will be a key member in a group of large corporations known as a keiretsu. The other members of a keiretsu are generally large commercial firms, although other financial institutions, such as insurance companies, may be included. The large Japanese banks do not dominate associated commercial firms in the manner of the large German banks. In fact, Japanese antitrust law prohibits a bank from owning more than 5% of the shares of a commercial firm. Nonetheless, Japanese banks are key members of their keiretsu. During the early post-World War II period, Japanese industry was heavily dependent on bank loans to finance capital investment. In more recent years, the emergence of the Japanese stock market as one of the world's leading financial centers and high corporate earnings have provided Japanese commercial firms with alternative sources of funds. However, a large bank within a keiretsu still provides important commercial loan services to its fellow members."

Responding to the economic and financial change after the oil crisis, the Banking Law underwent total revision and the current Banking Law[19] came into effect in 1981. The current law does not have specific articles concerning the separation of banking and commerce, but the scope of business conducted by banks is limited (Article 10) and the license requirements for entering banking are generally heavy.[20] The background idea of this separation derives from the experience of the banking crisis in 1927.

Current Law

Let us see the current system in detail. Banking regulation is generally heavier than commercial regulation except for some regulated industries such as electronic power providers. Under the Banking Law, "none shall engage in banking unless licensed by the Prime Minister (Article 4). To qualify for a license, the applicant must have a certain financial capacity, possess competent knowledge, and experience to carry out banking business and have adequate social credibility."[21] This "banking business" that distinguishes banks from others is called "typical bank business" that includes three principal businesses permitted to banks (Article 10 Clause 1): (1) the acceptance of deposits and/or installment savings; (2) the lending of money or discounting of bills; and (3) the conducting of exchange transactions (funds transfer).[22] Article 2 Clause 2 defines "banking" as the above "(1) plus (2)" or "(3)" or "(1) plus (2) plus (3)," and those who engage in banking without license will be punished (Article 61). In addition, a banking license cannot be transferred automatically. Article 30 of the Banking Law stipulates that mergers, splits, or business transfers require approval from the Prime Minister.

Therefore, the entry of commercial companies to the banking business is difficult, but there are some exceptions. Article 10 Clause 2 stipulates that banks can engage in about 20 other businesses ancillary to banking including "Receiving Public Money" business, meaning receiving, paying and conducting other monetary operations on behalf of national or local governments, public bodies, companies, and so forth. Not only banks, but also non-banking companies can engage in such ancillary businesses, and thus convenience stores, credit card companies, and other businesses are already engaged in the business of receiving public money, which resembles "funds transfer."[23]

In addition, non-bank's entry to banking was specifically permitted in August 2000.[24] With the development of the Internet and electronic commerce, such service providers began wanting to enter the banking business with fewer license requirements for providing electronic payment services for their customers. Responding to their requests and a national need to develop IT industries, the Japanese government clarified the policy in August 2000 that a non-bank's entry will be permitted if the parent company fulfills the adequacy requirement and the bank fulfills the bank subsidiary's profitability requirements, and limits its scope of business to dedicated Internet Bank that does not have physical branches. Promoting entry to banking is expected to promote innovation of the existing banking business not only in IT businesses, but also in other businesses. The Japan Net Bank commenced operations in October 2000 as Japan's first dedicated Internet bank, and this was followed by the launching of IY Bank (corporate name changed to Seven Bank in October 2005), Sony Bank, and eBank Corporation. Further, Incubator Bank of Japan launched operations in April 2004 focusing on financing for smaller and emerging companies. The Tokyo Metropolitan Government also set up ShinGinko Tokyo in April 2005. ShinGinko Tokyo focuses on financing of small and medium-sized companies.

On the other hand, the Banking Law limits the banking activities in four categories: (1) typical bank business; (2) ancillary business; (3) securities business (Article 11); and (4) other business permitted to banks under specific laws. Business aside from these four is prohibited in Article 12.

As a result, the current system allows "one-way" entry from commerce to banking only.

Banks' Proposal of Entering Into Commerce

With the financial deregulation and the development of securities markets, the Japanese keiretsu banking system has been weakened and the core banking business has become less profitable. Thus, many Japanese banks have been seeking more profitable opportunities in other financial businesses. They are promoting further deregulation by abolishing the barriers among banking, securities, and insurance in order to create a synergy effect by making financial conglomerates.

Further, some Japanese bankers[25] even seek to enter into non-banking business such as real estate, Internet business, and asset-based lending (ABL), by changing the current Japanese banking regulation from "one-way" regulation to "two-way" regulation.

According to Umeda, A. (2006), the current "one-way" regulation which does not permit entry from banking into commerce is a problem as a regulation because fair competition is not secured under current "one-way" regulation and it is desirable for the regulation to be revised from such a viewpoint. Benefits cited include enhanced customer benefits, strengthened international competitiveness, revitalized financial markets, and promotion of competition. On that basis, Umeda insists that it is necessary for restrictions on the scope of business conducted by banks and limits on share holding of general companies to be reconsidered, because the purpose of the restriction on banks engaging in different lines of businesses can be covered with such rules that set a limit on credits granted to one person, and the "arm's length" rule.[26]

Umeda, A. (2006) claims that the "one-way" regulation contains the following problems in terms of securing fair competition. Commercial companies are allowed to enter banking under the current "one-way" regulation, and it is possible for Internet-related companies to sell financial products, provide loans, and enhance the appeal of their own Web site as well as taking in commission revenue gained from settlement services, which will increase as online shopping expands, into their group companies. However, compared with the companies in different industries, discounting commission fees is not difficult for Internet-related companies and such companies can take advantage in price competition because an increase of the number of accesses directly links to increase of advertising revenue. In case mutual entry is permitted, it would be possible for the banks to enter into the Internet business and to participate in price competition adopting a similar business model. However, it is a cut-throat competition limited to the banking business under "one-way" regulation, and it causes a problem from the perspective of securing the banking system.

Legislation prohibiting entry of a bank into other businesses include such regulations that limit the scope of business conducted by bank's affiliate companies (Article 16 Clauses 2, 52, and 23, Banking Law) and regulations that limit acquisition of voting rights of business corporation by banks and by bank holding companies (Banks can hold up to 5% and bank holding companies can hold up to 15%, Article 16 Clause 3, Article 52 Clause 24, Banking Law) as well as aforementioned regulation that prohibits banks from engaging in other businesses (Articles 10-12, 52 Clause 21, Banking Law). In addition, not only the Banking Law but Antitrust Law limits bank's shareholding of a business corporation to 5% from the perspective of preventing industry control by bank (Antitrust Law Article 10). The purpose of these regulations is to assure sound management including: (1) to achieve optimal efficiency by concentrating on banking, (2) to prevent transactions that would prejudice the interest of the banks, (3) to avoid risks in other businesses from affecting the banking business.

According to Umeda, A. (2006), however: (1) A bank may gain higher efficiency in the sense of enhancing management efficiency by risk dispersal and by synergy effect and in the sense of diversifying revenue when working on multiple businesses than when concentrating only on the banking business, (2) Regarding transactions that would prejudice the interest of the banks, the restriction in case a business corporation becomes the main shareholder of a bank should be adopted in the case when a bank becomes the main shareholder of a business corporation, and issues regarding transactions that would prejudice the interest of the banks can be resolved with the existing arm's length rule that bans preferential treatment towards certain parties involved, and

(3) Regarding risk blocking, restrictions in the case that a business corporation becomes the main shareholder of bank should be adopted in the case when a bank becomes the main shareholder of a business corporation, and the issue of risk blocking can be resolved with regulation that sets a limit on credits granted to one person, in which the amount of credit granting to the same person or the same organization is limited to a certain proportion of equity capital, or with restriction of banks' shareholding (where the amount of shares held by banks is limited within the range of Tier 1), which was introduced in September 2006.

On the other hand, there may be an opinion that leakage of rent caused by excessive banking regulation which arises from a bank's operating other businesses should be prevented, because a bank which operates a settlement system receives benefits from the safety net including deposit insurance. However, such an argument that restriction on the scope of business conducted by a bank should be maintained does not make sense in the context of having already permitted business corporations to own banks, and the issue of preventing leakage of rent caused by excessive banking regulation can be resolved by adopting the arm's length rule or with other regulations. In spite of the worry of industry control by banks, now that bank's competitive superiority and influence is declining, following actual circumstances, it does not make sense from the perspective of securing fair competition. That is to say, a business corporation can hold all shares of another business corporation's shares while holding bank equity as a main shareholder, but a bank holding company is permitted to own up to 15% of another business corporation's share, and a business corporation is permitted to a become main shareholder of a bank, but a bank may hold business corporation's equity up to 5% under the antitrust law. Therefore, Umeda, A. (2006) insists that the regulations mentioned should be relaxed and bare minimum limits on share holdings should be introduced by adopting regulations on granting a large amount of credit or with other regulations.

Umeda, A. (2006) recommended to change the current regulations in which the entry of banks into commerce is not permitted right from the beginning and to expand the degree of freedom of banks in scope of business and in shareholding to further enhance customer benefits and strengthen international competitiveness while setting a bare minimum of ex ante regulations including a limit on credits granted to one person. Umeda, A. (2006) states the following fields as those from which we can expect a synergy effect: (1) to make real estate a financial product (securitization of real estate, real estate non-recourse loan, and so on), (2) chattel collateral finance, and (3) Internet-related business.

CONSIDERING THE JAPANESE SEPARATION POLICY

Considering the Japanese Bankers' Proposals

However, this new bank proposal by Umeda, A. (2006) to enter into commerce requires careful consideration by considering the following three points, at least.

First, the way that banks could enter into commerce is not limited to holding shares. If banks want to start new non-banking business with commercial companies, they can collaborate with such companies by advising them on business plans, sending staff members, and proposing joint business projects. In fact, Japanese banks controlled their keiretsu commercial companies strongly in the post-war era. This control has been weakened with financial liberalization and securitization, and a creative partnership between banking and commerce has become important. For example, Internet business providers have been seeking the advice of banks in developing electronic payment schemes. Thus, many economists consider that banks' additional holding of commercial companies' shares is not needed.

Second, the reality is not simply the same as the cross-country legal comparison of "one-way," "two-way," and "no-way" regulations. Under the EU Banking Directive, banks can invest in a single commercial company up to 15% of their capital, and commercial companies up to 60%. Thus, the regulations of Germany, France and other major EU companies are considered "two-ways." However, commercial companies have not positively entered into banking, and banks have influenced but not positively entered into commercial businesses. Under the U.S. "no-way" regulation, banks cannot hold commercial companies' shares and bank holding companies can only hold up to 5% of a commercial company's voting shares. By enacting the Gramm-Leach-Bliley Act of 1999, commercial companies are prohibited from buying unitary thrifts, which can engage in non-financial activities such as Real Estate, Hotels, Telecommunications, Travel Agency, and Auto Sales.[27] However, unitary thrifts continue to be able to engage both financial and non-financial activities.

Third, the synergy effects are estimated to be less when banks enter into commerce than when commercial companies enter into banking. Regarding the economy of scale, banks can increase synergy effects when they use their huge customer information database for non-banking business. However, such information exchange is limited by the various regulations for avoiding conflict of interests and for protecting customer privacy. As for developing new financial products by combining banking and commerce, such as promoting real estate securitization, it is not always necessary for banks to hold shares. In addition, there is concern about the "conglomerate discount" problem in which a conglomerate's stock price undervalues the sum of the intrinsic value of each of the subsidiary companies in a conglomerate. Bigger is not always better.

Therefore, there is not yet an urgent need to reform Japanese law. If business opportunities arise in the boundary field between banking and commerce, we need to prepare adequate laws to take advantage of them. However, it is hard to prepare for them by anticipating future business developments.

Comparison of the U.S. and Japan

The progress of discussions in Japan and in the U.S. differs. In the U.S., the discussion starts from "no-way" regulation in which both entry from commerce to banking and entry from banking to commerce are not permitted. However, in Japan, the discussion starts from "one-way" regulations where entry from commerce to banking has already progressed to a certain level. Therefore, in Japan, securing fair competition is the primary concern. For example, according to Umeda, A. (2006), it is asserted first of all that Japan should change its policy to the "no-way" regulation of the U.S. or to the "two-way" regulation of EU from the perspective of securing fair competition. Then, firstly, Umeda, A. (2006) proposed to change to "two-way" regulation, asserting that both the existing ownership by business corporations of banks as affiliate companies and integration of banking and commerce should be considered. In the U.S., there is a discussion between the Federal Reserve Bank (FRB) and the Department of the Treasury, which prefer to maintain "no-way" regulation, and the private sector, which insists that limitation of entry should be relaxed, but the focus of the discussion is risk prevention and determination of synergy effect. On the other hand, in Japan, it seems that people put first priority on fair competition.

In addition, in Japan where control of industry by banks has a long history, entry of commerce into banking is not so much seen as a problem and it is rare that a bank as an affiliate company of a business corporation threatens existing banks. However, a sense of caution towards entry from banking into commerce is still strong and this is why the real estate industry shows strong resistance to banks' entering into their business.

On the other hand, in the U.S., regional banks see entry from commerce into banking by big companies like Wal-Mart as a problem. Therefore, in spite of having theoretically same problem, Japan and the U.S. have completely different backgrounds. However, neither of them face such an urgent situation that would force them to remove controls. For example, we have not seen such situations that only European banks and business corporations take advantage by entering into business areas where a synergy effect of commerce and banking is expected, while Japan and the U.S. are disadvantaged in competition. As a result, both in Japan and the U.S., the issue of restrictions to segregate banking and commerce remains a theoretical conflict that has yet to become real.

Furthermore, in Japan, the banking industry's main concern is entry into the security business and the insurance business, because a practical response to financial conglomeratization in which a bank enters into other financial businesses including the security business and insurance business is delayed, while in the U.S. it is highly advanced. In addition, banks in Japan are actually in the stage of seeking new revenue opportunities because financial conglomeratization is not always desirable due to the issue of the "conglomerate discount." Many efforts can be seen now that banks are considering entering into commerce where it is uncertain whether or not a synergy effect is expected.

International Trends

According to the survey on 151 countries (including the U.S. territory of Puerto Rico) conducted by the World Bank in 2000 and 2003,[28] the international trends of this issue of banks' owning non-financial firms, are as follows: the ratio of countries where a bank may own 100% of the equity of a non-financial firm is 12% (including the UK), the ratio of countries where a bank may own 100% of the equity of a non-financial firm, but ownership is limited based on a bank's equity capital is 38% (including Germany and France), the ratio of countries where a bank can only acquire less than 100% of the equity in a non-financial firm is 44% (including Japan), the ratio of countries where a bank may not acquire any equity investment in a non-financial firm accounts for 6% (including Puerto Rico). As is shown by the survey result, most countries put a certain level of restrictions.

On the other hand, in relation to non-financial firms' owning banks, the ratio of countries where a non-financial firm may own 100% of the equity in a bank is 34% (including the U.K., France, and Germany), some prior authorization or approval is required in 31% of the countries (including Puerto Rico and Japan at the time of the survey in 2003), limits are placed on ownership, such as a maximum percentage of a bank's capital or shares in 31% of the countries including Japan, and no equity investment in a bank is permitted in 3% of the countries, including China. The survey results revealed a general trend that a tolerant attitude is taken toward entry from commerce into banking, while a cautious stance is taken on the banks' entering into commerce.

According to Watanabe (2006), who examined in depth the World Bank's survey of 2000 and of 2003, (1) Among developed countries, Japan takes a notably stern attitude toward restriction on the scope of business conducted by banks and the regulation is still stern when compared to the stage of development of the banking industry, so there is room for the restriction on scope of business conducted by banks to be relaxed; (2) Regarding the relationship between commerce and banking, regulation of the entry from commerce into banking is laxer than the entry from banking into commerce and "one-way" regulation is not confined to Japan but is common in many countries; (3) There is tendency that revenue of banks is recovered and that the banking sector is developed with relaxation of restriction; (4) It is often the case in the countries where restriction on the scope of business conducted by banks is lax that there are fewer nonperforming loans and financial crises, in addition, the safety net including deposit insurance is reduced.

However, Watanabe's analysis raises some questions in the following points which are difficult to agree on: (1) Watanabe's analysis doesn't consider the U.S., a developed country where restriction on the scope of business conducted by banks is stern, (2) Watanabe's analysis compared only limited figures, including the ratio of minimal shareholding by banks, bank's ROA and ROE, and ratio of nonperforming loans, when forming a conclusion and differences of bank's power of industry control, history and business practices are not considered. For example, (a) it is not Japan but the U.S. where restriction on scope of business conducted by bank is extremely stern, (b) it is dangerous to determine the level of entry only with the ratio of minimal shareholding by banks and not considering individual circumstances, (c) it is doubtful whether the general theory that relaxation of restriction on scope of business conducted by banks leads to revenue improvement can be adopted to this case in a situation where the synergy effect of banking and commerce is realistically not so much expected, and (d) even though a lack of nonperforming loans is related to easing of restrictions on the scope of business conducted by banks, a casual linkage between few nonperforming loans and relaxation of restriction on scope of business conducted by bank cannot be confirmed. Considering the points mentioned, it seems that there is not enough material to consider prompt revision of the law and that it is desirable to judge the time to be right to revise the law while watching development of business opportunities.

CONCLUSION

Now, it is difficult to find a case in which a synergy effect could not be achieved by a means other than a bank's ownership of non-financial firms through holding equity. Under these circumstances, it is not so unnatural for the supervising authorities of both Japan and the U.S. to still worry seriously about reducing the existing measures against risks. It seems that there is not a strong necessity to ease regulations until such cases, in which a synergy effect is fully achieved by a bank's entry into commerce, occurs in Europe where "two-way" regulation is adopted. If banks in Japan and the U.S. want to actively seek the chance to achieve a synergy effect, they have only to do it through their affiliate companies in Europe. However, as the pace of change in the economic environment is fast in the IT society, Japanese and American governments, from the perspective of global competition, will have to work on developing legislation quickly when they see the appearance of a field where some synergy effect is expected. Therefore, it is important to continue theoretical discussion.

FUTURE RESEARCH DIRECTIONS

Unlike European nations, separation between banking and commerce has been maintained in Japan and the U.S. because: though managing both banking and commerce (shareholding) has such advantages as (1) economies of scale, (2) risk dispersal, and (3) smaller cost for consumers to collect information (one-stop shopping); it also has such disadvantages as (1) diseconomies of scale, (2) fear of control over industry, and (3) more complexity and higher cost of financial supervision. Today, in light of IT advancement and changes in the financial environment, demand for entry has been increasing, from banking to commerce in Japan, and from commerce to banking in the U.S. For instance, in Japan, the banking industry claims that banks' entry to commerce would not cause the above disadvantages thanks to regulations requiring competition among banks, market rules, and the arm's length rule, and that banks' dual operation of real estate business, online-trade-related business, or personal security finance business would produce a synergy effect, which would also benefit consumers. However, banks effectively can enter into commerce without holding shares, and many are doubtful about the extent of the claimed synergy effect. So, it is essential to measure and verify actual advantages and disadvantages as much as possible to decide the degree of deregulation of share-holding limits.

On the other hand, as the issue is closely connected with other issues including IT advancement and Islamic finance development, future environmental changes and political factors may affect the course of separation of banking and commerce.

First, in online banking, the money economy that does not go through the bank system is spreading. For example, it is estimated that about one trillion yen worth of points are issued annually in Japan only; and in the market of RMT, exchange of online game currency and real currency is said to have expanded to over the 15 billion yen scale. It means that commerce has already been running a large part of the account settlement business, which is in theory to be operated by banks, by means of issuing points and game currency, thus making a foray to banking business. Separation rules of banking and commerce may be compelled to approve the move.

Second, as Islamic finance grows, moves to invite the Islamic economy are active in many nations worldwide, such as the United Kingdom, Singapore, and Malaysia. Interest (*riba*) is prohibited in the Islamic economy and commercial dealings (al-bay) are allowed instead of regular financing operated by banks of other countries. Islamic banks operate *murabaha*, which is purchase and resale of ordinary merchandise, and *ijara*, which is similar to leasing. In case Japan or the U.S. invites Islamic banks and grants them banking licenses, legal arrangements are needed to exempt *murabaha* and other dealings of goods from bans on banks' commercial business operation. Separation rules of banking and commerce may face revision in light of such moves.

REFERENCES

Brown, J. (2002). *The separation of banking and commerce*. GIS for Equitable and Sustainable Communities, last modified on October 7, 2002. Available at http://www.public-gis.org/reports/sbc.html

Caprio, G., Levine, R. E., & Barth, J. R. (2001, November). Bank regulation and supervision: What works best? Policy Research Working Paper 2725. The World Bank. Available at the World Bank Web site.

Cocheo, S. (1997, October). What's at stake with unitary thrifts? *ABA Banking Journal*, http://www.banking.com/aba/unitary_1097.asp

FRBSF. (1998, July 3). *The separation of banking and commerce*. Federal Reserve Bank of San Francisco (FRBSF) Economic Letter. Available at http://www.sf.frb.org/econrsrch/wklyltr/wklyltr98/el98-21.html

Iwahara, S. (2003). *Denshi Kessai to Hou* (Electronic Payments and Law in Japanese). Yuuhikaku., p. 625.

Japanese Bankers Association. (2006). *The banking system in Japan*. Zenginkyo. p.161 & p. 19.

Kaizuka, K., Kousai, Y., Nonaka, I. (Eds.). (1996). *Nihon Keizai Jiten* (Dictionary of Japanese Economy in Japanese). Nihon Keizai Shinbunsha. p. 1387.

Kinyu Chousa Kenkyu Kai (KCKK: Financial Research Study Group in Japanese). (2006, July). *Kinyu No Conglomerate Ka Tou Ni Taiou Shita Kinyu Seido No Seibi*. Creating A New Financial System. The Financial Research Study Group (Report No. 36). original is in Japanese only.

Office of Thrift Supervision. (2006, November 8). *Historical framework for regulation of activities of unitary savings and loan holding companies.* http://www.ots.treas.gov/docs/4/48035.html

Seaman, R. (1998). *English translation of Japanese banking law.* (updated January 1998). http://www.japanlaw.info/banking/1981.htm

Umeda, A. (2006, April). *Ginkou to Shougyou no one-way Kisei Ni Tsuite (Regarding "One-way" regulation of banking and commerce in Japanese).* Mizuho Research Institute. p. 18.

Watanabe, T. (2006, July). *Ginkou No Gyoumu Han-i Kisei Ni Tsuite (On Regulations of the Scope of Bank Business Activities in Japanese).* Kinyu. pp. 3-11.

World Bank. (2000, 2003). *Bank Regulation and Supervision: Finance and Private Sector Research.* http://www.worldbank.org

ADDITIONAL READING

Munir, A. B. (2004). *Internet banking: Law and practice.* LexisNexis Butterworths.

Richmond Law & Tax Ltd. (2005). *Financial Services Regulation in Europe.* p. 760.

Scott, H. S. (2004). *International finance: Law and regulation.* Thomson Sweet & Maxwell.

Vernados, A. M. (2006). *Islamic banking & finance in South-East Asia* (2nd ed.). World Scientific.

ENDNOTES

[1] To maintain the soundness of banking, the Japanese Banking Act has the following regulations: Section 10, 11, 12, and 52 (21) prohibit bank and bank holding companies from engaging in other business; Sections 16 (3) and 52 (23) restrict banks and bank holding companies from having subsidiaries and affiliates that engage in commerce; Sections 16 (3) and 52 (24) ban banks from having more than 5% and bank holding companies from having more than 15% of shares of commercial companies in total.

[2] To promote free and fair competition, the Japanese Antimonopoly Code, Section 11 prohibits banks from having more than 5% of shares of commercial companies.

[3] In the U.S., commercial companies obtaining more than 25% of bank shares are deemed to be "bank holding companies" and must separate non-financial businesses in principle. Banks cannot hold commercial companies' shares and bank holding companies cannot have more than 5% of shares of commercial companies.

[4] This technical term is firstly introduced in the financial research study conference held at the Japanese Bankers Association on March 10, 2006. See p. 3 of Kinyu Chousa Kenkyu Kai (2006).

[5] Ibid.

[6] Ibid.

[7] In some major European countries, commercial companies can hold up to 100% of bank shares if they meet the requirements for major stockholders, and banks can also hold up to 100% of commercial companies shares if they meet the capital requirements.

[8] The Clayton Antitrust Act of 1914, October 15, 1914, ch. 323, 38 Stat. 730, codified at 15 U.S.C. § 12-27, 29 U.S.C. § 52, 29 U.S.C. § 53.

[9] 48 Stat. 162 (1933).

[10] 12 USCS 1841-1850.

[11] For details, see Office of Thrift Supervision (2006).

[12] Pub. L. No. 106-102, 106th Cong., 1st Sess. (1999).

[13] See pp. 61-63 at Japanese Bankers Association (2006).

[14] See p.37 at Kaizuka, K., Kousai, Y., Nonaka, I., Eds. (1996).

[15] See p.42 at Id.

[16] See p.37 at Id.

[17] Though the Tokyo Watanabe Bank did not fail, the Minister of Finance, Mr. Kataoka said by mistake that "the Tokyo Watanabe Bank failed at around noon today" in the Diet meeting in March 14, 1927. See p.42 at Id.

[18] See pp.37-42 at Id. (1996).

[19] Law No.59 in 1981. For English translation of this law, see Seaman, R. (1998).

[20] Article 4 of the Banking Law stipulates that none shall engage in banking unless licensed by the Prime Minister. To qualify for a license, the application must have a certain financial capacity, possess competent knowledge, and experience to carry out banking business and have adequate social credibility. See p.64 at Japanese Bankers Association (2006).

[21] See pp.66-69 at Id.

[22] According to p.66-67 at Id, "the Japanese Banking Law is unique in that it defines not only taking deposits but also fund transfers as typical bank business. The bulk of transfers are between deposit accounts for settlement purposes. It is a measure of the reliability of banks and the banking system that settlement, which occupies a vital position in the flow of funds, is entrusted only to banks and other depository financial institutions."

[23] For details, see Iwahara (2003).

[24] For details, see pp.17-18 and p.40 at Japanese Bankers Association (2006).

[25] For example, see Umeda, A. (2006).

[26] This rule was first introduced in 1992 to ban transactions with the subsidiary that would prejudice the interest of the bank. With the 1998 amendments, the range of businesses was expanded open to bank subsidiaries and affiliates, and the scope of the arm's length rule was extended. The 2001 amendments made major shareholders subject to this rule in step with the addition of the regulations on major shareholders. See article 13-2 and pp. 70-71 at the Japanese Bankers Association (2006).

[27] For details, see Cocheo, S. (1997).

[28] See World Bank (2000, 2003).

Chapter IV
Laws and Regulations on Proprietary Trading System (PTS) in Japan:
Japanese Alternative Trading System (ATS)

Motoaki Tazawa
Meijo University, Japan

ABSTRACT

In order to improve convenience for investors through competition among stock exchanges, operation of Proprietary Trading Systems (PTS) was authorized as a form of securities business under the Securities and Exchange Act. The Japanese PTS is equivalent to ATS (Alternative Trading System), ECN (Electronic Communications Network) in the United States and MTF (Multilateral Trading Facilities) under MiFID in the EU. In 1998, ATS and ECN had already started in the United States and Japan's PTS followed the U.S. model. Telecommunication and information technologies and computer technologies made PTS possible, and PTS makes the border between the market and brokers ambiguous. Traditional regulations on broker-dealers and stock exchanges will inevitably be reviewed and regulations on securities markets will have to be reformed.

INTRODUCTION

Under the Financial System Reform of 1998, the no off-exchange trade rule which had been imposed on the sales of securities listed on such stock exchanges as the Tokyo Stock Exchange and the Osaka Securities Exchange was abolished. As a result, it became possible for securities companies which are the members of stock exchanges to trade the listed stocks through off-exchange trades. In connection with this, in order to improve the convenience of investors through competition among stock exchanges, operation of Proprietary Trading System (PTS) was authorized as one of the securities businesses under the Securities and Exchange Act. The Japanese PTS is equal to Alternative Trading System (ATS) and Electronic Communications Network (ECN) of the United

States and MTF (Multilateral Trading Facilities)[1] of MiFID of the EU (Shimizu, 1997; Shimizu, 2000; Osaki, 1999; Konishi, 2000; Yanaga, 2006[2]). In 1998, ATS or ECN had already begun operating in the United States and PTS of Japan followed the U.S. model (Kawashima, 2001)[3].

In June 2006, the Securities and Exchange Act was revised and in 2007, the Securities and Exchange Act will be revised to the Financial Instruments and Exchange Act and regulatory framework will be modified to that of financial service law or investment service law.[4] The securities business will be modified to the "financial instruments business" and the same definition of the PTS will be provided in the Financial Instruments and Exchange Act as one of the financial instruments businesses (Art. 2(8) (X)).

Current regulations on the PTS will generally be succeeded after being transferred to the Financial Instruments and Exchange Act.

BACKGROUND OF INTRODUCING PTS

Abolition of No Off-Exchange Trade Rule

The Financial System Reform Act (Act No. 107 of 1998) shaped the concepts and recommendations of the final report of the Securities and Exchange Council, "Comprehensive Reform of Securities Market—Towards the Realization of a Prosperous and Diverse 21st Century" (June 13, 1997)[5], etc, and so forth. The final report recommended abolition of the no off-exchange trade rule and authorization of the off-exchange trading of listed securities from the viewpoint of meeting diversified needs of investors.

Conventionally in Japan, trading of securities listed on stock exchanges was required to be executed on the market for exchange-listed securities established by the stock exchange not only for trades by securities companies, the members of the stock exchange, but also for trades by non-member securities companies.

That is, securities companies, the members of the stock exchange were prohibited from trading of securities listed on the stock exchange off the market for exchange-listed securities by the articles of association of the stock exchange.[6] Non-member securities companies of the stock exchange were supposed to execute trading of listed securities on the market for exchange-listed securities through consignment to member securities companies pursuant to the regulations of business and services by the minister of finance. Therefore, with respect to the listed securities of the stock exchange, there was no room for execution of trading off the market for exchange-listed securities (Kanzaki, 2000).

Abolition of the no off-exchange trade rule and introduction of the PTS are generally stated as follows in "Framework for Reliable and Efficient Transaction" (May 16, 1997)[7], the report of Market Working Party, which was established under the Securities and Exchange Council.

The roles of securities markets are to "efficiently and fairly" perform management of financial assets and distribution of funds to capital needs and securities market reform must ensure that securities markets can play such roles sufficiently and appropriately. In order for asset management and funding to be made "efficiently," it is essential to introduce the principle of competition and it is also necessary to review how the regulated market should be in connection with this. The prime reason for abolition of the no off-exchange trade rule was (1) the promotion of competition among stock exchanges, and secondarily, there were the following reasons: (2) response to diversified needs of investors, [8] (3) development of information and telecommunications technologies, [9] (4) response to globalization of stock exchanges.[10]

The no off-exchange trade rule has been established to give volume to the regulated market as well as to contribute to fair price discovery. Stock exchanges are granted a special position in securities market, to which the antitrust law was not applied and as a Self Regulatory Organization (SRO) under the Securities and Exchange Act, it was authorized to impose certain restrictions on the actions of member securities companies. Among the regulations of stock exchanges, however, it has been pointed out that the no off-exchange trade rule under the articles of association restricted competition. In terms of promoting competition among stock exchanges, it was considered to be necessary to drastically review the regulations restricting execution of customer's order by securities companies, including their abolition (Osaki, 2000; Fuchita, 1999[11]).

Trade as Off-Exchange and in Regulated Market

In the report of the Market Working Party, if an off-exchange trade was authorized to securities companies by abolishing the no off-exchange trade rule, it was an issue whether (a) a National Market System was to be formulated or (b) the system in which stock exchanges still occupied the main market status was to be formulated.

a. The National Market System is based on the following concept. If it authorizes securities companies to execute not only in a regulated market but also off-exchange, as the method for enabling to work competitive principles in execution of purchase and sale orders, secure fair price discovery and obtain the best execution of the customer's orders, it is necessary to enable securities companies to execute purchase and sale orders based on such a quote information system as following: the quote information system which covers all quote information not only in stock exchanges but also off-exchange and publishes it in real time.

It apparently seems that fragmentation of the market arises under this scheme, however, as any quote information is intensively published and securities companies can execute purchase and sale orders based on it, it is functionally conceivable that price discovery is made as trades in one comprehensive market.

However, it requires an enormous cost and considerable time for preparation to arrange such infrastructures. There is also concern that dispersion of supply and demand to off-exchange trading will reduce the liquidity of exchanges, major markets, and fair price discovery would also be hindered. Therefore, while it is one of the options to have a market with such a system as to how the Japanese securities market should be in the future, judging from the current conditions of Japan, it was considered that it would be more efficient and preferable to formulate a framework which would make the most of the price discovery function of stock exchanges and the adoption of this National Market System was thus passed over.

b. The system in which stock exchanges still occupy a main market status takes a position that the price discovery function by auction method in the market for exchange-listed securities as a main market is maintained and that trading off the market for exchange-listed securities shall be conducted using the above function. Under this system, execution of purchase and sale orders from customers on listed securities will be made on the market instructed by the customers, they shall be executed on the market for exchange-listed securities if the instructions of customers are not specifically given to off the market for exchange-listed securities. Trading off the market for exchange-listed securities shall be executed within a certain scope of the price based on the price discovered on the market for exchange-listed securities. In order for customers to make a reasonable choice and give instructions on whether to execute their orders on the market for exchange-listed securities or off the market for exchange-listed securities, it is important for them to precisely know the outline of the trading off the market for exchange-listed securities and the price information of listed securities. Therefore, after abolition of the no off-exchange trade rule, as a part of trade regulations, securities companies shall explain to customers the outline of trading off the market for exchange-listed securities and provide customers with the price information of the listed securities.

The report of the Market Working Party supported such a concept (b) mentioned. Therefore, when the Financial System Reform Act of 1999 introduced the PTS, the priority rule of markets for exchange-listed securities in execution of customer's orders by securities companies was simultaneously embodied in the Securities and Exchange Act as following. Except cases that customers specifically instructed their orders to be executed off the market for exchange-listed securities, execution of purchase and sale orders from customers on listed securities shall be executed on the market for exchange-listed securities.[12] And arrangements for price discovery and execution of the PTS were limited to price-importing reference market method and negotiation method in 1998. In 2000, limit order matching method and market maker method were added. As a result, this legal framework provided for protection of market for exchange-listed securities and did not promote competition among stock exchanges including PTS. This situation was inconsistent with the objective of the financial system reform (Kinyu Ho Iinkai, 2002[13]).

Considering, the Securities and Exchange Act was revised in 2005 (Yukizawa, 2005; Nakanishi & Ogura, 2005)[14]. The priority rule of markets for exchange-listed securities was abolished[15] and duty of best execution, which means securities companies are obliged to execute orders on terms most favorable to customers, was introduced. Auction method was added to arrangements for price discovery and execution of the PTS, however, volume regulations were imposed on auction method. The PTS still does not enjoy an equal status of stock exchanges in securities trading. Details of these will be discussed later.

PTS

According to the report of the Market Working Party, it has been pointed out that if the no off-exchange trade rule is abolished, as establishment of a Proprietary Trading System (PTS) is expected, it is also necessary to take legal measures for ensuring fairness of trading for a new form of trading.

In such an event, if the new trade system has a similar high price discovery function as stock exchanges, such a system must naturally be regulated as the stock exchange. As it is expected that under such a system for the time being, however, the price discovery function of a stock exchange will be utilized and a similar high level of the price discovery function will not work, it is appropriate to position it as a securities business not a stock exchange; provided, however, that minimum rules must be imposed in terms of prevention of unfair trading depending on the nature of the forum of trading in addition to regulations on securities companies.

The concepts reported by Market Working Party are now considered not to be consistent with the policy to promote competition among stock exchanges. This is the prime reason for abolition of the no off-exchange trade rule. This recognition explains the addition of auction method to one of the arrangements for price discovery and execution of the PTS in 2005, which details are in the following.

PTS AS THE SYSTEM UNDER THE SECURITIES AND EXCHANGE ACT

By the Financial System Reform Act (Act No. 107 of 1998) in 1998, the Securities and Exchange Act (Act No. 25 of 1948) was revised and the PTS was added to securities businesses (Art. 2(8) (vii)). Thereafter, as stated, with respect to the arrangements for price discovery and execution, addition was made two times. The first addition was made by revision and implementation of the Ordinance of the General Administrative Agency of the Cabinet in 2000.[16] The second addition was made by the Revising Act (Act No. 97 of 2004) of the Securities and Exchange Act, which came into force in April 2005.[17] As in effect in 2006, the following provisions are enacted for the PTS in the laws and regulations.

Definition of PTS

Art. 2(8) of the Securities and Exchange Act (hereinafter referred to as "SEA") provides for the definition of what kind of business securities business performs and provides for the contents of business which securities companies may perform (Nikko Shoken Homubu, 1999[18]). PTS is defined in SEA, Art. 2(8) (vii) as one of the securities businesses. That is, PTS is defined as "purchase and sale of securities or its intermediation, brokerage, or agency which is carried out by the method for determining the execution price of an order set forth below or similar methods, simultaneously setting multiple parties as either party or both parties through the use of electronic information processing system."

Criteria for Regulatory Authorization of PTS

Securities companies are business corporations which are registered as securities business with the Prime Minister (SEA, Art. 2(9) and Art. 28). In order for securities companies to perform PTS, however, registration for the securities business is insufficient because performance of PTS by securities companies requires expertise in business and a high level of risk management and securities companies must receive regulatory authorization from the Prime Minister for performance of PTS (SEA, Art. 29(1) (iii)).

Criteria for regulatory authorization are as follows (SEA, Art. 28-4):

1. It has arranged appropriate systems and rules concerning risk management of losses related to businesses for which it intends to receive regulatory authorization.
2. Minimum capital requirement for securities companies which perform ordinary purchase and sale, and so forth, of securities is JPY50 million, but the minimum capital requirement for securities companies which perform PTS is JPY300 million.
3. Amount of net assets is over the amount set forth in item 2, JPY300 million.
4. Capital adequacy regulation ratio is over 120%.
5. The method for determining the execution price of an order, the method of delivery and other settlement, standards for start of trade with customers and method of customer management, method of operation of electronic information processing system, method of preparation, and retention of trade records are necessary and appropriate for public interest and investor protection.

Difference between Regulated Securities Market and PTS—Degree of Price Discovery Function

It is provided that on the stock exchange to establish a securities market, the permission of the Prime Minister is required (SEA, Art. 80(1)). In a securities company starting PTS, the regulatory authorization of the Prime Minister is required

(SEA, Art. 29(1)(iii)). For the market for Over-The-Counter traded Securities (OTC market), as it is provided that the Securities Dealers Association itself, which establishes the market, requires the regulatory authorization of the Prime Minister (SEA, Art. 80 (1) and Art. 68 (2)).

In the background of the above provisions, there seems to be a difference between the subject of establishing a market and PTS, which have similar functions to the market. Securities businesses (securities companies) which establish the PTS are under the registration system and the Securities Dealers Association is under the regulatory authorization system and stock exchanges are under the permission system and the contents of regulations therefore are naturally different.

While stock exchanges and the Securities Dealers Association have broad authority in self-regulation, it is a significant issue that securities companies which establish PTS do not originally have a self-regulatory function such as ensuring fair trade against market participants.

A securities market may not be established by other than those who obtained permission from the Prime Minister, except for the Securities Dealers Association. On the other hand, in the event that securities companies, and so forth, perform purchase and sale and its intermediation, brokerage, or agency of securities, permission is not required (SEA, Art. 80).

That is, in the event that securities companies, and so forth, perform purchase and sale of securities, it does not fall under establishment of the securities market, which requires permission.

The concept suggested by the Securities and Exchange Act is that it exempts the securities business from application of a permission system, while it brings into its view that a securities business might be inherently a market. Such a method of provision is perceived that conducting the securities business collectively on the Internet and special online terminals, using a specific method for determining the execution price of an order, is not regarded as securities business under the registration system, but it is the purpose of the Act to make them subject to more sophisticated regulations under the permission system.

That is, there was such line drawn as those with a more sophisticated price discovery function require permission and if it is not so sophisticated, it is sufficient to receive registration as a securities business or regulatory authorization of PTS. It may be understood, in essence that the presence of a sophisticated price discovery function is added as an element for determining whether it is a securities market or not in SEA. This explains the reason why auction method applied to PTS is subject to volume regulations and conditions for regulatory authorization of PTS prescribe quantitative criteria concerning trade volume, which details are discussed later.

ARRANGEMENTS FOR PRICE DISCOVERY AND EXECUTION

As of 2006, arrangements for price discovery and execution in PTS have the following five methods. In 1998, when the provisions of PTS were newly enacted in SEA, only the price-importing reference market method and negotiated method were the methods to determine the execution price of an order of PTS. Supply and demand in securities trading are not reflected in prices of these methods, which did not have a price discovery function. Thereafter, as already explained, in order to promote competition among stock exchanges including the PTS, limit order matching method and market maker method were added in 2000, and auction method was added in 2005.

Price-Importing Reference Market Method[19]

It is a crossing system, and does not discover prices itself but import prices from the stock exchange market/OTC market where the securities to be traded are listed. For example, a transaction is concluded based on the closing price or VWAPVolume Weighted Average Price of the stock exchange market/OTC market where the securities to be traded are listed.

Negotiation Method[20]

It is a kind of order-driven method. Bid and ask quotes are collected and displayed to PTS participants. They respond, enter into negotiations, and conclude a trade under the agreed terms within the system. Orders are not matched automatically. PTS provides facilities and opportunities to negotiate and execute. This method would be appropriate for large block trades.

Limit Order Matching Method[21]

If a limit order price to sell and a limit order price to buy are matched, those orders are executed based on that limit order price. It is an order-driven method, however, it is different from an auction method applicable to stock exchange trades because a market order and *Itayose* method[22] are not allowed and orders are executed just through matching limit orders placed by PTS participants. A PTS that executes orders by this method is considered not to have a price discovery function sufficiently comparable to that of a market for exchange-listed securities.

Market Maker Method[23]

In a quote-driven, market maker system, transactions are concluded between investors and market makers. The latter continuously quotes binding bid and ask prices for certain securities, however, a market maker of the PTS is not obliged to do so, thus, he does not guarantee that securities can be traded immediately at any time. This is a material difference between a market maker of a PTS and that of the market for the Over-The-Counter traded securities. Therefore, a PTS using this method is considered not to have as much a sophisticated price discovery function as the market for OTC traded securities.

If a PTS operator is obliged continuously to quote binding bid and ask prices for certain securities, as it is no different from the price discovery function through market making in the regulated OTC market, it is required to be subjected to legal regulations of the regulated OTC market and it may not be performed as a securities business. Only the Securities Dealers Association, which was incorporated by regulatory authorization from the Prime Minister, may establish the market for OTC traded securities. This is currently the Japan Securities Dealers Association (JSDA).[24]

Auction Method[25]

By the revision of the Securities and Exchange Act[26], from April 1, 2005, the auction method was introduced as a method for determining the execution price of an order and it has been in effect up to the present. In terms of formulating an efficient and competitive market as a part of improvement in the institutional framework of competition among stock exchanges, equal footing on competing conditions between stock exchanges and PTS was intended to be secured and the same method for determining prices by the auction method as stock exchanges was introduced to PTS. Since PTS may perform purchase and sale of securities by the Auction method similar to that of stock exchanges, purchase and sale by the *Itayose* method[27] or market order became possible. Under this scheme, there is no longer a difference in the method of purchase and sale between PTS and stock exchanges, the only difference is the trade volume and the degree of the price discovery function.

On other methods to determine the execution price of an order, volume regulation is not imposed under the Securities and Exchange Act, but in the case of the auction method, it is provided, "it is limited to the volume of purchase and sale of securities which does not exceed the criteria determined by the Cabinet Order." (SEA, Art. 2(8) (vii) (a)). This Cabinet Order is "Criteria in the case of the Auction Method" provided by Art. 1-9-2 of the Cabinet Order for Enforcement of the Securities and Exchange Act (Cabinet Order No. 321 of 1965) and it has the following content (Nakanishi & Ogura, 2005[28]).

The average amount of the gross trade amount per business day concerning purchase and sale of exchange-listed securities and OTC traded securities performed by the Auction method in the past 6 months is 1% of the average amount of the gross trade amount per business day concerning purchase and sale of exchange-listed securities and OTC traded securities performed by the market for exchange-listed securities and the market for OTC traded securities in the past 6 months.

The average amount of gross trade amount per business day concerning each item of exchange-listed securities and OTC traded securities performed by the Auction method in the past 6 months is 10% of the average amount of the gross trade amount per business day concerning purchase and sale of exchange-listed securities and OTC traded securities performed by the market for exchange-listed securities and the market for OTC traded securities in the past 6 months.

Due to the described quantity regulation, it is perceived that PTS using the auction method does not have such a sophisticated price discovery function as the market for exchange-listed securities. However, in the event that the criteria are exceeded, acquisition of permission for establishment of the market for exchange-listed securities as the stock exchange shall be required.

In this regard, it is to be noted that when the securities company receives regulatory authorization for PTS business from the Prime Minister stated, "quantitative criteria concerning the trade volume" [29] which are attached to the conditions for regulatory authorization are different from the described criteria.

GUIDELINES FOR ESTABLISHMENT OF PTS

With respect to a new form of securities business, PTS, it was expected that there might be various problems that were not anticipated in the traditional securities business in terms of securing fair trade and investor protection.

Accordingly, the Financial Services Agency has recognized the need for promoting environmental improvements contributing to the digitalization of securities exchanges based on the viewpoint of investor protection and the Financial Services Agency published the "Guidelines for Establishment of Proprietary Trading Systems" on November 16, 2000. Regulatory authorization of the PTS business, based on revised ordinances under these guidelines and administrative guidelines, was enforced as of December 1, 2000 at the same time as the enforcement of the revised Securities and Exchange Act. These Guidelines consist of the following content (Osaki, 2001; Yoshino, 2001[30]).

Enhancement of Arrangements for Price Discovery and Execution in PTS Business

In addition to the conventional price-importing reference market method and negotiated method, the described "limit order matching method" and "market maker method" were newly authorized. Specifically, the Ordinance of the General Administrative Agency of the Cabinet concerning definitions prescribed by Article 2 of the Securities and Exchange Act[31] was revised and the provisions of Art. 8-2, titled "Arrangements for price discovery and execution of PTS operation business" was enacted. As a result of the addition of two types of price discovery methods, limit order matching method and market maker method, PTS acquired a certain price discovery function. Accordingly, the quantitative criteria described were established so that it would not have such sophisticated price discovery function as the market for exchange-listed securities and the market for OTC traded securities. Since Art. 80 of the revised SEA defines by dividing into those who require permission for establishment and those who may establish with regulatory authorization without permission, at the enforcement of the revised SEA as of December 1, 2000, the Financial Services Agency performed the work to determine among the contents of established markets the scope where it is performed as PTS, one of the securities businesses, and the scope where it may be performed only with the permission for securities exchange and it was summarized as the quantitative criteria based on the trading volume.

Improvement in Rules for Securing Fair Trade: Conditions for PTS Regulatory Authorization

Since securities companies have no self-regulatory function, if a certain price discovery function arises due to addition of the method for determining execution price of an order, there may be the possibility of problems on securing fair trades and investor protection. Therefore, in terms of preventing unfair trade, it is necessary to impose rules depending on the nature of the forum where such trades are conducted, including the nature of handling securities. The quantitative criteria based on trading volume share and the external announcements of price information were introduced as conditions for regulatory authorization of the PTS. These rules were provided in the administrative guidelines of the Financial Services Agency[32] in the beginning of December 2000, but the guidelines were abolished as of July 15, 2005 and the same contents were provided in the "Comprehensive Surveillance Guidelines for Securities Companies" of the Financial Services Agency, published on the same date.

External Announcement of Price Information, and so forth

In securing fair trade in off exchange trades, including the PTS business, it is necessary for the price discovery to be made fairly and transparently. For that purpose, factors such as reporting, concentration, and announcement of price information are essential. Therefore, in the PTS business handling share certificates, publication is required by the method externally accessible in real time in the form which is able to compare the best quote and trading prices with those of the PTS operated by other securities companies and it is a condition for regulatory authorization of the PTS business that it has the mentioned form.[33] It seems to be a provision, considering the U.S. National Market System (NMS), but integration of quote information of the same item is not required unlike the U.S. Consolidated Quotation System (CQS). It is sufficient that quote information of the PTS operation companies is "comparable."

Such conditions for regulatory authorization are limited to those handling so-called equity securities, including stocks and warrant bonds (securities provided for in Art. 59-2 of the Cabinet Office Ordinance concerning Securities Companies). These conditions are not imposed on debt securities, including corporate bonds. This takes into consideration the characteristics of bond trading, where there are a great variety of debt securities, including corporate bonds and besides it is technically difficult to publish individual quote and trading information, it is relatively easy to evaluate the validity of price from interest rates and credit ratings.

As the system enabling the publication, the PTS Information Network[34] operated by the Japan Securities Dealers Association (JSDA) started operation on April 30, 2002.[35] JSDA decided to formulate the system satisfying the conditions, as response to request of the Financial Services Agency and in light of its position of managing and regulating the purchases and sales through off-exchange trades of securities listed on stock exchanges.

Introduction of Quantitative Criteria based on Trading Volume Shares

Since securities companies do not have a self-regulatory function, in the event that trade participants increase and the size (trade volume share) expands beyond a certain level as a result of introducing a certain price discovery function to the PTS, the problems may arise in terms of securing fair trades as well as the liquidity of stock exchanges, and so forth, a major market. These may result in disturbance of fair price discovery. Therefore, for the PTS business which covers stocks and warrant bonds (only those listed on stock exchanges or registered with an OTC market), if trade volume shares exceed a certain level, a certain measures shall be required based on this, which are the conditions for regulatory authorization.[36]

Specifically, they are as follows:

1. In the past 6 months, if the ratio of "the daily average trading value at PTS" of stocks and warrant bonds which are listed on the market for exchange-listed securities or the market for OTC traded securities to the "total trading value on the stock exchange market or OTC market" is over 10% as to any of an item and over 5% of the total securities handled by PTS, the following measures shall be taken.
   a. In order to secure fairness in trades, the system (organization and personnel) which is in charge of trade management and examination shall be enhanced and improved.
   b. In order to secure the certainty of performance of settlement, a system similar to a reserve for compensation for default loss of stock exchanges shall be prepared.
   c. In order to secure safety and certainty of the system capacity, and so forth, sufficient checks shall be regularly conducted.
2. In the past 6 months, in the event that the ratio has exceeded 20% as to any of an item and 10% of the total securities handled by the PTS, permission for establishment of securities market shall be obtained.

The Financial Services Agency is supposed to confirm the ratio set forth in item 1 and 2 monthly. The reason for bonds not being the subject of these quantitative criteria is as follows: that is, from the reality of bond trading that such bonds as government bonds and corporate bonds are traded almost all through OTC trading even if they are listed securities, it is not appropriate to determine the level of regulation based on the trading volume at stock exchanges.

In addition, with respect to both the PTS which cover stocks or warrant bonds listed in the stock exchange market or the OTC market and other PTS, if it is necessary for public interest and investor protection corresponding to the expansion of trading volume, new criteria may be established to that extent.

Review of Regulatory Authorization Criteria and Periodic Reporting

It is expected that new forms of the securities business will be developed, which was not expected in the traditional securities business, along with the expansion of the scope of the PTS business. Therefore, in terms of investor protection, and so forth, as the response of examination and supervision of regulatory authorization of a new form of the PTS business, necessary reviews were made for the criteria of regulatory authorization described and periodic reporting, and so forth. Specifically, it was provided in the Administrative Guidelines[37] and Article 10 of Ordinance of the

General Administrative Agency of the Cabinet concerning Securities Companies[38].

First, it was noted that attention should be given to the following points in determining whether it falls under the PTS or not.

a. The system in which brokerage of the purchase and sale of securities on the market for exchange-listed securities or the market for OTC traded securities is conducted or brokerage of the purchase and sale of securities to another single securities company is conducted, is considered as not falling under the Proprietary Trading System and the market for exchange-listed securities.

This means the transmission system of order information such as online trading services on the Internet provided to individual investors by each securities company, which does not accompany the execution of orders, does not fall under the PTS. "System which conducts brokerage of the purchase and sale to another single securities company" is considered to mean the mechanism, in which non-member securities companies of the stock exchange conduct brokerage to the member securities companies and to the market makers off a stock exchange. "System which conducts brokerage to other multiple securities companies" may cause the possibility of falling under PTS by market maker method.

b. In the cross system in which the purchase and sale of securities is conducted between customers, with respect to the system which concludes the purchase and sale based on the posted quotation that summarized the demand and supply of securities by various orders, the Proprietary Trading System may fall under the market for exchange-listed securities.

It is the provision anticipating rather special circumstances where the securities company performs market making alone. It means securities companies which perform market making are considered to change quotations, taking into consideration the status of orders from customers and its own position. It shows recognition that if quotation is presented in conformity to the ordered price of customers after confirming the equilibrium of supply and demand, collecting orders for the purchase and sale from customers in advance (so-called leave order), it is actually the same as matching the orders of customers. And if there is such a reality, it falls under the PTS. Since this provision exists, it is clear that ordinary sole market making requires regulatory authorization for the PTS business.

Next, it was pointed out to pay attention to the following points in regulatory authorization for the business.

1. Enhancement of the Internal Management System
   a. In principle, a person in charge of the PTS business has over 5 years of experience in the securities business and the department performing the PTS business are assigned organization and personnel required for performance of the business.
   b. Method of identifying the person is established in the PTS business.
   c. Method and system of excluding the purchase and sale which hinders fair trades, including insider trading in PTS business have been established.
   d. Internal rules, which are in accordance with the laws and regulations including the Securities and Exchange Act, are prepared in relation to PTS business.

2. Obligation of Full Explanation to Customers of Trading Rules, including the method for determining execution price of an order. In explanation of the business to customers,

the system, which can make prior full explanation about the following matters, are prepared.
    a. Purchase and sale price discovery method
    b. Trading rules from order to execution and settlement
    c. Handling of default
    d. Execution possibility at the quoted price
3. Securing Safety and Certainty of System Capacity, and so forth. The following matters are prepared with respect to securing the safety and certainty of system capacity related to the business.
    a. Forecast of the number of future orders and execution, and so forth, shall be reasonably made and the system capacity corresponding thereto shall be secured.
    b. Based on the forecast, testing shall be sufficiently conducted.
    c. Monitoring method and the system, which enables prevention and early discovery of excess of system capacity and failures, and so forth, are prepared.
    d. Method and the system of countermeasures (explanation to customers and communication method, etc.) in the case of system failure are established.
    e. System is duplicated (back-ups exist).
    f. Assessment of a third party (external organization) was made and the safety and certainty of the system was confirmed with respect to the described matters. In fact, examination of regulatory authorization considerably puts focus on the safety of the system.
4. Preventive Measures for Confidentiality of Trading Information[39] With respect to confidentiality of trading information of customers related to the business, sufficient measures are taken, including the following matters.
    a. Personnel who are engaged in the business shall be clearly separated between the business department and other departments.
    b. It is prohibited that the personnel engaged in the business perform the business using the information related to other business or that the personnel engaged in other business perform other business, using the information related to the business.
    c. Measures for not divulging the trading information of customers to the outside are precisely taken.
    d. Internal rules are prepared for the described measures.

These are the measures for preventing acts with conflict of interests, including intentional crossing when securities companies perform simultaneously the purchase and sale as brokerage and trading with having positions as dealers. For example, if the order placed with PTS has arrived via the dealing department of the securities company, by looking at the order of the customer, it is possible for the securities company to intentionally match the position of the securities company or the orders of other customers, while the company finds out the price on the stock exchange is favorable to the customer. The system intends as practicable as possible to exclude the room for occurrence of acts hindering fairness of trades by establishing appropriate walls in the securities company for the trading information of customers related to the PTS business.

Response in Surveillance

After the regulatory authorization for the PTS business, the following points were supposed to be noted in response to surveillance.

a. Confirmation of the trading volume shall be made by report, and so forth, as to whether the conditions for regulatory authorization are satisfied.
b. Confirmation of the performance condition of the measures examined in regulatory authorization shall be made by requiring a report as appropriate.
c. In the event that the methods of business, including delivery and other settlement method, are intended to be changed after the regulatory authorization, request shall be made for prompt application for regulatory authorization pursuant to the laws.

PRESENT SITUATION AND PROSPECTS OF PTS

On June 30, 2000, the bond trading market system of e-Bond Securities, Inc. obtained the first regulatory authorization for a PTS in Japan. Since only 10 financial institutions participated in this PTS, it was unsuccessful as a securities business, which was liquidated in April 2001. As of October 31, 2006, there are 273 domestic securities companies and 35 foreign securities companies in Japan, a total of 308 securities companies, out of which only 12 securities companies obtained regulatory authorization for a PTS business. Nine companies[40] obtained regulatory authorization for a PTS as a bond trading system out of the 12 companies.

Three companies, Monex, Inc., Kabu.com Securities Co., Ltd. and Instinet Japan Limited, which operate respective PTS for securities trading, obtained regulatory authorization for a PTS for the trading system of equity securities. PTS of Instinet has institutional investors, securities companies, and business companies as its customers and trading is performed during the daytime from 8:00 to 17:00. Negotiation method, market maker method, and price-importing reference market method are adopted as arrangements for price discovery and execution. It seems to mainly deal with large block trades and basket trades by PTS.

In contrast, Monex and Kabu.com cover individual investors and provide after-hours trading. Monex adopts the price-importing reference market method. Kabu.com obtained the regulatory authorization for a PTS business on July 11, 2006 and started a PTS business on September 15. Kabu.com has gained attention as the only PTS adopting the auction method at present. The trading value of Kabu.com in the after-hours market was only JPY90,050,000 a day on average for the 19 business days between September 15 and October 13. The total trading value of PTS was only 0.1% of the total trading of all securities and only JPY50 billion to JPY60 billion a month. At this point, it cannot be said that it is active as participants and items of securities for PTS trading are limited (Ozaki, 2006[41]).

The biggest reasons for the sluggish trading are as follows: (1) Participants in the market are limited to individual investors. Participation of institutional investors whose order volume is large per order has not been authorized as a result of prior consultations with the Financial Services Agency until steady operation of the system can be confirmed. As the trading volume is small, the price significantly fluctuates when a large order is placed for a particular security, which makes it difficult for individual investors to use. (2) Margin trading has not been introduced and adoption of cash trading is another reason. It is for avoiding confusion among investors, but as margin trading cannot be used, which consists of 60-70% of the Internet traded securities by individual investors, it has been regarded as being inconvenient for use on the market.

As breakthrough measures, introduction of margin trading, extension of trading hours and increase in the number of items of securities traded and part of them have been realized. Fortunately, system failure, which was a concern initially, did not occur since trading volume was small. Therefore, the Financial Services Agency is said to be considering a policy of permitting participation of institutional investors, whose order volume is large, in a PTS in the future.

As was stated, PTS is in low gear in Japan, but in the Unites States, ATS and ECN, the equivalents to PTS of Japan have been very successful. The reason for the success was inefficient market structure of the United States. The NYSE still has a physical trading floor[42] and NASDAQ employs a market maker system. Both have inherent inefficiencies and investors incur unreasonably high trading costs. Due to the structural inefficiencies, ATS and ECN which provide more efficient services have been successful in the United States.

However, major markets of the world other than the United States have adopted central limit order system (best execution by auction) not a market maker system and have sufficiently computerized access without a physical trading floor. Therefore, they are regarded as adequately efficient markets, which is considered to be the reason for such a system as ATS or ECN not being required in other parts of the world. That is, ATS and ECN are merely systems in a transitional stage to transfer more efficient markets (Miyoshi, 2000[43]). Therefore, under the present condition in which other markets of the world are transferring to more efficient profit earning structures, ATS and ECN cannot be the significant elements in the markets (Mühlberger, 2005[44]).

Today, as telecommunications and information technologies have highly developed, we have an environment in which orders from domestic customers can be easily executed abroad and it is expected with stock exchange markets in each country, PTS and ATS will compete over whether they can provide services which attract orders from customers beyond borders not only within the country (Osaki, 2005[45]). In fact, such competition among markets in the EU is beginning. A group of seven global investment banks have agreed to establish a pan-European equities trading platform known as Multilateral Trading Facilities (MTF) that will compete with the region's domestic stock exchanges following the introduction of the EU's Markets in Financial Instruments Directive (MiFID) in November 2007. The seven investment banks include Citigroup, Credit Suisse, Deutsche Bank, Goldman Sachs, Merrill Lynch, Morgan Stanley, and UBS. This project is responding to the MiFID legislation by creating an integrated pan-European trading platform where equities can be traded more cost effectively, obtaining significant liquidity with greater efficiency for each and every participant in the equity markets.

In Japan, in which direction will PTS develop? Unlike the inefficient market structures of the United States, trading is concentrated in one market, where over 90% of the trading volume of all stock exchanges is executed on the Tokyo Stock Exchange. It is also an efficient market adopting the full auction method under an automatic matching system by computer. If PTS intends to compete over execution of an order at the best price, there is little room left over. Therefore, PTS can find its significance not in the "alternative" market of the exchange market but in the "supplementary" market to respond to the diversified needs of investors, including after-hours trading.

Lastly, the remaining problems of PTS in Japan will be stated.

Under the present Japanese legal system, a framework of regulation has been adopted, which distinguishes securities markets and PTS by the particular method for determining price, positioning the particular method for determining price as inherently having a sophisticated price discovery function, but it is doubtful. The level of strictness of regulations on a trading system must be determined, focusing attention on such factors as trading volume, number of participants, and composition.

If PTS will develop in the future, an integrated quotation information publication system such as NMS or CQS shall be necessary as an infrastructure not the present "publication of quotation information in comparable form" in order to prevent a schism in the market.

It is believed that a low liquidity situation where the trading volume of PTS is small will continue in the near future. As liquidity is low, stock prices tend to fluctuate significantly even in a not so large trade by speculation and rumor, it is necessary to prepare a system of monitoring unfair trades, including market manipulation. The provisions of the Securities and Exchange Act, which regulate market manipulation, have the part which provides for subjecting exchange trade (e.g., SEA Art. 159(2)(ii) & Art. 160, etc.), which has a statutory drawback that it is not applicable to PTS.

If such price sensitive information as a merger is announced at night, there are such problems as whether a trading halt can be flexibly made or monitoring of insider trading can be sufficiently made.

Telecommunications and information technologies and computer technologies realized PTS, and PTS is making the borders between markets and brokers ambiguous. Traditional regulations on broker-dealers and stock exchanges will be inevitably reviewed and the regulations on securities markets will be unable to avoid reform (Osaki & Kozuka, 2001[46]).

FURTHER RESEARCH DIRECTION

Japanese securities law tried to distinguish regulated securities markets and PTS by keeping auction method exclusive to regulated markets. The rationale was that a sophisticated price discovery function should be given only to a regulated securities market. PTS was introduced to Japan with the purpose of promoting competition among securities markets. From this viewpoint, there is little justification for keeping auction method exclusive to regulated markets. This is the reason of revision made to the Securities and Exchange Act in 2004 that introduced auction method to PTS. However, trading volume regulation was simultaneously introduced, and distinction between regulated securities markets and PTS are prescribed not by method for determining price but by trade volume under auction method.

It is wrong to formulate legal framework with implicit premise that PTS is inherently differs from regulated markets. Development of information technology makes it possible for securities companies to perform function of stock exchange and boundary between a stock exchanges and a securities company becomes ambiguous. Now it may be said that both are "markets." The difference between them is whether it has self regulatory function which secures fair trade on the market to protect investors. In the U.S., new SEC rule, Regulation - ATS broadens the definition of stock exchange so as to include ATS, and ATS may be registered as not a stock exchange but a broker-dealer with subject to certain conditions such as becoming a member of a self regulatory organization, and so forth.

In the U.S. system, ATS is a market without self-regulatory function, and may be registered as a broker-dealer. The U.S. regulation seems a practical approach at the sacrifice of theoretical consistency. There arises an issue concerning how to regulate a whole market structure comprising different types of markets.

On the other hand, a stock exchange is also changing its character. Traditionally it is a non–profit membership organization consisting of market participants with self regulatory function. However, recently demutualization of a stock exchange is a world-wide trend. It means that a stock exchange becomes a non-membership organization for profit, a business corporation. A stock exchange is a business corporation, and can a business corporation properly perform a self regulatory function? In Japan, the same question was discussed before introducing PTS as a securities business.

Now both a stock exchange and a securities company are business corporations for profit, and both operate a securities market. The boundary between them becomes more ambiguous. The issue is how to implement and secure self regulatory function or its substitute measures in order to protect investors. Although a stock exchange still maintains its character as a self regulatory organization, its function may be considered weakened by demutualization. Taking into account of investor protection and competition among securities markets, the combination puzzle of a market, a stock exchange, a securities company, and a self regulatory function increases its complexity. Designing a whole market structure with consistency is not easy.

REFERENCES

Bessembinder, H., & Venkataraman, K. (2003). Does an electronic stock exchange need an upstairs market?*Journal of Financial Economics*, *73*(1), 3-36.

Fuchita, Y. (1999). Regulations on stock exchanges and regulations on proprietary trading system. *Jurist, 1155,* 185-191.

JSDA (Japan Securities Dealers Association). (2002). Development on JSDA regulations related to announcement system of quotation, etc. of proprietary trading system. *Shoken Gyoho, 615,* 6-13.

Kanzaki, K. (2000). Abolition of no off–exchange trade rule. In Shouken Torihiki Hou Kenkyu Kai (Securities Law Study Group) (Ed.), *Kin'yu shisutemmu kaikaku to shoken torihiki seido* (pp. 145-160). (Financial System Reform and Securities Trading System). Tokyo: Nihon Shouken Keizai Kenkyujyo..

Kawashima, I. (2001). Electronic securities trading system and securities law (Issues on Civil & Commercial Law No. 10). *Senshu Daigaku Hogaku Kenkyujo Kiyou, 26,* 31-73.

KINYU HO IINKAI (Financial Law Committee). (2002). Interim organizing of issues concerning the concept of "Securities Market". *Jurist, 1225,* 38-50.

Konishi, N. (2000). Regulations on electronic securities market: Focusing on ATS (Alternative Trading System) Regulation. *Sandai Hogaku, 33*(3&4), 326-360.

Miyoshi, H. (2000). *Shoken shijo denshika no subete* (All about computerization of securities market). Tokyo: Tokyo Shoseki Kabushikigaisha.

Mühlberger, M. (2005). Alternative trading systems: a catalyst of change in securities trading. *Deutsche Bank Research, 47,* 1-12.

Nakanishi, K., & Ogura, T. (2005). Outline of development of cabinet orders, etc., with respect to introduction of obligation of best execution under the Securities and Exchange Act. *Shoji Homu, 1726,* 31-37.

Nikko Shoken Homubu (Ed.). (1999). Provision of definitions concerning securities, etc. *Shoji Homu, 1528,* 28-35.

Osaki, S. (1999). Electronic Communications Network (ECN). *Shihon Shijo Quarterly, 3*(2), 49-61.

Osaki, S. (2000). *Kabushiki shijo kan kyoso-NASDAQ no sekai senryaku to nihon* (Competition among stock exchanges: Global strategy of NASDAQ and Japan). Tokyo: Diamond Corp.

Osaki, S. (2001). New PTS (Proprietary Trading System) Regulation on Japan. *Shihon Shijo Quartlerly, 4*(3), 66-75.

Osaki, S. (2005). Progress in borderless transactions on securities exchanges and market regulations. In K. Egashira & Y. Masui (Eds.), *Tokeru sakai koeru ho 3 shijo to soshiki (Market and Organization)* (Melting border and flowing out of laws No.3). (pp. 85-203). Tokyo: Tokyo Daigaku ShuppanKai.

Osaki, S. (2006). PTS for night trading of stocks in Japan: Significance and issues. *Nomura Capital Market Review, 9*(4), 16-24.

Osaki, S., & Kozuka, S. (2001). Electronic securities trading and issues on legal system. *Jurist, 1195*, 98-103.

Shimizu, Y. (1997). Proprietary trading system (PTS) in US and competition among markets. *Shoken Keizai Kenkyu, 7*, 121-140.

Shimizu Y. (2000). Alternative trading system (ATS) in US and SEC regulations. *Shoken Keizai Gakkai Nenpou, 35*, 83-88.

Yanaga, M. (2006). PTS regulations in European countries. *Shoji Homu, 1781*, 4-19.

Yoshino, I. (2001). Current situation and issues concerning establishment of proprietary trading system (PTS) in Japan. *Gekkan Shihon Shijo, 188*, 57-70.

Yukizawa, K. (2004). Obligation of best execution in the Securities and Exchange Act. *Shoji Homu, 1709*, 4-23.

ADDITIONAL READINGS

Amaro, R. J. (2002). European Union Regulation of electronic communication networks: Stifling global integration of securities markets. *Wisconsin International Law Journal, 20*, 397-414.

Avgouleas, E. (2005). A critical evaluation of the new EC financial-market regulation: Peaks, troughs, and the road ahead. *The Transnational Lawyer* (University of the Pacific, McGeorge School of Law), *18*, 179-229.

Badway, E. E., & Busch, J. M. (2005). Ending securities industry self-regulation as we know it. *Rutgers Law Review, 57*, 1351-1376.

Beny, L. N. (2002). U.S. secondary stock markets: A survey of current regulatory and structural issues and a reform proposal to enhance competition. *Columbia Business Law Review, 2002*, 399-473.

Borrelli, M. (2001). Market making in the electronic age. *Loyola University Chicago Law Journal, 32*, 815-908.

Bronfman, C., Lehn, K., & Schwartz, R. A. (1994). SYMPOSIUM: MARKET 2000: The SEC's Market 2000 Report. *The Journal of Corporation Law* (University of Iowa), *19*, 523-551.

Chtaneva, A. (2002). Alternative trading systems: Impact of technology on securities market structure. *Banking & Finance Law Review, 17*(3), 342-378.

Cohen, P. D. (1999). Securities trading via the Internet. *Stanford Journal of Law, Business & Finance, 4*, 1-38.

Collins, A. L. (2002). Regulation of alternative trading systems: Evolving regulatory models and prospects for increased regulatory coordination and convergence. *Law and Policy in International Business, 33*, 481-506.

Dombalagian, O. H. (2005). Demythologizing the stock exchange: Reconciling self-regulation and the national market system. *University of Richmond Law Review, 39*, 1069-1154.

Fleckner, A. M. (2006). Stock exchanges at the crossroads. *Fordham Law Review, 74*, 2541-2620.

Frase, D., & Parry, H. (2001). *Exchanges and alternative trading systems*. Sweet & Maxwell.

Gallagher, D. M. (1998). Move over tickertape, here comes the cyber-exchange: The rise of integrated-based securities trading systems. *Catholic University Law Review, 47*, 1009-1056.

Karmel, R. S. (2002). Turning seats into shares: Causes and implications of demutualization of stock and future exchanges. *Hastings Law Journal, 53*, 367-430.

Klock, M. (1999). The SEC's new regulation ATS: placing the myth of market fragmentation ahead of economic theory and evidence. *University of Florida Law Review, 51,* 753-797.

Macey, J. R., & O'Hara, M. (1999). Regulating exchanges and alternative trading systems: A law and economics perspective. *The Journal of Legal Studies, 28,* 17-54.

Macy, J. R., & O'Hara, M. (2005). From markets to venues: Securities regulation in an evolving world. *Stanford Law Review, 58,* 563-599.

Matus, G. (2001). The regulation of alternative trading systems: Market fragmentation and the new market structure. *New York Law School Law Review, 44,* 583-604.

Maynard, T. H. (1992). What is an "exchange?" Proprietary electronic securities trading systems and the statutory definition of an exchange. *Washington and Lee Law Review, 49*(3), 833-912.

McCarroll, E. (2000). Regulation of electronic communications networks: An examination of Tradepoint Financial Network's SEC approval to become the first non-American exchange to operate in the United States. *Cornell International Law Journal, 33,* 211-262.

Nyquist, P. (1995). Failure to engage: The regulation of proprietary trading systems. *Yale Law & Policy Review, 13,* 281-337.

Poser, N. S. (2001). The stock exchanges of the United States and Europe: Automation, globalization, and consolidation. *University of Pennsylvania Journal of International Economic Law, 22,* 497-540.

Rubin L. (1998). *What is an exchange?* Oxford University Press.

Thompson, A. R. (1999). Taming the frontier?: An evolution of the SEC's regulation of internet securities trading systems. *Columbia Business Law Review, 1999,* 165-205.

ENDNOTES

[1] 'Multilateral trading facility (MTF)' means a multilateral system, operated by an investment firm or a market operator, which brings together multiple third-party buying and selling interests in financial instruments—in the system and in accordance with non-discretionary rules—in a way that results in a contract in accordance with the provisions of Title II of MiFID.

[2] See, SHIMIZU (1997) pp.121-140, SHIMIZU (2000) pp.83-88, OSAKI (1999) pp.49-61, KONISHI (2000) pp. 326-360, YANAGA (2006) pp.4-19.

[3] For detailed comparison and analysis, KAWASHIMA (2001) pp. 31-73.

[4] Brief descriptions of this revision are explained in: http://www.fsa.go.jp/en/policy/fiel/20060621.pdf

[5] http://www.fsa.go.jp/p_mof/singikai/shoken/top.htm This site page is Japanese text only.

[6] No off-exchange trade rule is provided as a rule under the Securities and Exchange Act but was implemented through (a) the provisions of articles of association of stock exchanges and (b) provisions of the regulations by the Ministry of Finance concerning business method of securities companies. These provisions of the articles of association and the regulations on business method were abolished in December 1998.

[7] See, supra note (5).

[8] For example, large block trades and basket trades of institutional investors have difficulty in efficiently executing trades depending on the auction method under conventional

principles of price priority and time priority. The auction method requires much time for execution of large block orders and basket orders and has a problem that bulk execution of orders is impossible. Economic analysis on this matter shows the same result. See, Bessembinder & Venkataraman (2003) p. 27.

[9] As a result of significant development of telecommunications and information technologies, as it became necessary to prepare such market infrastructure for a new trading system as ATS in the United States, it is necessary to take measures for the no off-exchange trade rule not being an obstacle to market infrastructure improvements.

[10] As globalization of securities trading has continued to develop, trades that prove difficult to execute in Japan will easily flow out abroad to seek an opportunity to execute abroad. In order to maintain the vitality of the securities market in Japan, it is necessary for the Japanese securities market to be attractive and convenient for investors. No off-exchange trade rule imposes restrictions on trades executed by market intermediaries (securities companies) and it should be reviewed for prevention of outflow of trading overseas.

[11] See, Osaki (2000) pp. 173-198, Fuchita (1999) pp. 185-191.

[12] SEA Art. 37.

[13] See, KINYU HO IINKAI (2002) pp. 38-50.

[14] See, Yukizawa (2005) pp. 14-23, Nakanishi, & Ogura (2005) pp. 31-37.

[15] SEA Art. 37 was deleted by Act No. 97 of 2004 concerning Amendment of the Securities and Exchange Act, which came into force in April 2005.

[16] See, infra note (21) and note (23).

[17] SEA Art. 2(8)(vii)(a).

[18] See, Nikko Shoken Homubu (1999) pp. 33-34.

[19] SEA Art.2(8)(vii)(b)&(c).

[20] SEA Art.2(8)(vii)(d).

[21] SEA Art.2 (8)(vii)(e); Cabinet Office Ordinance concerning Definitions prescribed by Article 2 of Securities and Exchange Act (Ordinance of Ministry of Finance No.14 of 1993) Art.8-2 (i).

[22] The order book prior to the start of the session is often complicated with offers (sell) at lower prices than bids (buy) and bids at higher prices than offers, as well as a mixture of market offers and bids. Under the *Itayose* method all orders reaching the order book are treated as simultaneous orders, in other words there is no time priority. Bids and offers are matched at a single price according to the principle of price priority.

[23] SEA Art.2 (8)(vii)(e); Cabinet Office Ordinance concerning definitions prescribed by Article 2 of Securities and Exchange Act (Ordinance of Ministry of Finance No.14 of 1993) Art.8-2 (ii).

[24] JSDA had operated the market for the Over-The-Counter traded securities known as JASDAQ since 1998. In 2004, JASDAQ market became a market for exchange-listed securities instead of a market for Over-The-Counter traded securities; Jasdaq Securities Exchange was created and all securities listed on the JASDAQ became the securities listed on Jasdaq Securities Exchange.

At present JSDA does not operate an OTC market.

[25] SEA Art.2(8)(vii)(a).
[26] Act concerning Amendment of the Securities and Exchange Act (Act No. 98 of 2004).
[27] See, supra note 24.
[28] See, Nakanishi, supra note (14) pp. 36-37.
[29] See, the Financial Services Agency, "Guidelines for Comprehensive Supervising for Securities Companies" III—2—2—1 (3)3.
[30] See, Osaki (2001) pp. 66-75, Yoshino (2001) pp. 57-70.
[31] Now it is renamed as the Cabinet Office Ordinance concerning Definitions prescribed by Article 2 of the Securities and Exchange Act (Ordinance of Ministry of Finance No.14 of 1993).
[32] Financial Services Agency, "Administrative Guidelines: On the matters to be noted in supervising securities companies, investment trust companies and investment corporations and securities investment advisers, and so forth. (Part I) Supervision of Securities Companies." As stated in the text, these Administrative Guidelines were entirely abolished as of July 15, 2005 when "Guidelines for Comprehensive Supervision for Securities Companies" was developed.
[33] See, the Financial Services Agency, "Guidelines for Comprehensive Supervision for Securities Companies" III—2—2—1 (3)a.
[34] http://www.pts-info.jp/
[35] Detailed rules can be found in JSDA, "Regulations concerning Off-Exchange Purchase and Sale, and so forth, of Exchange-Traded Securities, including Listed Stocks" (Fair Business Practice Regulations, No. 5) (established on November 18, 1998), Art. 7-Art. 10, JSDA "Detailed Rules relating to the Regulations concerning Off-exchange Purchase and Sale, and so forth, of Exchange-Traded Securities, including Listed Stocks." (established on November 18, 1998), and JSDA "On Handling of Report and Publication through Proprietary Trading System Price Information Publication System" (Resolution of the Board of Directors as of April 23, 2002). See, JSDA (2002) pp.6-13.
[36] See, the Financial Services Agency, "Guidelines for Comprehensive Supervision for Securities Companies" III—2—2—1 (3)3b.
[37] This is the current "Guidelines for Comprehensive Supervision for Securities Companies" III—2—2—1 (3)3.
[38] General Administrative Agency of the Cabinet and Ministry of Finance Ordinance No. 32 of 1998. As the General Administrative Agency of the Cabinet was reorganized to Cabinet Office in January 2001, the name of the ordinance is currently the "Cabinet Office Ordinance concerning Securities Companies."
[39] These are the measures for preventing acts with conflict of interests, including intentional crossing when securities companies perform simultaneously purchase and sale as brokerage and trading having positions as dealers. For example, if the order placed with PTS has arrived via the dealing department of the securities company, by looking at the order of the customer, it is possible for the securities company to intentionally match the position of the securities company or the orders of other customers, while the company finds out the price of the stock exchange is favorable to the customer. The

system intends as practicable as possible to exclude the room for occurrence of acts disturbing fairness of trade by establishing appropriate wall in the securities company for the trading information of customers related to PTS business.

[40] These nine securities companies are Japan Bond Trading Co., Ltd., ICAP Totan Securities Co., Ltd., Central Tanshi Securities Co., Ltd., Bloomberg Tradebook Japan Ltd., Yensai.com Co., Ltd., JBond Securities Co., Ltd., Japan Securities Agents, Ltd., BGC Shoken Kaisha Limited, and TradeWeb Europe Limited.

[41] See, Osaki (2006) pp. 16-24.

[42] Stock trading floors in Japan were abolished in December 1997 at Osaka Securities Exchange and in April 1999 at Tokyo Stock Exchange.

[43] See, Miyoshi (2000) pp. 135-138.

[44] See, Mühlberger (2005) pp. 8-9.

[45] See, Osaki (2005) pp. 185-203.

[46] See, Osaki & Kozuka (2001) pp. 98-103.

Chapter V
The Holding and Transfer of Interests in Securities in England and Japan:
Compared with the Holding and Transfer of Funds

Tomonori Fujiike
Hori & Partners, Japan

ABSTRACT

This chapter compares account-based securities settlement systems with payment systems in which funds are transferred through bank accounts in England and Japan and examines a desirable securities system to harmonize the relevant countries' jurisprudence considering U.S. securities system and relevant international trends. It argues that there should be two broad areas of similarity in both systems; compartmentalization of a legal relationship between related parties and the method of transfer of securities and funds. It also argues, however, that, due to the differences in the legal nature of both financial assets, there are some differences between both systems in order to response intermediary risk. The purpose of this chapter is not only to propose that similar legal issues in both systems should be resolved in the same ways as much as possible, but also to distinguish issues which could be resolved in commercial law from issues which should be resolved in the field of regulations by financial authorities in securities system.

INTRODUCTION

Traditionally, methods of holding and transferring securities have involved direct holding systems in which the owners of securities have a direct relationship with the issuers. Under such a system, in order to hold and transfer securities, the investor needs to be in physical possession of relevant certificates and then execute the physical delivery of them. However, such physical delivery is labor-intensive and time-consuming. There is also a risk that the certificates could be lost or stolen. These disadvantages triggered the evolution of securities systems under which the investor holds the interests in respect of the underlying securities indirectly. In such a system, the investor's interests are held via an account of an intermediary, which in turn has its interests recorded with another intermediary, and so on. This continues down the chain until some intermediary (CDS or central securities depositary) either: (1) is recorded as the owner of the securities on the issuer's register or (2) holds the certificates representing the securities (Bernasconi, et al., 2002i). This system is often known as an "indirectly held securities system" (this system will be referred to hereinafter as a "securities system," and the investor's interests under such a system will be referred to as "interests in securities"). Under securities systems, securities certificates are "immobilized" or "dematerialized," so that transfers of interests in securities are implemented through the adjustment of balances in relevant accounts instead of through the physical delivery of certificates.

The structure of securities systems appears similar to the system relating to the holding and transfer of funds. Deposits are recorded on the bank account. A funds transfer is made through a payment system to bypass the need to physically transport the money itself (the system of holding and transferring funds will be referred to hereinafter as "funds systems").

Obviously, interests in securities are different from interests in deposits in some respects. Traditionally, the legal nature of interests in securities has been regarded as proprietary rights whereas monetary deposits amount to mere personal rights enforceable against banks.

Notwithstanding such a difference, from a commercial transaction law viewpoint, both systems share many related risks and legal issues. This chapter, therefore, focuses on comparing securities systems with funds systems to examine whether the similar related risks and legal issues can be solved in the same way in the field of private commercial law.

Additionally, due to the rapid internationalization of securities transaction, a number of intermediaries in different countries can be involved in securities systems. Thus, laws of different countries are likely to seek to intervene across borders in interests in securities. For this reason, this chapter also aims, in comparing the legal systems of relevant countries, to harmonize the relevant in order to avoid the inconsistency of laws in cross-border securities transactions. In comparing national legal systems, Japanese law and English law (including applicable EU law) will be mainly considered because the contrast between Japanese law and English law in this area is so stark; that is, under Japanese law, the investor has a proprietary claim directly against the issuer, whereas, under English law, the investor has proprietary rights in respect of underlying securities held by its own intermediary as a trustee. Furthermore, as the need arises, consideration will be given to U.S. securities systems, which have influenced English securities systems and relevant international trends.

The structure of this chapter will be as follows:

1. A review of several legal issues in securities systems as compared to funds systems in the English and Japanese legal systems together with an examination of the similarities and differences in the risks relating to each system; and
2. An analysis of desirable securities systems to harmonize the relevant countries' jurisprudence.

EXAMINATION OF RISKS AND REVIEW OF LEGAL ISSUES

Intermediary Risk

Intermediary Credit Risk

Legal Nature of Interests in Securities
In both systems, the end-users, that is, depositors and investors, have their interests in deposits or securities through their immediate intermediar-

ies' accounts. There is therefore a risk that the intermediaries cannot maintain these interests for them should they become insolvent.

Under English and Japanese law, a customer who holds a deposit in a bank is deemed to have lent the bank the amounts standing to the credit of his account. Therefore, the customer only has a personal claim against the bank, which does not have priority against its general creditors if it becomes insolvent (Ellinger, et al., 2006; Kiuchi, 1989). As a result, this kind of intermediary risk is inevitable in the field of commercial law. For this reason, there are bank regulations including strict capital adequacy requirements and deposit insurance, and the central bank as a lender of last resort.

On the other hand, traditionally the legal nature of securities' interests with certificates has been regarded as a proprietary right. Similar to deposits, however, interests in securities are usually fungible in the sense that the interests are not individually traceable to the interests held by the upper-tier intermediaries and the securities certificates themselves because intermediaries normally hold interests in securities in fungible pools or accounts (Bernasconi, et al., 2002[3]). The question then arises whether interests in securities are regarded as contractual rights or proprietary rights. If the interests are proprietary rights, the legal or beneficial ownership of the assets held by the immediate intermediary in the account at the upper-intermediary will not be vested in the immediate intermediary. As a result, the creditor of the immediate intermediary cannot reach those assets.[4]

In England
Under common law, it was well established that proprietary rights could not exist over an asset held in a fungible account.[5] Therefore, there had been some doubts as to whether the customer's interests in securities were proprietary (Goode, 1987; Horrocks, 1991; Morishita, 2001[6]). Yet, in the High Court of the Hong Kong SAR Court of First Instance with regard to the matter of *CA Pacific Securities Ltd.*,[7] it was held that each individual customer had an individual proprietary claim to the securities in a fungible securities account rather than a collective interest with all other customers.

Nevertheless, this decision has been much criticized because the subject matter of the trust is too uncertain to establish a valid trust on particular shares for an individual investor irrespective of the fungible nature of shares (Hayton, 1994[8]). On this ground, the prevailing view as to these issues seems to be that the investor has *pro rata* beneficial rights in respect of underlying securities (or interests in securities against its upper-tier intermediary) held by its own intermediary for all of its customers, while the intermediary holds the underlying (interests in) securities (Financial Markets Law Committee, 2004; Benjamin, 2000; Goode, 1996[9]). Under this view, there is no uncertainty of subject matter because a single trust property in respect of the same type of asset comprises the entire client holding of that type of asset, so that all customers together beneficially co-own the pool of assets in the intermediary's hands (Benjamin, 2000[10]).

According to this view, the nature of interests in securities (proprietary rights) is different from that of the depositor's right (personal rights) although interests in securities are similar to depositor's rights in that these interests or rights lie against its immediate intermediary.

In Japan
In Japan, stocks, government bonds, corporate bonds, and commercial papers had been settled under various different legal systems on an "immobilized securities" basis. However, a move to drastic reform regarding dematerialized securities began in 2001. First, in 2001, the *Book-entry Transfer of Commercial Paper Act*[11] recognized paperless commercial papers on the basis of a single-tier book-entry system. Secondly, in 2002, the title of this Act was altered to the *Book-entry Transfer of Corporate Bonds Act*, which extended dematerialized securities to include government

and corporate bonds and offered a statutory basis for multi-tiered holding systems. Furthermore, in 2004, this Act and the Commercial Code were revised, so that the definition of dematerialized securities was extended to include stocks and the title of the former was changed to the *Book-entry Transfer of Corporate Bonds and Shares Act*. This revision compels the listed companies to dematerialize their shares until 2009.

Under the Act, "book-entry transfer institutions" are situated at the top of the system as CSDs (Article 8), and, at the lower tier, "account management institutions" hold accounts both for themselves and for their customers at CSDs or other account management institutions (Articles 44 and 45).

With regard to the nature of interests in securities, the Act provides that the investor has a proprietary claim directly against the issuer (Articles 66, 88, and 128), unlike its counterpart in England (Takahashi, Ed., 2003[12]). Thus, neither book-entry transfer institutions nor account management institutions have any rights to securities in respect of which they maintain accounts for their customers.

Intermediary Wrongdoing Risk

The deposited funds are owned by the bank; thus, the bank can utilize the funds for its own purposes such as lending and investments. Interests in securities, on the other hand, should not be utilized by the intermediary for its own purposes. Under English law, so long as an intermediary is regarded as a trustee for its customers' interests, it will be a fiduciary. A fiduciary is generally required to put the client's interests above his own interests.[13] Therefore, the status of the intermediary is different from that of a bank which is normally not a fiduciary relationship. Under Japanese law, the intermediary cannot dispose interests in securities without the consent of investor as well because it does not have any rights to interest in securities at all.

However, even if interests in securities are construed as proprietary rights under English law and Japanese law, the investors inevitably assume the risk of not maintaining the interests where the intermediary does not hold enough assets corresponding to assets credited in the investors' account at the intermediary because of its wrongdoing or miscalculation (Dalhuisen, 2004; Roger, 1996[14]). Thus, in order to response such intermediary wrongdoing risk, the financial authority should supervise the intermediary to achieve the segregation of its customers' assets with its own assets.[15]

The Influence of the Default of an Intermediary Other Than the Immediate Intermediary

Vertical Intermediary Risk and Horizontal Intermediary Risk

Vertical Intermediary Risk

In the case of bank deposits, there is no legal linkage concerning assets in accounts between banks.[16] In contrast, in the case of securities systems, there should be linkage between relevant intermediaries. An immediate intermediary is required to keep the customers' interests in securities segregated from its own assets through the credit entry responding to the interests in a relevant account at the next upper-tier intermediary. The upper-tiered intermediary also maintains the interests in an account of a further upper-tiered intermediary, including a CSD or international central securities depositories (ICSDs).[17] In such multi-tiered systems, there is, thus, a link between lower-tier intermediaries and upper-tier intermediaries. Therefore, it is possible that the interests of investors would be substantially reduced *pro rata* if the assets which the investor's intermediary credits to its account with its upper-tier intermediary are damaged. One legal issue then arises whether the immediate intermediary should assume the responsibility for maintaining the substantial interests in securities credited in its account (referred to hereinafter as a "vertical intermediary risk" issue.).

Horizontal Intermediary Risk
As far as a funds transfer is concerned, where the originator's bank and beneficiary's bank are different, the payment order and funds are transferred between banks. If the originator's bank and beneficiary's bank are not correspondent, one or more intermediaries between those banks could be involved. A funds transfer, therefore, is "a chain" of shifting the payment order and funds from the originator, via the intermediaries, to the beneficiary (Sommer, 1998[18]).

On the other hand, the transfer of interest in securities does not depend on the performance of other intermediaries where the investor sells or buys interests in securities. In such a case, the immediate intermediary buys the interests from him or sells them to him, with the price determined by certain market-mechanisms (Sommer, 1998[19]). Thus, in the case of the trading of interests in securities, there seems to be no chain relationship between the seller and buyer (Dalhuisen, 2004[20]).

However, in the case of transfers of securities as collateral, the transfer of interests in securities is performed between identifiable end-users ("a transferor" and "a transferee"), via intermediaries (Sommer, 1998[21]). Thus, this kind of transfer resembles a funds transfer; the chain of shift of transfer orders and credits in accounts is similar.

In this case, under both systems, the default or failure of an intermediary other than the originator's bank or immediate intermediary can directly influence the performance of a payment order or a transfer order because if one of the intermediaries fail to pass on an order and transfer funds or securities, then the chain of the orders and the transfers will be cut. Therefore, in both systems, a question could occur whether an immediate intermediary should be liable for the default or delay of any other intermediaries in the chain concerning a payment order or transfer order (this will be called a "horizontal intermediary risk" issue).

In England

Funds Systems
In funds systems, a payment order is regarded as the originator's mandate for the originator's bank, and the originator's bank and the correspondent bank are considered to be an agent and sub-agent of the originator respectively.[22] On this ground, with regard to horizontal intermediary risk, the originator's bank could be vicariously liable for the negligence or default of the correspondent bank unless it takes reasonable care to engage the latter as a reliable intermediary.[23] Nevertheless, in practice, originator's banks usually provide for clauses in standard payment instruction forms disclaiming any liability for the default of any correspondent bank (Sealy, Hooley, 2003[24]).

These exemption clauses may, however, be invalid pursuant to the *Unfair Contract Term Act 1977* and the *Unfair Terms in Consumer Contracts Regulations 1999*, particularly where the originator is a consumer[25]. Furthermore, "money back guarantee" adopted by the *Cross-Border Credit Transfer Regulations 1999*, implementing *Directive 97/5/EC on cross-border credit transfers*[26] can apply to certain retail cross-border credit transfers within the EU and EEA. In the case of certain delay in a fund transfer, the originator may request a refund from the originator's bank (Regulation 9).

Nevertheless, except for such retail payments, in fund transfers, the immediate intermediary does not assume horizontal intermediary risk.

Securities Systems
The equitable co-ownership of an investor in a fungible pool is a proprietary right only to the extent that securities are still in the pool maintained by the immediate intermediary with its account at its upper-tier intermediary. Thus, where the securities in the pool have been disposed of by the fraudulent or negligent acts of an upper-tier intermediary, the proprietary interests of the investor will decrease (Goode, 1996[27]). In such a case, in theory, it is

possible that the investor could assert personal claims against the immediate intermediary to maintain the securities. However, in practice, the immediate intermediary is generally exempt from any such claims as set out in its agreement with its clients. Under English law, it appears that such exemption clauses are valid because *section 23 of the Trustee Act 2000* relieves a trustee from liability for the acts of its custodian unless he has failed to comply with the duty of care applicable to him (Benjamin, 2000; Goode, 1996, Mentha, 2000[28]). Therefore, it is possible that an immediate intermediary will not undertake vertical and horizontal intermediary risk.[29]

In Japan

Funds Systems
The prevailing view in Japan understands a funds transfer in the context of a mandate. According to this view, the originator has commissioned the originator's bank to transfer funds while the originator's bank has agreed thereto (Article 643 of the Civil Code ("cc"), Kiuchi, 1989; Koyama, 2004[30]). On this basis, in respect of horizontal intermediary risk, the majority's view is that the originator's bank acts as the originator's agent and the correspondent bank is the originator's sub-agent, so that the originator's bank is liable for the sub-agent's act or omission only if it does not appoint and supervise the correspondent bank properly (Article 105 cc).[31] Furthermore, the model agreement between banks and its customers relating to funds transfers[32], proposed by the Japan Bankers Association in 1995, provides that the originator's bank is not liable for other financial institutions' defaults (section 11). Therefore, in Japan, it appears that the originator assumes horizontal intermediary risk.

Securities Systems

Vertical Intermediary Risk
As far as vertical intermediary risk is concerned, the Act provides as follows:

1. Where an intermediary has incorrectly increased credit entries, a good faith purchaser will acquire good title concerning the incorrectly increased credit entries (Article 77)
2. As a result, the nominal amount of the title of securities will increase
3. The intermediary who executed incorrect entries should obtain the excessive amount of securities from the market and acquit all the liabilities for the securities (Articles 78, 79 and 134)
4. Until then, because the issuer does not assume obligations for the excessive interests (Articles 80 to 81), the interests which the investors hold at lower-tier intermediaries' accounts are reduced *pro rata*
5. Thus, from the viewpoint of the protection of investors, the intermediary having committed the mistake assumes the obligations to fulfill the redemption of principal of and payment of interests in respect of excessive bonds (Articles 80 to 82) or to provide compensation to the investors in respect of excessive shares (Article 153)
6. It may, however, be too much of a burden for general investors to seek the payment of liabilities from upper-tier intermediaries (Takahashi, Ed., 2003[33]), thus, the Act provides that the immediate intermediary will assume joint and several responsibility for the upper-tiered intermediary's liabilities (Article 11-2)
7. Furthermore, where both the upper-tier intermediary and the immediate intermediary become insolvent, the beneficiary rights of the trust for the purpose of protection of investors will be to some extent vested in the investors (Takahashi, Ed., 2003[34])

Horizontal Intermediary Risk
With regard to horizontal intermediary risk, there is neither any provision in the Act nor any views of commentators as far as have been able to be located. However, to draw an analogy with funds transfers, presumably, the transferor's intermedi-

ary's liability for the other intermediary's default is likely to be exempted by disclaimer clauses.

Unauthorized Order

Protection of a Good Faith Purchaser

In both systems, the end-users' assets are held in accounts at their intermediaries, and are transferred through the order initiated by those end-users. Thus, an unauthorized order by a fraudster who pretends to be a genuine account holder may cause assets in the accounts to be transferred. The question then arises whether a person who acquires the assets transferred to his account with good faith should be protected.

If a bona fide acquisition is not protected, it will give rise not only to insecurity in the transfer of funds and securities but also "systemic risk" mentioned due to the revocability of the transfer (Rogers, 1996[35]).

In England

Funds Systems

Restitutionary Claims

The originator or originator's bank may request the beneficiary or the beneficiary's bank to repay funds transferred by way of an unauthorized payment order on the ground of the common law action for money had and received, which is now often referred to as a restitutionary claim at common law.[36]

However, the House of Lords in *Lipkin Gorman v Karpnale Ltd*[37] held that the beneficiary and the beneficiary's bank could have a defense of change of position in good faith. In this case, Lord Goff stated that "the defence is available to a person whose position has so changed that it would be inequitable in all the circumstances to require him to make restitution, or alternatively to make restitution in full."

In addition to this defense, it is well established that tracing[38] money at law through a mixed fund is impossible.[39] On this basis, the Court of Appeal in the *Agip* case[40] approved of Millett J.'s decision at first instance that the originator could not trace funds received by the defendant because the funds were mixed with other funds during the clearing process. Thus, tracing at law in funds systems would be difficult in practice because, in most cases, funds transfers are executed through a clearing system (Brindle, et al, Eds., 2004[41]).

Equitable Remedies

Even if tracing at law is impossible, tracing in equity may be available even though funds are transferred through a mixed fund.[42] Thus, the originator may assert a proprietary right to the wrongfully transferred funds against its recipient who retains the funds (Sealy, Hooley, 2003[43]). Furthermore, where the recipient does not retain the funds, the originator can invoke tracing in equity in order to seek a personal equitable remedy on the basis of "knowing receipt" if the defendant received trust assets for his own benefit with knowledge of breach of the trustee's duty (Sealy, Hooley, 2003[44]).

Nevertheless, the beneficiary, which obtained legal title, could have a bona fide purchaser defense[45] against such equitable claims as well as the defense of change of position, as mentioned (Sealy, Hooley, 2003[46]). This bona fide purchaser defense is available to a person who obtained a legal title for value without notice of an equitable interest.[47] Thus, the beneficiary who acquired a legal claim against the beneficiary's bank for value could be protected by this defense unless he receives funds with knowledge of an adverse claim.

Securities Systems

Restitutionary Claims

The holder of a negotiable instrument in due course can acquire good title from a thief. However, interests in securities cannot be negotiable instruments. Therefore, a defence of "negotiability" is not available in relation to securities systems. However, as with funds transfers, a transferee or buyer or their intermediary has a "change of position" defense. Furthermore, as with funds transfers, tracing interests in securities mixed with other assets at law is impossible (Benjamin, 2000[48]). It therefore seems to cause the difficulty in tracing the interest in securities which are often traded through the clearing system.

Equitable Remedies

Even if tracing at law is impossible, tracing in equity could still be available. For this reason, as is the case with funds transfers, the original holder and/or its intermediary may assert an equitable proprietary right or seek a personal equitable remedy against the buyer or the transferee or their intermediary.

Notwithstanding that the buyer and the transferee run such a risk, it is submitted that the defense of a bona fide purchaser is not generally available to them because they do not obtain legal interests but merely equitable ones (Financial Market Law Committee, 2004; Benjamin, 2000[49]). Therefore, it would appear that a good faith purchaser could only rely on other general defenses, such as "change of position."

In Japan

Funds Systems

In the case of an unauthorized order, case law has suggested that the beneficiary acquires the right to deposits against the beneficiary's bank, independently of the underlying relationship between the originator and the beneficiary, in order for banks to deal smoothly with a number of funds transfers with security and speed and at reasonable cost.[50]

However, the originator and the originator's bank will have a personal restitutionary claim against the beneficiary, based on the principle of unjust enrichment (Articles 703 and 704 cc).[51] A beneficiary acting in good faith, nevertheless, should repay only the existing enrichment in his hands (Article 703 cc). Although it is not clear that a full defense is available to the beneficiary himself, a third party who has received the funds for payment of an underlying monetary obligation from the beneficiary in good faith and without gross negligence will have a full defense for any restitutionary claim.[52]

Securities System

The Act provides that the investor shall be presumed to own the interests in securities recorded in his account (Article 76). The Act also provides that the investor who received the record of the increase of interests in securities in his account shall acquire the interests attached to that record unless he received the record in bad faith or with his gross negligence (Article 77). Therefore, the investor who received the interests in his account can normally obtain their legal title without any investigation into the title.

Systemic Risk

Multilateral Netting

In both systems, payment orders and transfer orders between intermediaries are often exchanged and netted out or offset multilaterally in a clearing house and then the net positions of participant intermediaries are settled multilaterally. However, if the multilateral netting process is legally invalid, it is more likely that the failure of one member of the clearing system to meet its required obligations could cause other members to be unable to meet their obligations when due. The chain of failures incurred as a result, might threaten the stability of the financial system as a whole. This is called "systemic risk." In order to respond to the threat of systemic risk, it is crucial that the finality of settlement in a clearing system should be maintained. Therefore, it is of great importance that the irrevocability of multilateral netting is legally established (BIS, 1990[53]).

In England

Under common law, although bilateral netting effectively withstands the failure of a participant in the system through the right of set-off in an insolvency, the effectiveness of such a set-off in a multilateral netting process is uncertain because a valid set-off requires mutuality, so that, multilateral netting could be challenged by a participant's liquidator in the funds or securities system due to the lack of mutuality.[54]

For the reason, in order to minimize the disruption created by the insolvency proceedings of a participant in settlement systems, the European Parliament and Council introduced *Directive 98/26/EC on settlement finality in payment and securities settlement systems*.[55] This Directive has been implemented in the UK by the *Financial Markets and Insolvency (Settlement Finality) Regulations 1999*.[56] Article 3(1) of the Directive provides that payment or delivery orders and any relevant netting shall be legally binding on third parties even in insolvency proceedings. Additionally, Article 3(2) stipulates that there should be no unwinding of a netting due to the laws which void the transaction executed before the moment of opening insolvency proceedings.

In Japan
Article 505 cc provides that a statutory offset requires the existence of the same kind of two opposing claims between two parties. Thus, multilateral offsets, which can be effectively agreed between the parties, are invalid as against receivers in bankruptcy proceedings. Therefore, multilateral netting is unlikely to be legally effective in Japan (Kubota, 2003[57]).

For this reason, in the Foreign Exchange Yen Clearing System for yen funds settlements in foreign exchange and the domestic fund transfers through the Zengin System for interbank settlements for small value transfers, the Tokyo Bankers Association (TBA) provides services to assume obligations regarding interbank settlements between the participants as a Central Counter Party (CCP) in order to secure legal effects for multilateral settlements by implementing bilateral offsets between TBA and each participant bank. Under this system, TBA will assume obligations, not claims, in relation to settlement among participants as a CCP. After acquiring claims in consideration for assuming the obligations, TBA will carry out bilateral netting for each participant in relation to the assumed obligations and acquired claims (Kubota, 2003[58]).

With regard to securities systems, the *Securities Exchange Act* was revised in 2002 to improve systems for securities settlement organizations (these provide settlement guarantees for netting results in both securities deliveries and funds transfers as the CCP of multilateral settlement). This Act provides that the settlement organization will assume obligations for both securities deliveries and funds transfers and perform bilateral netting between the settlement organizations and each participant in the same manner as the settlement by TBA.

Cross-Border Risk

Conflict of Laws
In both funds systems and securities systems, a number of intermediaries in different countries could be involved in a cross-border transaction, so that the laws of various jurisdictions could apply to a holding or a transfer of financial assets. The existing national laws may contain ambiguities when applied to both systems. Therefore, it is critical to clarify the conflict of laws position.

In England

Funds System
The general rule is that the law governing the bank-customer contract is the law of the place where the account is maintained unless there is an agreement to the contrary.[59] This rule is not altered by *The Contracts (Applicable Law) Act 1990* which implements the *Rome Convention on the Law Applicable to Contractual Obligations 1980*.[60]

Securities System
The traditional rule for proprietary rights is that the applicable laws are determined by the law of the place where a thing is located—the *lex*

situs.[61] Case law suggests that the *lex situs* rule applies to intangible as well as tangible assets.[62] On this basis, the Court of Appeal in *Macmillan v Bishopsgate (No. 3)*, in relation to indirectly held securities, held that the law of the jurisdiction in which the underlying securities themselves were deemed to be located was applicable.[63]

However, such a "Look-Through-to-Underlying Securities" approach will face some difficulties in its application. First, the location of global instruments (which are generally held by ICSDs) is usually unknown by their participants and irrelevant to interests in securities. Secondly, where international portfolios of securities are used as collateral, the relevant global instruments may be held in a range of different jurisdictions. In such a case, it is unworkable in practice to ensure the validity of the collateral in each jurisdiction (Benjamin, 2000[64]).

Claims are considered to be legally located where they are enforceable (Collins, Ed., 2000[65]). Interests in securities are recorded and transferred on the book of an intermediary. On this ground, even if the *lex situs* rule is applicable to indirectly held securities, leading academics submit that interests in securities should be treated as located in the jurisdiction of the office of the intermediary where the account is maintained (Benjamin, 2000[66]). This approach is known as the "The Place of the Relevant Intermediary Approach" (PRIMA).

In addition, Article 9(2) of the *Settlement Finality Directive*,[67] which was introduced for the purpose of reducing risks in payments and securities settlements, stipulates that, with regard to interests in securities provided as collateral to central banks of Member States the European central bank and/or the participants in EU settlement systems, the determination of the rights of such entities as holders of collateral shall be governed by the law of the Member State where the account is located. This Directive supports the PRIMA, and was implemented in the UK by the *Financial Markets and Insolvency (Settlement Finality) Regulations 1999*.[68]

Therefore, the governing law of interests in securities is likely to be the law of the place of the relevant intermediary, so that any agreement to the contrary seems to be invalid, unlike funds systems.

In Japan

Funds Systems

Deposits, which are personal claims, will be governed by the law chosen by the parties under the principle of party autonomy concerning contracts (Article 7 of Law Application Principles Act[69]). If no law has been expressly chosen, the place of the bank's branch where the relevant account is maintained will be deemed to have been impliedly chosen as the jurisdiction (Yamada, 2003[70]).

Securities Systems

Under Japanese private international law, the law which governs interests in securities is unclear. A proprietary right should be governed by the *lex situs* (Article 13 of the Act). For this reason, traditionally, securities have been governed by the law of the place where the certificates are located. It is submitted that the *lex situs*, however, cannot exist in the case of dematerialized securities under the Act. On the other hand, it is conceivable that interests in securities should be regarded as contractual rights and should be governed by the law chosen by the parties, as is the case with deposits. Nonetheless, this would be tenaciously criticized by those holding the orthodox view that interests in securities have proprietary effects which can affect the rights of third parties. Therefore, under Japanese law this issue of the governing law of interests in securities is unsettled.

ANALYSIS OF DESIRABLE SECURITIES SYSTEMS

The Legal Nature of Interests in Securities

In contrast to the depositor's right which is no more than a personal claim, interests in securities are regarded as proprietary rights to the underlying securities directly or indirectly in England and Japan for an investor to avoid intermediary credit risk. Nevertheless, the legal nature of interests in securities in England is different from that in Japan in the sense that the rights of investors lie against their immediate intermediaries. The question then arises which approach will be more appropriate in seeking the harmonization in international securities dealings.

The fundamental concept of interests in securities in England is similar to that of "securities entitlement" introduced in the U.S. in 1994 through the revised Article 8 in the *Uniform Commercial Code* ("UCC"). "A securities entitlement" is defined as a package of rights held by investors, including a mixture of personal rights, such as the right to require the immediate intermediary to deliver or transfer the assets and to obtain receipt of dividends and distributions on the investor's behalf, and a *pro rata* proprietary right in the totality of the interests in the financial assets held by the immediate intermediary, whether on its own account or for its account holders, to the extent necessary to satisfy all the security entitlements of the account holders (§ 8-503).

Such a concept, which denies investors any direct rights against the issuer, would be of great surprise to general investors (Rogers, 1996[71]). Nevertheless, this idea is not necessarily more disadvantageous to the investor than the idea of a direct right against issuers. As indicated, both ideas can avoid intermediary credit risk so far as the assets responding to a customer's interests are segregated from the intermediary's own assets. Furthermore, under the UCC, even if the intermediary has not segregated its customer's assets from its own assets, the customer would hold proprietary rights to the intermediary's assets to the extent necessary to satisfy all the security entitlements of the account holders (Rogers, 1996[72]).

The reason behind the UK/U.S. model is that, even if the investor has direct rights against the issuer, investors would often find it difficult to exercise such rights. This is because the exercise of their rights is often limited under securities issuance agreements, and, even without such agreements, the investor would be forced to go up the hierarchy of intermediaries step by step to prove their rights (Rogers, 1996[73]). For this reason, as Mr. Sommer pointed out, intermediation in securities systems has given rise to "compartmentalization of legal responsibility" on an accounts basis, where the account basis rights create "discrete pairwise relations between parties" which "enjoy strict privity," as is the case with funds systems (Sommer, 1998[74]).

It seems that such a concept of compartmentalization is of great significance particularly in international securities transactions because the legal structure of interests exercisable against issuers could cause a complex issue. Suppose that a Japanese investor orders a Japanese broker to buy foreign securities, which in turn orders an English wholesale broker to buy the securities. The Japanese broker may obtain interests in securities against the English broker under English law. The Japanese broker will then book credit entries on the account of the investor. In this case, what rights does the investor hold? As mentioned, the applicable law in respect of interests in securities is not clear in Japan. However, even if the Hague Convention mentioned is ratified, under Japanese law (the law of the place of the relevant intermediary), the investor would not hold direct rights against the issuer because the *Book-entry Transfer of Corporate Bonds and Shares Act* is only applied to the securities which are entered on the books of book-entry transfer institutions designated by competent ministers (Article 3). As a result, the investor's interests may be mere personal rights against his immediate intermediary.

In order to avoid intermediary credit risk, one solution might be that the relationship between the investor and the intermediary in international transactions should be interpreted as a trust[75] under the *Trust Act* in Japan. In explaining why Japan had not adopted the UK/U.S. model, the draftsmen of the *Book-entry Transfer of Corporate Bonds Act* states that the "trust method" based on the UK/U.S. model was difficult to incorporate into a system where shareholders may exercise their rights directly against companies (e.g., the rights to shareholders' representative lawsuits). However, they also acknowledged that such issues could be resolved by the use of a special system to identify substantial shareholders (Takahashi, Ed., 2003[76]). Therefore, such a solution is worth being considered. Another solution could be that the Act should apply the international securities transaction *mutatis mutandis*. Under this interpretation by analogy, the immediate intermediary does not have any rights to underlying securities, so that intermediary credit risk can be avoided. However, the Act would not bind a foreign company or intermediary at all. As a result, the Japanese investor can assert his rights to interests in securities under the Act only against an intermediary in Japan. Therefore, under both solutions, the reality is that investor's interests in securities lie against his immediate intermediary.

Hence, in order to clarify the ambiguity and inconsistency in the substantive law, a special statute should be enacted using a similar legal structure to the UK/U.S. model to achieve "compartmentalization of legal responsibility" at least in the international sphere.[77]

The Responsibility of the Immediate Intermediary for the Defaults of Other Intermediaries

Horizontal Intermediary Risk

In England and Japan, banks are usually contractually exempt from the defaults of their correspondents in funds transfers with exception of certain retail payments in England. In both countries, moreover, the intermediary in securities systems will not be responsible for acts and omissions of other intermediaries. Thus, in both systems, the customer assumes horizontal intermediary risk.

Vertical Intermediary Risk

Under English law, the intermediary will not be liable for the default of its upper-tier intermediary in principle whereas, under Japanese law, an immediate intermediary undertakes vertical intermediary risk by assuming joint and several liabilities to its customers for its upper-tiered intermediary's mistakes through the aforementioned Act. However, the Act will not apply to an international dimension of securities transactions, so that the intermediary could avoid vertical intermediary risk through exemption clauses. Therefore, the investor could assume vertical intermediary risk at least in international transactions.

The end-user in securities systems is usually in no position to know the intermediaries other than his immediate intermediary. In this sense, it is to some extent reasonable that the intermediary which selects its upper-tier intermediary assumes its risk. In international sphere, however, it seems to be unreasonable for the intermediary to accept the risk of the default of the international wholesale custodians, so called global custodians because the loss could be too enormous for them to bear it. Therefore, it seems to be inevitable for the investor to assume vertical intermediary risk in the international dimension.

Protection of a Good Faith Purchaser

Under English common law, in both systems, restitutionary claims of the original holder and his immediate intermediary are difficult to bring successfully where a clearing system is involved. However, in equity, although the proceeds in the hands of the beneficiary and transferee are traceable through a clearing system, in the case of securities systems, a bona fide purchaser defense is not available. Thus, in securities systems, the status of a transferee may be insecure.[78]

In this respect, the UCC provides that an adverse claim cannot be asserted against a purchaser for value of an interest in a security entitlement who obtains control and does not have notice of the adverse claim (§8-510). Additionally, where a securities intermediary disposes of an entitlement holder's interest in violation of the latter's rights, a purchaser for value who obtains control and does not act in collusion with the intermediary is protected (§8-503(e)). The purpose of these provisions is to secure the transfer of securities entitlements and to maintain finality in securities settlements in order to avoid systemic risk (Rogers, 1996[79]).

Japanese draftsmen referred to these provisions and explained that article 77 of the *Book-entry Transfer of Corporate Bonds Act* contributes to secure transfers and the finality in settlements as much as the UCC provisions because they argue that the requirement of "collusion" in the UCC is equal to the concept of bad faith or gross negligence in the Act from the perspective of Japanese courts' practice.[80]

The Validity of Multilateral Netting

In England, the effectiveness of multilateral netting is established in both systems although this is not yet the position in Japan. In response to existing circumstances in Japan, multilateral settlement has been kept legally effective by the implementation of bilateral netting between TBA and participants, as mentioned. However, if a Japanese financial institution is permitted to remotely access a funds or securities settlement system unaccompanied by a CCP in foreign countries, and the financial institution goes bankrupt, the multilateral netting among participants in the settlement system could be ineffective under Japanese law. As a result, the effectiveness may not be claimed to a receiver of the financial institution (Kubota, 2003[81]).

To prevent systemic risks, it will be of great importance for every legal system to secure the effects of multilateral settlement under relevant substantive laws. For this reason, Japanese law should be revised so as to admit the legal effects of multilateral nettings in funds and securities settlement.

The Conflict of Laws Rule

Under both English and Japanese law, the governing law for a funds transfer will be determined by the choice of the parties concerned, and, if their intention is not clear, the funds transfer will be governed by the laws of the place where the relevant account is located.

In comparison, in securities systems, the traditional *lex situs* approach (i.e., the law of the place of securities certificates) is much criticized. In England, to respond to the criticism, PRIMA seems to be being introduced although the position in Japanese private international law is still unclear.

In this respect, in the U.S., due to the extensive adoption of the principle of party autonomy, interests in securities are now being treated much more like deposits.[82] The *Hague Convention on the Law Applicable to Certain Rights in respect of Securities Held with an Intermediary* (2002) recognized PRIMA as determined by account agreements with intermediaries and substantially introduced the principle of party autonomy.[83]

In respect of interests in securities under substantive laws, if the relation between the tiers of such interests is decided separately according to each tier, it will be appropriate that the governing law be decided based on the place of the accounts, as in the case of deposits, or otherwise the governing laws should be left to the choice of the parties of each tier. In other words, compartmentalized relationships between parties from the perspective of substantive law are likely to lead to the determination of the governing law for each pairwise relationship in the field of conflict of laws (Sommer, 1998[84]). The issue that then arises is which approach is appropriate, PRIMA or party autonomy.

Some commentators oppose the principle of party autonomy being broadly introduced because investors' interests in securities are proprietary in nature, thus possibly causing unforeseeable damage to third parties in relation to those interests in securities (Goode, 1998[85]).

However, even if the principle of party autonomy is adopted, the validity of interests in securities acquired by the acquiring party (or secured party) will be decided according to the governing laws agreed upon between the acquiring party and its immediate intermediary. For example, if X having an account at Intermediary A has offered corporate bonds as security to Y who has an account at Intermediary B, the validity of the acquisition by Y of the interests in securities will be decided by the governing law agreed upon between Y and B. As a result, in deciding the validity of the interests in securities, Y will not need to refer to any laws said to apply between X and A. Therefore, regardless of any governing laws applicable to X and A, Y seems to be able to be kept out of unexpected damage.

Therefore, it seems that the adoption of the principle of party autonomy would not actually have such a harmful effect on the rights of third parties. Hence, it seems that the Hague Convention should be ratified at least by the county where the conflict of law is still unclear, like Japan.

CONCLUSION

In conclusion, as a result of the analysis of desirable legal securities systems, there are two broad areas of similarity in both systems: (1) the compartmentalization of a legal relationship between two parties; (2) the method of transfer of financial assets.

Compartmentalization of a Legal Relationship Between Two Parties

First, interests in securities should be rights against the immediate intermediary, like deposits, in order to avoid serious inconsistencies in the relevant countries' jurisprudence.

Secondly, the applicable law in respect of interests in securities should normally be the law of the state in which the intermediary maintains accounts for its customers; however, if there is an agreement contrary to this rule between the investor and its immediate intermediary, the law agreed should be applied, as is the case with funds systems.

Method of Transfer of Financial Assets

First, horizontal intermediary risk is not in principle assumed by the bank and intermediary.

Secondly, the account-based transfer is executed and the protection of a good faith purchaser should be clearly established in both systems.

Thirdly, the validity of multilateral netting should be robust in both systems.

Despite such similarities, whereas a deposit is a mere personal right, interests in securities should be proprietary rights to avoid intermediary credit risk. Furthermore, in order to response to intermediary wrong doing risk and vertical intermediary risk, there should be linkage between the interests held by a lower-tier intermediary and an upper-tier intermediary. In other words, both should maintain enough (interests in) securities with their upper-tier intermediaries and segregate them form their own assets. Nonetheless, custodians sometimes reserve rights to dispose interests in securities for their own purposes. This could provide instability for securities transaction. Hence, international cooperation among financial regulators in the supervision of custodians could be a critical issue to stabilize securities transactions and settlements.

FUTURE RESEARCH DIRECTIONS

This chapter, to a certain extent, suggests that securities systems and funds systems share some similar risks and legal issues, which can be resolved in the same way in the field of private commercial law. It also indicates, however, that there are some differences between both systems in order to response intermediary risk.

The customer who holds deposits in a bank has a mere personal claim against the bank, which does not have priority against its general creditors if it becomes insolvent. As a result, the intermediary risk is inevitable in the field of commercial law. In the viewpoint of regulations, therefore, there are bank regulations including strict capital adequacy requirements and deposit insurance, and the existence of the central bank as a lender of last resort. On the other hand, if interests in securities are regarded as proprietary rights in the field of commercial law, the investor could avoid intermediary credit risk where its immediate intermediary becomes bankrupt. However, unless the intermediary segregates customer's interests from its own assets and maintains enough interests at its upper-tier intermediary, then the intermediary wrongdoing risk would occur, so that the proprietary rights of the investor would be *pro rata* reduced. In the viewpoint of regulations, therefore, the segregation of the customer's assets from the intermediary's assets is of great importance. This chapter focuses on the field of private commercial law. Therefore, a future research may be conducted into the differences between both systems from the point of view of regulations by a government.

In addition, even though the immediate intermediary of investors maintains interests in securities at the account of its upper-tier intermediary, if the upper-tier intermediary does not maintain enough interests in securities and becomes bankrupt, the rights of immediate intermediary against the upper-tier intermediary would be *pro rata* reduced. As a result, so long as there is an exemption clause for wrongdoing risk of the upper-tier intermediary, the interests of investors would be *pro rata* reduced as well. Therefore, in order to response such a vertical credit risk, it is indispensable that all the related government strictly requires the segregation of the assets of each intermediary. For this reason, a future research could be carried out into the cooperation among financial authorities of leading nations and the harmonization of their regulations.

REFERENCES

Benjamin, J. (2000). *Interests in securities*. Oxford University Press.

Bernasconi, C., Potock, R., & Morton, G. (2002). General introduction: Legal nature of interests in indirectly held securities and resulting conflict of laws analysis. In R. Potok (Ed.), *Cross border collateral: Legal risk and the conflict of laws*. London: Butterworths Lexis Nexis.

BIS. (1990). *Report of the Committee on Interbank Netting Schemes of the central banks of the Group of ten countries (Lamfalussy Report)*. Retrieved March 22, 2007, from http://www.bis.org

Brindle, M., & Cox, R. W. (Eds.). (2004). *Law of bank payments* (3rd ed.). London: Sweet & Maxwel.

Collins, L. (Ed.). (2000). *Dicey & Morris on the conflict of laws* (13th ed.). London: Sweet & Maxwell.

CREST. (2001). *The international framework*. Retrieved March 22, 2007, from http://www.cresto.co.uk

Cresswell, P., Blair, W. J. L., Hill, G. J. S., Wood, P. R., Phillips, P. M., Hooley, R. J. A., Brent, R., Mcquater, E. A., & Sheridan, M. B. G. (Eds.). (looseleaf). *Encyclopaedia of banking law*. London: Butterwoths.

Dalhuisen, J. (2004). *Dalhuisen on international commercial, financial and trade law.* Oxford: Hart Publishing.

Ellinger, E. P., Lomnicka, E. Z., & Hooley, R. (2006). *Modern banking law* (3rd ed.). Oxford: Oxford University.

Financial Markets Law Committee. (2004, July). *Analysis of the need for and nature of legislation relating to property interests in indirectly held investment securities, with a statement of principle for an investment securities statute.* Retrieved March 22, 2007, from www.fmlc.org

Fletcher, I. F. (1999). *Insolvency in private international law.* Oxford: Clarendon Press.

Geva, B. (2001). *Bank collections and payment transactions comparative study of legal aspects.* Oxford: Oxford University Press.

Goode, R. (1987). Ownership and obligation in commercial transactions. *Law Quarterly Review, 103*, 433.

Goode, R. (1996). The nature and transfers of rights in dematerialised and immobilised securities. *Journal of International Banking and Financial Law, 4*, 167.

Goode, R. (1998). Security entitlements as collateral and the conflict of laws. *The Oxford Colloquium on Collateral and Conflict of Laws, Special Supplement to Journal of International Banking and Financial Law, 1998*(7), 22.

Hayton, D. (1994). Uncertainty of subject-matter of trusts. *Law Quarterly Review, 1994*, 335.

Hayton, D. (2003). *Underhill and Hayton law relating to trusts and trustees* (16th ed.). London: Butterworths.

Horrocks, D. (1991). Insolvency and the Eurobond market. *Journal of International Banking and Financial Law, 2*, 51.

Iwahara, S. (2003). *Electronic payment and law.* Tokyo: Yuhikaku.

Kiuchi, Y. (1989). *Financial law.* Tokyo: Seirin Shoin.

Koyama, Y. (2004). *Banking law.* Tokyo: Kinzai.

Kubota, T. (2003). *Legal issues of Japanese funds payment systems.* Tokyo: Kokusai Syoin.

Mentha, J. (2000). Legal risks associated with acting as a global custodian—Mitigating the risks. *Journal of International Banking and Financial Law, 2000*(4), 122.

UK Law Commission Report. (1995). *Fiduciary duties and regulatory rules.* (Report No 236.). London: HMSO.

Morishita, T. (2000). Legal issues in respect of international securities settlements (1). *Jyochi Hougaku Ronsyu, 44*(1), 1.

Morishita, T. (2001). Legal issues in respect of international securities settlements (2). *Jyochi Hougaku Ronsyu, 44*(3), 35.

Morishita, T. (2002). Legal issues in respect of international securities settlements (3). *Jyochi Hougaku Ronsyu, 45*(3), 149.

Pullen, K. (1999). Fungible securities and insolvency. *Journal of International Banking and Financial Law, 1999*(7), 286.

Rogers, J. (1996). Policy perspective on revised U.C.C. Article 8. *UCLA Law Review, 43*, 1431.

Sealy, L. S., Hooley, R. J. A. (2003). *Commercial Law Text, Cases and Materials* (3rd ed.). London: LexisNexis UK.

Shinomiya, K. (1989). *Trusts law new ed.* Tokyo: Yuhikaku.

Sommer, J. (1998). A law of financial accounts: modern payment and securities transfer law. *Business Lawyer, 53*, 1181.

Takahashi, Y. (Ed.). (2003). *Article by article commentary of the book-entry transfer of corporate bonds act.* Tokyo: Kinzai Institute for Financial Affairs.

Takahashi, Y. (Ed.). (2004). *Article by article commentary of the book-entry transfer of corporate bonds and shares act*. Tokyo: Kinzai Institute for Financial Affairs.

Yamada, R. (2003). *Private international law* (2nd ed.). Tokyo: Yuhikaku.

ADDITIONAL READING

The American Law Institute, National Conference of Commissioners on Uniform State Laws, *Uniform Commercial Code, Official Text—2000, revised art 8 (1994 revision)*.

Bank of Japan. (2003). *Response to the disclosure rramework for securities settlement systems*. Retrieved March 22, 2007, from http://www.boj.or.jp

Benjamin, J., et al. (2002). *The law of global custody* (2nd ed.). London: Butterworths.

BIS. (1993). *Central bank payment and settlement services with respect to cross-border and multi-currency transactions* (Noël Report). Retrieved March 22, 2007, from http://www.bis.org

BIS. (1995). *Cross-border securities settlements, by committee on payment and settlement systems*. Retrieved March 22, 2007, from http://www.bis.org

BIS. (1996). *Settlement risk in foreign exchange transactions*. Retrieved March 22, 2007, from http://www.bis.org

BIS. (1998). *Reducing foreign exchange settlement risk: a progress report*. Retrieved March 22, 2007, from http://www.bis.org

BIS. (1999). *Securities lending transactions: market development and implications*. Retrieved March 22, 2007, from http://www.bis.org

BIS. (2000). *Clearing and settlement arrangements for retail payments in selected countries*. Retrieved March 22, 2007, from http://www.bis.org

BIS. (2001a). *Core principles for systemically important payment systems*. Retrieved March 22, 2007, from http://www.bis.org

BIS. (2001b). *Recommendations for securities settlement systems*. Retrieved March 22, 2007, from http://www.bis.org

BIS. (2003). *A glossary of terms used in payments and settlement systems*. Retrieved March 22, 2007, from http://www.bis.org

BIS. (2004). *Recommendations for central counterparties*. Retrieved March 22, 2007, from http://www.bis.org

Financial Law Board. (2000). *Interim note on legal rules relating to book-entry securities settlements*. Retrieved March 22, 2007, from http://www.flb.gr.jp

Geva, B. (looseleaf). *The law of electronic funds transfer*. New York: Matthew Bender.

Goode, R. (1996). The nature and transfer of rights in dematerialised and immobilised securities. *Journal of International Banking and Financial Law, 1996*(4), 167.

Goode, R. (1998). Proprietary right in commercial assets: Rethinking concepts and politics. In R. Goode (Ed), *Commercial law in the next millennium*. London: Sweet & Maxwell.

Goode, R. (2004). *Commercial law* (3rd ed.). London: LexisNexis UK,.

Hayton, D., Pigott, H., & Benjamin, J. (2002). The use of trusts in international financial transactions. *Journal of International Banking and Financial Law, 2002*(1), 23.

Honda, M. (2001). Legislation in respect of the Transfer of Financial Assets. *Minshoho Zashi 123*(6), 1.

McIntyre, H. (2000). *How the U.S. securities industry works*. New York: The Summit Group Press.

Moshinsky, M. (1998). Securities held thorough a securities custodian—Conflict of laws issue. The Oxford Colloquium on Collateral and Conflict of Laws. *Journal of International Banking and Financial Law, 1998* (Special Supplement 7), 18.

Reed, C., Walden, I., & Edgar, L. (2000). *Cross-border electronic banking* (2nd ed.). London: LLP.

Rogers, J. (1998). Of normalcy and anomaly: Thoughts on choice of law for the indirect holding system. The Oxford Colloquium on Collateral and Conflict of Laws. *Journal of International Banking and Financial Law, 1998(Special Supplement 7),* 47.

Ryan, R. (1990). Taking securities over investment portfolio held in global custody. *Journal of International Banking Law, 10,* 404.

Schwarcz, S. L. (2001). Indirectly held securities and intermediary risk. *Uniform Law Review, 2001/2,* 283-299.

Scott, H. S. (2004). *International finance: Law and regulation.* London: Sweet & Maxwell.

The Society for the Study of Securities Exchange Law. (2004). *Theory and practice in respect of paperless securities.* Tokyo: Syojihomu.

Tennekoon, R. (1991). *The law and regulation of international finance.* London: Butterworths.

Tyson-Quah, K. (1996). Cross-border securities collateralisation made easy. *Journal of International Banking and Financial Law 1996*(4), 177.

UK Law Commission Report. (1995). *Fiduciary duties and regulatory rules* (Report No. 236). London: HMSO.

UNIDROIT. (2003). *The Position Paper of The UNIDROIT Study Group on Harmonised Substantive Rules Regarding Indirectly Held Securities.* Retrieved March 22, 2007, from http://www.unidroit.org

UNIDROIT. (2004). *Preliminary Draft Convention on Harmonised Substantive Rules regarding Securities Held with an Intermediary: Explanatory Notes.* Retrieved March 22, 2007, from http://www.unidroit.org

Vroegop, J. (1990), The role of correspondent banks in direct funds transfers. *Lloyd's Maritime and Commercial Law Quarterly.*

Wood, P. (1995). *Comparative law of security and guarantees.* London: Sweet & Maxwell.

ENDNOTES

[1] Bernasconi et al. (2002), pp. 7-13.
[2] Ellinger et al. (2006), pp. 124. Kiuchi (1989), p. 161.
[3] Bernasconi et al. (2002), p. 13.
[4] The universally recognized axiom of *nemo dat quod non habet* (one who has not cannot give) means that, as its corollary, there is a fundamental principle that a creditor qua creditor cannot validly claim more rights than its debtor has in property. Fletcher (1999) pp. 61-62.
[5] In *Re Wait* ([1927] 1 Ch 606 at 623), *Re London Wine Co (Shippers) Ltd* [1986] PCC 121 and *Re Gold Exchange Ltd (in receivership)* [1995] 1 AC74m. Pullen, 1999, p. 287.
[6] Goode (1987), p. 451ff. Horrocks (1991), p.52ff. Morishita (2001), p. 37ff.
[7] [2000] 1 BCLC 494.
[8] Hayton (1994), p. 355 ff.
[9] Financial Markets Law Committee (2004), p. 10ff. Benjamin (2000), p. 31ff, p. 321ff. Goode (1996), p. 171ff.
[10] Benjamin (2000), pp. 52-59.
[11] Heisei 13 Ho75.
[12] Takahashi, Ed. (2003), p. 21.
[13] UK Law Commission Report (1995).
[14] Dalhuisen (2004), p. 711. Roger (1996), p. 1511ff.

[15] In Japan, the Act provides that book-entry transfer institutions shall settle a trust for investors with the funds contributed by account management institutions as a safety net (Articles 51 to 65). The cap of compensation is 10 million yen, equivalent to that in deposit insurance (Article 60 of the Act, Article 6 of the Enforcement Regulations of the Act).

[16] Of course, one cannot deny some economic linkage because a bank could receive some economic impact by its correspondent bank's default which might cause the chain-reaction bankruptcy of the bank.

[17] For example, Clearstream and Euroclear.

[18] Sommer (1998), p. 1203.

[19] Sommer (1998), p. 1203.

[20] Dalhuisen (2004), p. 711, p. 719.

[21] Sommer (1998), p. 1204.

[22] *Royal Product v Midland Bank Ltd* [1981] 2 Lloyd's Rep. 194, Queen's Bench Division.

[23] *Royal Product v Midland Bank Ltd* (supra footnote 22).

[24] Sealy, Hooley (2003), p. 706.

[25] Sch 2, para 1(b). Cresswell et al. (looseleaf), D1, para 853.

[26] [1997] OJL43/25

[27] Goode (1996), p. 174.

[28] Benjamin (2000), p. 231. Goode (1996), p. 174. Mentha (2000), p. 123 states, in order to be commercially competitive, it is most likely that the custodian accepts liability for the default of the sub-custodian. However he does not deny the legal validity of the exemption clauses.

[29] The consumers and small business may not be as well protected in securities systems as in funds systems. However, as mentioned, the horizontal risk occurs only in the case of transfers of securities as collateral which are usually not executed by consumers and small business.

[30] Kiuchi (1989), p. 319ff. Koyama (2004), p. 161.

[31] The judgment of the Tokyo High Court on 28 October 1987 (Hanji No1260,p. 15). Cf. Iwahara (2003), p.407ff. Geva (2001), p. 256ff.

[32] Although the model agreement does not have any legal effect, most banks follow it.

[33] Takahashi, Ed., (2003), p. 26, p.88.

[34] Takahashi, Ed., (2003), p. 27.

[35] Rogers (1996), pp. 1461-1462.

[36] *Westdeutsche Landesbank Girozentrale v Islington London Borough Council* [1996] AC 669 at 683, per Lord Goff.

[37] [1991] 2 AC 548.

[38] Tracing is neither a claim nor a remedy but a process for identifying the path of value from the claimant to the defendant (*Boscawen v Bajwa* [1995] 4 All ER 769 at 776, per Millett LJ).

[39] *Tayler v Plumer* (1815) 3 M&S 562; *Re Diplock* [1948] Ch 465.

[40] *Agip (Africa) Ltd v Jackson* [1991] Ch 547.

[41] Brindle, et al, Eds. (2004), paras 3-115, 3-116.

[42] *Agip (Africa) Ltd v Jackson* [1991] Ch 547.

[43] Sealy, Hooley (2003), p. 563.

[44] Sealy, Hooley (2003), p. 655ff.

[45] *Pilcher v Rawlins* (1872) 7 Ch App 259.

[46] Sealy, Hooley (2003), p. 565.

[47] *Cave v Cave* (1880) 15 Ch D 639. Hayton, 2003, p. 984ff.

[48] Benjamin (2000), pp. 46-47.

[49] Financial Market Law Committee (2004), p. 13. Benjamin (2000), p. 49.

[50] The judgment of the Supreme Court on April 24, 1996 (Minsyu 50-5, p. 1267). The judgment of the Tokyo High Court on November 28, 2004 (Kinpo 1667, p. 94).

[51] The judgment of the Tokyo District Court on March 5, 1993 (Hanji 1508, p. 132)

[52] The judgment of the Supreme Court on September 26, 1970 (Minshu 24-7, p. 909).

[53] BIS (1990), section 1 of the Lamfalussy Report.

[54] *British Eagle International Airlines Ltd v Compagnie National Air France* [1975] 1 WLR 758, HL.
[55] [1998] OJL166, p. 45.
[56] SI1999/2979.
[57] Kubota (2003), p. 167ff.
[58] Kubota (2003), p. 169ff.
[59] *Libyan Arab Foreign Bank v Manufactures Hanover Trust Co* [1988] 2 Lloyd's Rep 608.
[60] *Sierra Leone Telecommunications Co Ltd v Barclays Bank plc* [1998] 2 All ER 821, at 827, per Cresswell J.
[61] *Cammell v Sewell* (1858) 3 H&N 617.
[62] *Re Maudslay* [1900] 1 Ch 602. *Jabbour v The Custodian* [1954] 1 All ER 145.
[63] [1996] 1 WLR 387.
[64] Benjamin (2000), p. 162.
[65] Collins, Ed. (2000). Rule 112(1) provides that 'Choses in action generally are situate in the country where they are properly recoverable or can be enforced.'
[66] Benjamin (2000), p.160. Collins, Ed. (2000), para. 24-064.
[67] Directive 98/26/EC of the European Parliament of the Council of 19 May 1998 on Settlement Finality in Payment and Securities Settlement systems.
[68] SI 1999/2979.
[69] Heisei 18, Ho78.
[70] Yamada (2003), p. 336.
[71] Rogers (1996), p. 1511.
[72] Rogers (1996), pp. 1514-1519. Morishita (2000), p. 31ff.
[73] Rogers (1996), p. 1455. Benjamin (2000), p. 26ff.
[74] Sommer (1998), p. 1184.
[75] In Japan, with respect to securities in custody in foreign countries, it is considered that investor receive a depositary receipt instead of the foreign securities from Japanese broker. Such substitute securities could be interpreted to represent beneficial interests in trust where Japanese brokers having ownership of the securities were trustees (Shinomiya, 1989, p. 30). On this basis, it seems to me that interests in securities could also be construed as beneficial rights against the immediate intermediaries.
[76] Takahashi, Ed. (2003), p. 21.
[77] Registered securities including equities, gilts, corporate debts, and money market instruments can be settled through the procedures available at CREST Co (CREST), the operator of a settlement system in the UK. The securities settled in CREST are dematerialized on the ground of the *Uncertificated Securities Regulations 2001* (SI2001/3755). Under this system, with regard to UK securities, a member of CREST holds its securities rights directly against the issuer (Benjamin, 2000, p. 205.). In order to form a cross-border link, the sub-custodian CREST International Nominees Ltd. and the depositary CREST Depositary Ltd. were established. Whereas the former becomes a participant in foreign systems and holds the title to foreign securities on a bare trust for the latter, the latter issues a new form of security, a CREST Depositary Interest (CDI) for CREST members. Thus, CDIs represent beneficial interests in respect of the relevant foreign securities . CREST (2001), p. 3ff., Global Deed Poll in Appendix 2 of the document. T. Morishita (2002).
[78] Financial Market Law Committee (2004), p. 9ff acknowledges that the protection of the bona fide purchaser is not very clear.
[79] Rogers (1996), p. 1469ff.
[80] Takahashi, Ed. (2003).
[81] Kubota (2003), p. 167ff.
[82] UCC §8-110(e).
[83] See Article 4 of the Convention.
[84] Sommer (1998), pp. 1184-1185.
[85] Goode (1998), p. 27.

Section II
E–Payment

Chapter VI
Global Trends of Payment Systems and the Next-Generation RTGS Project in Japan

Masaaki Nakajima
Reitaku University, Japan

ABSTRACT

This chapter investigates the evolutionary process of the payment system against the background of structural changes. At the early stage, most payment systems were Designated-Time Net Settlement (DTNS) systems. Then, Real-Time Gross Settlement (RTGS) systems were introduced, which had the merit of reducing settlement risks. This first trend was followed by the deployment of Hybrid systems and Integrated systems. The Bank of Japan (BOJ) is proceeding with the Next-Generation RTGS (RTGS-XG) project. This project is regarded as a typical enhancement of payment systems following the global trend. The features and benefits of the RTGS-XG are closely analyzed.

INTRODUCTION

When the author worked for the Bank for International Settlements (BIS) several years ago, he got to know a senior official of a central bank in Europe, who was the head of the payment systems division. One day, he said to him, "Payment systems are not the most fascinating topic in the world." The author was very surprised to hear that. But the senior official continued, "However, the least fascinating topics are by no means the least important." The author fully agreed with his opinion then, and still believes his remarks are absolutely true. Payment systems are the indispensable infrastructures for financial markets and business activities.

BACKGROUND

A payment system is a mechanism that facilitates smooth transfer of funds among financial institutions. Generally, it consists of a set of instruments, procedures, rules, and technical bases like computers and networks. It is sometimes referred to as an interbank funds transfer system.

Payment systems[1] are the important social infrastructures that support the whole national economic activities. Every commercial trade and financial transaction is finalized only when the final settlement is made through payment systems. If malfunctions ever happen in a payment system, which prevent the smooth transfer of funds, the national economy and financial markets would be thrown into extreme confusion and seriously damaged. Therefore, safe and efficient payment systems are critical to the effective functioning of national economies and financial systems.

This chapter is structured as follows. The first section explains the structural changes in the payment system field. The second section describes the global trends of payment systems. The third section focuses on the Next-Generation RTGS Project in Japan. The fourth section analyzes the features and benefits of the Next-Generation RTGS system.

STRUCTURAL CHANGES IN PAYMENT SYSTEM FIELDS

In recent years, some significant structural changes have occurred in the payment system fields (Nakajima, Masashi, and Junichi Shukuwa, 2005; Nakajima, Masashi, 2003).

Rapid Growth of Settlement Values and Accompanying Settlement Risks

First of all, settlement values of payment systems in industrialized countries have increased in a very rapid pace which is faster than that of economic growth. The progress in globalization and labialization of financial trade had a direct impact on the rapid growth of settlement amount. The settlement values of payment systems in an industrialized country are as much as 50 to 80 times as the nominal GDP of each country. This fact means that the settlement value of a payment

Table 1. Settlement values of payment systems as a percentage of GDP (as of 2004)(in %)

Country	Payment System	Settlement values relative to Nominal GDP
France	TBF	65.8
	PNS	10.6
Germany	RTGSplus	57.0
Japan	BOJ-NET	41.2
	FXYCS	8.7
United Kingdom	CHAPS Euro	19.1
	CHAPS Sterling	44.9
United States	Fedwire	40.0
	CHIPS	29.5

Source: Statistics on payment and settlement systems in selected countries, Bank for International Settlements, March 2006

system in only a week is larger than the nominal GDP of the nation for a whole year. It is worth mentioning that larger settlement values would be accompanied with larger settlement risks (Bank of Japan, 2006b).

Activities of the BIS for Settlement Risk Awareness

Secondly, the BIS published several important reports for the reduction of payment system risks. A range of risks could arise in payment systems, which include credit risk, liquidity risk, legal risk, operational risk, and systemic risk. These risks are collectively referred as "settlement risks." Important reports of the BIS for mitigating the settlement risks include Lamfalussy Report, DVP Report, Noël Report, Allsopp Report, RTGS Report, and Core Principles Report (Bank for International Settlements, 2001). These educational campaigns of the BIS increased the awareness for the settlement risks gradually across the globe. Then, the overseers and operators of the payment systems became to actively work for the reduction of settlement risks, which lead to the evolution of payment systems as well as the improvement of risk management.

Competition between Payment Systems

Thirdly, competitions between payment systems have been the driving forces for the innovation of payment systems. In some cases, the competition has taken place between the two payment systems in one country. The competition between the Fedwire and the CHIPS in the U.S. would be a good example. Major U.S. banks can use one of two payment systems, depending on the urgency of the payment and request of the customers.

In other case, cross-border competition has occurred among the several national payment systems. The typical cross-border competitions have been observed in EU, where the single currency Euro was introduced in 1999 and legacy currencies, like Deutsche Mark and French Franc, were abolished. As a result of introduction of single currency, more than 20 payment systems were converted from the payment systems of legacy currencies to the Euro payment systems. Then, they had to compete with each other in the same currency zone, namely the Euro zone.

These competitions have been conducive to the improvement and radical changes of payment systems. In order to survive in the competition,

Table 2. List of the BIS reports for reducing the settlement risks

Date of publication	The name of the report
November 1990	Report of the Committee on Interbank Netting Schemes of the Central Banks of the Group of Ten Countries (Lamfalussy Report)
September 1992	Delivery versus Payment in Securities Settlement Systems (DVP Report)
September 1993	Central Bank Payment and Settlement Services with respect to Cross-border and Multicurrency Transaction (Noël Report)
March 1996	Settlement Risk in Foreign Exchange Transactions (Allsopp Report)
March 1997	Real-time Gross Settlement Systems (RTGS Report)
January 2001	Core Principles for Systemically Important Payment Systems (Core Principles Report)

some payment systems introduced very innovative and enhanced payment mechanisms, which promoted the evolution of the payment systems.

Innovation of Information Technology

Fourthly, the progress of information technology (IT) also made significant contribution to the enhancement of payment systems (Bech, Morten, L., & Hobijn, Bart, 2006). Advanced processing capability of computers enabled the settlement in very sophisticated ways, such as the continuous netting and queue management with complex algorithms. In addition, enhanced communication networks enabled real-time exchanges of messages as well as real-time monitoring of liquidity and interactive management of the queue.

GLOBAL TRENDS OF PAYMENT SYSTEMS

During the past 15 years, payment systems have evolved in the environmental changes mentioned. Three movements could be pointed out as the global trends of payment systems.

Introduction of RTGS systems

RTGS System and DTNS System

The first trend was the introduction of the Real-Time Gross Settlement (RTGS) systems. There are two features of the RTGS system. The first feature is that the settlement of funds occurs on a gross basis, which means payment instructions are processed one-by-one basis without netting. The second feature is final settlement is made on a real-time basis during the day.

Before the changeover to the RTGS systems, many countries adopted the Designated-Time Net Settlement (DTNS) systems. The DTNS system is a net settlement system, thus the settlement of funds occurs on a net basis. In concrete terms, a net position of each participating bank is calculated, which is defined as an amount of difference between the sum of the outgoing payments and the sum of the incoming payments. If the amount of out going payments is larger than the amount of incoming payments, the participant has a net debit position and has to pay the net amount before the settlement time. The DTNS system is a designated-time settlement system, in which the final settlement takes place at a designated-time, usually at the end of the day. In short, in the DTNS system, the final settlement of net positions occurs at the end of the day.

Merits of the RTGS System

The RTGS system has two merits in reducing settlement risks. Firstly, unsettled payment instructions accumulate until the end of the day in the DTNS system. Therefore, until the final settlement is completed at the end of the day, the settlement risks still exist. Compared with this, the RTGS system processes each payment instruction one-by-one and makes them final during the daytime. Thus, the RTGS system can effectively reduce the settlement risk.

Secondly, "systemic risk" is the key word. This is the risk that the failure of one participant to meet its required obligation will cause other participants to be unable to meet their obligations when due. Such a failure may cause widespread liquidity or credit risk problems and, as a result, might create total chaos in financial markets. As overseers of payment systems, central banks are particularly concerned with the systemic risk. The DTNS system has potentiality of systemic risk, because if one participant is unable to settle its net debit position at the end of the day, the payment system has to recalculate a new set of net positions for each of the remaining participants by deleting the payments involving default participant. This procedure is called "unwinding." The unwinding could lead to unexpected changes to the net positions of remaining participants, which could result in further knock-on effects or a cascade of settlement failures. On the contrary, there is no possibility of systemic risk in the RTGS system, because each transfer of funds becomes final instantly during the day and there is no need for unwinding.

Hence, the RTGS system is more robust to settlement risk than the DTNS system. However, the elimination of risk comes at the cost of an increased demand for intraday liquidity. In fact, there is a certain trade-off between the settlement risk and the cost of liquidity. Needs for much more liquidity is the only and non-negligible demerit of the RTGS system. Usually, central banks provide intraday credit to the participants in the RTGS system. Most commonly the intraday credit is provided with no fee, but the intraday liquidity is not cost-free because collaterals are required for the intraday credit.

Adoption of the RTGS System

In the 1980s, only a few countries adopted the RTGS systems, namely the Fedwire in the U.S., the SIC in Switzerland, and the EIL-ZV in Germany. In the 1990s, a number of countries introduced the RTGS systems. This trend was apparent especially for the payment systems which central banks operated, because huge amount of funds were settled through central bank operating payment systems and it was the urgent task for the central banks to reduce the settlement risks.

Additionally, the central banks of the European Union (EU) were obliged to introduce the RTGS system as a precondition to link to the TARGET[2] system and reconstructed their payment systems as the RTGS systems in 1996-1997, one after another. Influenced by these movements, some Asian countries also introduced the RTGS systems in the late 1990s. The use of the RTGS also grew outside industrialized countries. Some

Table 3. Timing of the introduction of RTGS system in selected countries

Country	Payment System[1]	Timing of the introduction of RTGS system
United States	Fedwire	1982
Switzerland	SIC	1987
Germany	EIL-ZV	1988
United Kingdom	CHAPS	1996
Belgium	ELLIPS	1996
France	TBF	1997
Italy	BI-REL	1997
Netherlands	TOP	1997
Korea	BOK-Wire	1994
Hong Kong	CHATS	1996
Singapore	MEPS	1998
Australia	RITS	1998
Japan	BOJ-NET	2001

[1] *The name of payment system at the time of introduction of RTGS system.*

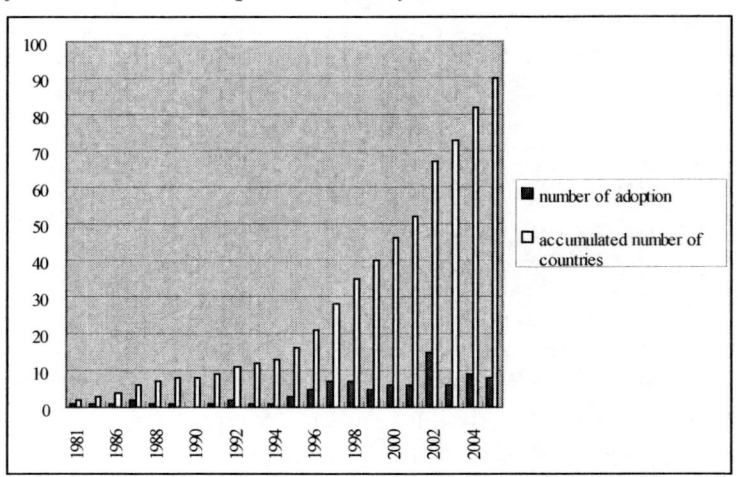

Figure 1. Number of countries that adopt the RTGS system

countries in Eastern Europe, CIS countries, and Latin America were similarly reported to have the RTGS systems. These countries were characterized to construct the electronic payment systems from scratch as RTGS systems. According to the survey of Federal Reserve Bank of New York, 90 out of the 174 countries in the world adopted a RTGS system at the end of 2005. By this means, the adoption of the RTGS system became the global trend of payment systems.

In Japan, the Bank of Japan (BOJ) reconstructed the BOJ-NET as a RTGS system in January 2001. The case of the BOJ-NET was rather special, because the BOJ-NET already had two functions of the DTNS mode and the RTGS mode. But, the RTGS mode was seldom used by participants due to the higher liquidity cost. For this reason, the characteristics of the old BOJ-NET was basically regarded as the DTNS system. The BOJ changed the BOJ-NET into the RTGS system by abolishing the DTNS mode.

HYBRID SYSTEM

Feature of the Hybrid System

The second evolution of the payment system was the emergence of the Hybrid System. The Hybrid System means the combination of the best features of the DTNS system and the RTGS system.

The Hybrid System derived from the DTNS system, in which final settlement takes place only once at the end of the day. In the Hybrid System, net settlements are made at frequent intervals or continuously and transfer of funds become final at the time of frequent net settlements. The DTNS system has a disadvantage that transfer of funds become final only at the end of the day, even though it has an advantage that settlement can be made with small liquidity only for the net position. With the frequent net settlements, the Hybrid System keeps the merit of the DTNS system, that is, the settlement capability with small liquidity, and additionally realizes the merit of the RTGS system, that is early finality. That is the reason why this kind of system is called Hybrid[3] system. This system is sometimes referred as the Continuous Net Settlement (CNS) system, compared to the DTNS system.

Examples of the Hybrid System

The first Hybrid System in the world was the EAF2 in Germany. It became the Hybrid system from the DTNS system in March 1996. In EAF2, bilateral netting settlements were made

Table 4. Introduction of hybrid system

Country	Payment System	Timing of the introduction of Hybrid System
Germany	EAF2	March 1996
Canada	LVTS	February 1999
France	PNS	April 1999
United States	CHIPS	February 2001

every 20 minutes for the whole morning and two multilateral netting settlements were made in the afternoon. The settlements became final at each netting settlement.

Following the EAF2, the LVTS in Canada, the PNS in France, and the CHIPS in U.S. became Hybrid Systems during 1999-2001. In this way, the introduction of the Hybrid system for net settlement systems became the trend in industrialized countries.

The CHIPS is the latest and the most advanced Hybrid System, in which the system judges the capability of net settlement for each payment instruction and net settlement is made continuously, if possible. The system, which is called "balanced release engine," selects the processing mode from the three types: the individual release, the bilateral release, and the multilateral release, according to the available balances of payer and payee and incoming and outgoing payment situation. The individual release is a simple processing of a payment instruction without netting. The bilateral release is just like bilateral netting between two participants. The multilateral release is a kind of multilateral netting among three or more participants.

Situation in Japan

In Japan, the FXYCS (Foreign Exchange Yen Clearing System) is still operated as a simple DTNS system. We find ourselves with no choice but to feel uneasy to look at the out-of-date net settlement system. To our relief, however, the project is going on to enhance the FXYCS and reduce the settlement risk. This project will be described.

INTEGRATED SYSTEM

Feature of the Integrated System

The next evolution of the payment system was the transition to the Integrated System. The Integrated System is defined as the payment system which has both the RTGS mode and the Hybrid mode. Participants of the Integrated System can use both modes as the situation demands. For example, participants can use the RTGS mode for the urgent payment and time-critical payment, while they can use the Hybrid mode for non-urgent payment. The Hybrid mode executes continuous or frequent settlement as mentioned. The Hybrid mode in the Integrated System is often referred as "liquidity saving mode," because participants can make their payment with smaller amount of liquidity by using frequent netting.

Integrated System and Hybrid System are sometimes collectively referred as "Advanced System," since both systems implement advanced technologies and complex handling method of payment instructions.

The LVTS in Canada

The pioneer of the Integrated System was the Large Value Transfer System (LVTS) in Canada. The LVTS started its operation in February 1999. The LVTS has two functions of payment. One is called Tranche 1, which is the RTGS mode. The other is called Tranche 2, which is the liquidity saving mode. Participants can select either Tranche 1 or Tranche 2 and send their payment instructions to the appropriate Tranche.

The PIS in France

The second Integrated System was the Paris Integrated System (PIS) in France. France has two large-value payment systems of Euro. One is the Paris Net Settlement (PNS) operated by CRI,[4] which became the Hybrid System from the DTNS system in April 1999. Another is the Transferts the Banque de France (TBF), which is the RTGS system operated by Banque de France. In April 1999, CRI developed "liquidity bridge" between the TBF and the PNS. Liquidity bridge is the scheme that participants can transfer liquidity between the two payment systems at any time of the day. In this way, the PNS and the TBF became closely linked. So even though these are two separate payment systems, they appear as one combined payment system to the participants. Therefore, these two systems are called the PIS (Paris Integrated System) as a whole and regarded as a kind of Integrated System.

The RTGS^{plus} in Germany

The RTGS^{plus} in Germany was the third Integrated System, which started operation in November 2001. RTGS^{plus} has two modes; the EX payment mode and the Limit payment mode. The EX payment mode is the RTGS settlement for high priority payment. And the Limit payment mode is liquidity saving element with continuous offsetting settlement. When a payment instruction is sent to the system, a special algorithm searches the central queue to see if some set of payment instructions might offset each other. Once such a set of payment instructions is found, these instructions are settled in the form of offsetting.

"Offsetting[5]" means the simultaneous booking of outgoing payment and incoming payment, and the effect of the offsetting is quite similar to the netting. In the Limit payment mode, participants can set sender limit bilaterally or multilaterally to control their own liquidity. Participants can manage their liquidity in a single liquidity pool and can use two modes according to the priority of the payment.

Other Examples

Bank of Italy added the same kind of liquidity saving mode to their RTGS system BI-REL, and made it into the Integrated System in April 2004, which was called "new BI-REL."

Integrated system came into use in Asia. Monetary Authority of Singapore (MAS) has been operating the RTGS system since 1998, which is called MEPS (MAS Electronic Payment System). They have developed liquidity saving mode in MEPS and make it into the Integrated System. This new system is called "MEPS+." MEPS+ is the first Integrated System in Asia and started the operation in December 2006.

Table 5. Introduction of integrated system

Country	Payment System	Timing of the introduction of Integrated System
Canada	LVTS	February 1999
France	PIS: PNS and TBF	April 1999
Germany	RTGS^{plus}	November 2001
Italy	new BI-REL	April 2004
Singapore	MEPS+	December 2006

NEXT-GENERATION RTGS PROJECT IN JAPAN

Following the evolutionary movements, the Bank of Japan (BOJ) plans to enhance its RTGS system to a sophisticated system. This project is called the Next-Generation RTGS (RTGS-XG) Project of the BOJ-NET.

Background of the RTGS-XG Project

In Japan, there are three payment systems: the Bank of Japan Financial Network System (BOJ-NET[6]), the Foreign Exchange Yen Clearing System (FXYCS), and the Zengin Data Telecommunication System (Zengin System). The BOJ-NET is operated by the BOJ, and two private-sector payment systems, the FXYCS and the Zengin System, are operated by Tokyo Bankers Association (TBA).

The BOJ-NET

The BOJ-NET is a RTGS system and used mainly for the funds transfers for money market transactions and government bond transactions, settlement of net positions of private-sector netting systems, and funds transfers arising from BOJ's open market operations. Payment instructions processed in the BOJ-NET are mainly inter-bank transactions and are very high value payments. As mentioned earlier, the BOJ-NET became the RTGS system from the DTNS system in January 2001.

The FXYCS

The FXYCS is basically a DTNS system that handles yen payments to settle foreign exchange transactions. Most of the transactions that are processed by this system are yen leg settlements of foreign exchange transactions and international treasury settlements. The FXYCS has the RTGS mode as well as the DTNS mode, although the use of the RTGS mode, which includes the payment for CLS bank, is quite limited.

The Zengin System

The Zengin System is a nationwide electronic fund transfer network. Almost all financial institutions in Japan, more than 2,000 financial institutions, participate in the Zengin System and use this system mainly for customer payments. As many of the payments made through this system are consumer and commercial payments, the transaction volume are extremely large, but the amount of each payment is rather small. In addition to single payments, the system also supports batch payments file containing a number of payments, such as payroll and pension payments. The Zengin System is a DTNS system, whose final settlement of net positions takes place at the end of the day at the current account of the BOJ.

Sharing of Roles Among Three Systems

The BOJ-NET and the FXYCS are mainly for the inter-bank payments and characterized as large-value payment systems. On the other hand, the Zengin System is mainly for the customer payments and regarded as a retail payment system. But, we have to pay some attention that some large-value payments are also processed in the Zengin System. That is because of a historical reason; international related payments are assigned to the FXYCS by the law of foreign exchange control, and domestic payments are handled by the Zengin System.

Proposal of the RTGS-XG Project

Proposal of Japanese Bankers Association

In March 2004, Japanese Bankers Association[7] (JBA) published a report, "Proposal for Reorganizing Fund Transfer Systems in Japan—Introducing a Large Value Settlement System" (Japanese Bankers Association, 2004). This report proposed the introduction of a "Large Value Settlement System." The aims of the proposal were to reduce the settlement risk, to comply with the international standards, and to improve the efficiency of fund settlement.

The proposal envisages the integration of large-value fund settlements in Japan. If this proposal was realized, fund transfer systems in Japan, which consists of the BOJ-NET, the FXYCS, and the Zengin System would be reorganized into a Large Value Settlement System and the Zengin System would be specialized in small value payments.

The JBA submitted the report to the BOJ for further consideration, because the restructuring of the BOJ-NET was the key factor for realizing the proposal. Therefore, one can argue that the RTGS-XG project took root in private sector initiative.

BOJ's Proposal

In response to the proposal of JBA, after deliberate consideration (Imakubo, Kei, & McAndrews, J. J., 2005), the BOJ announced its proposal for the Next-Generation RTGS (RTGS-XG) in November 2005 (Bank of Japan, 2005). Following the public consultation process, the BOJ decided to implement the project and started the system development phase in February 2006 (Bank of Japan, 2006a). The purpose of this project was to further enhance the safety and efficiency of large-value payment systems in Japan,

Outline of the RTGS-XG Project

The RTGS-XG project consists of two sub-projects. The first sub-project is to add liquidity-saving features (LSF) to the pure RTGS mode of the BOJ-NET. The second sub-project is to incorporate large-value payments currently handled by two private-sector DTNS systems, the FXYCS, and the Zengin System, into the new BOJ-NET with the LSF.

Sub-Project A

The sub-project A is to add the LSF into the BOJ-NET. The LSF consists of Centralized Queuing Function and Offsetting Function.

Centralized Queuing Function

As the current BOJ-NET doesn't have a centralized queue, if a bank does not have enough liquidity at the current account at the BOJ, the payment instruction is rejected by the system and sent back to the sending bank. Once the centralized queue is constructed in the BOJ-NET, the payment order that is not covered by adequate liquidity would be suspended in the queue. Each participant can actively control the payment instructions in the queue for the efficient settlement, which includes monitoring, setting the priority, reordering, and cancellation of the payment instructions.

Offsetting Function

Offsetting means the simultaneous processing of outgoing and incoming payment orders. The offsetting algorithm searches for the participants who have submitted payment orders for each other and calculates the net amount of inflow and outflow. If the net outflow is sufficiently covered, which means the credit balance of the debited participant is larger than the net outflow, the system process the incoming and outgoing payment order simultaneously. The outcome of the offsetting is exactly the same as the netting of the two payment orders. The only difference is whether two payment orders are processed individually in a gross basis or the net amount is simply processed.

In the RTGS-XG project, two kinds of offsetting are planned to be introduced. One is "bilateral offsetting," in which payment orders are processed between the two participants. Bilateral offsetting is regarded as the main function for settlement, and the algorithm will run when certain movements take place in the system, including submission of a new payment instruction, increase in credit balance, and settlement, reordering or cancellation of a top-queued payment.

The other is "multilateral offsetting," in which payment orders are processed among three or more participants. Multilateral offsetting is regarded as the complementary function to the bilateral offsetting, and the algorithm will run at designated times of the day. The execution times of multilateral offsetting will be set when there are fewer events initiating bilateral offsetting, since while the multilateral algorithm runs, the receipt of the new payment orders will be suspended. With these two offsetting functions, real-time gross settlement will be possible in a faster pace with lower amount of liquidity.

LSF Account

Participants who use the LSF should open the special account, the LSF account, in the RTGS-XG.. The LSF account is independent from the current account of the BOJ-NET, thus each participant should manage the respective liquidities of two accounts[8].

Participants can transfer the liquidity at anytime during the daytime between the current account and the LSF account. Although the overdraft is not admitted at the LSF account, participants can obtain liquidity from the BOJ through the overdraft facility at the current account. While the operating hours of the current account is from 9:00 to 17:00[9], participants can use the LSF account from 9:00 to 16:30. At 16:30, all the balances at the LSF accounts will be automatically transferred back to the current accounts, which mean the balance of the LSF will be zero at the end of the day. If there are some remaining payment orders in the queue, these orders will be cancelled automatically.

The incoming and outgoing payment to/from a LSF account should be processed only against the LSF account of other participants and can not be processed against the current accounts of other participants.

Most transactions between participants can be processed through the LSF account. Although some transactions should be executed at the current account, which includes 1) the transactions involving the BOJ and the government, 2) the net settlements of clearing systems (the Bill and Check Clearance and the Zengin System), and 3) the Delivery versus Payment (DVP) settlements of Japanese Government Bonds (JGB) and corporate bonds.

Sub-Project B

Current Situation of Large-Value Payment in Japan

Currently, the large-value payments in Japan are divided into three payment systems. First of all, the BOJ-NET is the main settlement channel of large-value payments and settled 88.3 trillion yen on a daily average basis in 2005. The second one is the FXYCS, which handles mainly foreign exchange related payments. The FXYCS settled 16.4 trillion yen per day in 2005. The last one is the Zengin System, which is usually regarded as a retail payment system. However, a part of payments in the Zengin System, 0.2% of total volume, are large-value payments that are 100 million yen and up. These 0.2% large-value payments accounted for 65% of total value, which is equivalent to 6.2 trillion yen per day in 2005.

These divided large-value payments lead to some issues. Among them, there is a duplication situation. The Zengin System and the FXYCS are both the same kind of payment system, that is, the DTNS at the end of the day. It used to be the request of the law[10] to divide foreign exchange related payments from domestic payments, but the law was radically revised in 1996 and there is no need for the distinction any more. This environmental change created the duplication as a result, more specifically, to operate and maintain the two same kind of end of day net settlement systems.

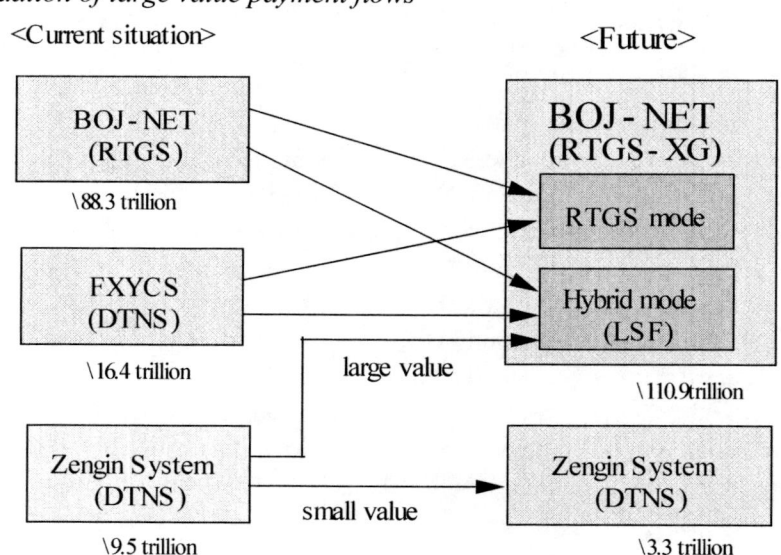

Consolidation of Large-Value Payment Flows

The sub-project B of the RTGS-XG project is to incorporate large-value payments on the FXYCS and the Zengin System into the new BOJ-NET. The two benefits are pointed out for incorporating the payments in the private-sector DTNS systems into the BOJ-NET. Firstly, participants can obtain intraday finality with the continuously settlement of the LSF. It is a significant risk mitigation compared to the current scheme of end of day finality in the private-sector systems. Secondly, the RTGS-XG achieves greater efficiency in liquidity usage. The LSF can save the liquidity by offsetting the outgoing payment and incoming payment compared to the pure RTGS system, in which all the settlement is made on gross basis.

Under the RTGS-XG, the FXYCS payment will be forwarded to the BOJ-NET via the FYXCS. And the main function of the FXYCS, the DTNS mode, will be abolished. As for the Zengin System, a newly developed interface will pick up the large-value payments and send them to the BOJ-NET, while the remaining small-value payments are processed in the Zengin System as before, in the DTNS method. When the interface sends large-value payments to the BOJ-NET, only interbank payment information will be sent, while customer information will be kept in the Zengin System.

Implementation Timetable

Phased implementation is planned for the RTGS-XG project. As for the phase 1, the development of the LSF and the modification of the FXYCS will be finished and the new system is planned to be launched in fiscal year[11] 2008.

With regard to phase 2, the modification for large-value Zengin payments, including the development of interface to the BOJ-NET, will

Figure 2. Consolidation of large value payment flows

Note: Settlement values are daily averages in 2005

be completed in 2011, when the next upgrading of the Zengin System is planned.

THE RTGS-XG PROJECT AND THE GLOBAL TREND

Feature Analysis of the RTGS-XG

As features of the RTGS-XG, three characteristics could be identified, which include Integrated system, two-account system, and offsetting system.

Integrated System

The RTGS-XG of BOJ-NET will have two modes for settlement. At the current account, participants will be able to make a simple RTGS, just as the same as the current BOJ-NET. This mode can be called the "pure RTGS mode." On the other hand, at the LSF account, continuous settlement with liquidity saving feature will be possible. The latter mode, the "liquidity saving mode," is a Hybrid mode, where offsetting is executed on a continuous basis.

Having both the RTGS mode and the Hybrid mode, the RTGS-XG will be defined as an Integrated System. Participants will be able to select the mode of settlement according to the character of the payment. It is expected that most of the payment will be made in liquidity saving mode, because participants can make settlement with fewer amount of liquidity, which means the cost-saving for the participant. As for the urgent payment or time-critical payment, it is expected to be processed in the pure RTGS mode. Also some transactions, including BOJ and government related transaction and DVP settlement of JGB, are assigned to the pure RTGS mode.

In the evolutionary process of payment systems, the RTGS-XG will be one of the cutting edges of the world payment systems, along with RTGS^{plus} in Germany, PIS in France, new BI-REL in Italy, and LVTS in Canada.

Two-Account System

The RTGS-XG will have two separate accounts in one system: the current account and the LSF account. Participants will have to monitor and manage the two liquidities in each account during the day. In some Integrated Systems, like RTGS^{plus} in Germany, single liquidity pool is adopted, and participants can control the liquidity in the single account. The single liquidity pool would be more user-friendly than two-account system. But, the RTGS-XG will allow participants to transfer the liquidity flexibly between the two accounts during the day (all day liquidity bridge). Thus, it is presumed that management burden of two liquidities would not be significant. It is apparent when compared to the case of the EAF2 in Germany, which allowed transferring the liquidity only once every hour.

In terms of two accounts, the RTGS-XG has similar structure to the PIS in France, where liquidity bridge combines the PNS account and the TBF account.

In the case of the RTGS-XG, consideration for the system development was the major factor to choose the separate LSF account. The BOJ-NET provides not only fund transfer service but also government bond settlement service. Therefore, the current account already has a very sophisticated link with the JGB account in the BOJ-NET through DVP mechanism and self-collateral scheme. It seemed concerned that to add the LSF to the current account might make the account structure too complicated.

Offsetting System

The RTGS-XG adopts the offsetting scheme. As mentioned earlier, there is not much difference between netting scheme and offsetting scheme, with regard to the outcome of the processing. In both cases, the difference of outgoing payment and incoming payment would be added or debited from the participants' account.

The concept of offsetting was introduced to the RTGS^{plus} in 2001 for the first time in the world. It was because the RTGS^{plus} would be a part of the TARGET, and only RTGS systems were allowed to link to the TARGET. So to avoid becoming a netting system that could not be liked the TARGET, Deutsche Bundesbank invented the concept of offsetting, which means the simultaneous booking of offsetting payment flows.

In the case of the BOJ-NET, there is no such a constraint. But only a situation was BOJ abolished, the netting mode in 2001 when the BOJ-NET became a pure RTGS system. So it would presumably be rather difficult for the BOJ to explain the LSF as adding a netting function again only several years after. It is just conceivable that this might be a sort of reason to adopt the offsetting concept instead of netting concept.

Benefits of the RTGS-XG Project

Upon the characteristics of the RTGS-XG mentioned, let us see the benefits this project would bring.

To Achieve Earlier Settlement and Reduce the Risk

The first benefit is to realize the earlier settlement and the finality in the daytime, which lead to the risk reduction. Large-value payments that are currently processed in the FXYCS and the Zengin system obtain the finality of payment only at the end of the day. After incorporating all large-value payments into the RTGS-XG, all the settlements will be made on a real-time basis and get the finality during the day. It is called "intra-day finality." It is a major benefit of the RTGS-XG to give every large-value payment intra-day finality and reduce the settlement risk.

To Reduce Liquidity Cost

The second benefit is the reduction of the liquidity cost for the participants. With the LSF, participants can make continuous gross settlement with small amount of liquidity by offsetting their outgoing payments with incoming payments from other participants. Although the BOJ provide the intra-day overdraft with no fee, participants have to pledge collaterals to get the overdraft. Thereafter, the RTGS-XG reduces the cost for participants by reducing the liquidity necessary for the settlement.

To Prevent Gridlock

The third benefit is to prevent gridlock in the payment system. In the pure RTGS system, participants tend to wait for the incoming payments before sending out their outgoing payments, or sometimes try to send the payment instructions as late as possible in order to save their liquidity. If many participants try to do the same thing, the circulation of liquidity in the system would be blocked and prevents a substantial number of instructions from being executed. This kind of situation is called "gridlock." With the LSF, the

Table 6. Implementation timetable of the RTGS-XG project

Phase	Sub-Project	Estimated time
Phase1	Development of LSF in BOJ-NET Modification for FXYCS payments	Fiscal 2008
Phase2	Modification for large-value Zengin payments	2011

RTGS-XG matches the offsetting payment flows and saves the liquidities of both sides. This will substantially reduce the necessity for participants to hold off on sending payment instruction. Accordingly, participants are expected to send their instructions earlier and overall earlier settlement in the system would be accomplished.

To Comply with the International Standard

The compliance with the international standards is another essential benefit. In January 2001, the Bank for International Settlements (BIS) published "Core Principles for Systemically Important Payment Systems (Core Principles)" and these principles are regarded as an essential international standard to be observed. Core Principle IV describes "The system should provide prompt final settlement on the day of value, preferably during the day and at a minimum at the end of the day." The first part, achieving final settlement by the end of the day, is regarded as a "minimum standard" which every country should observe. Fortunately, three Japanese payment systems, the BOJ-NET, the FXYCS, and the Zengin System meet the requirement.

On the other hand, the latter part, achieving intra-day finality, is regarded as a "best practice" which is recommended for the advanced countries. The Core Principles report also mentioned "Providing intra-day finality is particularly desirable in countries with large volumes of high-value payments and sophisticated financial markets." No one might want to contend that the Japanese market is not included in this definition. Thus, intra-day finality would be desirable for the payment systems in Japan, but the FXYCS does not meet this requirement: finality is provided only at the end of day.

Actually, it was the starting point of the discussion for the reform plan of large-value payment systems. The discussion on how to comply the intra-day finality requirement lead to the proposal of the JBA and developed to the RTGS-XG project.

The RTGS-XG will settle all the large-value payment with intra-day finality, which will meet the requirement of Core Principles. This is another important benefit of this project.

FUTURE TRENDS

Ahead of BOJ, the Monetary Authority of Singapore (MAS) successfully implemented "MEPS+" in December 2006. MEPS+ was the first Integrated System in Asia, which replaced the previous national inter-bank payment system, MEPS.

The remarks of the managing director of MAS would give us a practical suggestion. He mentioned that changes in the financial landscape had led to a need for more efficient liquidity management, improved risk management and more streamlined payment flows, and MEPS+ was designed to meet these needs. If the market demand works in the same way, it is highly possible that the payment systems would continue an evolutionary progress with the aid of technological innovation in order to meet the market needs.

Shortly after the RTGS system was invented, only a handful of countries adopted this innovative system, which was quite effective in reducing the settlement risks. However recently, the number of countries that adopt the RTGS system is getting close to 100. Therefore, one can predict that these "Advanced Systems" would gradually become the prevailing system throughout most of the world. It should be added that the RTGS system took more than 20 years to become the prevailing system.

CONCLUSION

Technological progress and market needs push ahead with deployment of new types of payment systems, which include the Hybrid System and the Integrated System. These Advanced Systems bring a better combination of risk reduction and efficient settlement. The Next-Generation RTGS Project in Japan would be a good example of such ongoing progress. This trend for sophisticated payment systems is believed to continue and become widespread. We should keep a sharp eye on the progress and analyze how the new wave of payment systems would affect on the risk control and liquidity management.

Future Research Directions

As mentioned in this chapter, the designs for the payment systems are changing, which created the new type of Advanced Systems. This progress was the reaction to the market needs that seek more sophisticated liquidity control and risk management. The market needs and historical background vary from country to country and the technologies that can be adopted would differ at the time of implementation. As a consequence, the Advanced Systems vary in the system designs and functions, especially queue management, payment matching, liquidity control, account structure, and so on. These kinds of diversity should be analyzed further with the reason behind.

Liquidity and risk is the most important key words when discussing the payment systems. That is to say, how to reduce the settlement risk and how to make settlements with lower amount of liquidity was the two main subjects to improve the payment system. The payment systems have been progressed balancing the two factors. How did the Advanced Systems contribute to the improvement of the two factors? That would be another meaningful research topic.

This chapter focused on the large-value payment systems in the payment field. But major innovations are also taking place in the retail payment field, including electronic money, mobile payment, e-commerce, and micro-payment. These areas have numerous research topics to be done.

As a theoretical approach, some economists try to analyze payment systems using game theory, information economics, and theory of industrial organization. This area is called "Economics of Payments," which seems to be one of the promising area of research.

Last but not least, what is the most desirable payment system? It is widely alleged that there is no single solution for the ideal payment system. But someone may not be convinced with the common belief.

REFERENCES

Bank for International Settlements. (2001, January). *Core principles for systemically important payment systems.*

Bank of Japan. (2005, December). *Proposal for the next-generation RTGS project of the BOJ-NET funds transfer system.*

Bank of Japan. (2006a). *Framework for the next-generation RTGS project of the BOJ-NET funds transfer system.*

Bank of Japan. (2006b). *Outline of the 2005 Issue of the Payment and Settlement Systems Report.*

Bech, M. L., & Hobijn, B. (2006, September). *Technology diffusion within central banking: The case of real-time gross settlement.* Federal Reserve Bank of New York Staff Reports.

Imakubo, K., & McAndrews, J. J. (2005, August). *Initial funding levels for the special accounts in the new BOJ-NET.* Bank of Japan Working Paper Series.

Japanese Bankers Association. (2004). *Proposal for reorganizing fund transfer systems in Japan—Introducing a "large value settlement system" (overview).*

Nakajima, M., & Shukuwa, J. (2005). *All about payment systems* (2nd ed.). (in Japanese). Toyo Keizai Inc.

Nakajima, M. (2003). *Global trends in payment systems and their implications for Japan*. Forum of International Development Studies, Nagoya University.

ADDITIONAL READING

Bank for International Settlements. (1989, February). *Report on netting schemes (the Angell Report)*.

Bank for International Settlements. (1990, November). Report of the Committee on Interbank *Netting schemes of the central banks of the group of ten countries (the Lamfalussy Report)*.

Bank for International Settlements. (1993, September). *Central bank payment and settlement services with respect to cross-border and multi-currency transaction (the Noël Report)*.

Bank for International Settlements. (1996, March). *Settlement risk in foreign exchange transactions (the Allsopp Report)*.

Bank for International Settlements. (1997, March). *Real-time gross settlement systems (the RTGS Report)*.

Bank for International Settlements. (1998, July). *Reducing foreign exchange settlement risk: A progress report*.

Bank for International Settlements. (1999, September). *Retail payments in selected countries: A comparative study*.

Bank for International Settlements. (2000, September). *Clearing and settlement arrangements for retail payments in selected countries*.

Bank for International Settlements. (2001, January). *A glossary of terms used in payments and settlement systems*.

Bank for International Settlements. (2003, March). *Policy issues for central banks in retail payments*.

Bank for International Settlements. (2003, April). *Payment and settlement systems in selected countries*.

Bank for International Settlements. (2003, August). *The role of central bank money in payment systems*.

Bank for International Settlements. (2005, May). *Central bank oversight of payment and settlement systems*.

Bank for International Settlements. (2005, May). *New developments in large-value payment systems*.

Bank for International Settlements. (2006, January). *Cross-border collateral arrangements*.

Bank for International Settlements. (2006, January). *General guidance for national payment system development*.

Bank for International Settlements. (2006, November). *Statistics on payment and settlement systems in selected countries: Figures for 2005 (Annual)*.

Bech, M. L., & Hobijn, B. (2006, September). *Technology diffusion within central banking: The case of real-time gross settlement*. Staff Report, Federal Reserve Bank of New York.

European Central Bank. (2006, December). *Payment and securities settlement systems in the European Union and in the acceding countries*.

European Central Bank. (2006, August). The evolution of large-value payment systems in the Euro area. *ECB Monthly Bulletin*.

Fry, M. (1999, February). Risk, cost, and liquidity in alternative payment systems. *Bank of England Quarterly Bulletin*.

Fry, M., Kilato, I., Roger, S., Senderowicz, K., Sheppard, D., Solis, F., & Trundle, J. (1999). *Payment systems in global perspective*. Routledge International Studies in Money & Banking.

Hollanders, M. (2006-2007). Issues Shaping the future of payment systems. *SPEED*, *1*(3).

Pringle, R., & Robinson, M. (2002). *E-money and payment systems review*. Central Banking Publications Ltd.

Humphrey, D. B. (1995). *Payment systems—Principles, practice, and improvements*. The International Bank for Reconstruction and Development.

Martin, A. (2005). Recent evolution of large-value payment systems: Balancing liquidity and risk. *Economic Review* (First Quarter). Federal Reserve Bank of Kansas City.

McAndrews, J., & Trundle, J. (2001, December). New payment system designs: Causes and consequences. *Financial Stability Review*, Bank of England.

Millard, S., & Saporta, V. (2005, December). The future of payments. *Financial Stability Review*, Bank of England.

ENDNOTES

[1] Payment systems are generally divided into two categories: large-value payment systems (LVPS) and retail payment systems. LVPS facilitate payments, generally of very large amounts, which are mainly exchanged between banks and usually require urgent and timely settlement. Retail payment systems handle mainly consumer payments of relatively low value and urgency. As LVPS are the most significant payment systems for the national economy, hereinafter payment system means LVPS in this chapter, if not otherwise specified.

[2] TARGET (Trans-European Automated Real-time Gross settlement Express Transfer) system. TARGET links the RTGS systems of EU countries to facilitate the cross-border settlement of Euro. Only RTGS systems were permitted to be linked to TARGET system because TARGET was designed as a RTGS system as a whole.

[3] Hybrid means something that consists of or comes from a mixture of two or more other things.

[4] Centrale des Règlements Interbancaires. Created in January 1995, CRI manages the PNS. The shareholders of CRI are French credit institutions and Banque de France.

[5] The concept of offsetting was adopted by RTGS^{plus} first time ever in the world.

[6] The BOJ-NET comprises two systems: A system for funds transfer (BOJ-NET Funds Transfer System) and a system for the settlement of Japanese Government Bonds (BOJ-NET JGB Services). In this chapter, BOJ-NET Funds Transfer System (FTS) is referred simply as BOJ-NET.

[7] JBA is a premier financial organization whose members consist of banks and bankers association in Japan. The Association had 249 members at the end of 2006. JBA is involved in the planning of some clearing systems. The Tokyo Bankers Association (TBA), the biggest regionally based bankers association and one of the Special Members of JBA, operates the Zengin System and the FXYCS. As the secretariat of TBA is the same as that of JBA, JBA is the substantial operator of the two clearing systems.

[8] Reasons to set up independent LSF account include the considerations for transaction processing performance and for smooth system development.

[9] Participants can extend the operating hours until 19:00 with permission from the BOJ.

[10] Foreign Exchange and Foreign Trade Control Law used to strictly restrict the foreign exchange transactions. In 1996, the law was drastically revised and foreign exchange transaction was fully deregulated.

[11] The Japanese fiscal year starts in April and finishes at the end of the next March.

Chapter VII
Technical and Legal Concerns about Global Card Payments

Fernando Barrio
London Metropolitan University, UK

ABSTRACT

Well into the first decade of the twenty-first century, it is fair to say that card payments are the cyberspace payment method by definition and, therefore, in order not to deter the development of commercial transactions carried out by electronic means, they should be accepted globally in the same or similar manner, which also means that the technology and rules applicable to them should be the same or closely harmonized. However, as this chapter tries to explain, while there are some characteristics that have made cards' acceptance truly global in scope, there have been historical, economic, and regulatory forces that resulted in different jurisdictions favoring the use of different technologies and different legal architectures for the deployment and control of cards as a means of payment, which may both obstruct the possibility of extending the benefits derived from the use of card payments and avoid the extension of the negative features associated with their utilization.

INTRODUCTION

Well into the first decade of the twenty first century, it is fair to say that card payments are the cyberspace payment methods per antonomasia and, therefore, in order to not imply a deterrence to the development of commercial transactions carried out by electronic means, they should be accepted globally in the same or similar manner, which also means that the technology and rules applicable to them should be the same or closely harmonized. However, as this chapter tries to explain, while there are some characteristics that have made cards' acceptance truly global in scope, there have been historical, economic, and regulatory forces that resulted in different jurisdictions favoring the use of different technologies and different legal architectures for the deployment and control of cards as a mean of payment, which may both confabulate with the possibility of extending the benefits derived from the use of card payments and avoid the extension of the negative features associated with their utilization.

The phenomenon of card use, its technological features, and its regulation, can be addressed from a vast array of points of view and with focus on different aspects of it, and for many of those aspects and points of views the present article borrows from the existing literature. It recognizes that there are far more technical and legal concerns that those that can be treated in a single book, not to mention the impossibility of doing it properly in one chapter of a book devoted to Cyberlaw for Global E-business. Accordingly, the chapter starts presenting different technologies used to facilitate credit and debit card payments and their use in different countries to then analyze the feasibility of global convergence in this matter. It does not, however, enter into the details of the information and communication technologies used to process different forms of card payments but it concentrates in different technologies used to make the payment possible, as for example, PIN and PIN-less credit and debit cards, and their implication in an online environment.

Card payments, in all their forms and manners, are subject to and allow the use of a myriad of regulatory techniques and methods, but this chapter concentrates in those that, it can be argued, generate greater disparities between jurisdictions and are in more urgent need of harmonization, referring to the type of card payments that make up the vast majority of transactions: credit and debit cards. One of those issues, and one that probably permeates most analysis of legal regulation on cyberspace, is represented by the unsolved problem of establishing jurisdiction in online transactions. The general topic of Internet jurisdiction has been the focus of previous work (Barrio, 2007) and here reference is made only to the difficulties arising from conflicting regulations or lack of within the specific realm of card payments. The same kind of divergence can be observed in privacy and personal data protection, which arguably has the potential to severely damage the card payment system because the essence and main advantage of it resides in a very efficient transmission and use of data (Mann, 2006).

The rise and growth of electronic commerce and the importance of information and communication technologies for trade, economic growth and development are both well documented phenomena (UNCTAD, 2006), to such level that it could be argued that they are already part of the common knowledge not needing reference or citation, and they complement the also acknowledged value and impact of information in the current global environment. From the multiple examples of the later, the way that Stetson Kennedy used information to successfully combat the renaissance of the Ku Klux Klan can be chosen as one that underlines information's power in a colorful manner (Levitt & Dubner, 2006). The significance of information technologies per se can be assimilated to a new industrial revolution (Castells, 2000) and the broader impact on people, companies, and countries economic life can be explained in terms of increased productivity (van Ark, 2006), better access to markets (Kula & Tagotlu, 2003) and sophistication of marketing techniques, and product innovation (Davidson & Copulsky, 2006). In the same way, the importance of the existence and the expansion of electronic payments and its subtype card payments for the mentioned growth and diversification of electronic commercial transactions should not be underestimated.

In the United States, for example, the Federal Reserve reported that in 2003, electronic payments surpassed for the very first time check payments, and that card payments totaled more than 77% of those electronic payments (2004). It is important to note that in the U.S., due to historical and regulatory constraints, the paper check has had an unparalleled role as the preferred method of payment across the society (Mann, 2006), but that long standing tradition cannot, in the long term, compete with the benefits and efficiencies brought about by electronic payments in general and card payments in particular, although it is true that a cashless and checkless society "has a long way to go" (Evans & Schmalensee, 2005, p. 5).

A detailed and long explanation about the features that give electronic and card payments a unique advantage over other forms of payment goes beyond the scope and intention of this chapter and only some comparison is needed when explaining the technological characteristics of the different types of card payments. However, it is important to note that most independent studies about different aspects of the evolution and growth of cards as a method of payment tend to conclude that some form of regulation is needed and, even those that started from the hypothesis that the market would do a better job than legislators and regulators, as Mann (2006), have reached the same pro-regulation conclusion. This is not to say that regulation would be innocuous and that it would not probably slow down the growth of the most efficient method of payment, the card, but the same researchers have also found that the side effects resulting from the spread of the use of cards can have substantial negative social effects that outweigh some of the potential benefits, which implies a benefit in the slowing down process (Manning, 2000; Evans & Schmalensee, 2005; Mann, 2006). Still, taking into account the importance in volume and the economic and social impact that card payments have in modern markets, some of the main aspects of card payments are largely unregulated, being Denmark the only European country with specific legislation covering card payments other than credit cards (Cranston, 2005).

This chapter takes the issue where other authors had left it and building upon the recognized need of legal regulation to cards payments, the differences on jurisdictional rules applied to electronic card payments, and different treatment for personal data in different jurisdiction, argues that moves toward international convergence and harmonization would have the multilayered effect of ameliorating some of the negative aspects of cards' usage, improve the legal certainty and thus the profitability of the card sector in the mid and long term and would also help break inertial forces that preclude proper domestic regulation in some countries due to either ideology or short-term economic gain.

THE PARTICIPANTS AND THE TECHNOLOGY OF DIFFERENT CARD PAYMENTS

In this chapter, as it was mentioned before, card payments are treated as a subtype of electronic payments, but excepting for comparative purposes other electronic payment forms are ignored. The explanation that follows is centered in the fact that since the main card networks started using electronic processing for their transactions in early 1970s, (Mann, 2006), most if not all card transactions, even those conducted in person, are electronic payments, which explains why continuous references are made to situations predating the development of electronic commerce and cyberspace as are known in 2007. It is also important to remember that although for practical purposes different payment forms are called "card payments" due to the physical object that represent that form, these represent different legal and financial instruments with some different and some similar characteristics, even though arguably they share the same technical features. The shape and size that most physical representations of the mentioned payment forms take are based on the ANSI X4.13, "American National Standard for Financial Services—Financial Transaction Cards" that also defines the place and size of the magnetic band or stripe, signature panel, and the area for making the card more distinctive.

Probably most people automatically associate card payment with credit cards, although the rate of growth of other card payment methods is quite higher than that of credit cards in most developed countries (Bank of International Settlements, 2003). When a credit card is presented or used for payment, that act implies a series of legal relations and financial activities supported by a broad and highly advanced technological infrastructure. The legal and financial aspects of that apparently simple act were well explained in the American case *Williams v United States* (1961), where the court was of the opinion that:

[presenting a credit card was] an indication to sellers of commodities that the person who ha[d] received a credit card from the issuer thereof [had] a satisfactory credit rating and that, if credit [was] extended, the issuer of the credit card [would] pay (or see to it that the seller of the commodity receive[d] payment) for the merchandise delivered. A credit card signifie[d] that the legal owner thereof [was] a good credit risk and the issuer guarantee[d] payment for goods, wares and merchandise sold and delivered on the basis of the card. (pp. 99-100)

In the case of the seller accepting the card, a complex cycle of authorization, processing and settlement takes place, which involves a series of participants that can be unrelated but connected by the different card networks. There are different ways to separate those participants, but they are generally grouped into consumers, merchants, card networks, issuer, and acquirer. There are other entities that provide services necessary for the successful completion of a credit card transaction, but they are not relevant for the purposes of the legal relation between the buyer, the seller and the card itself. These are third party processors as regional and national switches, payment support providers and intermediaries between the merchant, the issuer, and or the acquirer.

The card or networks are bodies that set up standards for involvement in the credit card system and they usually give authorization to other institutions, mostly banks, to issue cards bearing their brand, upon acceptance of the network rules. These rules normally include the right and obligation of the network to intervene in disputes arising from the system use. The network can belong to a private membership corporation as Visa, to a private share corporation that franchises the brand as MasterCard or to companies like American Express, Diners Club, or Discovery. Although the main product for which American Express is known is not technically a credit card but a charge card (does not involves revolving credit and the total sum spent needs to be settled when billed) it can be grouped with credit cards too, especially since it has franchised its brand to other issuers and it also started to offer products with revolving credit (Consumer Action, 2005). From the network point of view, the functioning is similar but in the case of card Visa and MasterCard, they do not issue credit cards directly and their brands are used by thousands of financial institutions that pay membership fees or receive a franchise in order to issue cards (Visa, 2007; MasterCard, 2007). The function of the card networks is extremely relevant because in their contract of adhesion to the network, there is almost no room to negotiate the terms, which if passed to the customers may be impacted differently by regulations on different jurisdictions. However, the card networks are mainly the operators of payment card systems, each of which "consists of a distinct set of computers and rules for processing transactions, seeking verification, getting approval, transferring funds, and capturing billing information" (Evans & Schmalensee, 2005, p. 12) and they play no direct role in the contractual relations arising from a credit card transaction (Ellinger et al., 2006).

The issuer of a credit card is normally a financial institution that can be a bank, a credit card company, as American Express or Diners Club, or a company created solely for that purpose, this later being called monoline. Different countries differ on the percentage of credit card belonging to each type of issuer, but it is acknowledged that in Europe most credit card issuers are also banks that hold deposits for their customers (Mann, 2006). The issuer usually grants credit lines and enters into a contractual relation with its customers, issue the credit cards, authorize purchases and other uses (as the withdrawal of cash in an ATM), and bills the customer through a monthly statement. The relation between the issuer and the cardholder and the impact that regulations to that relation have upon the relations that issuers have with other members of the credit card systems are the focus of the legal analysis in the last part of this chapter.

The acquirers are those that create the relation with merchants and their name originates in them acquiring those sellers for the network. They accept merchants' drafts and apply a discount, which covers their costs. Acquirers can be either financial institutions, credit car companies, or technology companies (Mann, 2006) and they are usually responsible for merchant fraud and failure, and they also have to respond in case of a legitimate dispute between the merchant and the cardholder (Ellinger et al., 2006). This later feature varies between jurisdictions and some of the options are mentioned in the section dealing with contract design.

In the case of debit cards, the participants do not differ substantially, but the legal relation between them differs substantially. It also important to add that in debit card transactions there are other players that occupy the role of the network, although the market has undergone a deep process of consolidation and in most countries debit card and credit card networks have converged (Mann, 2006). The main difference between credit and debit cards resides in the fact that when a cardholder uses a debit card, he/she is giving an order to the issuer to deduct in that moment funds from their account while in the situation of the credit card, the aforementioned explanation of *William v. United States* (1961) always applies. In the former situation, the law treats the transaction as an electronic funds transfer and, therefore, the level of protection in most jurisdictions for the cardholder is considerably lower. In the case of United States the weaker Electronic Funds Transfer Act of 1978, codified to 15 U.S.C. 1601, applies to debit card transactions while the more robust Truth in Lending Act of 1968, also codified to 15 U.S.C. 1601, pertains to credit card transactions and results in, for example, greater scope of protection from unauthorized charges made to the card in question. In the case of English law, it seems clear that credit cards are understood as credit tokens in the sense referred by the Consumer Credit Act of 1974 and therefore subject to all its regulations, but it also seems to be clear, although no tested in court, that debit cards are not covered by that piece of legislation (Ellinger et al., 2006). However, it can be argued that within both credit and debit cards, a very important aspect of relevance to transactions conducted via electronic networks is the technology that they use for authentication.

In that respect, following partially Mann (2006), it is possible to group both credit and debit cards in those requiring a Personal Identification Number or PIN and those that do not, or PIN-less (Mann, by focusing mainly in the American market does not pay much attention to credit cards requiring PIN, which are now common in many European countries). Card payments requiring PIN do not complete the transaction unless the user or cardholder enters the secret number and the transaction is, in that form, conducted online. PIN-less cards work off-line and rely on the presentation of the card and the cardholder's signature. It is important to note that PIN technology decreases the risk of fraud substantially and the introduction of PIN-based credit cards in England is credited with the substantial reduction of card fraud reported in 2005 (APACS, 2006). On the other hand, the instances of card-not-present fraud, or CNP, have registered an important increase, and those are the cases that mostly involve payment through Internet (Leyden, 2006).

Due to the technology involved, most payments carried out in cyberspace use the less secure PIN-less cards, which could explain to a degree, the constant rise of Internet fraud. The normal approach in most jurisdictions has been to leave the market to decide which technology is better suited to deal with issues arising in the fast-moving digital scenario, and regulation has been enacted to deal with the result of the use of such technology (Biegel, 2003), but it can be argued that due to the important financial, economic, and social costs of online fraud, some sort of regulation can be imposed to either directly require or to indirectly foment the use of PIN-based technology in online transactions. Activities complementary to existing private initiatives could include state support to research into PIN-based online authentication systems or the release into the public domain of on-hand government owned high tech authentication methods and techniques. However, one of the main issues is the global harmonization of standards, since once the PIN-based cards become adopted and widely used in one country, fraudsters are able to carry out their activities via CNP transactions in and from other countries (Leyden, 2006). One of the possible solutions resided on the broad utilization of EMV chip card specifications, which provides the basis for global, interoperable chip-based card transactions.

EMV is the set of specifications devised by Europay, MasterCard, and Visa (EMVCo)—created with the aim of supporting global interoperability between chip cards and readers. To drive this new standard, the card schemes are mandating that the liability for fraudulent card-present transactions will shortly shift to the non-EMV-compliant party in the transaction. (Davies, 2004, p. 3)

In any case, it is clear that the technology currently used to authenticate most CNP generally, and Internet transactions in particular, is not the most satisfactory and there are other options available within the reach of the card payment networks and issuers, and that any delay in its adoption can only result in further social costs represented by economic inefficiencies represented by higher insurance premiums and by increasing consumer distrust in electronic commerce, which most research suggests is one of the main obstacles to its further growth and development (Bruin, 2002). Accordingly, both the actual and potential economic and social costs and the effect over electronic commerce development should justify the need for some form of incentive or obligation toward the use of PIN-based card payments at global scale.

JURISDICTION, PRIVACY, AND DATA PROTECTION IN CARD PAYMENTS

Assuming that every network and every issuer in every country had adopted the more secure PIN-based cards and that the technology for PIN-based authentication in CNP transactions were made widely available, there would still be some constraints to the development of electronic commerce transactions at global scale. Those limitations are represented by differences in the legal treatment of certain issues, which add legal uncertainty to the already existing technological and trust-related uncertainties faced by consumers and card companies. As explained before, the law treats differently a long list of aspects affecting commercial transactions carried out through digital networks paid by card, but this section focuses on jurisdiction, privacy and data protection, and certain contract design issues due to the centrality of these topics to the aforementioned form of trade.

Jurisdiction

The jurisdiction to which the card payment relation is subjected is fundamental and, unfortunately, cannot be easily implied from the current legislation. While the jurisdiction of the contract between the cardholder and the issuer is usually easy to establish due to the almost normal requirement for the cardholder to be a resident of the jurisdiction where the card is issued, the problem arises with the jurisdiction of the legal relation created during an Internet transaction paid with a credit card. It can be said that the issue is not distinct to any international Internet transaction regardless of the method of payment, but with card payment the question resides in whether the cardholder has a domestic contract with the issuer, which implies the use of all consumer protection legislation available in that jurisdiction, the issuer has a domestic contract with the network and the network, due to its global presence, has an international contract with the acquirer, which in term has a contract with the seller. Assuming this hypothetical chain of contracts as the correct one, it is possible to observe that such a situation would create an unquantifiable risk for the card networks.

In some jurisdictions, as in England, consumers enjoy certain legal protections that can not be waived or modified by any contractual clause, as what it is stipulated in the Consumer Protection Act of 1987. Therefore, it would follow that in the case of an English consumer using an English credit card from England to carry out an Internet purchase abroad, and since the contract in which the consumer has entered, the cardholder-issuer has been concluded in England, the issuer would have to guarantee the same level of protection than the afforded when products are bought in England. For example, if the consumer-cardholder has purchased a good, the issuer would have to guarantee that the seller has had proper title and quiet possession, that the goods match the description, and that they are of satisfactory quality according to the Sale of Goods Act of 1979, sections 12, 13, and 14 respectively. The apparent solution given by *Office of Fair Trading v Lloyds TSB Bank plc and others* (2004), fails to clarify the issue. While it is true that in the case of the example given by the defendant and repeated by Mrs. Justice Gloster DBE, a hypothetical plastic surgery paid in New York with an English credit card, the inapplicability of section 75 of the Consumer Credit Act of 1974, which imposes liability to the issuers for breach of contract or misrepresentation of the supplier, is almost obvious, the extension of the same principle to Internet transactions, as mentioned in paragraph 43, seems to be erroneous. By introducing Internet transactions, it could be argued that Gloster, J. should have elaborated into the nature of the contract created by electronic means, because from the analysis of her ruling there is not much scope for doubt about the existence of an affirmation that purchases carried out in Internet from a foreign supplier become foreign contracts, which would contradict basic principles of the English contract law. If Web sites are either advertisement or display of goods, following *Partridge v. Crittenden* (1968) and *Fisher v. Bell* (1960) respectively, Web sites constitute an invitation to treats, which would imply that the consumer is the one making the offer that needs to be accepted by the seller. Acceptance must be effectively communicated and it becomes valid, in the case of electronic communications, in the place where is received, read, and understood, following *Entores Ltd v. Miles Far East Corporation* (1955), which leads to the univocal conclusion that a contract for the purchase of goods carried out via Internet when the purchaser is in England, is formed in England. It could be argued however, that the contract in question may include a choice of law clause pointing to the foreign jurisdiction, but here again, since the Consumer Protection Act of 1987 forbids its exclusion from consumer contracts such a choice of law clause would be void by implication. Furthermore, since in most, if not all Internet consumer contracts, the terms are unilaterally imposed by the seller, Unfair

Contract Terms Act of 1977 and Unfair Terms in Consumer Contracts Regulations of 1999 would be applicable, especially sections declaring invalid standard terms in consumer contracts.

In the case of the United States the situation seems to be simpler due to the prevalence of choice of law clauses and a more entrenched respect for freedom of contract, but it could be only in appearance. In general terms the U.S. Supreme Court has held that forum selection clauses are generally enforceable because a person can consent to personal jurisdiction, as in *Burger King v. Rudzewicz* (1985). However, courts decide whether those clauses are enforceable on a case-by-case basis, and in The *Bremen v. Zapata Off-Shore Co.* (1972), the Supreme Court indicated that forum selection clauses must be fair and reasonable to be enforced. These same principles also apply to a choice of law provisions and *Caspi et al. v Microsoft Network* (1999) can be used to show that these principles still work in the online environment.

Many transactions conducted via Internet, especially for small amounts and with smaller sellers, do not count with detailed contractual provisions, even when the substantial reduction in the prices of card terminal allows those smaller merchants to receive credit card payments. This result in the need to resort to the common law rules of jurisdiction, which have inconsistency as the only thing that is consistent (Barrio, 2007). It is not clear if in the case of disputes arising from purchases paid with cards, the use of the card would be considered enough interactivity, as in *Cody v. Ward* (1997), and therefore jurisdiction be found in either the place of residence of the cardholder, the seat of business of the merchant, or even the forum where the issuer is located. If, on the other hand, the card activity is not regarded as interactivity per se separated from the main contract, the form of payment would be irrelevant and the jurisdiction would be decided following the usual inconsistent existing rules in which different courts have held opposite views in almost the same set of issues and very similar facts (Barrio, 2007). An interesting possibility would be given by the possibility of finding jurisdiction following the product liability theory of stream of commerce, as in *Luv N' Care v. Insta Mix* (2006), which would also invalidate the previously referred Mrs. Justice Gloster DBE reasoning in the English case *Office of Fair Trading v Lloyds TSB Bank plc and others*. If following such theory, a court can find jurisdiction over a defendant based on the defendant being upstream of the business relation, nothing would preclude the application of the mentioned section 75 of the English Consumer Credit Act of 1974 to a global card network that operates in the UK, giving the possibility to the issuer to recoup what has paid to the cardholder for the merchants breach of contract or misrepresentation in a foreign transaction (which anyway is normally contemplated in the agreement with the network). Furthermore, the U.S. has sought before to impose extraterritorially its laws and regulations to foreign transactions carried out using cards, even when the cardholder, the issuer, and the transaction are all outside the United States, as when in 2002 several UK residents received a notice from their credit card issuers, owned by an American company, that their credit cards would not be valid in Cuba, probably due to provisions of the 1992 Cuban Democracy Act (Torricelli Law). The situation went even further due to other credit card issuers using an American company, MBNA, to process their transactions, which had also impact on the cards use because of an assertion of the ban on subsidiary trade with Cuba (Wilkinson, 2002).

In Australia, the widely publicized case *Dow DowJones & Co. v. Gutnick* (2002), where the High Court of Australia subjected Dow Jones to suit in Australia for defamation in that country under Australian law arising from a Web posting on a U.S.-based server, was based partially on the fact that that there were at least 1,700 WSJ.com subscribers with Australian credit cards.

The case of Japan has certain similarities in what regards to extra-territorial application of domestic law when the cardholder is Japanese. The 1907 version of the Japanese Penal Code, in its Chapter 23 dedicated to gambling and lottery-related crimes (this part was not modified during the 1947 reform) establishes that "[a]ny individual who engages in gambling is subject to fines and penalties not to exceed 500,000YEN" (article 185), "[a]ny individual who engages in habitual gambling is subject to up to 3 years' imprisonment" (article 186.a), and also that "[a]ny individual or group who operates a gambling establishment or enters into a relationship with a gambling establishment operator to make a profit through gambling is subject to 3 months to 5 years imprisonment" (article 186.b), which would make online gambling illegal (there is an exception to horseracing carried out by the Japan Racing Association, prefectural and city governments, and designated municipalities, which was established by the Horseracing Law of 1890). The problem would arise if a Japanese cardholder decides to bet in a foreign online betting site while being in a foreign country. Following the logic of Gloster, J. in the already mentioned English case *Office of Fair Trading v Lloyds TSB Bank plc and others*, such a transaction would be a foreign transaction subject to a foreign jurisdiction, but credit cards in Japan that allow international transactions, that is, Visa, MasterCard, American Express, Diners Club, and JCB, "have prohibited gambling transactions and immediately cancel a participating merchant's contract if the merchant is determined to be acting as a betting agent" (Kominami, 2003, p. 2), which clearly implies a extraterritorial application of Japanese law when the cardholder and/or the issuer are residents of Japan.

Since the mentioned cases and situations can be combined to find that more than one court has the right to exert jurisdiction over the same dispute, cardholders enter into legal relations without knowing for certain what law applies and merchants and card issuers need to make previsions for an immeasurable legal risk. The previous analysis seems to project an uncertain picture about what rules of jurisdiction would apply when cards are used to pay for online transactions, which added to the current and increasing uncertainty over general jurisdictional issues in Internet commerce (Barrio, 2007), conspires against the aim of promoting the development and growth of electronic commerce. It is fair to conclude that some form of international harmonization should be sought to deal with the issue.

Privacy and Data Protection

The former analysis is consistent with Nolan (2003), who points out, that doing business online has jurisdictional consequences and raises an array of issues which would not apply in a domestic context, like the possibility of consumers placing themselves outside the protections afforded them by their local consumer protection laws. Unfair marketing practices, unsafe products, insecure payment methods, and loss of personal privacy are among the "threats" faced by cardholders as online consumers (Alboukrek 2003).

The rise of citizens' privacy violation due to recent advances in information and communications technology (Vaz, 2003) has part of its origin and is potentially augmented by the use of cards as a method of payment. The use of cards erases the possibility of anonymous transactions and users have to cope with the threat of losing control over their personal information (Beltramini, 2003); control that can be restored though privacy and data protection legislation, where there are great disparities between different jurisdictions (OECD, 2006).

In the United States, the main source of protection to invasions of privacy and data protection in online transactions is to be found in the Fair Information Practices (Federal Trade Commission, 1998), which constitute a mere guide to formulating privacy policies in the use of databases comprising online consumer information.

It can be argued that the information regarding a transaction, including the personal identifiable information of the consumer, is owned as much by the merchant, card issuer, and network as by the individual and the merchant is not obliged by the Gramm-Leach-Bliley Act, as the issuers and networks are. The cardholder is left with the choice as to which businesses have proper privacy and data protection policies, according to what the business in question has disclosed. In case of an online merchant displaying a privacy policy and not complying with it, the Federal Trade Commission Act, gives to the FTC, the power to put a stop to unfair methods of competition and unfair or deceptive acts or practices in or affecting commerce, which allows the FTC to take action against business companies that not comply with their own privacy policies or otherwise misrepresent their information management practices. This Commission can also deal with unfair misuse of personal information where the practice (a) inflicts substantial harm on consumers that they cannot reasonably avoid and (b) does not offer offsetting benefits to consumers or competition, as established in 15 U.S.C. § 45(n). However, it would appear that with too much flexibility given to e-business, the consumer is left at a great disadvantage and the American freedom-of-choice ideals should not deny the consumer's need for proper privacy protection when transacting online (Barrio & Santiago, 2007).

In Europe, the right to privacy and the protection of personal data is covered by a complex, comprehensive, and superimposing regulatory framework. The European Convention of Humans Rights and Fundamental Freedoms of 1950, in its article 8.1, establishes that "[e]veryone has the right to respect for his private and family life" and that has been widely interpreted as creating a strong right to privacy within the signatory states, although the operational measures to put the right to privacy into practice were left to the individual states. However, with the expansion of far-reaching automatic data processing systems, the need to tackle the handling of personal data within such systems became evident (Lloyd, 2004). In 1981 the Council of Europe adopted the Convention 108 for the protection of individuals with regard to the automatic processing of personal data and in 1995 the European Union adopted the Directive 95/46/EC on the processing of personal data. This Directive instituted the basic principles for the collection, storage, and use of personal data to be respected by governments, businesses, and any other organizations or individuals engaged in handling personal data, which has deep impact on the card payments' system. The principles deal with transparency, data quality, collection and use of the data, security safeguards, subject access, and transborder data flows. Member states, in turn, have materialized this into domestic laws that may result in stricter rules for as long as the minimum standards set by the directives are met (Bainbridge, 2004). It is these minimum standards that bring a sense of uniformity insofar as the EU is concerned. The Privacy and Electronic Communications (EC Directive) 2003 of the UK provides, in essence, that no person shall use subscriber's information unless the purpose is made clear to the latter and he is given the choice to refuse. In other words, an informed consent is required. In this example, there is all the more reason to for e-business firms to display privacy policies on their Web sites.

In Japan, the new Personal Information Protection Law, effective April 1, 2005, applies to any business with offices in Japan that stores personal data on 5,000 or more individuals including the company's employees, and the personal data's definition includes a person's name, address, date of birth, sex, home and/or mobile phone numbers, and also a person's e-mail address if that address can be linked to the person's name. The law states a set of obligations for companies handling personal data, and the Japanese Ministry of Economy Trade and Industry (METI) has issued a set of guidelines on how to maintain data security. Among the new rules that companies must follow, they must specify for what purpose information is being collected, obtain consent from individuals before using the information for any other purpose than the one originally stated, and take measures to prevent data being leaked and stolen. Companies must also deal with complaints and correct mistaken data. It is important to note that the law does not deal with transborder data flows (OECD, 2006).

Clearly, each regulatory approach can have arguments for and against it, but it can be argued with confidence that the difference between the different jurisdictions cause uncertainty and increases the sensation of insecurity (Barrio, 2006), insecurity that most research show as a main concern of consumers (OECD, 2006). Accordingly, in the search for a common global standard that would enhance the usage of efficient payment systems as cards, the concept of self-regulation would appear to be the lesser choice (Harrington, 2004). While there are certainly those who argue that self-regulation is the answer to consumer concerns and that the market can find an adequate solution (Aguilar, 2000), it seams clear that without government intervention, there is no stopping for these firms from formulating self-serving policies, thus opening the doors to fraud and other violations of consumer rights, increasing consumer lack of trust and, therefore, reducing the use of card payments and hampering the growth of commercial transactions carried out in cyberspace (Barrio & Santiago, 2007). Lack of confidence in e-business firms is cited as the main reason for this (Schwaig, Kane, & Storey, 2005), and Taylor (2001) emphasizes this point by stating that the 'brick-and-mortar retailers' still prevail in winning the consumers' confidence. This would suggest the need for government intervention precisely to build consumer confidence and consequently aid e-business growth.

CONCLUSION

The analysis that precedes, points towards the confirmation of the need of some sort of regulation to ensure that card payments keep their pace of growth and collaborate to guarantee a smooth development of electronic commercial transactions at global scale. However, through the selected topics, it is also evident that there are differences both in the type of regulation used and in the content of them when the regulation is carried out by law. From the type of regulation point of view, although those favoring self-regulation and those championing legal intervention seem to take into account the need to balance the interest of business and consumers, it seems more appropriate to choose a legislative approach while continuing to implement a strategy of balance. It is clear from the analysis that, even in cases where some form of legal regulation has taken part, legal rules enacted by legislative bodies are paramount in affirming consumer rights, which derives in better consumer confidence and consequently in a better business environment for card issuers, acquirers, and networks.

Compliance with a myriad of laws presents itself as a problem for e-business firms in general and card payment ones in particular, which leads back to the advocated need for harmonization in legal regulation, either via international cooperation or some fort of international agreement.

Future Research Directions

The chapter explored the issues arising from the technological and regulatory environments surrounding the use of card payments in online transactions and by doing so opened the door for further exploring the topic with a more prospective and normative focus. Future research would focus on the reactions that the topics treated in the chapter have originated in different jurisdictions, especially those that in order to solve some of the perceived problems created by the use of cards on electronic commerce transactions' payments have created new barriers for the global use of that means of payment. For example, the requirement to use the Zip code belonging to the address where the card bill is received in certain jurisdiction seems to introduce an unnecessary hurdle for the use of non-domestic cards, while the security that adds needs to be properly assessed. This type of situation could multiple due to regulators and card companies rushing to address consumers concerns over security and research needs to be conducted on the different options been pondered or applied. The focal point will remain to be the harmonization or not of different regulatory and technological solutions to the problems presented by the use of card payments, but through the analysis of those being actually deployed in different jurisdictions.

REFERENCES

Aguilar, J. (2000). Over the Rainbow: European and American consumer protection policy and remedy conflicts on the Internet and a possible solution. *International Journal of Communications Law and Policy, 4*, 1-57.

Alboukrek, K. (2003). Adapting to a new world of e-commerce: The need for uniform consumer protection in the international electronic marketplace. *The George Washington International Law Review, 35*(2), 425-460.

APACS. (2006). *Fraud: The facts 2006*. Available at http://www.apacs.org.uk/resources_publications/documents/FraudtheFacts2006.pdf

Bainbridge, D. (2004). *Introduction to computer law* (5th ed.). Harlow, UK: Longman.

Bank of International Settlements. (2003). *Payment and settlement systems in selected countries*. Available at http://www.bis.org/publ/cpss53.pdf

Barrio, F. (2006). Regulación o autorregulación de los derechos del consumidor en Internet? Esa es la cuestion., Revista de Derecho, Comunicaciones y Nuevas Tecnologias, Number 2, Bogota, Colombia: GETCI

Barrio, F. (2007). The consistent inconsistency in defining cyberspace spatial boundaries, Revista Académica Facultad de Derecho de la Universidad La Salle Año IV No. 8, Mexico, pp. 83-100

Barrio, F., & Rosario, Santiago, M. O. (2007). Consumer protection, the regulation of privacy across the Atlantic and the creation of a business-friendly environment. *Script-ed, 4*(4). Edinburgh, Scotland.

Beltramini, R. (2003). Application of the unfairness doctrine to marketing communications on the Internet. *Journal of Business Ethics, 42*(4), 26-27.

Biegel, S. (2003). *Beyond our control? Confronting the limits of our legal system in the age of cyberspace*. Cambridge, MA: MIT Press.

Bruin, R. (2002). *Consumer trust in electronic commerce*. London: Kluwer Law International.

Consumer Action. (2005). *Credit cards: What you need to know*. Available at http://www.consumer-action.org/downloads/english/2005_CC_terms_en.pdf

Cranston, R. (2005). *Principles of banking law* (2nd ed.). Oxford, UK: Oxford University Press.

Davies, M. R. (n.d.). *Chips cards in banking: Optimizing the migration strategy, IBM Consulting*. Available at http://www-03.ibm.com/industries/wireless/doc/content/bin/wl_chip_cards_in_banking_1.pdf

Ellinger, E. P., Lomnicka, E., & Hooley, R. J. (2006). *Ellinger's modern banking law* (4th ed.). Oxford, UK: Oxford University Press.

Evans, D. S., & Schmalensee, R. (2005). *Paying with plastic* (2nd ed.). Cambridge, USA: MIT Press.

Federal Reserve System. (2004). The 2004 Federal Reserve Payments Study. Analysis of Noncash Payments Trends in the United States: 2000-2003.

Federal Trade Commission (1998). Privacy online: A report to Congress. Available at http://www.ftc.gov/reports/privacy3/priv-23a.pdf

Harrington, D. (2004). Consumer vulnerability on an all-IP world. *Intermedia, 32*(4), 26-27.

Kominami, K. (2003). Report on the 29th Asian racing conference's business session on wagering. *Japan Association for International Horse Racing Journal*. Available at http://www.jair.jrao.ne.jp/journal/v11n2/cover.html

Levitt, S. D., & Dubner, S. J. (2006). *Freakonomics*. London: Penguin Books.

Leyden, J. (2006, November 7). *UK credit card fraud down to GBP209.3 m. The Register*. Available at http://www.theregister.co.uk/2006/11/07/credit_card_fraud_stats/

Lloyd, I. J. (2004). *Information technology law* (4th ed.). Oxford: Oxford University Press.

Mann, R. J. (2006). *Charging ahead: The growth and regulation of payment card markets*. New York: Cambridge University Press.

Manning, R. D. (2000). *Credit card nation: The consequences of America's addiction to credit*. New York: Basic Books.

MasterCard. *Corporate Overview*. Available at http://www.mastercard.com/us/company/en/docs/Corporate%20Overview.pdf

Nolan, S. (2003). Freedom from contract. *Ebusinesslex.net*. Retrieved from http://www.ebusinesslex.net/front/dett_art.asp?idtes=94>

OECD. (2006). *Report on the cross-border enforcement of privacy laws*. Available at http://www.oecd.org/dataoecd/17/43/37558845.pdf

Schaig, K., Kane, G., & Sorey, V. (2005). Privacy, fair information practices and the Fortune 500: The virtual reality of compliance. *The Data Base for Advances in Information Systems, 36*(1), 49-63.

Taylor, M. (2001). E-tail watchdog. *CIO, 14*(9), 48.

Vaz, S. (2003). Internet and personal data protection. *Ebusinesslex.net*. Retrieved from http://wwwebusinesslex.net/front/dett_art.asp?idtes=94>

Visa Corporation. *Visa facts*. Available at http://www.usa.visa.com/download/about_visa/press_resources/company_profile/visa_facts.pdf

Wilkinson, S. (2002, October 22). British credit cards hit by US sanctions. *Cuba Si*, available at http://www.cuba-solidarity.org/cubasi_article.asp?ArticleID=13

ADDITIONAL READING

Abrazhevich, D. (2004). *Electronic payment systems: A user centered perspective and interaction design*. Eindhoven, The Netherlands: Universiteitsdrukkerij Technische Universiteit Eindhoven.

Chatterjee, C. (2002). *E-commerce law for business managers*. Kent, UK: Financial World Publishing.

Gkoutzinis, A. (2006). *Internet banking and the law in Europe: Regulation, financial integration and electronic commerce*. Cambridge, UK: Cambridge University Press.

Hiller, J., & Cohen, R. (2002). *Internet law and policy*. NJ: Pearson Education.

Jackson, P., Harris, L., & Eckersley, P., (Eds.). (2003). *E-business fundamentals*. London: Routledge.

Khosrowpour, M. (Ed.). (2005). *Advanced topics in electronic commerce*. Hershey, PA: Idea Publishing Group.

Kou, W. (2006). *Payment technologies for e-commerce*. Heidelberg, Germany: Springer-Verlag.

Lessig, L. (2000). *Code and other laws of cyberspace*. Basic Books Publishing.

Radu, C. (2002). *Implementing electronic card payment systems*. Norwood: Artech House.

Reed, C. (2004). *Internet law, text and materials* (2nd ed.). Cambridge: University Press.

Spindler, G., & Börner, F. (Eds.). (2002). *E-commerce law in Europe and the USA*. Springer.

Winer, J. (2001). If the U.S. is from Mars and the EU is from Venus, What do you do in cyberspace? *Privacy and Information Law Report, 1*(8), 8.

Chapter VIII
The Regulation of New Forms of Electronic Fund Transfers in Japan Focusing on Electronic Money

Takashi Nakazaki[1]
Anderson Mori & Tomotsune, Japan

ABSTRACT

In this chapter, after surveying existing Japanese public laws that regulate the transfer of funds via the Internet, and focusing on electronic money in particular, It will be discussed how these existing regulations may apply to new electronic payment methods that may not have been accounted for when these regulations were established, whether the regulations are sufficient to both provide convenience to the user and protect their safety, and whether these regulations are desirable as business conditions for developing electronic money. Through these discussions, certain objectives will be developed, which should be taken into account when developing regulations in Japan on the transfer of funds via the Internet. Also, this chapter discusses anti-money laundering regulations applicable to transfers of funds on the Internet, focusing on electronic money, and will examine how Japanese money laundering regulations may apply to cross-border transfers of funds using overseas electronic money services. Through this examination, the chapter will attempt to suggest desirable money laundering regulations on domestic electronic money in the near future. Furthermore, this chapter discusses real money trade and point-rewarded programs in view of function of payment or transferring funds electronically in extended research sections, and closes by predicting future research directions.

Copyright © 2008, IGI Global, distributing in print or electronic forms without written permission of IGI Global is prohibited.

INTRODUCTION: WHY ELECTRONIC MONEY NOW?

Electronic Money has Increasingly become a Part of Personal Lives in Japan

The use of Electronic Money has been expanded in Japan in recent years, and it has come to be used transactions in various goods and services. As the commercial online transactions quickly spread among general consumers, the necessity for establishing electronic payment methods has increased. Also, as the domestic player population of online games continues to expand, intermediate agents on the Internet specialized for Real Money Trading (hereinafter referred to as "RMT"), meaning the exchange of virtual currency within online games with the currency of the real world, has also appeared. Meanwhile, in the real world, in order to avoid the time and effort involved in using cash at vending machines, convenience stores, and so forth, IC chips that act as Electronic Money devices have been introduced. IC chips working as Electronic Money have become a standard function of cellular phones and cellular phones themselves, which are widely used by the Japanese, have an Electronic Money function. The integration of IC chips into cellular phones brought about an increase in the number of users of Electronic Money. Moreover, it did not stop only at transactions with entrepreneurs supplying goods and service, also allowed users to transfer the electronic value recorded on IC chip to each other. In addition, the number of shops that accept Electronic Money from existing Electronic Money issuers has increased rapidly, thanks to associations with other issuers. Furthermore, large-sized mass home electronics retailers and airline companies have started a service which converts points and mileage into Electronic Money issued by other entities.

How has the Japanese Government Responded to the Spread of Electronic Money?

As a social phenomenon, Electronic Money has started to spread to general consumers, rather than merely being confined to special-use groups. Therefore, the introduction of legislation regulating Electronic Money in order to protect consumers has become increasingly urgent. From the 1990s, members of the Japanese government have frequently advocated the introduction of full-scale legislation on Electronic Money and have issued research reports. Although these reports are available to the public, since Electronic Money has not yet become fully widespread, the legislation which covers Electronic Money widely has not yet been established. In this situation, the Working Group on Information Technology Innovations and Financial Systems (hereinafter referred to as the "Working Group") under the Sectional Committee on Financial System of the Financial System Council of Financial Services Agency (FSA) has held several hearings from providers of prepaid-type electronic payment services, focusing on the detailed content of their services and their safety measures. The Working Group released a memorandum from the chairman[23] (FSA, 2006, the "Chairman Memorandum") to the public entitled "Issues facing the Development of New Electronic Payment Services" in April, 2006. The Chairman Memorandum is primarily a summary of: (1) matters to be considered by service providers and (2) issues to be studied by the government in the future.

However, the Chairman Memorandum covers only prepaid-type electronic payment services, summarized and categorized into "electronic payment services using IC chips" and "electronic payment services over the Internet" and does not cover the newest forms of electronic funds transfer, such as point cards or air miles. Moreover, the Working Group approached the matter mainly from the view point of how to raise the reliability of prepaid-type electronic services through more stable payments and stronger user protection, not from the view point of the right to issue currency only being permitted by the nation, financial policy, and balancing with strict regulations on banks.

The Aim of this Chapter

In this chapter, after surveying existing Japanese public laws that regulate the transfer of funds via the Internet, and focusing on Electronic Money in particular, it will be discussed how these existing regulations may apply to new electronic payment methods that may not have been accounted for when these regulations were established, whether the regulations are sufficient to both a provide convenience to the user and protect their safety, and whether these regulations are desirable as business conditions for developing Electronic Money. Through these discussions, certain objectives will be developed, which should be taken into account when developing regulations in Japan on the transfer of funds via the Internet.

Also, this chapter discusses anti-money laundering regulations applicable to transfers of funds on the Internet, focusing on Electronic Money, and will examine how Japanese money laundering regulations may apply to cross-border transfers of funds using overseas Electronic Money services. Through this examination, this chapter will attempt to suggest desirable money laundering regulations on domestic Electronic Money in the near future.

Lastly, the extended research sections discuss real money trade and point-rewarded programs, focusing on the use of such services to make payments or transfer funds electronically, and the final section predicts future research directions.

WHAT IS "ELECTRONIC MONEY"?

Discussions So Far

When considering regulations on Electronic Money, it is necessary first to clearly identify the subject of the regulations. The common understanding of the term "Electronic Money" varies widely in Japan. One view insists that Electronic Money means electronic payment methods or general payment methods using advanced information communication technology. The other view claims that the Electronic Money means the electronic data itself which has monetary value. By way of illustration, the understandings of Electronic Money indicated in the two reports issued by the first[4] and the second[5] (June 1998) round-table conferences on the theme of Electronic Money are very different. The first report divides the digitalization of payment services into 1) the means of payment and 2) the method of payment. In this context, "means of payment" means the instruments that have monetary value, such as cash, and "method of payment" means the mechanisms for transferring "means of payment," such as payment by debit card and wire transfers using online banking. The first report defines Electronic Money quite narrowly, as electronic data itself having monetary value within the category of "means of payment." The second report, on the other hand, explains that Electronic Money is a payment mechanism performed by the transfer or updating of an electronic record issued corresponding to funds provided prior to issuance, or the electromagnetic record itself. In summary, the second report assumes that the meaning of Electronic Money varies from electronic data to method of payment, depending on the context. In revising the 1998 Foreign Exchange and Foreign Trade Law (*Gaikokukawase oyobi Gaikokubouekihou*, Law No. 228 of 1949, as amended, the "FEL"), it intends to include both electronic payment services using IC-chip-embedded devices, such as IC cards and mobile phones (hereinafter referred to as "IC-chip type service") and electronic payment services in which electronic value data is centrally managed solely on the service provider's server (hereinafter referred to as "Server-Managing type service") into the definition of "means of payment" applied by the said law, and sets out the definitions in the FEL accordingly.[6] The FEL is the only piece of legislation where Electronic Money is defined. The FEL definitions were, however, created in the context of the FEL, and are only used in this article for reference purposes.

The Chairman Memorandum does not use the term Electronic Money, but uses "Electronic Payment Services" instead. This seems to try to clarify the subject of prospective regulations in the near future, by excluding the vague and multiple meanings corresponding to the term Electronic Money.

Position of this Article on How to Analyze the Term Electronic Money

Although the expression Electronic Money is used in this chapter, it is not realistic to pursue a singular strict definition of the term here, as such definition has long been debated and remains controversial.

In order to determine how increasingly prevalent Electronic Money transactions should be regulated, it would be useful to determine and analyze the core elements of Electronic Money that are common to all understandings of the term. In the following section, such core elements will be discussed, after providing a loose definition of the concept of Electronic Money.

Definition of Electronic Money in this Chapter

What Range Should Electronic Money Cover?

Should Electronic Money mean only "means of payment" or include both "means of payment" and "methods of payment"? For the purposes of this chapter, "methods of payment" in the definition of Electronic Money will not be included because many "methods of payment" such as wire transfers and credit payments through the Internet have become widely used in Japan, and have already been thoroughly discussed; it would be unnecessary to argue further that they should be regulated. Once we assume that Electronic Money does not include "methods of payment," the next question is whether Electronic Money is limited to data having monetary value in and of itself, or in addition, whether it should include a payment scheme using electronic means of payment, that is, data with monetary value. A payment scheme using electronic means of payment differs from electronic methods of payment using non-electronic means of payment insofar as in the former system, users directly control the data with monetary value. Users of electronic methods of payment using non-electronic means of payment may only give instructions to the entities actually controlling the non-electronic means of payment, such as cash, that is, banks and credit card companies. Even if the meaning of Electronic Money is limited to data having monetary value in and of itself, it cannot be determined how Electronic Money transactions should be regulated without also analyzing the effect of payment by transferring such data.

Does Electronic Money Need Versatility?

Whether it is necessary for Electronic Money to be versatile is arguable. The opinion of the author is that it is unnecessary. Whether Electronic Money needs versatility, namely, whether payment by Electronic Money should be a perfect substitute for payment using cash currency, is primarily a political and theoretical issue, and is distinct from issues of finding the solution to a social phenomenon. By "a political and theoretical argument," it is meant that Electronic Money functioning as a perfect alternative for cash currency will infringe the exclusive right of nations to issue currency, or contravene currency laws and regulations. However, making Electronic Money absolutely equivalent to cash by endowing it with versatility and cashability has been the aspiration of Electronic Money advocates. In addition, as a social phenomenon, some of the existing payment services which may be used only for purchasing certain goods or services tend to be versatile to some extent, through the relationship between service providers. This tendency makes it difficult to draw a line regarding versatility.

Core Elements of Electronic Money

The three core elements which are generally common to all definitions and understandings of Electronic Money are as follows:

i. The issuer's issuance of electronic data (money value information) corresponds to funds provided by users prior to issuance (issuing Electronic Money corresponding to funds provided prior to issuance).
ii. The holder of money value information may transfer this data electronically, and, thereby, may use it in order to settle of debts, such as the price of a good.
iii. The holder of money value information may ask issuers and other service providers to convert such money value information into cash.

Regarding (i), many scholars stress the importance of prior funds being offered and base their arguments on the assumption that funds have been offered by cash or wire transfer before Electronic Money has been issued. It is indispensable for user protection to make payment capability dependent on an issuer's credit worthiness.

Regarding (ii), it is generally said that this element should be a core element from the view that it is desirable to provide versatility that can be used as a means of payment for purchasing various goods or services. In addition, this element seems to aim at protecting users from an issuer's bankruptcy risk.

Regarding (iii), cashability means that an affiliated store may receive cash from an electronic money service provider after a user has purchased goods or services, not that a user may request an electronic money service provider to convert electronic money into cash (hereinafter referred to as "General Cashability"). Professor Shigeyuki Maeda claims that General Cashability should be considered an essential element of Electronic Money in order to ensure that it is credible and versatile (Maeda, S.[7]). However, it cannot be denied that General Cashability may be in contravention of the Investment Deposit and Interest Law (*Shusshino Ukeire, Azukarikin oyobi Kinritouno Torishimari ni kansuru houritsu*, Law No. 195 of 1954, as amended; the "Deposit Law") and the Banking Law (*Ginkouhou*, Law No. 195 of 1954, as amended) (Sugiura, N., & Kataoka, Y., 2003[8]). In order for General Cashability to be permitted, it would be necessary for related regulation on banks to be applied to Electronic Money as well, under the auspices of financial policy, and that the users of electronic money be thoroughly protected (Iwahara, S., 2003[9]). It would take a significant amount of time to meet these conditions. The argument for General Cashability is merely a legislative theory at the moment.

ELECTRONIC MONEY AND ITS CLASSIFICATION

Classification According to Location where Electronic Value Information is Stored

Electronic Money may be classified into IC-chip type and Server-Managing type, depending on whether information is recorded on the IC-chip-embedded device itself or on a service provider's server.

Examples of IC-chip type Electronic Money includes "Suica," which is offered by East Japan Railway Company, and "Edy" which is offered by Bitwallet. They are already widely used in ordinary life as a means of transportation and at convenience stores.

Most prepaid money specialized for usage on the Internet belongs to the Server-Managing type. As stated, Server-Managing type Electronic Money is characterized by the administration of electronic value with respect to each user solely on the service provider's server, without issuing cards, and so forth, that carry electronic value.

This classification is generally said to greatly affect the application of the Prepaid Card Law (*Maebaraishiki Shouhyou no Kiseitou ni kansuru houritsu*, Law No. 92 of 1989, as amended).

Classification by Issuing Party

Regardless of whether Electronic Money is IC-chip type or Server-Managing type, it may be classified further into two types: Electronic Money used for purchasing good and services only provided by the relevant issuer (*Jika-gata*, hereinafter referred to as the "Internal type") and Electronic Money used for purchasing goods and services provided by any party (*Daisansha-gata*, hereinafter referred to as the "External type").

In the E.U., regulations on electronic money are applied only to External type prepaid cards, which have the potential of functioning akin to currency, and are not applied to the Internal type prepaid cards. Although the regulations contained in the Japanese Prepaid Card Law differ treat Internal type and External type differently, as mentioned later, it is common for the Prepaid Card Law to be applied to both, in contrast to E.U. regulations. The importance of regulations of Japan is to protect users from an issuer's bankruptcy or other financial distress, and this need exists equally for both the Internal and External types of Electronic Money (Morishita, T., 2005[10]). Since a network prepaid Internal type may be used for transactions related to RMT mentioned later, the Internal type market is expected to expand further.(Hiramatsu, M., 2006[11]).

Other Classification View Point

In addition, in Japan, online prepaid money may be divided roughly into two kinds of types, the ID type and the Wallet type, depending on the method purchasing and consuming electronic value. Mr. Yutaka Kodaira (2006) indicated that the advantages of these two types are said to be anonymity and security, respectively (Kodaira, Y., 2006[12]). Whether Electronic Money is classified as ID type or Wallet type does not affect the application of regulations in Japan.

EXISTING REGULATIONS ON ELECTRONIC MONEY: PART I: LEGISLATION AS THE BASIS FOR GOVERNMENTAL POLICY: THE PREPAID CARD LAW

Framework of Regulations: Application of the Prepaid Card Law

Since Electronic Money is data representing value issued based on prepaid funds by users, the Prepaid Card Law serves as underlying legislation for the regulation of Electronic Money, that is, the basis for the validity of governmental measures and policies.

Under Article 2, paragraph 1, item 1 of the Prepaid Card Law, a "Prepaid Voucher" (*maebaraishiki-shohyo*) is defined as any voucher or certificate which is issued corresponding to the receipt of an amount "that is either indicated on the voucher or certificate or stored in the voucher or certificate in an electromagnetic manner (electronic, magnetic, or other manners that cannot be recognized by human perception)" and can be used as payment. "Prepaid Voucher" should not be intangible because of the expression stated in item 1. According to such definition, an IC-chip-embedded device including monetary value information in an electromagnetic manner may be considered a "Prepaid Voucher."(Kanda, H., 2005[13]). IC-type devices are issued in correspondence with funds provided by users and can be used for payments by using appropriate reading devices.

In addition, Professor Shinsaku Iwahara (2005) points out that regulations under the Prepaid Card Law, such as obligations to fully indicate information on issuers and the amount to be used, are difficult to actually comply with on non-card type devices (such as a cellular phone, clock, etc.) that use an IC chip (Iwahara, S., 2005[14]).

Application to Server-Managing Type

Devices linked to electronic value data that is managed solely on the service provider's server and to Server-Managing type Electronic Money do not themselves contain data that is stored electromagnetically. Therefore, they should not be considered to be "Prepaid Vouchers."(Iwahara, S., 2003[15]). The Chairman Memorandum clearly supports this view.

Outline of the Contents of Regulations under the Prepaid Card Law

Introduction

The Prepaid Card Law aims mainly at consumer protection, paying attention to financial functions arising from the advance payment system, and does not have Electronic Money in mind. The Prepaid Card Law focuses on regulating the minimum standards for commencing the business of issuing prepaid cards, principally including financial regulations on minimum capital, the requirement to indicate the amount of prepayment money on a certificate or voucher, and a system for depositing issue guarantee money.

Notification / Registration Duties at the Commencement

When the total amount of non-consumed Electronic Money exceeds 7 million Japanese yen, Internal type service providers have to submit notice of the amount of non-consumed Electronic Money remaining after an issuance and the provider's information to the Prime Minister. Special limitations when commencing a business do not exist (Article 4 of the Prepaid Card Law).

External type service providers have to be registered by the Prime Minister before initiating their services (Article 6 of the Prepaid Card Law). At the time of registration, the corporation will be examined to determine whether it has sufficient capital to issue Electronic Money. When providing services available in two or more municipalities (i) the ratio of capital to net assets should be less than 90% and (ii) the capital must not be less than 100 million Japanese yen (Item 6, Paragraph 1, Article 6 of the Prepaid Card Law).[16]

Duties of Indicating Amount of Value Information on a Certificate or Voucher

On a certificate or voucher, a service provider has to display a publisher's information and the amount of non-consumed value (Article 12 of the Prepaid Card Law).

Duties of Posting a Bond

When the outstanding unused value of advance payment system certificates that the service provider has issued exceeds 10 million Japanese yen, the service provider is obliged to post a bond with a deposit office worth at least half of the outstanding amount yet to be used in order to protect its customers. Users may ask the Prime Minister to return deposited money in case of the service provider's bankruptcy (Articles 13 and 14 of the Prepaid Card Law).

Which Entities are Regulated by the Prepaid Card Law?

The Prepaid Card Law defines the entities under its purview simply as "issuers." Currently, one card or device may include multiple functions such as an electronic money IC-chip. In such case, it is very unclear which entity would be considered the "issuer," especially when providing "External" service. Professor Shinsaku Iwahara (2005) claims that an "issuer in the External service" (Paragraph 7, Article 2, the Prepaid Card Law) should be interpreted as an entity who owes an obligation compelling a goods or service provider to provide such goods or services to an user in exchange for data with monetary value.(Iwahara, S., 2005[17]). Also, Professor Shinsaku Iwahara insists that regulated entities should be limited to issuers, except that the duty of explaining obligations to users when selling should be imposed on distributors.

EXISTING REGULATIONS ON ELECTRONIC MONEY: PART II: VERSATILITY—THE BILL AND SIMILAR CERTIFICATES CONTROL LAW

Introduction

In the deliberation process for establishing the Prepaid Card Law, one of the most controversial arguments was whether the law conflicted with regulations prohibiting the issuance of certificates with functions similar to currency under Article 1 of the Bill and Similar Certificates Control Law (*Shihei Ruiji Shoken Torichimariho*, Law No. 51 of 1906, as amended). The same argument may be raised in respect of Electronic Money.

IC-Chip Type

The Bill and Similar Certificates Control Law prohibits only certificates having functions similar to currency and it is generally said that this prohibition focuses on whether the certificates work as a means of payment, i.e., whether they are sufficiently versatile to be expended by any person, at any location, and for any purchase. This standard seems to permit versatility to a great extent.(Maeda, Y. (2005), Iwahara, S. (2003)[18]). At this moment, there is no IC-chip type having such versatility.[19]

Server-Managing Type

Since Server-Managing type Electronic Money does not exist in the form of a tangible "certificate," it is generally accepted that the Bill and Similar Certificates Control Law is not applicable to Server-Managing type Electronic Money.

EXISTING REGULATIONS ON ELECTRONIC MONEY: PART III: CASHABILITY—THE DEPOSIT LAW

Introduction

In the deliberation process of establishing the Prepaid Card Law, one of the most controversial arguments was whether it conflicted with the prohibition on deposits contained in the second clause of Article 2 of the Deposit Law. The same argument may be raised in respect of Electronic Money.

Conflicts with the Deposit Law

Article 2 of the Deposit Law prohibits persons other than financial institutions and banks (see Article 3 of the Law) from taking "deposits" as its business. A "deposit (*azukari-kin*)" means: (i) the acceptance of a monetary deposit (*yokin*), savings (*chokin*), or installment savings (*teiki-tsumikin*) (Article 2, paragraph 2, item 1 of the Deposit Law) or (ii) acceptance of money from a numerous number of people as deposits, savings or installment savings, corporate bonds, debts, or other economic nature similar to that stated in the preceding item (paragraph 2, item 2)."

Although Electronic Money services are not, strictly speaking, monetary deposits (*yokin*), the question is whether the service has economic characteristics similar to monetary deposits and thus falls within the definition of a "deposit (*azukari-kin*)."

"Acceptance of money of an economic nature similar to that stated in the preceding item" means any acceptance of money on the promise that the principal amount will be refunded, which will be undertaken for retaining the value of the deposit, mainly for the depositor's convenience. In other words, deposits have the following economic features: (i) an amount equal to the principal or more is guaranteed and (ii) the money is kept for the depositor's convenience.[20] When generally understood as a return of promised principal, the service has similar economic characteristics to a monetary deposit (*yokin*) and thus it is very likely that Electronic Money services would fall within the definition of a "deposit (*azukari-kin*)." This is borne out by the fact that with respect to most major Electronic Money issued in Japan, in order (a) to reduce office costs and (b) to avoid criminal prosecution, issuers do not give refunds for purchased Electronic Money.

EXISTING REGULATIONS ON ELECTRONIC MONEY: PART IV—EXCHANGE TRANSACTIONS: THE BANKING LAW

Introduction

"Exchange transactions" under the Banking Law (Article 2, paragraph 2, item 2 and Article 10, paragraph 1, item 3 of the Banking Law) are included in the primary line of business of a bank, which can be conducted solely by a bank licensed in Japan (Article 4, paragraph 1 of the Banking Law).

First of all, although there is no definition of "exchange transactions" in the Banking Law, the Japanese Supreme Court held in a case of a so-called "underground bank" that it would be reasonable to define an exchange transaction as transferring funds between people in distant locations, which does not involve the transportation of actual currency, but instead the exchange of information, to be made upon the request of a customer (March 12, 2001 decision of third Petty Bench of the Japanese Supreme Court; Criminal Law Reports of Supreme Court No. 55-2 at 97).

As stated, Server-managing type Electronic Money tends to be used for online payments between people in distant locations. Also, IC-chip type Electronic Money may be used for online payments between people in distant locations via a card reader device connected to the Internet. These IC-chip type and Server-Managing type services that involve transfers of funds may fall within the definition of "exchange transactions."

Under either of the following two approaches, IC-chip type and Server-Managing type services that involve transfers of funds may not fall within the definition of "exchange transactions."

One approach is to break down the function of the services into legal relationships based on the contracts between the relevant parties. According to this explanation, it is generally said that the main purpose and role of Electronic Money services differs from that of fund transfers between people in distant locations, even if the services have the same result as transfers. A similar approach using an analysis of individual legal relationships was employed in two "no action letters" announced in 2004 by the FSA (FSA, 2004a, 2004b[21]).

In a "no action letter" published on July 9, 2004, the FSA published its answer indicating that a certain Server-managing type Electronic Money service "Catel" may not fall within the definition of "exchange transactions."

In the Catel system, each customer acquires "Catel" points directly, that is, via the Internet, from the Issuer of Catel ("Issuer Company" in this section hereafter) and consumes such Catel points in Catel's affiliated shops and stores. In the Catel system, a customer may select when he pays cash corresponding to Catel points prior to consuming such Catel points. Like Electronic Money services, a customer may pay cash to the Issuer Company, acquire Catel points, and purchase goods and enjoy services at affiliated stores and shops by the following procedure:

a. The customer applies to the Issuer Company to issue Catel points directly, that is, via the Internet
b. Issuer company issues Catel points to the customer by sending an e-mail indicating the issuing information, including how many Catel points have been issued.
c. Issuer Company delegates a telecommunication company to collect cash from the customer and transfer the cash to Issuer Company.
d. The customer will pay such cash by a means of bank transfer.
e. The customer will purchase goods and enjoy services at affiliated stores and shops by consuming his Catel points.
f. The relevant shop or store will charge Issuer Company for cash corresponding to the Catel points consumed.
g. Issuer Company pays cash to the relevant shop or store by a means of bank transfer.

In this scheme, there are four contractual relationships, as follows:

A. Binding Catel service terms and conditions concluded between Catel and each consumer:
 - Based on this contract, a customer will escape from his debt obligation to the Issuer arising from issued Catel points by paying the relevant amount of money to the telecommunications company responsible for the collection of receivables.

B. Contracts concluded between Catel and each affiliated shop or store delegating the collection of bills:
 - Based on these contracts, the Issuer will collect a bill for an affiliated shop or store through a telecommunications company.

C. Billing agency contracts concluded between Catel and a telecommunications company:
 - Based on this contract, the telecommunications company will collect bills from customers and transfer such money to the Issuer by way of a bank transfer.

D. Contracts concluded between each consumer and the telecommunication company delegating the collection of bills:
 - Based on this contract, a telecommunication company will collect a bill from a customer for the Issuer and an affiliated shop or store.

Remittance from the telecommunications company to the Issuer Company is no more than the performance of its obligation to deliver the receipts and does not constitute a remittance entrusted by consumers.

This is evident from the fact that no transfer destination is specified by consumers.

Furthermore, payment from the Issuer to an affiliated shop or store is not a remittance requested by a consumer or a telecommunications company.

Thus, no "transfer of funds" requested by a customer is involved in any of the transactions relevant to the Catel service between: (i) the consumer and the affiliate shop or store (ii) the affiliate shop or store and the Issuer (iii) the consumer and the telecommunication company or (iv) the Issuer and the telecommunications company. It cannot therefore be considered that the Cash Passport service constitutes "exchange transactions."

Moreover, the direction of fund transfers is not interactive but one-way. "Exchange transactions" are originally interactive transfers with offset. This fact also supports the above conclusion.

There are no articles or official views clearly stating that general Electronic Money services do not fall under the definition of "exchange transactions." However, similar explanations, as indicated in the no action letter, seem to be applied to interpretations of Electronic Money services.

Another approach to determining whether a service falls within the definition of "exchange transactions" involves an analysis of whether the subject of a transaction falls within the definition of "funds," that is, whether or not the relevant service has either General Cashability or versatility. Professor Iwahara has suggested that most Electronic Money services might fall within the definition of "exchange transactions" because they probably would have versatility in many cases (Iwahara, S., 2003; Fujiike, T., 2002[22]).

EXISTING REGULATIONS ON ELECTRONIC MONEY: PART V—MONEY LAUNDERING REGULATIONS

Introduction

It is possible that Electronic Money may potentially be used for money laundering (that is, concealing the profit of criminal activities), since it is easy to ensure anonymity. Anti-money laundering legislation in Japan mainly consists of the Anti-Organized Crime Law (*Soshikitekina Hanzaino Shobatsu oyobi Hanzaishuuekino Kiseitouni kansuru Houritsu*; Law No. 136 of 1999, as amended), the Customer Identification Law (*Kin-yuukikantouniyoru Kokyakutouno Honninkakunintouni kansuru Houritsu*; Law No.32 of 2002, as amended), and the Foreign Exchange and Foreign Trade Law (*Gaikokukawase oyobi Gaikokubouekihou*; Law No. 228 of 1949, as amended, the "FEL") (Nakazaki, T., 2007a[23]).

This chapter examines the possible application of these laws in the event that Electronic Money is used for money laundering.

The Anti-Organized Crime Law

The Service Provider's Responsibility

The concealment or disguise of proceeds of crime is prohibited and may lead to imprisonment with labor for up to 5 years or a fine of up to ¥3,000,000, or both (Article 10 of the Anti-Organized Crime Law). However, unless a service provider knowingly assists the concealment or disguise or proceeds of crime, it is not subject to this penalty.

Duty to Report Suspicious Transaction

Under Article 54 of the Anti-Organized Crime Law, if a financial institution suspects that certain assets or funds are proceeds of crime, such institution must report any suspicious transactions involving the assets or funds to the agency that has jurisdiction over it (in the case where such agency is the FSA, then to the Japan Financial Intelligence Office). Financial institutions are not allowed to disclose to the parties involved that such a report has been or will be made (Article 54, Para. 2 of the Anti-Organized Crime Law). The agency receiving the reports is required to forward it to the Japan Financial Intelligence Office.

The Anti-Organized Crime Law imposes reporting obligations concerning suspicious transactions on a wide range of relevant reporting institutions that receive money from customers such as banks, trust banks, insurance companies (including foreign insurance companies), securities companies (including foreign securities companies), Japan Post, money-lenders, futures trading companies, and investment trust management companies (the Anti-Organized Crime Law Article 54, Para. 1; Cabinet Order Concerning Reporting of Suspicious Transactions [*Utagawashii Torihikino Todokedeni kansuru seirei*; Cabinet

Order No. 389 of 1999, as amended; "COCRST"], Art. 1, Paras. 1&2). Electronic Money service providers are currently not required to report under the Anti-Organized Crime Law.

The Customer Identification Law

The Customer Identification Law imposes identification obligations in respect of certain transactions on a wide range of financial institutions that receive money from customers, such as banks (including foreign banks and trust banks), insurance companies (including foreign insurance companies), securities companies (including foreign securities companies), trust companies, money-lenders, futures trading companies, and investment trust management companies (The Customer Identification Law Art. 2). Electronic Money service providers are currently not subject to identification obligations under the Customer Identification Law.

The Foreign Exchange and Foreign Trade Law

When a consumer purchases overseas goods or services using Electronic Money issued by a Japanese Electronic Money service provider, the service provider will send cash to the entity providing the relevant goods or service at the end.

When an entity in Japan sends more than 30 million Japanese yen overseas or receives more than 30 million Japanese yen from overseas, such entity needs to report their name and address, the date of the transaction, and the amount of the transaction to a financial minister (Article 1 of the Ministerial Ordinance concerning Reports on Foreign Exchange, Transactions etc. [MOF No.29 Mar 19, 1998], Article 18-4 of the Foreign Exchange Order [Cabinet Order No. 260 Oct 11,1980], and Article 55 of the FEL). Even when 30 million yen or more is regularly sent or received from overseas in the same fashion and involving the same parties, the entity sending or receiving must report each and every transaction.

Since the IC-chip type and the Server-managing type of Electronic Money all correspond to "means of payment," Electronic Money service providers may be subject to Article 19 of the FEL.

NECESSITY FOR THE REEXAMINATION OF PUBLIC LAW: THE REGULATION OF ELECTRONIC MONEY

Electronic Payment Services that have Carried Out a Sudden Expansion

The Chairman Memorandum enumerates Server-Managing type services and escrow services as electronic payment services used for payments over the Internet, and IC-chip type services as electronic payment services mainly used for payment at shops, based on the result of interviews. Also the Chairman Memorandum indicates discussions on (i) matters to be considered by service providers and (ii) issues to be studied by the government in the future, regarding both the Server-Managing type and the IC-chip type. In addition to discussing the state of public law regulations, the Chairman Memorandum also comments on the contents of an article. The contents of the Chairman Memorandum have been outlined as follows.

Matters Deemed to Require Consideration by Electronic Payment Service Providers

A wide range of electronic payment services are expected to be developed and disseminated in the future, but there is currently no legislation regulating such electronic payment services across the board. For this reason, the Working Group has indicated that the following five matters should at least be considered by providers of electronic payment services in order to improve the reliability of services by ensuring the protection of users and stability in payment.

Clarification of Contractual Relationships, etc.

Service providers should clearly state, for example, the point in time at which the user's obligation to make a payment disappears, the responsibilities of the user and the service provider, and other such matters in an easy-to-understand manner for users in the terms and conditions of use.

Handling of Loss, Impairment, and Etc., of Electronic Value Data

Service providers should clearly state how electronic value data on IC chips and servers will be handled in the event that it is lost, impaired, and so forth, in the terms and conditions of use, and so forth, especially the conditions of re-issuance, and so forth.

Information Security and Ensuring Reliability of System Operation

In particular, services in which electronic value data is centrally managed solely on the service provider's server are deemed to be exposed to higher risks of hacking, unauthorized use, and other illicit acts. Therefore, countermeasures should be taken, such as devising an authorization mechanism.

Proper Management of Advances Received

In the case of electronic payment services which involve receiving a certain amount of money from users in advance, a service provider should have a mechanism to refund as much money as possible even if it goes bankrupt.

Protection of Personal Information

While this is not limited to electronic payment services, due caution needs to be exercised especially when using the usage log in other operations, and so forth, in order to protect personal information.

Issues Relating to Electronic Payment Services to be Studied in the Future

The government considers it necessary to continue to conduct studies on how to deal with the following three issues in the future. In conducting such studies, the government will take trends in other countries into account, while making sure the development of services in line with IT innovations will not be hindered, in light of the anticipated growth in electronic payment services.

User Protection in the Event that the Service Provider Goes Bankrupt.

Currently, the Prepaid Card Law does not apply to services in which electronic value data is managed solely on the service provider's server. The government has deemed in necessary to develop an appropriate user protection method to deal with cases where such a service provider goes bankrupt.

How Responsibility Should be Shared between Parties to Electronic Payment Services, etc.

The government deems it necessary to look into how responsibility should be shared between the service provider and the user in cases where some kind of problem arises in the electronic payment services (e.g., cases where electronic value data is lost or impaired or the payment is not completed or is delayed due to system failure) in order to protect users and ensure confidence in electronic payment services.

Future Shape of Electronic Payment Services

In furtherance of user convenience, it would be desirable to introduce new services that transfer electronic value between users and that convert electronic value into cash. However, such services would have to be compatible with the existing legislative framework and business practices regarding "exchange transactions" under the Banking Law and "deposits" under the Deposit Law.

Risks when General Cashability Provided, and Desirable Regulations

If General Cashability is provided in the future, as suggested, an Electronic Money issuer would be similar to a bank in the sense that it would store funds for the public and would have a payment function. Under the Banking Law, a licensing system and strict supervisory regulations are imposed on banks in order to protect depositors and maintain orderly credit conditions. Imposing the same regulations on Electronic Money issuers would have an adverse effect the spread of Electronic Money transactions. As long as Electronic Money transactions on involve the payment of a small sum, it may be unnecessary to impose the same regulations on Electronic Money service providers as on banks.

By providing General Cashability and enabling users to transfer value electronically, the possibility that Electronic Money may be used for money laundering will increase even more. Electronic Money transactions may become subject to such obligations as reporting obligations under the Anti-Organized Crime Law and identification obligations under the Customer Identification Law. As mentioned, Server-Managing Electronic Money would be an attractive vehicle for money-laundering due to its anonymity.

OTHER ONLINE PAYMENT SERVICES BY NON-FINANCIAL INSTITUTIONS[24]

Payment Service Development in Japan and the Banking Law

Other than electronic money, there emerge many payment services such as online escrow services and e-mail payment services, including Paypal. These services are likely to fall within the definition of "exchange transactions."[25] Because the definition includes the exchange of information, entities who exchange information leading to funds transfers between people in distant locations, using existing payment services provided by banks, may contradict with the Banking Law. The debate on this issue may be a useful reference for discussions on electronic money once it has General Cashability and versatility.

E-mail Payment Services, Including Paypal

General

E-mail payment services collect value for payment from the account of a person who wants to send value, and put the value into the credit card account of the opposing party. As opposed to with electronic money, the remaining value in the credit card accounts may be used as means of payment and has versatility, and therefore it is highly likely that such payment services would be interpreted as "exchange transactions" (Kubota, T., 2003[26]).

Cross Border Service: Why do We Need to Examine the Possible Application of Japanese Laws?

When an overseas payment enterprise provides a resident of Japan with service, unless the enterprise has a presence in Japan, article 61 of the Japanese

Banking law may be applied (Kubota, T., 2003[27]). Moreover, in the *Hourei,* the Law Application Principles Act, the rule governing the application of laws in private international law has been revised completely and will become effective in January, 2007. This new rule will make provisions of Japanese law that protect consumers apply to disputes between foreign companies and consumers living in Japan as much as possible, when a foreign company provides goods or services to consumers living in Japan. It is not clear whether Japanese regulations for consumer protection currently apply to overseas Electronic Money service providers because the arguments regarding this new general rule have not yet been fully explored.[28]

Online Escrow Service[29]

In an online escrow service, one party deposits his credit card or debit card having monetary value with an escrow agent. The agent delivers these deposits to the opposing party after the agent confirms that the opposing party has fulfilled his obligations. Moreover, although the fee for escrow services is consideration not for exchange services, but for temporary retention services, the target object of the service includes monetary value. This service may therefore be interpreted as an "exchange transaction."

Online escrow services may also contradict the Deposit Law (Kubota, T., 2003[30]).

WHEN OVERSEAS DIGITAL GOLD CURRENCY ENTERPRISES PROVIDES RESIDENTS OF JAPAN WITH SERVICE

Why do We Need to Examine the Possible Application of Japanese Laws?

For the purposes of this chapter, Digital Gold Currency is defined as any electronic currency issued by a private company to be used for international online payments, and involving international currency exchange. Most Electronic Money issuers limit domestic consumers to those within the same country as the one where the issuer resides. When an overseas Digital Gold Currency enterprise provides a resident of Japan with service, and the enterprise does not have a presence in Japan, Japanese law may be applied as stated. The next paragraph is based on the assumption that there is a theoretical possibility that Japanese regulations apply to overseas electronic money services.

The possibility of Public Law-Regulations being Applied to Overseas Digital Gold Currency

It will be examined whether Japanese regulations on Electronic Money apply to the services provided by overseas Digital Gold Currency companies to consumers living in Japan, taking e-gold as an example.[31] A commission is collected from the side receiving money at the time of receipt.

E-gold works as follows. A user pays cash into his account of e-gold in order to purchase e-metal, which is the Digital Gold Currency of the e-gold system, and stores such e-metal in his account. The worth of the e-metal in his account is displayed as a result of conversion into main currencies. Usually, e-gold backs the e-metal with gold equivalent to the worth of the e-metal and the conversion rate of e-metal in user accounts fluctuates according to changes in the market price of gold.

The components of e-gold are as follows: (i) e-gold issues e-metal, electronic data (money value information) corresponding to funds paid by e-gold users (ii) users holding e-metal can electronically transfer this to other users' accounts by giving directions to e-gold, and, thereby, can use such e-metal to settle debts, such as purchase goods and (iii) the holder of e-metal can request that e-gold the user's e-metal into cash. Component (iii) is equivalent to General Cashability.

E-gold seems to be comparable to Electronic Money issued in Japan with General Cashability and versatility, since the money-value information is recorded solely on the server of e-gold.

Since there is no certificate, the Prepaid Card Law and the Bill and Similar Certificates Control Law do not apply to e-gold transactions. However, there seems to be a risk that e-gold transactions would be contrary to the Deposit Law and the Banking Law.

BRIEF COMPARISON WITH REGULATIONS OF U.S. AND E.U.

General

In order to search for desirable countermeasures to the rapid spread of Electronic Money in Japan, it may be useful to study the "wait and see" regulations in place in the U.S. and the rigid and detailed regulations in the E.U., which, among other things, limit issuers to banks in the E.U.

U.S. and Japan

The principal legislative acts regulating electronic payment system in the U.S. are the Electronic Fund Transfer Act (ETFA) and its associated regulations (Regulation E). They basically target consumer protection and apply to "accountable" stored value systems. This "accountable" classification is decided based on whether monetary value information may be affected by a change in a consumer's bank account. As previously indicated, this chapter focuses on the unaccountable type. In state-level regulations, Money Transmitter Laws apply to non-banking payment services including electronically stored value. Only authorized transmitters and distributors may issue and sell certain types of means of payment. Authorized transmitters have to safely retain advance payment funds in full until used by a consumer. Authorized distributors have to send advance payment funds to authorized transmitters. These regulations preserving advance payment funds are stricter and cover more services than the regulations by the Japanese Prepaid Card Law, stated previously in part. This regulation for preserving advance payment funds may serve as a guide to Japanese authorities.

E.U. and Japan

In Directive 2000/46/EC of the European Parliament and of the Council of September 18, 2000 on the taking up, pursuit of, and professional supervision of the business of electronic money institutions (the "EC Directive on EM"), Electronic Money is defined as "monetary value as represented by a claim on the issuer which is: (i) stored on an electronic device (ii) issued upon the receipt of funds of an amount not less in value than the monetary value issued (iii) accepted as means of payment by undertakings other than the issuer" (Item (b), Paragraph 3, Article 1). This definition includes both the IC-chip type and the Server-managing type, however, as already written, E.U. regulations are applied only to the External type.

Under the EC Directive on EM, issuers of electronic money must obtain business licenses. In addition, the Directive regulates prohibitions on engaging in other businesses, initial and ongoing capital requirements, and limitations on investments. E.U. regulations are especially rigid in limiting issuers to banks only.

One of the principal differences between the electronic money regulations of the E.U. and Japan is redeemability (Article 3, the EC Directive on EM). Japanese electronic money issuers in Japan do not give refunds for purchased electronic money in order to avoid violating the Deposit Law. Based on the Chairman Memorandum, Japanese authorities may be favor of granting General Cashability to electronic money through discussions on the Deposit Law and the Banking Law.

POSSIBLE LEGISLATION ON ELECTRONIC MONEY IN THE FUTURE

The Chairman Memorandum does not specify how the government should legislate to protect consumers and encourage the development of the Electronic Money industry in Japan. Professor Shinsaku Iwahara suggests concrete ideas for amending the Prepaid Card Law (Iwahara, S., 2005[32]). Some practitioners argue that the government should divide the Prepaid Card Law into a part regulating electronic records and another part regulating all other prepaid vouchers, and establish new legislation covering electronic money. In order to determine ideal regulations, it is necessary to take into consideration point-based reward programs and Server-managing type services especially (Maeda, Y., 2005[33]).

In addition, establishing and amending legislation in response to the expansion of the online payment service business may grant legal legitimacy to non-financial institutions entering into the general payment business, including the online payment business. Some existing financial institutions, including banks, are not in favor of such expansion, and it will take a great deal of time to introduce radical regulations dealing with electronic money. The need for regulations protecting consumers is urgent, however, and therefore it seems reasonable to develop such regulations prior to other regulations.

EXTENDED RESEARCH I: REAL MONEY TRADE

Why do We Need to Examine the Possibility of Application to RMT?

An employee of an online game management company created virtual currency within an online game without proper authority, and obtained unjust profits that amounted to tens of millions.[34] The Ministry of Economy, Trade and Industry requested online game management industry to take a precaution. It is not yet clear whether the Ministry of Economy, Trade and Industry will establish a new regulation system involving virtual currency, introduce new guidelines, or suggest self-regulation by the online game management industry.

In November 2006, a foreign resident in Japan who sent 100 million yen to China without the proper certification was arrested and charged with being part of an RMT agency business. It is generally said that RMT broker payments should be regulated to some extent.

RMT Broker

RMT means exchanges of data corresponding to items and virtual currency in online games and user accounts in online games with assets, mostly real currency, in the real world. An RMT broker offers such services as mediating deals, escrow services for sale prices of items, buying items from sale candidates, and selling them to purchase candidates, and so forth.

Possibility of Regulations on RMT Broker

Service to be Examined

Among the various online payment services that use an RMT broker, the most likely to be regulated are escrow services, as they mediate money transfers between users who wish to purchase data or accounts and users who wishes to sell them.

Regulations by Public Laws Such as the Banking Law

Because the mentioned escrow service retains funds temporarily, there is a possibility that such services will be against the Deposit Law. Moreover, any payment between a purchase candidate who is the user of an online game, and a sale candidate may be against the Banking Law. The arguments in previously mentioned "online escrow service" apply here as well.

Foreign Payments: Money Laundering

An RMT broker is comparable to an Electronic Money entrepreneur in respect of the possible application of money laundering-related regulations. However, unlike with general Electronic Money, RMT brokers in Japan are numerous and are relatively small-scale, and their services are limited to the specific player with which a user is also engaged in RMT. If it is revealed later that the broker was temporarily used for money laundering purposes, it is more probable that a court will judge that the RMT broker recognized the fact that their service was used for money laundering at that time.

Domestic Deployment of Online Game Which Features Conversion Virtual Currency to Real Money

When an online game which can perform General Cashability into the currency of the real world from currency in a game is developed for Japan, the converting service concerned examines the possibility of conflicting with public law regulations in Japan.[35] As mentioned, even when the concerned online game management entrepreneur does not have a base in Japan, since the laws protecting consumer may be applied, they must be considered.

A user can purchase currency in a game, and can sell and buy within the game using such currency. Since dealing within a game remains directly in the currency of the game, and the likelihood of violating the Banking Law is not very high, the possibility that the game will be against the Deposit Law regarding subscription cannot be denied, depending on the system of structuring fund transfers and conversions into and from virtual currency.

EXTENDED RESEARCH II: POINT-BASED REWARDS PROGRAMS AND MILEAGE PROGRAMS

Spread of Point-Based Rewards Programs and Mileage Programs

Recently, the things to be provided for free under a points-based rewards program, air miles, and so forth, have become widespread and are similar to electronic money in having monetary value. When a consumer purchases goods and services, an entrepreneur gives the user points at no cost, and the consumer can use these points to purchase goods and services from the same entrepreneur later. Mileage is monetary value which an airline gives to the user using one of its airplanes.

The point-based reward system has conventionally only been used for purchasing goods and service from the entrepreneur who issued the points. Increasingly, however, many issuers of points and Mileage are forming business partnerships and these monetary value systems have become more versatile. In response to the expansion of this versatility, it will also be necessary to consider the application of public law regulations on Electronic Money to point-based or mileage systems.

Discussions So Far

The Prepaid Card Law does not apply to point-based or mileage systems, as an entrepreneur delivers points or miles to consumers at no cost, that is, accumulating points is not prepayment (FSA, 2004a[36]).

Subjects to be Studied Towards in the Future

Points and miles are property rights exchangeable for goods or services. If a holder expects their points or miles to become more versatile, the necessity for consumer protection may arise (Sugiura, N., 2003[37]). In recent years especially, when an entrepreneur offers a points with high trade-in value as an incentive for consumers to buy, consumer purchasing increases, and the points become more valuable. If different point-based rewards programs become more closely associated, versatility will increase considerably in the future. It may thus become necessary to consider the regulations from the viewpoint of consumer protection.

The excessive regulations may be cumbersome for small-scale retail stores, and such stores may be forced to discontinue point-based reward systems (Maeda, S., 2005[38]). The author's opinion is that such regulations may apply only to services that issue points or Mileage with a certain level of versatility, hold a certain amount of non-consumed monetary value in their system, or are regarded as currency-like by the public. Whether or not a service is regarded as currency-like may depend on various characteristics, including how long issued points or Mileage are available after issuance and further versatility obtained through different issuers' partnerships. Regarding the amount of non-consumed monetary value, it seems rational to set criteria much higher than the number indicated by the Prepaid Card Law because many issued points and Mileage could very possibly expire.

FUTURE RESEARCH DIRECTIONS

The Nomura Research Institute predicted that the economic market size of points and mileage issued by companies will be over 450 billion yen in the 2005 fiscal year (Nomura Research Institute, 2006b[39]). Since 2005, the institute has advocated a new concept: "business currency issued by private companies" including points and mileage broadly and has urged establishing new legislations for "private currency" including consumer protection (Nomura Research Institute, 2006a[40]). However, such new legislation is likely to impose excessively burdensome and unnecessary costs on points and mileage systems. Points and mileage are essentially a part of the promotional activities of private companies and excessive burdens may unfairly constrain those commercial activities. The FSA does not seem to have taken a positive view of this new concept either.

One related interesting theme in the near future is how to resolve the issues of virtual economic transactions such as Second Life in relation to existing financial and consumer-protecting regulations. As stated, there are many legal uncertainties regarding economic activities in Second Life (Nakazaki, T., 2007b, 2007c, 2007d[41]). The FSA seems interested in these issues. These issues include taxation issues, online gambling regulations, general consumer protection regulations, and promoting regulations other than ones related to the legal issues discussed so far in this chapter.

Another theme is how to deal with virtual property, including intellectual property. In the U.S., there are several famous full-fledged published discussions on laws related to this latter theme (Lemley, M. A., 2002; Wu, T., 2003; Grimmelmann, J. T. L., 2004; Fairfield, J., 2005[42]). Of course, Japanese legislation based on the civil law system differs very much from U.S. legislation based on the common law system. However, Japan also needs to determine how to apply existing legislation and regulations on physical property to virtual property, and should consider the experience of the U.S.

Furthermore, the Japanese government is continuing to introduce a new system of electronic registration of accounts receivable, which will enable businesses to assign accounts receivable electronically, (the "Electronically Registered Receivables" *[Denshi Touroku Saiken]*). This new system is originally designed for B2B businesses, not B2C businesses such as Electronic Money. It has been pointed out that this new system may be used as a method of issuing Electronic Money. However, the report published by the Working Group on Information Technology Innovations and Financial Systems, Sectional Committee on Financial Systems of Financial System Council to the public entitled "Towards the Establishment of an Electronically Registered Receivables Law (provisional name): Focusing on Approaches to the Establishment of an Electronically Registered Receivables Management Body" in December, 2006, clearly stated that it is unlikely that the new system may be used as a method of issuing Electronic Money (FSA, 2007[43]). In design, an amendment to or a replacement of the Electronic Money regulations, the Electronically Registered Receivables system ought to be considered.

REFERENCES

FSA. (2004a). *Financial Advisory Agency No Action Letter of April 20, 2004 to Barclay Vouchers K.K.* Retrieved March 15, 2007 from http://www.fsa.go.jp/common/noact/kaitou/001/001_06b.pdf

FSA. (2004b). *Financial Advisory Agency No Action Letter of July 9, 2004 to K.K. Daiichi-Bussan.* Retrieved March 15, 2007 from http://www.fsa.go.jp/common/noact/kaitou/001/001_08b.pdf

FSA. (2006). *June 2006 newsletter in English* (pp.2-3). Retrieved March 15, 2007 from http://www.fsa.go.jp/en/newsletter/2006/06a.html#01

FSA. (2007). *March 2007 newsletter in English* (pp.23-25). Retrieved March 15, 2007 from http://www.fsa.go.jp/en/newsletter/2007/02.pdf

Fairfield, J. (2005). Virtual property. *Boston University Law Review, 85*, 1047-1102.

Fujiike, T. (2002). Public regulations on settlement services by operating companies, i.e., not financial institutions. *Kinyu-houmu-jij, 1631*, 19-26. Tokyo: Kinzai.

Grimmelmann, J. T. L. (2004). Virtual worlds as comparative law. *New York Law School Law Review, 47*, 147-184.

Hiramatsu, M. (2006). The urgency of protecting electronic money users: issues related to prepaid electronic payments on the internet. *Kinyu-zaisei-jijo, 2708*, 18-21. Tokyo: Kinzai.

Iwahara, S. (2003). *Electronic payment and legislation* (p. 594). Tokyo: Yuhikaku.

Iwahara, S. (2005). The ideal future of regulations on electronic money. In The First Subgroup of the Study Group on the Financial System of the Japanese Bankers Association (Zenginkyo). *E-money legislation* (pp. 68-76). Tokyo: Zenginkyo.

Kodaira, Y. (2006). The urgency of protecting electronic money users: Japanese government has to develop legislation in anticipation of electronic money issuer's bankruptcy. *Kinyu-zaisei-jijo, 2708*, 22-25. Tokyo: Kinzai.

Kubota, T. (2003). *Legal issues related to fund settlement systems*. Tokyo: Kokusai-shoin.

Lastowka, F. G., & Hunter, D. (in press). The laws of the virtual worlds. *California Law Review*.

Lemley, M. A. (2002). Place and cyberspace. *California Law Review, 91*, 521-549.

Maeda, Y., Kanda, H., Morishita, T., Maeda, S., & Iwahara, S. (2005). *E-money legislation*. Tokyo: Zenginkyo.

Ministry of Finance. (1998). *The second electronic money round-table conference report*. Retrieved March 15, 2007, from http://www.fsa.go.jp/p_mof/singikai/kinyusei/tosin/1a1202.htm

Ministry of Finance. (1997). *The first electronic money round-table conference report*. Retrieved

March 15, 2007, from http://www.fsa.go.jp/p_mof/singikai/kinyusei/tosin/1a1201.htm

Nakazaki, T. (2007a). Anti-money laundering laws of Japan. *Anti-money laundering International law and practice.* pp. 680-701. London: Wiley & Sons.

Nakazaki, T. (2007b). *Converting in-game currency in U.S. Dollars at "Second Life" - is this violating the investment law?* Retrieved March 15, 2007, from http://www.itmedia.co.jp/bizid/articles/0702/15/news109.html

Nakazaki, T. (2007c). *Will a game contest offering big money prizes in the virtual world constitute an illegal gamble?* Retrieved March 15, 2007, from http://www.itmedia.co.jp/bizid/articles/0703/16/news046.html

Nakazaki, T. (2007d). *Will real money trading be a legitimate business?* Retrieved March 15, 2007, from http://www.itmedia.co.jp/bizid/articles/0701/26/news008.html

Nomura Research Institute. (2006a). *Business currency in 2010.* Tokyo: Toyo Keizai Inc.

Nomura Research Institute. (2006b). *Estimates for nine major industries in Japan for the 2005 fiscal year.* Retrieved March 15, 2007, from (http://www.nri.co.jp/english/news/2006/060816.html

Sugiura, N. (2003). Legal issues related to point-based rewards programs. *Kinyu-zaisei-jijo, 2561,* 41. Tokyo: Kinzai.

Sugiura, N., & Kataoka, Y. (2003). *Future Electronic Money and its legal infrastructure* (p.38). Retrieved March 15, 2007, from http://www.fsa.go.jp/frtc/seika/discussion/2003/20030828-2.pdf

Working Group on Information Technology Innovations and Financial Systems under the Sectional Committee on Financial System of the Financial System Council of the Financial Services Agency. (2006). *The chairman memorandum "Issues facing the development of new electronic payment services."* Retrieved March 15, 2007, from www.fsa.go.jp/news/newsj/17/20060426-5/01.pdf

Wu, T. (2003). When code isn't law. *Virginia Law Review, 89,* 101-170.

ADDITIONAL READING

Honda, M. (2001). Legislation on transferring financial assets. *Minshouhou-zasshi, 123,* 811-865.

Hori, H., Rokugawa, H., & Fujiike, T. (2001). Discussion on the legal framework for internet escrow settlements. *NBL,* 707, 29-39. Tokyo: Yuhikaku.

Iida, K. (1998). Brief summary and current situation of electronic money. *Jiyuu-to-seigi, 49*(3), 108-119. Tokyo: Japan Federation of Bar Assosication.

Ishikawa, T. (2006). The urgency of protecting electronic money users: issues related to prepaid electronic payments on the Internet. *Kinyu-zaisei-jijo, 2708,* 13-17. Tokyo: Kinzai.

Iwahara, S. (2007). Legal issues related to private laws on electronic money. *Future prospects of merchant law.* Tokyo: Shouji-houmu.

Kataoka, Y., & Seki, T. (1998). Legal issues related to public laws on electronic money. *Kinyu-houmu-jijo, 1503,* 38-44. Tokyo: Kinzai.

Kawamura, S. (1998). Diversification of settlements and predicted future of financial regulations. *Japan Research Review, 8,* 5-38.

Kubota, T. (2004). What is money? *Kinyu-houmu-jijo, 1702,* 9-19. Tokyo: Kinzai.

Maeda, Y., Iawahara, S., & Takeuchi, H. (1990). Discussion meeting: Legal issues related to prepaid cards. *Jurist, 951,* 18-33. Tokyo: Yuhikaku.

Masuda, S. (1998). Legal issues related to private laws on electronic money. *Kinyu-houmu-jijo, 1503*, 45-52. Tokyo: Kinzai.

Masuda, S., Iida K., & Uchiyama, R. (1998). P*ractice for electronic mone.* Tokyo: Shin-nihon-houki.

Morita, H. (1997). Legal framework for electronic money part I. *NBL, 616*, 6-12. Tokyo: Yuhikaku.

Morita, H. (1997). Legal framework for electronic money part II. *NBL, 617*, 23-30. Tokyo: Yuhikaku.

Morita, H. (1997). Legal framework for electronic money part III. *NBL, 619*, 30-37. Tokyo: Yuhikaku.

Morita, H. (1997). Legal framework for electronic money part IV. *NBL, 622*, 33-39. Tokyo: Yuhikaku.

Morita, H. (1997). Legal framework for electronic money part V. *NBL, 626*, 48-56. Tokyo: Yuhikaku.

Nomura Institute of Capital Markets Research. (1998). *A move towards the formulation of electronic money law.* Retrieved March 15, 2007, from http://www.nicmr.com/nicmr/report/repo/1998/1998aut07.pdf

Oguchi, H. (2002). The legal environment of electronic money. *IT Law Taizen*, pp.203-229. Tokyo: Nikkei BP.

Ozawa, T. (1997). Legal relations among electronic money transaction parties and loss allocation part I. *NBL, 623*, 6-12. Tokyo: Yuhikaku.

Ozawa, T. (1997). Legal relations among electronic money transaction parties and loss allocation part II. *NBL, 624*, 28-33. Tokyo: Yuhikaku.

Ozawa, T. (1997). Legal relations among electronic money transaction parties and loss allocation part III. *NBL, 625*, 39-48. Tokyo: Yuhikaku.

Shindou, K. (1998). Legal research intended for the realization of electronic money. *NBL, 640*, 6-39. Tokyo: Yuhikaku.

Sudou, O. (1997). The evolution of computer networks and related challenges. *Jurist, 1117*, 5-12. Tokyo: Yuhikaku.

Sugiura, N. (2004). The development of the legal infrastructure for electronic money. *Information Network Law Review, 3*, 68-95.

Tabuchi, T. (1996). Financial legal issues related to card-type electronic money. *Kinnyuu Torihiki Saisentan*, pp.3-14. Tokyo: Shouji-houmu.

Tachi, R. (1999). *Interim Report.* Retrieved March 15, 2007, from http://www.imes.boj.or.jp/japanese/zenbun99/kk18-3-1.pdf

Teramoto, S., Tanaka, Y., & Kunsen, G. (1997). Steps toward the practical use of electronic money part I. *NBL, 614*, 34-46. Tokyo: Yuhikaku.

Teramoto, S., Tanaka, Y., & Kunsen, G. (1997). Steps toward the practical use of electronic money part II. *NBL, 626*, 57-66. Tokyo: Yuhikaku.

Uchida, T., Kanda, H., & Dougauchi, M. (1997). *Discussion on private law sphere of Electronic Money.* Retrieved March 15, 2007, from http://www.imes.boj.or.jp/japanese/zenbun97/kk16-2-1.pdf

Yamana, N. (1998). Brief overview of the second electronic money round-table conference report. *Kinyu-houmu-jijo, 1523*, 56-60. Tokyo: Kinzai.

Yasui, T. (1997). Brief overview of the first electronic money round-table conference report. *NBL, 620*, 6-10. Tokyo: Yuhikaku.

Yasui, T. (1997). Brief overview of the first electronic money round-table conference report. *Kinyu-houmu-jijo, 1487*, 24-27. Tokyo: Kinzai.

Yasui, T. (1997). Brief overview of the first electronic money round-table conference report. *Jurist, 1117*, 120-125. Tokyo: Yuhikaku.

ENDNOTES

[1] I would like to thank Keiko Kaneko, a partner of Anderson Mori & Tomotsune (AM&T), for providing helpful comments. I am also grateful to Takaharu Totsuka, a legal associate, and Jonathan Ellison, a foreign legal clerk, of AM&T, for their assistance in preparing this article.

[2] The Working Group on Information Technology Innovations and Financial Systems under the Sectional Committee on Financial Systems of the Financial System Council of Financial Services Agency (2006). *The chairman memorandum "Issues facing the development of new electronic payment services."* Retrieved March 15, 2007, from www.fsa.go.jp/news/newsj/17/20060426-5/01.pdf (the "Chairman Memorandum")

[3] FSA. (2006). *June 2006 newsletter in English* (pp.2-3). Retrieved March 15, 2007, from http://www.fsa.go.jp/en/newsletter/2006/06a.html#01

[4] The first report was issued pursuant to "The round-table conference for Electronic Money and electronic payment" led by the Ministry of Finance (May 23, 1997). Retrieved March 15, 2007, from http://www.fsa.go.jp/p_mof/singikai/kinyusei/tosin/1a1201.htm

[5] The second report was issued pursuant to "The round-table conference for developing an environment for Electronic Money and electronic payment" led by the Ministry of Finance (June 17, 1998). Retrieved March 15, 2007, from http://www.fsa.go.jp/p_mof/singikai/kinyusei/tosin/1a1202.htm

[6] The FEL Article 6 (Definitions)
Item 1
(7) "Means of payment" shall mean any one of those instruments mentioned as follows:
(a) Banknotes, Treasury notes, notes of small denomination, and coins;
(b) Checks (including traveler's checks), bills of exchange, postal money orders, and letters of credit;
(c) Property values inputted in vouchers, electrical appliances or other instruments ......on electromagnetic system (electronic, magnetic or other systems that cannot be recognized by human perception) and which can be used for the payment among unspecified or a large number of persons (Limited to those whose usage circumstance is similar to that of currency as prescribed by a cabinet order).
(d) What corresponds to those mentioned in (a) and (b) as pre scribed in a cabinet order.
The Cabinet Order Article 2 (Definitions)
Item 1
(1) Promissory note (excluding the one coming under securities or instruments designated in the following paragraph)
(2) Of the one similar to either the one mentioned in Article, 6, paragraph 1, item (7)-(a) or item (7)-b of the Law or the one mentioned in the preceding item, the one which can be used for payments.

[7] Maeda, S. (2005). Regulations on electronic money. In The First Subgroup of the Study Group on the Financial System of the Japanese Bankers Association (Zenginkyo), *E-money legislation* (pp.48-67). Tokyo: Zenginkyo.

[8] Sugiura, N., & Kataoka, Y. (2003). *Future Electronic Money and its legal infrastructure* (p.38). Retrieved March 15, 2007, from http://www.fsa.go.jp/frtc/seika/discussion/2003/20030828-2.pdf

[9] The Chairman Memorandum; Iwahara, S. (2003). *Electronic payment and legislation* (pp.597, 599). Tokyo: Yuhikaku.

[10] Morishita, T. (2005). Electronic money in U.S. and Europe. In The First Subgroup of the Study Group on the Financial System of the Japanese Bankers Association (Zenginkyo), *E-money legislation* (pp. 18-47). Tokyo: Zenginkyo.

[11] Ms. Hiramatsu is the former chief of the research office of the planning division of the planning and coordination bureau of the Financial Services Agency. Hiramatsu, M. (2006). The urgency of protecting electronic money users: Issues of prepaid electronic payment on the Internet. *Kinyu-zaisei-jijo,* 2708, pp.18-21. Tokyo: Kinzai.

[12] Mr. Kodaira is the chief of the electronic payment service division in the innovative financial systems department of NTT Communications Corporation that issues Electronic Money under the name of "Cho-com." Kodaira, Y. (2006). The urgency of protecting electronic money users: Japanese government has to develop legislation in anticipation of electronic money issuer's bankruptcy." *Kinyu-zaisei-jijo,* 2708, pp.22-25. Tokyo: Kinzai.

[13] Chairman Memorandum; Kanda, H. (2005). The analysis of the first and second electronic money round-table conference reports. In The First Subgroup of the Study Group on the Financial System of the Japanese Bankers Association (Zenginkyo), *E-money legislation* (pp. 6-17). Tokyo: Zenginkyo; and Financial Supervisory Agency. *Points of concern for financial supervisory etc. guideline.* 3rd book, 5-1-1(1). Retrieved December 9, 2006, from http://www/fsa/go.jp/guide/guidej/kaisya/k005.hrml

[14] Please see 4.3.2 and 4.3.3 for details on these regulations. Iwahara, S. (2005). The ideal future of regulations on electronic money. In The First Subgroup of the Study Group on the Financial System of the Japanese Bankers Association (Zenginkyo), *E-money legislation* (pp. 68-76). Tokyo: Zenginkyo.

[15] Iwahara, S. (2003). *Electronic payment and legislation* (p.594). Tokyo: Yuhikaku.

[16] When providing service available in only one municipality, the capital must be not less than 10 million yen.

[17] Iwahara, S. (2005). The ideal future of regulations on electronic money. In The First Subgroup of the Study Group on the Financial System of the Japanese Bankers Association (Zenginkyo), *E-money legislation* (pp. 68-76). Tokyo: Zenginkyo.

[18] Maeda, Y. (2005). Ideal future legislation on electronic money. In The First Subgroup of the Study Group on the Financial System of the Japanese Bankers Association (Zenginkyo), *E-money legislation* (pp. 1-5). Tokyo: Zenginkyo. See also Iwahara, S. (2003). *Electronic payment and legislation* (p.596). Tokyo: Yuhikaku.

[19] The first report, "The round-table conference for Electronic Money and electronic payment" (May 23, 1997) concluded that the Bill and Similar Certificates Control Law would not apply to IC-chip type (pp.39-40). Retrieved March 15, 2007, from http://www.fsa.go.jp/p_mof/singikai/kinyusei/tosin/1a1201.htm

[20] Osaka District Court Judgment, September 14, 2001.

[21] FSA. (2004). Financial Advisory Agency No Action Letter of April 20, 2004 to Barclay Vouchers K.K. Retrieved March 15, 2007, from http://www.fsa.go.jp/common/noact/kaitou/001/001_06b.pdf and
FSA. (2004). Financial Advisory Agency No Action Letter of July 9, 2004, to K.K. Daiichi-Bussan. Retrieved March 15, 2007, from http://www.fsa.go.jp/common/noact/kaitou/001/001_08b.pdf

[22] Iwahara, S. (2003). *Electronic payment and legislation* (pp.596). Tokyo: Yuhikaku.
Mr. Fujiike, on the other hand, has suggested that Electronic Money will fall within he definition of "exchange transactions" only if is has both General Cashability and versatility together. This conclusion is realistic, however, the reasons why both the elements are necessary in order for Electronic Money to be classified as "exchange transactions"

are not clear. Fujiike, T. (2002). Public regulations on settlement services by operating companies, that is, not financial institutions. *Kinyu-houmu-jijo*. 1631, pp.19-26, Tokyo: Kinzai.

23. Nakazaki, T. (2007). Anti-money laundering laws of Japan. In *Anti-money laundering International law and practice*, pp. [uncertain, to be published by the end of March]. London: Wiley & Sons.

24. Kubota, T. (2003). *Legal issues related to fund settlement systems* (pp.179-208). Tokyo: Kokusai-shoin.

25. Please see the definition at the section A of "Existing Regulations on Electronic Money—Part III—Cashability—the Deposit Law."

26. Kubota, T. (2003). *Legal issues related to fund settlement systems* (p.191). Tokyo: Kokusai-shoin.

27. Kubota, T. (2003). *Legal issues related to fund settlement systems* (p.194). Tokyo: Kokusai-shoin.

28. Concretely speaking, Item 2, Paragraph 6, Article 7 of the new rule would be the point.

29. Kubota, T. (2003). *Legal issues related to fund settlement systems* (p.192). Tokyo: Kokusai-shoin.

30. Kubota, T. (2003). *Legal issues related to fund settlement systems* (p.193). Tokyo: Kokusai-shoin.

31. E-gold is one of famous worldwide e-currency companies and provides multinational online payment service backed up by gold and other metals. For more details, please visit the following URL: http://www.e-gold.com/

32. Iwahara, S. (2005). The ideal future of regulations on electronic money. In The First Subgroup of the Study Group on the Financial System of the Japanese Bankers Association (Zenginkyo), *E-money legislation* (pp. 68-76). Tokyo: Zenginkyo.

33. Maeda, Y. (2005). Ideal future legislation on electronic money. In The First Subgroup of the Study Group on the Financial System of the Japanese Bankers Association (Zenginkyo), *E-money legislation* (pp. 1-5). Tokyo: Zenginkyo.

34. The game was "Ragnarok Online," one of the most popular multiplayer online role playing games in Japan.

35. For example, "Second Life" (www.secondlife.com) officially announced starting their service in Japanese from April 2007 early 2007.

36. FSA. (2004). *Financial Advisory Agency No Action Letter of April 20, 2004 to Barclay Vouchers K.K.* Retrieved March 15, 2007, from http://www.fsa.go.jp/common/noact/kaitou/001/001_06b.pdf

37. Sugiura, N. (2003). Legal issues related to point-based rewards programs. Kinyu-zaisei-jijo, No.2561, p.41. Tokyo: Kinzai. See also Sugiura, N., & Kataoka, Y. (2003). Future Electronic Money and its legal infrastructure (p.38). Retrieved March 15, 2007, from http://www.fsa.go.jp/frtc/seika/discussion/2003/20030828-2.pdf

38. Maeda, S. (2005). Regulations on electronic money. In The First Subgroup of the Study Group on the Financial System of the Japanese Bankers Association (Zenginkyo), *E-money legislation* (pp.48-67). Tokyo: Zenginkyo.

39. Nomura Research Institute. (2006). *Estimates for nine major industries in Japan for the 2005 fiscal year*. Retrieved March 15, 2007, from (http://www.nri.co.jp/english/news/2006/060816.html

40. Nomura Research Institute. (2006). *Business currency in 2010*. Tokyo: Toyo Keizai Inc.

41. Mr. Nakazaki. (2007). Three articles are listed as dealing with predictable legal issues arising from economic transactions in Second Life in one of the largest IT news portal Web sites in Japan, ITMediaBiz Web site (http://www.itmedia.co.jp/bizid/) as follows: Nakazaki, T. (2007). Will real money trading be a legitimate business? Retrieved

March 15, 2007, from http://www.itmedia.co.jp/bizid/articles/0701/26/news008.html; Nakazaki, T. (2007). *Converting in-game currency in U.S. Dollars at "Second Life"— is this violating the investment law?* Retrieved March 15, 2007, from http://www.itmedia.co.jp/bizid/articles/0702/15/news109.html; Nakazaki, T. (2007). *Will a game contest offering big money prizes in the virtual world constitute an illegal gamble?* Retrieved March 15, 2007, from http://www.itmedia.co.jp/bizid/articles/0703/16/news046.html

[42] Five articles are listed as follows: Lemley, M. A. (2002). Place and cyberspace. *California Law Review,* 91, pp.521-549;

Lastowka, F. G., & Hunter, D. The laws of the virtual worlds. *California Law Review,* forthcoming;

Wu, T. (2003). When code isn't law. *Virginia Law Review,* 89, pp.101-170;

Grimmelmann, J. T. L. (2004). Virtual worlds as comparative law. *New York Law School Law Review,* 47, pp.147-184;

Fairfield, J. (2005). Virtual property. Boston University Law Review, 85, pp.1047-1102.

[43] FSA. (2007). March 2007 newsletter in English (pp.23-25). Retrieved March 15, 2007, from http://www.fsa.go.jp/en/newsletter/2007/02.pdf

Chapter IX
Commodity Based Digital Currency:
A Legal Analysis

Evelyn Lim Meow Hoong
The Malaysian Institute of Chartered Secretaries and Administrators (MAICSA), Malaysia

ABSTRACT

Financial innovations bring new challenges and new risks besides advantages to the world of finance in cyberspace and in the real world. These innovations evolve alongside the development of cyberspace creating more e-business opportunities. One such innovation is digital currency. As cyberspace develops, this financial innovation allows more and more players into a formerly closed market of providing a medium of intrinsic purchasing power which was generally supplied by a nation's central bank in the form of money. What then, is the legal status of this digital currency in a nation?

INTRODUCTION

Digital currencies are denominations of intrinsic purchasing power medium that exist only in electronic information storage. Financial innovations such as digital currency bring new challenges and new risks besides advantages to the world of finance in cyberspace and in the real world. These innovations develop and evolve alongside the development of cyberspace creating more e-business opportunities.

As cyberspace develops, this financial innovation allows more and more players into a formerly closed market of providing intrinsic purchasing power medium which was generally supplied by a nation's central bank in the form of money. This poses a question, is this medium money?

This medium utilizes payment systems that are built over the Internet, and a need for supervisory and regulatory control arose as these innovations seem to defy the payment systems law of some countries. This need has spawned new e-business opportunities for creation of accreditation companies to evaluate digital currencies' providers. This chapter seeks to illuminate how far the supervisory and regulatory control over this industry.

Copyright © 2008, IGI Global, distributing in print or electronic forms without written permission of IGI Global is prohibited.

WHAT IS DIGITAL CURRENCY?

Digital currency is a term used by the researcher to refer to laissez-faire private virtual currencies or free banking concept virtual currencies that are used as medium of exchanges in cyberspace. There are three broad categories of digital currency—indexed based digital currency, asset or community based digital currency, and community digital currency. Index based digital currency is digital currency that does not have direct asset backing for its issuance, while asset or commodity based digital currency is backed by valuable assets or commodities for its issuance, and community based digital currency is the digitization of local currency concept, that is, Local Exchange Trading Systems.

What is Commodity Based Digital Currency?

Asset or commodity based digital currency, hereinafter will be abbreviated as CBDC, initially appeared in the Internet payment systems market in 1996 under the name e-gold. Since 1996, there are many companies issuing similar type of payment instrument established in cyberspace. E-gold is the brainchild of Douglas Jackson, an American physician.[1] This innovation is being used in the United States, Australia, Britain, and even Japan, to name some areas of usage. This type of payment system is run by non-bank private companies held by private individuals with no connection to any government.

Innovation such as CBDC assumes functions of money in cyberspace and challenges our traditional view of money. It modifies for use in cyberspace the old concept of commodity based receipt money, where receipts were given in exchange for gold held in deposit and these receipts are used to exchange for goods and services. CBDC issues payment instruments in exchange for gold held in trust by CBDC issuing companies.

Legal tender is monopolized by central banks or similar governmental institutions. In contrast, CBDC is found based on the notion of free banking and creation of money that is free from government monopoly. These non-bank private companies issue payment instrument or digital currency for use in their payment systems. They collect money in exchange for the denomination of intrinsic purchasing power medium that they supply and charge fees for the services they provide in administration and management of the medium. The issuance of CBDC type of digital currency must necessarily be supported by valuable assets or valuable commodities. This is the determining feature of this type of digital currency.

Capie (1999), an economic historian, noted that e-gold is an interesting development in cyberspace retail business, the gold industry, and free banking.[2] He advised that "It is important to be clear about what [e-payment] is."[3] Drawing from his advice, we need to be clear as to what e-payment is, what it does, what it cannot do, and why it is the way it is. To an ordinary user, he would say that one e-payment is the same as another. This is true insofar as to the functions they serve are concerned but not true in the area of legal rights, duties, and liabilities they carry due to differences in contractual set up of each e-payment.

Legal Concept of Money

CBDC is a medium of exchange but is not money, according to Mann's (1963) legal concept of money.[4] CBDC did not manage to qualify for even one out of the five criteria listed by Mann (1963). It is not a universal medium of exchange. It is not a chose in possession as well as a chose in action but only a chose in action. It does not come in certain denomination. It does not possess intrinsic purchasing power. Moreover, it is not a chattel created by law. Therefore, CBDC is not money and does not even come close to being called money. Although it emulates most features of money well, CBDC needs to contract with users/participants, some features of money that we have taken for granted—the feature of trustworthiness of money, the exclusion of user-to-user liability, and the privacy of transactions.

THE LEGAL STATUS OF CBDC

All titles of ownership and details of transfer transactions are necessarily handled by electronic means for CBDC. Digital currencies like CBDC are created to alleviate deficiencies of credit cards and bank related payment systems used in cyberspace. Credit cards and bank funds transfer payment methods still come with paper shuffling despite their transactions being electronically executed. For example, vendors need to mail paper transaction receipts to their acquirer in order to receive payments from the issuer. For banks that do not support Internet banking services, paper accounts statements are in use. Even for banks that offer Internet banking, there is still the option of requesting for paper accounts statement to be delivered to the account holder upon request. Further, collection of funds using through credit card payment method is sometimes slow. The use of bank funds transfer requires a lot of manpower to crosscheck and to confirm the payment by means of paper accounts statements or Internet banking. In contrast, digital currency increases the efficiency of Internet commerce where the transfers are immediately effective.

CBDC charges fees upon obtaining the currencies, exchange of the currencies, and seigniorage earned on the currencies in circulation. For CBDC, the transferee is charged a fee through deduction of fees from the amount received. CBDC further collects yearly maintenance fees for its operations from its users just like trust companies or may even be equated with warehouse rental fees.[5]

CBDC is convertible by way of a medium of exchange and through the conditional redemption clause or enforceable repurchase clause in their contracts with their users. As a medium of exchange, it can be convertible in two ways instead of one. The first way is by way of "spend" where users spend at merchants who accept e-gold as a medium of exchange, and the second way is through independent exchange services that sell e-gold for territorial currencies such as U.S. dollars, Canadian dollars, and so forth.

CBDC contracts come with conditional redemption.[6] The conditional redemption clause or enforceable repurchase clause is required to keep the risk of hyperinflation on the part of the issuer in check (Macintosh, K. L., 1998[7]). E-gold anticipates that if it is faced with a redemption request, it may be able to draw from its physical holding of assets held in trust, as the value of every issuance is 100% secured by assets held in trust of the same value.

CBDC is a commodity based currency in electronic form. CBDC is not based upon an abstract title to a commodity basket or an index as proposed under the Macintosh's (1998) "Global Electronic Currencies"[8] model (GEC) where GEC is a "digital promissory note" based on a basket of commodities or an index. Digital promissory note may be defined as a secure digital code attached to an electronically transmitted message from sender to receiver that signifies an unconditional promise made by the issuer of the digital code to pay absolutely and in any event, a certain sum of money either to, or to the order of, the receiver.

CBDC is a title, albeit in digital form, to commodity issued vis-à-vis real commodity held in trust.[9] CBDC is fully secured at all times by valuable commodity, such as gold, where the value of digital title is equivalent to the exact value of the physical valuable commodity claimed for. For example, the title in the property embodied in e-gold is a reference to gold held in trust. Historically, money existed in a similar form long ago when 'paper' receipt was issued for commodity money, normally gold held by sovereign, known as receipt money (Griffin, G. E., 1994[10]). This is the phase where commodity money such as gold is replaced by paper that represents ownership to commodity money.

CBDC type of digital currency may also be known as a payment system of "warehouse receipt for precious metals"(Macintosh, K. L., 2001[11]). The mechanism of the CBDC payment system incorporates the likeness of the commodities market. CBDC is a small commodity exchange by itself. It enables small investors to participate in the commodities market through the CBDC payment system by merely purchasing digital currency for use on the payment system without having to participate in existing large commodity exchanges. Depending on the commodity that the digital currency is based on, it is the commodity that is being traded in CBDC payment system/exchange. If it is based on gold, then gold is being traded by that CBDC payment system/exchange. Small investors purchase digital currency not for use as a medium of exchange but as an investment or store of value.

Since it is also a digital exchange, there is more flexibility in converting and managing the amount of digital currency held as long as users have access to the Internet. They are also not bound by commodity market time restrictions as long as there are independent service providers willing to sell or buy digital currency. Further, they are not bound by minimum amount restrictions of traditional commodity markets. In traditional markets, an investor needs to have access to a broker who is appointed to conduct transactions on his/her behalf. In contrast, there is no such need in the CBDC payment system. Therefore, it may be more convenient to participate in the digital currency payment system than to participate in traditional commodity exchanges.

CBDC brings commodities markets into your living room through cyberspace, with a difference. The difference is the degree of convertibility and transferability of the electronic title to assets or commodities held in trust. In other words, the uniqueness of this digital currency, as a medium of investment, is in its high degree of transferability or convertibility.

Another significant feature of the CBDC is that CBDC does not have an absolute unit of account. It is weighed out or set out in terms of national currencies as trade units to be used in the CBDC payment system.[12] If CBDC is gold based, this notion brings back the appealing gold standard that existed before the Bretton Woods system. CBDC might even be said to be similar to gold as a medium of exchange revisited instead, like the ancient times centuries ago, except that it need not be physically divided to be effective*.

Macintosh's (1998) GEC model proposes that the transnational unit of account need not be translated or calculated to be understood.[13] For this transnational unit of account to be effective it has to be legitimate and accepted by users. To have a legitimate transnational unit of account there would be government involvement. CBDC avoids this trap by not having any unit of account.

CBDC enables funds transfers which includes cross border funds transfers. For example, anyone may transfer their e-gold in whatever amount they like without fee, but the recipient will be charged a small fee (Smith, G., 2000[14]). CBDC competes with traditional bank-related funds transfers for domestic as well as cross border funds transfers. If there is only 'single world money' then, everywhere in the world everyone uses one type of money that can be used anywhere without having to go through foreign currency exchanges (Kindleberger, C. P., 1981[15]). Some analysts believe that a supranational currency or full dollarization will eliminate cross border transactions costs (Helleiner, E., 2003[16]). This may not be realized if supranational currency is still being used alongside some other territorial currencies. Exchange transactions between supranational currency and territorial currencies will still come with costs. Similarly, for exchanges from CBDC to some specified territorial currencies and vice versa, there are exchange costs depending on price difference fluctuations of territorial currencies to CBDC commodity.

The exclusion of liability is a taken for granted feature of money. This is the negotiability feature of money where the transfer is for the value and without notice of any defect of the title of the transferor. Due to the exclusion of liability in the user agreement, in the event of disputes between users, CBDC is transferable with or without another underlying obligation for goods or services. Since CBDC is not money but a product of a private company, this exclusion clause has to be expressly included in their contract with users.[17]

The structure of CBDC has yield surprising findings where it is found that CBDC adopts the structure of asset-based security and mainly revolves around the concept of bankruptcy remoteness. CBDC operates on an asset-backed security like machinery where a trust is being set up to manage pooled assets or commodities, securities are issued for funding the pooled assets where these securities are wholly secured by assets from the pool. CBDC issues digital currency for funding pooled assets or commodities and the digital currency is wholly secured by assets from the pool. These pooled assets are for securitization of the CBDC payment instrument and are held in trust for the benefit of CBDC users in general.[18]

Asset-backed security machinery is commonly run by a special-purpose entity or vehicle whose main business is to manage the pooled assets or commodities and ensure that the pooled assets or commodities are bankruptcy remote (Scott, H. S., & Wellons, P. A., 1999[19]). The special-purpose entity may be equated with the CBDC issuer who manages the pooled assets or commodities in relation to the issuance of CBDC.[20] This type of machinery revolves around central theme of bankruptcy remoteness. The responsibility to keep CBDC bankruptcy remote falls on its special purpose entity or issuer.

Bankruptcy remoteness is the essential theme of asset-backed security machinery where it reduces risks for its investors (Scott, H. S., & Wellons, P. A., 1999[21]). Efforts towards bankruptcy remoteness for CBDC could include setting up trusts for management of the pooled assets or commodities, preservation and enhancement of assets through contractual arrangements with independent third parties, and limitation of activities on CBDC companies, especially the issuer. CBDC companies should hold little or no debt or contingent liabilities associated to the assets held in trust.

The constitution of trusts is an essential structure of CBDC where it assures bankruptcy remoteness of this assets securitized digital currency. The involvement of an independent third party in the set up of CBDC trusts is equally important to ensure that there is no prejudice in management and handling of the trusts. The appointment of an independent third party escrow agent to handle physical assets or commodities of CBDC should be different from the trustee and will improve the integrity of CBDC trusts. By reducing the risk factor of CBDC, it would also attract more users to use CBDC and it would be an incentive for users to consider and use CBDC as a better alternative medium of exchange for their transactions.

The assets held under CBDC trust is generally for the benefit of CBDC users. Although CBDC uses the term "currency," in essence, legally it could instead be classified as a title to assets or commodities and a mere claim or even a warehouse receipt for assets or commodities held in trust. The trust settler is an issuer of CBDC and normally an independent third party or professional trust company may be appointed trustee of CBDC trusts. CBDC trusts are subjected to trust rules of the country in which they are created. This is where CBDC companies may exploit regulation arbitrage that exists in the world today to obtain the best possible solution for their cause.

There is no pre-labeled trustworthiness for either CBDC, unlike legal tender. Legal tender has territorial sovereign's backing and this gives the legal tender preconceived trustworthiness. Moreover, issues of transparency and third party auditing reporting have already been addressed in many legal tenders around the world through public reports in parliaments, congresses, or diets of some democracies. These features have been taken for granted though the results are often criticized. Every legal tender has its own standard ethics of transparency formalized through the legal framework and system of each territorial sovereign.

Similarly, transparency of digital currency operations will build confidence in users and should be done through voluntary self-disclosure efforts. High standard ethics of transparency should be made a required feature in private companies that deal with public service infrastructures. As CBDC and GEC are providing public infrastructure of medium of exchange, ethics of transparency should not be an option but should be made a requirement. Moreover, third party independent reporting for CBDC should also not be an option but a requirement. It would not be efficacious if independent third partys were employed by the company for advertising purposes as information published may be manipulated to make the company look more favorable than it actually is. Therefore, there should be supervision and regulation by territorial sovereigns over these companies on these issues.

SUPERVISORY AND REGULATORY CONTROL

At the time of this research, CBDC does not need to report its activities to any government and its main responsibility is towards its users only. In other words, CBDC is independent from any supervisory or regulatory authority in the world at this time (Smith, G., 2000[22]). Even "know your customer" background checks are not being enforced on CBDC. CBDC is currently not a designated payment system of any country nor is it a designated payment instrument of any country. Further, it is more difficult to supervise and regulate if CBDC is set up as an offshore private company, although efforts are being made in order to bring CBDC into the supervisory and regulatory radar of governments around the world.

It may be a matter of time before the CBDC type of businesses are brought within governments' radar as their operation grows (Smith, G., 2000[23]). For example, only reports of federal cash transactions of US$10,000 and above in cash are required according to the U.S. laws. Hence, any transactions or exchanges that do not involve U.S. dollars in cash are excluded from this reporting. CBDC users are excluded from this reporting requirement if they do not deal in U.S. dollar cash. If the government decides to extend its radars, then this requirement may be altered to say that all transactions of US$10,000 equivalent in any form must be reported.

The implementation of this regulation may be difficult on CBDC companies as they are non-bank companies and not financial institutions. These reports to Federal Reserve Banks are required from financial institutions; therefore, CBDC is exempted from this regulation. Furthermore, issues of money laundering abuse of CBDC and issues of consumer protection are not being properly addressed (Macintosh, K. L., 2001[24]). Efforts are being made towards bringing these non-bank companies into the supervisory and regulatory radar of the government though the approach differs from one government to another.

Due to the multinational nature of its structure, the complex web of the CBDC group of companies is free from political influences. The supply of CBDC is internally controlled by the issuer without regulation or supervision by any government in the world. Moreover, some analysts even believe it is difficult to regulate CBDC (Helleiner, E., 2003[25]). The individual companies in the CBDC group of companies are mobile. They may move their bases to exploit regulatory arbitrage for optimal operations with minimal or neither political nor governmental interferences. This amounts to the effort of reducing political risks based on the concept of bankruptcy remoteness.

CBDC competes with territorial currencies of the world as well as other payment systems providers to begin with.[26] CBDC is also based on the free market concept in its set up where merchants, exchange service centers, organizations, and private individuals are among users of this CBDC.[27] Further, most exchange service centers exist independently from the CBDC group of companies. They compete amongst each other for business without any interference from the CBDC issuer or group of companies and they even compete with the exchange service provider that is owned by the CBDC group of companies. The independent exchange services offer exchange between national currencies and e-gold.[28] These exchange services offer conversion from selected national or supranational currencies to e-gold and vice versa.[29]

The CBDC model is set up as a group of companies with each company performing different functions but sharing the same goal of maintaining their CBDC payment system. CBDC weaves itself around legal complexities and exists on a platform of trusts and legal entities to minimize physical, legal, and political risks. Moreover, CBDC does not limit itself to issuance of only one currency, that is, one issuer may issue more than one commodity backed CBDC within its stables.[30]

This is a paperless trust-structured commodity based digital instrument. Even though it is not a unit of account, it is convertible and capable of cross border funds transfers. This private service that collects fees for their usage is built up of a complex web of trusts and entities. CBDC strive to limit risk-taking activities, to have high ethics of transparency of operation and to practice a free market system. In short, CBDC is a payment system service that is uniquely set up to exist with minimum government and/or political influences over its activities.

CBDC is mainly used in cyberspace where CBDC replaces money for the purchase of goods and services from Internet merchants by its users, and the Internet merchants receive CBDC in exchange for their goods and services. They have made a niche in the Internet payment systems market by overcoming time constraints that are associated with credit cards and traditional electronic funds transfer services (Stankey, R. F., 1998; Macintosh, K. L., 2001[31]). CBDC provides payment solutions to Internet merchants. These payment solutions are necessarily linked to Internet merchants' point of sales systems also known as POS systems for effective value transfer.

In some instances, CBDC may be used outside cyberspace, for instance, paying of bills and transferring funds across borders, that is, a user in Canada may use CBDC to pay a non-user bill collector or a non-user beneficiary in Japan through independent exchange service providers physically located in Japan, who offer such services. The extent of CBDC being used outside cyberspace is at present still a novel feature yet to be explored.

CBDC places itself at the far end of the definition of legal tender and seems to defy laws of some countries, especially countries where there are payment system laws to supervise and regulate payment systems like in Malaysia and Australia. CBDC seems to challenge laws of some countries, especially countries where there are payment system laws to supervise and regulate payment systems like in Malaysia. Malaysia has recently enacted the Payment Systems Act (2003) to supervise and regulate payment systems in use by Malaysian residents including those found in cyberspace. Stringent requirements, supervision, and regulations prevail in this closely monitored market.

Payment systems, payment instruments, and financial instruments have always been within the ambit of central banks, stock market exchanges, commodities exchanges, and their related agents. As cyberspace develops, non-related agents are able to participate in this formerly closed market through innovations like digital currency. In order to prevent as well as to settle disputes, market supervision and regulations are required to ensure fair competition amongst players in the market, to prevent and remedy abuses, to ensure consumer protection, to prevent and remedy disasters from systemic risks, to prevent and control criminal activities in the market, and to remedy dysfunctional areas in the market.

E-gold Ltd. is classified as a virtual Point of Sales non-bank e-money issuer by the ePayment Systems Observatory (also known as ePSO), a project of the Institute for Prospective Technological Studies, an institute of the European Commission's Directorate General Joint Research Centre.[32] However, the researcher is wary of using the term e-money as this term is viewed normally in relation to legal tender denominated payment instruments, such as virtual wallets or electronic purses, which have relatively different contractual terms of use from CBDC.

Traditionally, banking institutions are the main users for systemically important payment systems in a nation and the main movers of large aggregate or large value transactions in the systemically important payment systems. Innovations like the e-money and digital currency have altered the borders of traditional financial markets and even global financial markets (Abdul Razak, A., 2001[33]). The increase in the use of Internet commerce proportionately increases the use of electronic payment systems. New types of Internet based electronic systems appeared as non-bank financial service providers. These alterations have brought evolved risks as well as new risks (Abdul Razak, A., 2001[34]). The needs for new legal framework arose in consequence to these alterations.

The core systems are what the Committee for the Payment and Settlement Systems (CPSS) of the Bank for International Settlements named as systemically important payment systems. These are the systems that constitute the main heart and arteries of an economy. The CPSS stresses the need to protect these systems from risks, especially risks transmitted via the system. If there is a failure occurring in any part of these systems, it might cause a collapse of the economy as a whole. Controlled competition for payment systems promotes safety of payment systems (Mortlock, G., 1999[35]). CDBC being competing payment systems belong to what is known as fringe payment systems. They do not pose direct risks to the core payment systems of a nation.

Non-bank corporations should be allowed to operate competing payment systems, but entry and exit as well as operations are supervised and regulated (Mortlock, G., 1999[36]). Depending on the level of risk carried by each type of payment system, the level of stringency of control differs accordingly. The higher the risk carried by the payment system, the more stringent is the control through supervision and regulation. The CBDC seems to hold a low level of risk in their payment system.

Payment systems are normally required to maintain a certain level of ex-ante and ex-post crisis management measures to alleviate the risks posed by their participation in the systems.

Generally, ex-ante crisis management measures delineate rights and obligations of every stakeholder in the systems as well as supervisory and regulatory requirements for prevention of crisis and to ensure the smooth running of payment systems. CBDC uses contractual relationships to establish the rights and obligations of every stakeholder in their payment system.

On the other hand, ex-post crisis management measures are failure-to-settle mechanisms (Mortlock, G., 1999[37]). This is the fire-brigade section of crises management of financial systems. Failure-to-settle mechanisms may be fail safe mechanisms, market intervention mechanisms, and/or mechanisms for seeking redress. The quick reaction of central banks as supervisors of a financial system may arrest any crisis that may arise from systemic influence. If reaction is required from the central bank, but the arms of the central bank can not be extended beyond their stated authority to arrest systemic failure occurring in some part of the financial system, then the risks will not be abated. In line with the trend of a market-oriented financial sector, powers of central banks need to be extended and enhanced to cope with changes. CBDC uses contractual obligations to control this risk. They included a clause for irreversibility of e-gold transactions to avoid the failure-to settle risk in their payment systems.

Cyberspace is fresh grounds for crimes; payment systems may contain fruits of a crime, be used in a crime, or be target of a crime. Formerly, crimes involving paper money or legal tender—such as fraudulent notes circulation, and crimes involving hard cash transfers—such as cash-in-transit robberies. If these were translated in cyberspace terminology, crimes involving digital currency would be password theft, fraudulent authentication and fraudulent transfers; and crimes involving value transfers would be fraudulently intercepted and redirected transfers to persons other than the intended parties. There are risks of criminals using technology to eliminate evidence of crimes committed; to commit fraud, cyber laundering, and other cyber crimes as well as those mentioned. Generally, supervision and regulation of payment systems have to take these issues into consideration besides having to promote efficient and secure payment systems, to check authenticity of payment systems and to ensure consumer protection.

Due to their inclination to be free from government interventions, CBDC has to fight the crimes that pose a direct threat to the integrity of their payment systems themselves. As for crimes that do not pose a direct threat to the integrity of their payment systems as being used as a medium for con-artists or a medium for money laundering, CBDC has the right to decide if they are willing to put in the mechanisms to prevent these activities or not. Criminal laws are basically very territorial in nature. It may be a crime in some countries and not a crime in others. CBDC being a truly virtual global medium of exchange for intrinsic purchasing power, would be onus on the territorial sovereigns to decide if CBDC has to adhere to their criminal laws or not.

CBDC such as e-gold exchange companies are seen to be very cooperative with financial authorities where the e-gold exchange centers for Australian dollars were voluntarily shut down as they do not hold the Australian Financial Services License to operate their business.[38] Although the Australian e-gold exchange is shut down, the users are still able to utilize their e-gold at other exchange centers until such a time when the Australian Securities and Investments Commission would issue a license to the exchange operators. CBDC faces this challenge in order to operate globally.

CONCLUSION

There is a need for public supervision of coordination among private and public payment systems as technological innovations increase. Private entities should be left free to experiment and come up with innovations. This creative freedom should be unrestricted. Although public sector authorities need to examine innovations as they are put into the market to prevent injury to the public by way of fraud, unfair terms of contract, hidden clauses, and other such abuses, will be a very great challenge to public sector authorities as CBDC is operating virtually and globally. One other way is to solve this by way of international law where private treaties or contracts be made directly with CBDC and the territorial sovereigns. As for parties involved in transactional contracts with CBDC issuers and exchange centers, whose rights are being breached, may need to settle their disputes in arbitration centers or through direct negotiations with the counterparties.

Future Research Directions

The researcher is currently looking into financial innovations in cyberspace that facilitates e-commerce and the legal implications of such innovations, how private and public entities collaborate or not in mobilizing financial innovations such as digital currency and frauds involving financial innovations in cyberspace. Regarding digital currency, future research should include reference to new types of e-money (see Chapter VIII). As for frauds and cybersecurity, please refer to Chapter I.

REFERENCES

Abdul Razak, A. (2001). The payment and settlement systems in Malaysia. In M.L. Torreja, Jr. (Ed.), *The payment and settlement systems in the SEACEN countries* (Vol. 2, pp. 105-162). Kuala Lumpur: The SEACEN Centre.

Capie, F. (1999, November 19). Strength and weakness of the international monetary system. In *Proceedings of the Conference on Gold and the International Monetary System in a New Era* (pp. 25-26). Paris: World Gold Council.

Griffin, G. E. (1994). *The creature from Jekyll Island—A second look at federal reserve.* [Review in Idaho Observer, June 2003]. Westlake Village, CA: American Media (pp. 133-170). Retrieved November 9, 2003, from http://proliberty.com/observer/20030603.htm

Hayek, F. (1990). *The denationalisation of money—The argument refined* (3rd ed.). London: Institute for Economic Affairs.

Helleiner, E. (2003). *The making of national money: Territorial currencies in historical perspective.* Ithaca: Cornell University Press.

Kindleberger, C. P. (1981). *International money, a collection of essays.* London: George Allen & Unwin Ltd.

Konvisser, J. B. (1997). Note: Coins, notes and bits: The case for legal tender on the Internet. *Harvard Journal of Law & Technology, 10,* 327-328,37.

Macintosh, K. L. (1998). How to encourage global electronic commerce: The case for private currencies on the Internet. *Harvard Journal of Law & Technology, 11*(3), 733-796.

Macintosh, K. L. (2001, January 5). Electronic cash—More questions than answers. Proceedings of the Association of American Law Schools, Annual Meeting held in San Francisco, Section on Law and Computers. *Boston University Journal of Science and Technology Law, 7,* 214-218.

Mann, F. A. (1963). *The legal aspect of money, with special reference to comparative, private and public international law* (2nd ed. reprint). Oxford: Clarendon Press.

Mortlock, G. (1999). *An assessment of the causes of financial instability and possible policy solutions* (Occasional Papers No.30). Kuala Lumpur: The SEACEN Centre.

Scott, H. S., & Wellons, P. A. (1999). *International finance: Transactions, policy, and regulation* (6th ed.). New York: Foundation Press.

Smith, G. (2000, April 3). Would global crisis make e-gold glitter? *BusinessWeek Online,* E.Biz: Perspective. Retrieved October 16, 2003, from http://www.businessweek.com/ebiz/0004/ep0403.htm

Stankey, R. F. (1998). Internet payment systems: Legal issues facing businesses, consumers and payment service providers. *CommLaw Conspectus, 6,* 11-15.

ADDITIONAL READINGS

Iwahara, S. (2003). *Denshi Kessai to Hou (Electronic payment and law).* Tokyo: Yuhikaku Publishing Co., Ltd.

Maruthavanar, K. (2000). Banking laws in Malaysia: The path to the future. *Journal of Malaysian and Comparative Law, 27*(1-2), 181-205.

Mayer, M. (2001). *The FED: The Inside story of how the world's most powerful financial institu-*

tion drives the markets. New York: The Free Press.

Ritter, L. S., & William, L. S. (1977). *Principles of money, banking, and financial markets.* New York: Basic Books.

Scott, H. S. (2004). *International finance: Law and regulation.* London: Thomson, Sweet & Maxwell.

Wardrop, A. (2004). Credit card regulation, interchange fees and the meaning of "payment system" in Australia. *Journal of International Banking Law and Regulation, 3,* 68-80.

ENDNOTES

[1] See e-gold Corporate History Web page, Available from http://www.e-gold.com/unsecure/aboutus.html, accessed November 02, 2004.

[2] Capie, F. (1999). "Strength and Weakness of the International Monetary System," in Gold and the International Monetary System in a New Era: Proceeding of the Conference held in Paris on November 19, 1999 by World Gold Council (Paris: World Gold Council, 1999), 25-26; Available from http://www.gold.org/sp_archive/pdf/parisconf.pdf, accessed November 11, 2004.

[3] *Ibid.* Capie, F. (1999) used the word electronic money in his advice. As the definition of electronic money is very general, the researcher changed the word "electronic money" into "e-payments" without a change in meaning to his advice.

[4] Mann, F.A. (1963). *The Legal Aspect of Money, with Special Reference to Comparative, Private and Public International Law* 2nd ed reprint. Oxford: Clarendon Press, 3-26.

[5] With an e-gold subscription, the user may hold as much e-gold as they want subjected to a yearly fee of 1% of the value of the holding what e-gold calls the Agio Fee. See e-gold fees Web page. Available from http://www.e-gold.com/unsecure/fees.htm, accessed June 30, 2004.

[6] For whatever reason, the user may exercise their right to redeem e-gold for the delivery of certified good delivery bullion bars under conditions specified under item 3.3 of the User Agreement (Appendix 1) except if the account of user is frozen under item 4.6.1 of the same agreement. The conditions attached to redemption covers specified redemption medium, threshold redemption quantity, shipping/handling and premium attached to the redemption.

[7] Macintosh, K.L. (1998). How to Encourage Global Electronic Commerce: the Case for Private Currencies on the Internet. *Harvard Journal of Law & Technology 11,* no.3 (Summer 1998): 752.

[8] Supra note 7, 739-777.

[9] e-gold is claimed by the founders as "an electronic currency 100% backed at all times by gold bullion in allocated storage repositories certified by the London Bullion Market Association." See e-gold Better money Web page. Available from http://www.e-gold.com/unsecure/qanda.html, accessed May 26, 2004. See also e-gold Examiner Web page. Available from http://www.e-gold.com/examiner.html, accessed June 30, 2004; e-gold's current total gold holdings as of June 30, 2004 is around 1,710 kilograms of gold valued at USD$12.642 per gram makes an equivalent to about USD$21.6 million in gold assets alone. See e-gold Examiner Web page. Available from http://www.e-gold.com/examiner.html, accessed June 30, 2004. See also e-gold Exchange rates Web page. Available from http://www.e-gold.com/currentexchange.html, accessed June 30, 2004; It claimed to have a velocity of 191.7kg of gold equivalent to USD$2.4 million in circulation velocity per 24 hours. See e-gold Examiner Web page, available from http://www.e-gold.com/examiner.html, accessed June 30, 2004; As of June 30, 2004,

this is just a small fraction compared to the Clearing House Interbank Payments System (CHIPS) daily processing of gross value USD $1.37 trillion. See the Clearing House Interbank Payments System homepage. Available from http://www.chips.org/, accessed July 14, 2004.

[10] Griffin, G.E. (1994). *The Creature from Jekyll Island – A Second Look at Federal Reserve* (Westlake Village, CA: American Media, 1994) 133-170; review in Idaho Observer June 2003, available from http://proliberty.com/observer/20030603.htm, accessed November 09, 2003; G. Edward Griffin, interviewed by James J. Puplava, May 29, 2000 Financial Sense Online—Newshour's Ask the Expert, San Diego, CA. [audio file online] Available from http://www.financialsense.com/Experts/2002/Griffin.htm, accessed July 08, 2004.

[11] Macintosh, K.L (2001). "Electronic Cash – More Questions than Answers," in Section on Law and Computers: Proceedings of 2001 Annual Meeting held in San Francisco on January 5, 2001 by Association of American Law Schools, *Boston University Journal of Science and Technology Law 7*, (Summer 2001), 218. Macintosh (2001) calls e-gold a payment system of "warehouse receipts for precious metals."

[12] The e-gold payment system uses specified weights of gold and also terms of eight major currencies as the trade unit used in the payment system, in example "10 troy oz worth of e-gold", "5.3 grams worth of e-gold", "US$100.00 worth of e-gold" or "CHF685.88 worth of e-gold". See e-gold Better money Web page. Available from http://www.e-gold.com/unsecure/qanda.html (Accessed May 26, 2004)

[13] Supra note 7, 758.

[14] Smith, G. (2000). "Would Global Crisis Make E-Gold Glitter?" *BusinessWeek Online*, E.Biz: Perspective, April 3, 2000 [magazine on-line] Available from http://www.businessweek.com/ebiz/0004/ep0403.htm, accessed October 16, 2003. Just by using e-mail, an e-gold customer may be able to send value to another person, to pay bill or buy something off the Internet. "…Many customers are members of libertarian and antigovernment groups, lawyers specializing in privacy and offshore trusts, or small-business owners who don't like to pay credit-card fees…"; Each Spend transaction of e-gold, a maximum of 0.05 AUG (gram of gold) per transaction will be charged to the recipient. Calculated at the rate as of June 30, 2004 of 1 AUG is equivalent to USD $12.642, the cost is roughly at USD $0.63 per transaction compared to 4 or 5 % per credit card transaction. The rates are available from http://www.e-gold.com/currentexchange.html, accessed on June 30, 2004 and the fees are available from http://www.e-gold.com/unsecure/fees.htm, accessed June 30, 2004.; Clause 3.7 of the e-gold account user agreement (refer Appendix 1) ensure that privacy of the user is secured unless there is "order by court or arbitration body of acceptable jurisdiction."

[15] Kindleberger, C.P. (1981). *International Money, a Collection of Essays.* London: George Allen & Unwin Ltd, 9-23.

[16] Helleiner, E. (2003). *the Making of National Money: Territorial Currencies in Historical Perspective.* Ithaca: Cornell University Press, 227.

[17] In their contract agreement with the users of the payment instrument, the e-gold Account User Agreement, e-gold Ltd specifically excludes liability in case of any disputes that arise between users. E-gold especially cautions that they are not an escrow service provider in the Account User Agreement. They do not provide any guarantees regarding purchases made when using the e-gold service, whether on quality, safety or legality or the completion of the transaction transacted with e-gold. The e-gold Account User Agreement is attached as Appendix 1 for further reference. See e-gold Direc-

tory disclaimer Web page. Available from http://www.e-gold.com/unsecure/links.htm, accessed May 26, 2004; See e-gold Account User Agreement, Privacy Policy. Available from http://www.e-gold.com/unsecure/terms.htm, accessed June 30, 2004; refer Appendix 1 item 2.5.2.

[18] The intention for creation of the trust for e-gold may be found in their user account agreement (refer Appendix 1) under item 1.1; the e-gold account holders collectively are named beneficiaries in three documents—item 1.1 in the user account agreement (refer Appendix 1), item 2 in the escrow agent agreement (refer Appendix 2), and item 4.1 in e-gold declaration of trust (refer Appendix 3).

[19] Scott, H.S., & Wellons, P.A. (1999). *International Finance: Transactions, Policy, and Regulation,* 6th ed. New York: Foundation Press, 707.

[20] The trust for e-gold is named the e-gold Bullion Reserve Special Purpose Trust. (This special purpose trust declaration is attached in Appendix 3). The e-gold has the constitution of trust inbuilt into its structure. e-gold asserts that no bullion in the form of certified good delivery bars held in trust may be removed or disposed of without signatures of both an e-gold and a third party escrow agent. Appendix 2 shows the agreement between e-gold Ltd and the escrow agent. See e-gold Escrow Agent Agreement Web page. Available from http://www.e-gold.com/contracts/egold-bbsc.3.htm, accessed June 30, 2004. The third party escrow agent of e-gold only handles the certified good delivery of gold, silver, platinum, and palladium bars and not the exchanges of e-gold over the Internet.

[21] Supra note 19, 708-709.

[22] Smith, G. (2000). "Would Global Crisis Make E-Gold Glitter?" *BusinessWeek Online*, E.Biz: Perspective, April 3, 2000 [magazine on-line] Available from http://www.businessweek.com/ebiz/0004/ep0403.htm, accessed October 16, 2003.

[23] Smith, G. (2000). "Would Global Crisis Make E-Gold Glitter?" *BusinessWeek Online*, E.Biz: Perspective, April 3, 2000 [magazine on-line] Available from http://www.businessweek.com/ebiz/0004/ep0403.htm, accessed October 16, 2003.

[24] Macintosh, K.L. (2001). "Electronic Cash—More Questions than Answers," in Section on Law and Computers: Proceeding of 2001 Annual Meeting held in San Francisco on January 5, 2001 by Association of American Law Schools, *Boston University Journal of Science and Technology Law 7,* (Summer 2001), 218. The Uniform Money Services Act has been approved by the United States National Conference of Commissioners on Uniform State Laws in 2000. This Act tries to control non-bank money services businesses and requiring them to be licensed and regulated by the state governments.

[25] Helleiner, E. (2003). T*he Making of National Money: Territorial Currencies in Historical Perspective* (Ithaca: Cornell University Press, 2003), 224; e-gold aspires to be the 100% gold backed single world money in cyberspace which is free from any political encumbrances.

[26] E-gold embraced Hayek's posit for reintroduction of the gold standard to bring in a stable currency to compete with the territorial currencies which would discipline the governments because a rational man with his own free will would choose the most stable currency.

[27] See e-gold Directory Web page. Available from http://www.e-gold.com/unsecure/links.htm, accessed June 30, 2004.

[28] See e-gold Bettermoney Web page. Available from http://www.e-gold.com/unsecure/qanda.html, accessed May 26, 2004; The users have a choice from about twenty independent exchange service providers that covers some major currencies in the world and located in different parts of the world. See e-gold Directory Web page. Available from http://www.e-gold.com/unsecure/links.htm,

[29] accessed June 30, 2004. G&SR Inc. owns and operates a currency exchange service under another legal entity called OmniPay. See e-gold Corporate History Web page. Available from http://www.e-gold.com/unsecure/aboutus.html, accessed May 26, 2004.

[29] The rates are determined independently by the operators themselves. See e-gold Directory Web page. Available from http://www.e-gold.com/unsecure/links.htm, accessed June 30, 2004.

[30] The e-gold payment system is used for other commodity based currency as well, such as silver, platinum, and palladium. See e-gold Examiner Web page. Available from http://www.e-gold.com/examiner.html, accessed June 30, 2004.

[31] Stankey, R.F. (1998). "Internet Payment Systems: Legal Issues Facing Businesses, Consumers and Payment Service Providers," *CommLaw Conspectus 6*, (Winter 1998): 11-15; Konvisser, J.B. (1997) "Note: Coins, Notes and Bits: The Case for Legal Tender on the Internet," *Harvard Journal of Law & Technology 10*, (Winter 1997): 327-328, 337; Macintosh, K.L. (2001). "Electronic Cash— More Questions than Answers," in Section on Law and Computers: Proceeding of 2001 Annual Meeting held in San Francisco on January 5, 2001 by Association of American Law Schools, *Boston University Journal of Science and Technology Law 7*, (Summer 2001), 214-215.

[32] This categorization is inferred from the Categorised Search Web page of ePayment Systems Observatory, Available from http://www.jrc.es/cfapp/invent/index.cfm?level1=8&level2=13&level3=25, accessed November 09, 2004; Details of who ePayment Systems Observatory is, can be found from about ePSO Web page under the heading of Objective. Available from http://epso.jrc.es/, accessed November 09, 2004. The ePayment Systems Observatory project ended in February 2002.

[33] Abdul Razak, A. (2001). "The Payment and Settlement Systems in Malaysia," in *the Payment and Settlement Systems in the SEACEN Countries*, Vol. 2, ed. Magno L. Torreja, Jr. Kuala Lumpur: The SEACEN Centre, 143-144.

[34] Supra note 33, 144-145.

[35] Mortlock, G. (1999). *An Assessment of the Causes of Financial Instability and Possible Policy Solutions*, Occasional Papers No.30 Kuala Lumpur: The SEACEN Centre, 30.

[36] *Ibid.*

[37] Supra note 35.

[38] Australia Securities and Investments Commissions acts to shut down electronic currency trading Web sites.

[*] The e-gold payment system uses specified weights of gold and also terms of eight major currencies as the trade unit used in the payment system, in example, "10 troy oz worth of e-gold," "5.3 grams worth of e-gold," "US$100.00 worth of e-gold," or "CHF685.88 worth of e-gold." See e-gold Better money Web page, http://www.e-gold.com/unsecure/qanda.html, accessed May 26, 2004.

Chapter X
Mistakes in Remittance to Account

Masao Yanaga
University of Tsukuba, Japan

ABSTRACT

Some courts have recently ruled in Japan with regard to mistakes in remittance to account. While the Supreme Court held that the recipient has become a depositor of a savings deposit as much as the remitted amount of the receiving bank as a result of a remittance, and the recipient obtains a bank deposit in the amount equivalent to the transferred amount, even where there was no legal relationship which could be used as a legal basis for the remittance between the person who requested the remittance and the recipient, it held that the person who made a demand for repayment of a bank deposit while knowing that there was a remittance to account made into its bank account by error, and received the repayment shall be guilty of fraud. In addition, some lower courts held that it is fair and equitable to interpret that the receiving bank must directly refund to the originator with regard to the originator's claim to refund, as much as the amount of the erroneous remittance as unjustified enrichment. Thus, the position of Japanese courts is still in disarray in respect to the legal consequences of mistakes in remittance to account.

INTRODUCTION

Some courts have recently ruled in Japan with regard to mistake in remittance to account (*furikomi*). However, it seems that the reasoning adopted in civil cases might not be consistent with the reasoning adopted in criminal cases. In addition, the grounds for the court decisions in case of the seizure by a creditor of the named recipient might not necessarily be compatible with those in case of the setoff by the receiving bank. In this chapter, those court decisions and some explanations will be analyzed.

BACKGROUND

Remittance to account is a system by which an originator remits funds to a recipient's account at the bank at which the recipient has his accounts (*hishimuke ginko*). The originator's bank (*shimuke ginko*) accepts cash from the originator and requests the receiving bank to credit the account of the recipient's, and thereby the money remitted to the account will be credited to the recipient's account by the receiving bank (Maeda, 1976[1]). The account to which money is remitted usually must be a current account or ordinary savings account.

In other words, he/she who would like to remit funds to another person goes to a bank, tenders cash (or requests to withdraw his/her current or ordinary savings), and supplies such information as the receiving bank, the branch, the account number, name and address of the recipient, and the amount to be remitted.

It is the widely accepted opinion (Makiyama, 1996[2]) that the legal nature of remittance to account is mandate (*inin*, Article 643 of the Civil Code) or quasi-mandate (*jun-inin*) while some scholars argue that it is a contract for the third party. A judicial precedent[3] also rejected the argument that remittance is a contract for the third party. "A wire fund transfer contract is not necessarily a contract for the third party, recipient of the remittance, as long as there are no special circumstances. While the receiving bank contractually owes the obligation to pay the remitted money to the beneficiary of remittance in the relation to the paying bank, it owes no obligation to the recipient in question but has an authority to pay the remitted money to the named recipient for account of the paying bank."

A remittance involves a complex array of multiple contracts. According to a famous professor, it consists of seven components (Iwahara, 1985[4]): (i) the underlying relationship (debtor-creditor relationship) between the originator and the recipient, (ii) the remittance transaction agreement between the originator and the originator's bank, (iii) the originator's request of remittance to the originator's bank, (iv) the contact for remittance between the originator and the originator's bank, (v) the exchange instruction given by the originator's bank to the receiving bank, (vi) the exchange contract between the sending and receiving banks, and (vii) the settlement of the remittance between the two banks based on the exchange contract. The originator makes instruction (iii) on the precondition of the contracts (ii), (iv), and (v) and the receiving bank credits the remitted amount to complete settlement.

The relationship between the originator and the recipient is usually the underlying relationship for the remittance to the account of the named recipient. The originator tenders cash and there will be a quasi-mandate contract to remit money to the recipient's account at his bank (receiving bank) between the originator and the originator's bank. Between the originator's bank and the receiving bank, there is relationship based on the exchange contact between each financial institution that joins the Domestic Exchange System, and is assumed to be a contract to mandate the receiving bank to credit the recipient's account as provided by the Domestic Exchange System.

Finally, the rules and regulations for current account or ordinary savings account transactions, to which the clients of financial institutions are subject, provide that funds remitted to the account be accepted by the financial institution as a deposit. Accordingly, once money is remitted to an account of a customer at the receiving bank, the customer acquires a deposit claim[5] against the receiving bank.

SUPREME COURT DECISION OF APRIL 26, 1996[6]

The court held that the recipient has become a depositor of a savings deposit as much as the remitted amount of the receiving bank, as a result of a remittance, and the recipient obtains a bank deposit in the amount equivalent to the transferred amount even where there was no legal relationship which could be used as a legal basis for the remittance between the person who requested the remittance and the recipient.

Summary of the Facts

On April 28, 1989, Benkan Ltd. (plaintiff and appellant) was the lessee of an office building and requested Omori branch of Dai-Ichi Kangyo Bank to remit 5,583,030 yen in order to pay the rent to the lessor, *Tooshin*. However, Benkan supplied the paying bank with wrong information on the recipient, such as the recipient's bank, branch, and account number because the name of the erroneous named recipient was the same in pronunciation as that of the intended recipient, with the difference identified with two Chinese characters. Thus Fuji Bank credited the same amount to the ordinary savings account of the named recipient at its Ueno branch. As Benkan owed no debt to the named recipient at that time, it asked the paying bank for reversal of payment (*kumimodoshi*). Before the paying bank got approval of reversal of payment, the named recipient was bankrupt and its representative became missing. On July 31, 1989, Genda (defendant and appellant), who had the notarial deed for the loan claim against the named recipient, filed for a seizure on the ordinary savings of the named recipient. Then, in order to prevent the compulsory execution of the seizure by Genda, Benkan filed a lawsuit as the third party objection.

Reasoning

The ordinary savings agreement provides that the receiving bank will accept the transferred amount as a deposit of the recipient. There are no provisions in the agreement that suggest that the recipient obtains a bank deposit only when there is legal relationship that could be a legal basis for the remittance to account between the recipient and the person who requests the remittance to account. In the process of remittance to account, the involving banks may accomplish their tasks without taking the existence or content of the legal basis for the remittance into consideration in order to process a large sum of fund transfers inexpensively, safely, and smoothly.

Moreover, the person who has made the mistake in requesting a remittance to account has the claim for the restoration of an unjustified enrichment as much as the remitted amount but does not have a right to disturb the transfer of the deposit, even when there was no underlying relationship for the remittance.

Former Lower Courts Decisions

Before this Supreme Court decision, several lower courts decisions were published with regard to mistake in remittance to account.

Decision of Nagoya High Court of January 28, 1976[7]

Marubeni (plaintiff) would like to request the headquarters of Fuji Bank (defendant) to remit to the account of "Howa Kogyo Ltd.," but the name of the recipient was, by mistake, described as "Howa Sangyo Ltd." on the remittance request. In addition, this name was displayed as "Houwasangyou" in *katakana*[8] when Fuji Bank communicated by telex, and neither the account number nor other descriptions was given. Nagoya branch of Fuji Bank interpreted that "Howa Sangyo Ltd."(it was same in pronunciation with the intended recipient, with the difference identified with Chinese characters), which was a client of Nagoya branch, was the designated recipient, credited to the ordinary savings account of Howa Sangyo Ltd. Then Marubeni filed a seizure on the deposit of Howa Sangyo Ltd. and a claim to Fuji Bank for the payment of the deposit. The Nagoya High Court admitted that the relationship between the receiving bank and the recipient is a mandate and bailment for use contract. Then it held that the recipient had no deposit claim against the defendant bank (receiving bank) because the recipient had no intention to accept the remitted fund as his deposit in cases where there no underlying relationship for remittance. The court argued that it could not be admitted that there was an "intention to accept as a deposit" because the existence of an underlying relationship resulting from transactions, which made the recipient as a due recipient in substance, is a precondition of "the intention of the acceptance stipulated in the rules for the ordinary savings account."

Decision of Kagoshima District Court of November 27, 1989[9]

Sharp Finance Ltd. (plaintiff) entered into an affiliation contract with Kyowa Communications Construction Ltd. and San chic Limited Liability Company (hereinafter, referred as "San chic") respectively. Though Sharp Finance would like to remit funds to the current account of Kyowa Communications at Uedori branch of Higo Bank, but, by mistake, requested to remit to the ordinary savings account of San chic at Nishida branch of Kagoshima Bank (defendant). Accordingly, Kagoshima Bank credited the remitted amount to the ordinary savings account of San chic and set off the amount maintained in the savings account of San chic against the amount of its loan to San chic. Thus, Sharp Finance brought the case to the court, requesting to refund the amount of the remitted money as unjustified enrichment. The court followed the theory that the Nagoya High Court had taken and held that the defendant bank was not allowed to set off because the deposit claim of the recipient is invalid in cases where there are no underlying relationships for remittance between the originator and the recipient.

Doctrine

Argument before this Ruling

Before this decision, there had been arguments for and against the mentioned lower court decisions.

The majority had taken the position that deposit claim of the named recipient is invalid when no underlying relationship exists between the originator and the named recipient, supporting such lower court rulings.

It is less thoughtful to think that an instruction is not erroneous in a banking transaction legally, even where the originator makes an instruction for remittance with the wrong description of the recipient's bank account or the named recipient. It is doubtful that the receiving bank has an intention to owe a deposit debt to the named recipients when it credits to the recipient designated by mistake. Moreover, it is difficult to admit that the person specified as a named recipient by mistake, has the intention to accept the remitted funds as a deposit for himself, even when it is clear to him that the remittance was done by a third party who has no transaction relationship with him (Shiozaki, 1991[10]). To allow the creditor of the named recipient to collect from the deposit resulting from a remittance made by mistake will force the sacrifice on the originator that made the mistake when he requests remittance. The disadvantage as a result of the mistake may be excessive for such a slight mistake (Kinami, 1991[11]). Where the receiving bank pays deposit back to the named recipient or the creditor in good faith, the bank will be sufficiently protected under Article 478 of the Civil Code[12]. There is little need to recognize the validity of the deposit claim of the named recipient who has no proper interests (Takizawa, 1993[13]).

On the other hand, some had spoken against such lower court rulings. It is quite fair that 'the person who makes a mistake abide by the disadvantage resulting from it'. It may also be fair to interpret that the originator should request the named recipient to refund the unjustified enrichment outside the remittance procedure while the deposit contract is valid, even when the remittance was made by mistake (Goto, 1990[14]). As the essence of the remittance procedure is that remittance is independent from its underlying relationship and is processed automatically, the validity of the deposit claim is unrelated to presence of the underlying relationship (Makiyama, 1990[15]). It is also pointed out that it is impossible for banks to investigate and confirm whether there is an underlying relationship of commercial transactions between the originator and the named recipient (Suzuki, 1991[16]). In addition, where the receiving bank is advised by the originator that there is no underlying relationship for the remittance, it is very difficult for the bank to judge whether the assertion by the originator is true or not (Kawada, 1992[17]).

Argument against this Ruling

The majority of academics have put forward an argument against this Supreme Court decision. Firstly, it is pointed out that there is little doubt that a judgment like this decision can be derived from the fact that there are no provisions in the rules and regulations for current or ordinary savings accounts that suggest the validity of deposit claims and depends upon the existence of any creditor-debtor relationship (underlying relationship) between the originator and the recipient. Some argue that it is rather natural that the provisions in such rules and regulations do not cover exceptional and pathology cases where mistakes are made in the process of remittance to account. It is pointed out as well that it is not persuasive reasoning for the ruling that remittance to account "is a means to transfer funds safely, at a low price, and promptly through the remittance procedure between interbank and the bank branches" because this is not more than the socio-economic function of remittance to account and is a little bit weak as grounds of a legal interpretation concerning a erroneous transfer and the validity of the deposit contract (Shiozaki, 1996; Hata, 1997[18]).

Secondly, one of the most famous Japanese commercial law professors has produced a powerful argument against this Supreme Court decision. "As long as the third party objection lawsuit concerned, the bank doesn't owe judgment risk because it only has nothing but to follow the ruling of the third party objection lawsuit. I cannot help but have sense of discomfort at this decision that gives a windfall profit to the creditor of the named recipient because this decision disregards honest profits of the originator for the protection of banks"(Iwahara, 1996; Takeuchi, 1999[19]).

Thirdly, it is also recognized that we cannot necessarily find an intention to accept remitted funds as deposit in cases where the remittance was done without any underlying relationship when taken into consideration that remittance to account is a means for the settlement of the underlying debtor-creditor relationship (Takeuchi, 1999[20]).

In addition, a famous civil law scholar argues that this case cannot be solved by the means 'Interpretation of contract' though this decision derives the conclusion through interpretation of contract (Maeda, 1997[21]).

Argument for this Ruling

On the other hand, bank workers have made out a case for this decision. "I want to welcome it as a decision that has an epoch-making significance, protecting dynamic safely of the fund system in the banking transaction and stability of the settlement" (Kawada, 1996[22]). Another bank worker thinks that a bank should not be held responsible because the mandated clerical work has been completed when the bank has credited the named recipient. Moreover, it is way off balance that a bank takes a heavy responsibility when an erroneous remittance is executed in the light of cheap transfer fee (Yoshioka, 1997[23]). It is also pointed out that the contract for remittance should not be interpreted as one affects on the relationship between the originator and the recipient (underlying legal relationship of funds transfer) and a bank neither assumes responsibility to inquire an underlying relationship between the originator and the named recipient nor undertakes a duty to confirm the identity of the named recipient. If a deposit resulting from erroneous remittance is deemed as invalid, the receiving bank might assume the risks and bear the costs in cases where the wrong recipient does not refund voluntarily, which is irrational (Hayakawa,1997[24]). It is preferable for banks that remittance is a neutral transaction independent from the underlying relationship between the originator and the recipient, because banks which intermediate funds transfer, should take judgment risks and responsibility to inquire if the validity of deposit claims is deemed as dependent upon the underlying relationship (Makiyama, 1996[25]). It will be uncertain whether the amount credited can be treated as a deposit and the stability of the deposit settlement system will be ruined if a deposit should be deemed as invalid because of any defect in its underlying relationship (Ito, 1996[26]). If the validity of remittance is independent from the underlying relationship, the dispute related to the underlying relationship should be settled among the persons concerned because exchange transactions, including remittance, are only payment measures. Even if customers expect to settle through the bank, banks have not agreed to take such responsibility (Matsuoka, 1997[27]).

SUPREME COURT DECISION OF MARCH 12, 2003[28]

Ruling and Reasoning

The court held that the person who made a demand for repayment of a bank deposit while knowing that there was a remittance to account made into its bank account by error and received the repayment, shall be guilty of fraud.

According to the decision, a process called '*kumimodoshi* (reversal of payment)' which restores the status of the bank accounts to the status before the remittance to account, when it is requested with the consent of the recipient of the remittance to account, exist in the banking practice, even if the deposit into the recipient's account is completed, when there is a request from the person who made a remittance to a wrong account. Even in the case where the recipient notifies the bank of erroneous remittance, the bank takes certain steps such as, while verifying its own process for crediting the account, making inquiries to the bank which received the remittance and, through such bank, and to the person who requested the remittance, as to whether there was any mistake in the remittance.

Such steps conforming to the objectives of the ordinary savings rules and the remittance rules, and so forth, are beneficial for maintaining a safe remittance system, and are necessary in order to avoid the bank being involved in disputes between the person who has requested the remittance and the recipient of the remittance. They are also important for the society because they would prevent unnecessary disputes among the parties involved, such as the person who requested the remittance and the recipient of the remittance. Therefore, whether the bank deposit repayment which was requested was based on an erroneous remittance or not is important information for the bank in order to decide whether or not it should immediately repay the bank deposit. From the recipient's perspective, it has the duty to act in good faith, as a person who has continuing deposit transactions with the bank under ordinary savings transaction agreement, and to notify the bank of the erroneous remittance when it came to the knowledge of it in order to allow the bank to take the steps stated. Such notice obligation is self explanatory under reason of the social standards because the recipient of an erroneous remittance shall, by himself, refund it to the person who requested the remittance and has no actual right to definitively treat the amount transferred by the error as his own. Thus, a demand for repayment of a bank deposit made by the recipient who knew of the erroneous remittance while pretending as if he did not, is an act of deceit which is a factor in the criminal offence of fraud, and a mistake on the existence of erroneous remittance, is a mistake which is also a factor in the criminal offence of fraud, and the recipient shall be charged for such an offence when the recipient receives the repayment of the bank deposit from the mistaken bank receptionist.

Based on the findings, the defendant that did not tell the bank receptionist at the time he made a demand for repayment, about the erroneous remittance to his bank account although he knew it and received cash from the receptionist, can be charged for the criminal offence of fraud.

Consistency with the Supreme Court Decision of April 26, 1996

The 1996 Supreme Court decision overturned the precondition of the former court decisions[29] and doctrines (Otani, 1985[30]) with regard to crimes that the wrong recipient did not have a deposit claim resulting from erroneous remittance. Accordingly, after the 1996 Supreme Court Decision, it had been considered as difficult to explain that the wrong recipient is guilty of fraud or theft where he/she withdraws the deposit. Unless the interpretation with regard to civil law has no influence on the interpretation with regard to criminal law (Maeda, 1999; Kimura, 2003[31]), academic doctrines recognized that the recipient would be guilty of embezzlement of lost property (Otani, 1985; Ida, 2002; Hayashi, 1999; Sone, 2001[32]) or would not be guilty (Saeki & Dogauchi, 2001; Matsumiya, 2001; Kawaguchi, 2000; Matsuoka, 2003[33]).

However, in 2003, the Supreme Court held that the deposit resulting from erroneous remittance belongs to the wrong recipient, along the lines with the 1996 decision, but the recipient who took out the deposit shall be guilty of fraud. Then it is a good problem whether the 1996 decision and the 2003 decision are contradicted or not.

Criminal law scholars have tried to give some explanations. For example, Nishida, one of the most famous professors in Japan, has interpreted that the reach of the 1996 decision is limited because the decision aimed at the protection of the interests of banks, and the possession of money remitted by mistake belong to the bank (Nishida, 2002[34]). Some argue that the 2003 decision might be compatible with the 1996 decision if the 1996 decision only admitted the validity of the deposit claim resulting from erroneous remittance but did not mention the named recipient's right to withdraw the deposit at the receiving bank. However, it is natural to interpret that the recipient may request the receiving bank to pay the deposit back if he/she has a deposit as credited to the account, including the amount of erroneous remittance from the viewpoint of the civil law (Saeki & Dogauchi, 2001[35]). That is, it seems that the bank should pay to the depositor (named recipient) on demand[36] where the named recipient advises the bank that the remittance was an erroneous one but refuses to give consent to '*kumimodoshi*'.[37] Accordingly, the 2003 decision lays the risks on the shoulder of the receiving bank, which might be incompatible with the balancing of interests in the 1996 decision.

EMERGING TREND

Nagoya High Court Decision of March 17, 2005[38]

Sobue Commercial Development Ltd. (plaintiff and appellant) requested Sobue branch of Ohgaki Kyoritsu Bank (originator's bank) to remit 668,780 yen to the current account of Yukando Ltd. at UFJ Bank (defendant and appellant). However, Sobue Commercial Development recognized that it made a mistake in instructing the payee's bank account, and requested '*kumimodoshi*'. However, the receiving bank, UFJ Bank refused to do '*kumimodoshi*' because it had already credited the remitted amount to the account of Yukando. Insisting that an underlying relationship for the remittance did not exist between Sobue Commercial Development and Yukando, this remittance was a erroneous one, and the Yukando's deposit claim to UFJ Bank was invalid, Sobue Commercial Development argued that UFJ Bank was obtaining unjustified gain by the loss of Sobue Commercial Development, and requested the payment of 668,780 yen, equivalent to the amount of the erroneous remittance. UFJ Bank notified Yukando that it had set off the loan to Yukando, against the deposit of Yukando, though Yukando had already given consent in writing to do '*kumimodoshi*' to Sobue Commercial Development.

The Nagoya High Court held as follows:

Where an originator has requested the originator's bank to remit to the deposit account of a named recipient without any underlying relationship between the originator and the recipient that justifies the remittance and the receiving bank has credited the current account of the named recipient as a result of a so-called erroneous remittance, as a rule, the current deposit contract between the named recipient and the receiving bank is valid regardless of the nonexistence of the underlying relationship between the originator and the named recipient. Therefore, it cannot be said that the receiving bank has gained as much as the remitted amount.

However, where the originator has requested 'kumimodoshi' to the receiving bank due to an erroneous remittance and the named recipient has admitted that the remittance was made by mistake, and given a consent to 'kumimodoshi,' it can be interpreted that the named recipient expresses his will to refuse the credit by an erroneous remittance by the originator (or, abandons, in fact, the deposit as much as the credited amount to his current account). Moreover, in such a case, as the recipient does not have an idea to exercise the deposit claim as much as the remitted amount, the receiving bank actually enjoys an unjustified enrichment. In addition, where the receiving bank has known that the remittance was made by mistake, it is not necessary to take the protection of the receiving bank into consideration for smooth processing of frequent transfers of a large sum of funds inter-bank and between the bank branches, because it will not make the receiving bank involved in the dispute over the underlying relationship between the originator and the recipient, and lead the receiving bank to a difficult standpoint. Where both the receiving bank and the named recipient have recognized that the remittance was made by mistake, it is not fair that the originator should submit to the disadvantage resulting from an erroneous remittance. Above all, it is possible to take the procedures of 'kumimodoshi' individually.

Therefore, it is fair and equitable for this case to interpret that a deposit contract between the named recipient and the receiving bank is invalid in substance, the receiving bank gains resulting from the loss of the originator, and, accordingly, the receiving bank must directly refund to the originator, with regard to the originator's claim to refund as much as the amount of the erroneous remittance as an unjustified enrichment.

This is because it is not appropriate that the originator, who has done an erroneous remittance, should exercise the claim for a refund of an unjustified enrichment against the named recipient and the recipient should always withdraw the deposit at the receiving bank, which is roundabout as a solution of a dispute, leading to the outcome that he who is not to be duly protected may be protected, and causes useless confusion, even in cases where the recipient himself has admitted that he/she has no deposit claim as much as the remitted amount and the receiving bank has no duly grounds to refuse to take measures of 'kumimodoshi' of the remitted amount.

Tokyo District Court Decision of September 26, 2005[39]

In order to settle with Masuyama Industry Ltd. Musashi Steelworks (plaintiff) requested the Tokyo Central branch of the Bank of Mitsui-Sumitomo Bank, to transfer 1,190,385 yen but specified the savings account of Vector Ltd. at the Mejiro branch of the Bank of Tokyo-Mitsubishi (defendant) by mistake. Therefore, 1,190,385 yen was credited to the deposit account of Vector. Then Musashi Steelworks requested the Tokyo Central branch of the Bank of Mitsui-Sumitomo Bank for 'kumimodoshi' of the amount of the erroneous remittance, but the Mejiro branch of the Bank of Tokyo-Mitsubishi answered that 'kumimodoshi' for the plaintiff could not be proceeded because the Mejiro branch could not contact Vector and it was unable to obtain the consent of Vector. Musashi Steelworks tried to contact Vector in vain because the telephone line to Vector was suspended, and former personnel of Vector answered that Vector was in a state of bankruptcy and he/she did not know where the representative of Vector was. Afterwards, the deposit of Vector, including the erroneous remittance amount was counterbalanced against the loan claim on Vector of the Bank of Tokyo-Mitsubishi. Then, Musashi Steelworks argued that the Bank of Tokyo-Mitsubishi gained unjustifiable profits, as much as the amount of the erroneously remitted money, and requested the payment to the Bank of Tokyo-Mitsubishi as unjustified enrichment.

Tokyo District Court held as follows:

Because the named recipient has become the depositor of the deposit as much as the remitted amount, even if the underlying relationship of the remittance between the originator and the named recipient, where there is a funds transfer to the savings account of the recipient at the recipient's bank, from the originator, the validity of the attachment for the creditor of the named recipient on the deposit or the setoff made by the receiving bank against the deposit, are not denied as long as there are no special circumstances that made them the abuse of the rights.

However, it is not desirable that the redress for an originator who makes a mistake in requesting a remittance is limited to the unjustified enrichment claim to the named recipient, even in cases where the originator is unable to obtain consent of the named recipient to 'kumimodoshi' because the named recipient is missing. It is desirable that the receiving bank, as an operator of the remittance system, should take appropriate measures to confirm whether the remittance has been made by mistake and distinguish the credited amount resulting from such remittance from the original deposit of the recipient, meanwhile in order to leave an opportunity for the originator's effective redress, where the originator has given the receiving bank sufficient explanation of the situation, that the named recipient has been missing and the originator has not been able to obtain consent from the recipient.

Accordingly, it is fair to interpret that the bank has gained without a lawful cause, and the gain should be interpreted as unjustified enrichment with regard to the originator where the receiving bank has collected the debt owed by the named recipient, through setoff between the credit to the named recipient and the recipient's deposit resulting from the erroneous remittance without confirmation whether the remittance was made by mistake or not, though the receiving bank has been considerably advised by the originator that he/she could not obtain the consent of the named recipient to 'kumimodoshi' because the recipient has been missing.

Therefore, the Bank of Tokyo-Mitsubishi owes the obligation to pay Musashi Steelworks.

Consistency with the Supreme Court Decision of April 26, 1996

These decisions give priority to the interests of the person who made an erroneous remittance more than to the interests of the receiving bank while the 1996 Supreme Court decision emphasized the interests of the receiving bank. These judgments might be based on the thought that it is not fair for the receiving bank to enjoy the windfall profits. If this balancing of interests is appropriate, it is not persuasive to give the windfall profits from the erroneous remittance to the creditor of the named recipient. Moreover, though the 1996 Supreme Court decision held the validity of the deposit contract between the receiving bank and the named recipient, in order to protect the interests of the receiving bank, the receiving bank does not become advantageous according to these decisions, even if the deposit contract is deemed to be valid. The interpretation rather, might bring disadvantage to the receiving bank. Where the receiving bank is advised by the originator that there is no underlying relationship for the remittance, it is very difficult for the bank to judge whether the assertion of the originator is true or not. The receiving bank might assume the risks and bear the costs in cases where the wrong recipient does not refund voluntarily.

Thus these decisions might be inconsistent with the 1996 Supreme Court decision.

CONCLUSION

The position of the Japanese courts is still in disarray in respect to the legal consequences of mistake in remittance to account. Though the conclusion of the court decisions might be equitable in each case, the judgment of value expressed by recent lower court decisions seems to be different from the 1996 Supreme Court Decision. The reasoning given in the 2003 Supreme Court Decision might be inconsistent with that given in the 1996 Supreme Court Decision because the receiving bank will not suffer losses by repaying a named recipient-depositor according to the 1996 Supreme Court Decision and, therefore, it is not always persuasive that the depositor owes a duty to tell the receiving bank, for the benefits of the receiving bank, that his deposit is the result of mistake in remittance to account.

If the value judgment in the 2003 Supreme Court Decision and some recent lower court decisions should be accepted, the reasoning and conclusion given in the 1996 Supreme Court Decision should be reconsidered.

Future Research Directions

It is a challenge to find whether the 2003 Supreme Court Decision and some recent lower court decisions are consistent with the 1996 Supreme Court Decision and, if so, how to give coherent interpretation of the decisions. In addition, the Supreme Court ruling on the cases of the setoff by the receiving bank is still expected, as the defendant has appealed to the Supreme Court against the Nagoya High Court Decision of March 17, 2005.

REFERENCES

Goto, K. (1990). Recent court decisions and problems concerning remittance. *Kin'yu Homu Jijo, 1269*, 10-17.

Hata, M. (1997). The validity of deposit claim in cases where remittance was made to different person by mistake made by the originator. *NBL, 618*, 78-83.

Hayakawa, T. (1997). Erroneous remittance and validity of deposit. *Kansai Daigaku Hogaku Ronshu, 47*(3), 449-483.

Hayashi, M. (1999). *Keiho Kakuron* (Specifics of Criminal Law). Tokyo: Tokyo Daigaku Shuppankai.

Ida, R. (2002). *Keiho Kakuron* (Specifics of Criminal Law). Tokyo: Kobundo.

Ito, H. (1996). Validity of ordinary savings contract relating to the remittance in cases where there are no underlying relationship of the remittance between the originator and the named recipient. *Kin'yu Shoji Hanrei, 1001*, 43-51.

Iwahara, S. (1985). Computer-aided settlement and law. *Kin'yu Ho Kenkyu* (Financial Law Research), *1*, 9-59.

Iwahara, S. (1996). Is the originator allowed to insist the third party objection against the seizure on the deposit claim of the recipient resulting from erroneous remittance? *Kin'yu Homu Jijo, 1460*, 11-16.

Kawada, E. (1992). The issues on the validity of Deposit resulting from remittance by mistake. *Kin'yu Homu Jijo, 1324*, 4-5.

Kawada, E. (1996). The validity of deposit by an erroneous remittance by the originator. *Kin'yu Homu Jijo, 1452*, 4-5.

Kawaguchi, K. (2000). Erroneous remittance and fraud. *Nara Hogakukai Zasshi, 13*(2), 1-34.

Kimura, M. (2003). *Enshu Keiho* (Exercises in criminal law). Tokyo: Tokyo Daigaku Shuppankai.

Kinami, A. (1991). Remittance by mistake and validity of deposit. *Kin'yu Homu Jijo, 1304*, 7-10.

Maeda, M. (1999). *Keiho Kakuron Kogi* (Lectures on specifics of criminal law) (3rd ed.). Tokyo: Tokyo Daigaku Shuppankai.

Maeda, T. (1976). Furikomi (Remittance to account). In I. Kato, R. Hayashi, & I. Kawamoto (Eds.), *Ginko Torihiki Ho Koza* (Lesson on the law for bank transactions), *Vol. 1*. Tokyo: Kin'yu Zaisei Jijo Kenkyukai.

Maeda, T. (1997). The case where a deposit claim against a bank was established through credit to the recipient's account resulting from mistake made by the originator. *Hanrei Jiho, 1585*, 192-200.

Makiyama, I. (1990). The case where the recipient did not acquire deposit claim where the originator designated wrong recipient. *Kin'yu Homu Jijo, 1267*, 12-19.

Makiyama, I. (1996). The validity of ordinary savings contract through remittance in cases where there was no underlying relationship for the remittance. *Kin'yu Homu Jijo, 1467*, 12-19.

Matsumiya, T. (2001). Erroneous remittance and interpretation and legislation of crimes with regard to properties. *Ritsumeikan Hogaku, 278*, 999-1024.

Matsuoka, H. (1997). Validity of deposit claims resulting from remittance with error in the recipient's name. *Jurist*, (extra edition), *113*, 73-74.

Matsuoka, H. (2003). Tangle of criminal law and civil law. *Keiho Zasshi, 43*(1), 90-102.

Nishida, N. (2002). *Keiho Kakuron* (Specifics of criminal law) (2nd ed.). Tokyo: Kobundo.

Otani, M. (1985). Illegal use of cash cards and crimes relating to properties. *Hanrei Times, 36*(12), 84-89.

Saeki, H., & Dogauchi, H. (2001). *Keiho to Mimpo no Taiwa* (Dialogue between criminal law and civil law). Tokyo: Yuhikaku.

Shiozaki, T. (1991). Seizure on deposit resulting from remittance by mistake and permissibility of the third party objection by the originator. *Kin'yu Homu Jijo, 1299*, 11-19.

Shiozaki, T. (1996). Erroneous remittance by the originator and validity of deposit contract between the recipient and the bank. *Ginko Homu 21*(523), 4-11.

Sone, T. (2001) *Keiho Kakuron* (Specifics of criminal law) (3rd. ed.). Tokyo: Kobundo.

Suzuki, M. (1991). Remittance by mistake and finding of depositor. *Hanrei Times, 42*(6), 103-106.

Takeuchi, T. (1999). The case where a deposit claim of the recipient is deemed to be valid through an erroneous request for remittance without an underlying relationship. *Toin Hogaku, 5*(2), 137-157.

Takizawa, M. (1993). Validity of deposit claims resulting from remittance by mistake and permissibility of the third party objection by the originator. *Jurist, 1018*, 118-121.

Yoshioka, S. (1997). Erroneous remittance without its underlying relationship and validity of deposit. *Ginko Homu, 2*(529), 38-46.

ADDITIONAL READINGS

Anazawa, D. (2005). Offences against property in cases of so-called erroneous remittance and book entry. *Jochi Hogaku Ronshu, 48*(2), 322-286; *48*(3-4), 428-384.

Honda, M. (2005). Erroneous remittance and setoff by the receiving bank. *Kin'yu Homu Jijo, 1733*, 37-47; *1734*, 48-58.

Nagai, M., & Watanabe, Y. (2004). Duty of disclosure of "erroneous remittance" and integration of criminal law and civil law. *Yokohama Kokusai Keizai Hogaku, 13*(1), 1-44.

Okamoto, M. (2005). Erroneous remittance and setoff by the receiving bank. *Kin'yu Homu Jijo, 1751*, 9-14; *1752*, 37-45.

Yamaguchi, A. (2004). Erroneous remittance and offences against property. *Hogaku Kyoshitsu, 283*, 82-88.

ENDNOTES

[1] Maeda (1976). p. 298.
[2] Makiyama (1996). p. 13.
[3] Sakuyama v. Daiichi, Supreme Court Decision of December 5, 1968, *Minshu* (Supreme Court Civil Cases Reporter), Vol.22, No.13, p. 2876.
[4] Iwahara (1985). p. 9.
[5] Bank deposit has been interpreted to be bailment for use (*shohi kitaku*, Article 666 of the Civil Code).
[6] Benkan Ltd. v. Genda, *Minshu*, Vol. 50, No. 5, p. 1267.
[7] Marubeni Ltd. v. Fuji Bank, *Kin'yu Homu Jijo*, No. 795, p. 44.
[8] *Katakana* are Japanese characters adapted from Chinese characters.
[9] Sharp Finance Ltd. v. Kagoshima Bank, *Kin'yu Homu Jijo*, No. 1255, p. 32.
[10] Shiozaki (1991). p.15.
[11] Kinami (1991). p. 9.
[12] A performance rendered to quasi-possessor of an obligatory right is effective only if it was done in good faith.
[13] Takizawa (1993). p. 120.
[14] Goto (1990). p. 16.
[15] Makiyama (1990). p. 14.
[16] Suzuki (1991). p. 105.
[17] Kawada (1992). p. 5.
[18] Shiozaki (1996). p.10. *See also* Hata (1997). p..82.
[19] Iwahara (1996). p. 14. *See also* Takeuchi (1999). p. 151.
[20] Takeuchi (1999). p. 147.
[21] Maeda (1997). p. 194.
[22] Kawada (1996). p. 5.
[23] Yoshioka (1997). p. 44.
[24] Hayakawa (1997). p. 67.
[25] Makiyama (1996). p. 17.
[26] Ito (1996). p. 48.
[27] Matsuoka (1997). p. 74.
[28] *Keishu* (Supreme Court Criminal Cases Reporter), Vol. 57, No. 3, p. 322.
[29] Though most of the court have found guilty of fraud (e.g., Sapporo High Court Decision of November 11, 1976, *Keisai Geppou*, Vol.8, No.11/12, p.453) or theft (e.g., Tokyo High Court Decision of September 12, 1994, *Hanrei Jiho*, No.1545, p. 113: Withdrawal through ATM) in cases where a wrong recipient withdrew the deposit resulting from erroneous remittance, one decision found guilty of embezzlement of lost property (Tokyo District Court Decision of October 19, 1972, *unpublished*).
[30] Otani (1985). p. 87.
[31] Maeda (1999). p. 173, Kimura (2003). p. 274.
[32] Otani (1985). p. 88, Ida (2002). p. 127, Hayashi (1999). p. 279, Sone (2001). p. 172.
[33] Saeki & Dogauchi (2001). pp. 26ff., Matsumiya (2001). pp. 1013ff., Kawaguchi (2000). pp. 22ff., Matsuoka (2003). p. 99.
[34] Nishida (2002). p. 226.
[35] *See* Saeki & Dogauchi (2001).
[36] However, it is probable that the court will dismiss the claim of the named recipient if he/she brings this to court, due to the principle of good faith and sincerity and the abuse of rights.
[37] The consent of the named recipient is indispensable for the procedure of '*kumimodoshi.*' The Supreme Court Decision of March 9, 2000, *Kin'yu Shoji Hanrei*, No.1091, p. 12.
[38] Sobue Commercial Development Ltd. v. UFJ Bank, *Kin'yu Homu Jijo*, No. 1745, p. 34.
[39] Musashi Steelworks Ltd. v. Bank of Tokyo-Mitsubishi, *Hanrei Jiho*, No. 1934, p. 61.

Section III
E–Contracts and Dispute Resolution

Chapter XI
Doing International Business Online for the Small and Medium Enterprise

Sam Edwards
Nagoya University, USA and Japan

ABSTRACT

This chapter addresses the primary difficulties that small and medium enterprises face when doing business online with international partners. The guidance provided in this chapter is primarily for owners of small and medium enterprises rather than legal for professionals. The two main problems inhibiting online transactions are a lack of trust between the parties and the risk inherent in the exchange. This chapter analyzes ways to address these problems. Many of the practical suggestions in this chapter are inspired not by million dollar deals but by playground transactions between children. Often the simple solutions are the best ones.

INTRODUCTION

Scene One

You run a small shop that specializes in imported art from native artisans. Although you do not have the budget to travel to every place that might have interesting items, you still want to offer a variety of goods. While surfing the Internet, you locate a site that shows items that look to be perfect but the seller appears to be located in Kenya. How can you do business with someone you will never meet face-to-face? From the small digital pictures and limited descriptions, how can you be sure the goods will be as portrayed? How can you protect yourself from all of the scams you hear about on the net? If you decide to buy, how can you resolve any disputes that might arise?

Copyright © 2008, IGI Global, distributing in print or electronic forms without written permission of IGI Global is prohibited.

Scene Two

Your uncle produces hand-carved wooden statues and sells them in his small stall in a Nairobi market. Since the statues have proven popular with foreign tourists, he has asked you to help expand his business. Being a computer savvy student, you quickly put together a Web page with pictures of his works in hopes of exporting them. After a few months, despite having an ever-growing page hit count, you have not received any orders. What can you do to improve the chances of selling? How can you protect yourself from all the scams that exist in the wilds of the Internet?

Increasingly small and medium businesses are expanding to do business on the Internet. This is nothing new, however, as more people gain access to the Internet, international transactions for these smaller businesses will increase. For a large company, experienced teams handle international transactions. These teams normally travel and meet their counterparts face-to-face. Smaller enterprises do not have the resources and must rely on remote communications if they wish to do international business. Can the same Internet that facilitates finding potential trade partners help to solve some of these problems with international transactions and disputes?

This chapter focuses two aspects of online commerce: 1. how the various e-commerce systems can increase trust and reduce risk, and 2. should a dispute arise, how online dispute resolution can efficiently resolve problems.

In addition to direct business-to-business transactions, this chapter will examine private marketplaces such as eBay. With eBay recently signing up its 200,000,000th member, eBay has become, by population, the fifth largest "country" in the world (Whitman, 2006). Given eBay's dominance, this chapter will examine the practices that help mitigate risk in international transactions. Moreover, eBay's acquisition of Skype, a voice over IP telephony service, opens up the potential for much more interesting features to help bring buyers and sellers closer in spirit, if not space.

This chapter will conclude with recommendations for small and medium businesses looking to engage in international business through the Internet.

TWO BASIC PROBLEMS INHIBITING ONLINE TRANSACTIONS

In our examples, the two biggest problems facing our parties are: trust and risk. First, neither party trusts the other. Moreover, there is a general distrust of Internet based businesses. Second, there are substantial risks when dealing online. The combination of low trust and high risk creates substantial barriers. Using a variety of techniques and resources, the parties can eliminate or at least reduce these two fundamental concerns.

BUILDING TRUST BEFORE THE EXCHANGE

500 years ago Tusser sagely observed, "[a] fool and his [or her] money are soon parted" (1557). This sage advice is no less true today. In fact, one can become parted from one's e-money in a single, careless click on the Internet. Just how can one trust someone in cyberspace?

Know Thy Partner

Who exactly is the person at the other end of the transaction? Knowing someone is part of building trust. In a face-to-face exchange just getting to "look someone in their eyes" can help build trust. Online this can be accomplished in a variety of ways.

Communication

The more communication between the parties the easier it is to build trust. Communication falls into two broad categories: synchronous and asynchronous. The primary difference is that in synchronous communication the parties communicate in real time. In asynchronous communication the message is sent and later received by the other party. Synchronous communication includes: text chat, voice chat, video chat, and any other real time communication. Asynchronous communication includes: e-mail, voice mail, video mail, and any other communication that does not link the parties in real time.

Synchronous communication can be more affective in building trust since it allows more information to pass between the parties. For example, if the seller hesitates when asked if her carvings are real ebony wood, the buyer might question the seller's claims. While synchronous communication is preferable, asynchronous communication can be more convenient given the time differences when dealing with global transactions. Moreover, parties operating in their second (or more) language are often more comfortable with asynchronous communication.

There are also other advantages to text-based communication. Epstein (2001) suggests that parties are less likely to lie when their comments are "on the record" in writing. Epstein was discussing attorneys in negotiations but the principle remains the same; having a permanent record of all communications can be an effective deterrent to parties engaging in untruths.

For example, a seller can build trust with potential buyers by offering several methods of communication such as live text chat, a "VOIP me"[1] button on their Web site, and e-mail. Regardless of the method, prompt responses to all inquires are important in building trust. An e-mail that goes unanswered for weeks would dissuade the most interested buyer. Further, the more personal the communication, the better it will help build trust. For example, a personal e-mail rather than an automatically generated response from the seller generates much more trust.

In addition to personalized responses, the content of the communication is also important in building trust. For example, in asynchronous written communication, it is difficult to judge the feelings of the author since the reader only has the sterile words. In fact there is evidence that even the wording of something as simple as the closing "Sincerely, Best, Cheers" can significantly affect the tenor of the communication (Ogunnaike, 2006).

Judge a Person by Their Past

By looking to someone's history you can learn what to expect from them. If you find out that a local seller has a reputation for good quality you are more likely to trust them. Use the Internet to research the history of a seller or buyer. Private auction sites such as eBay incorporate history of users into their site. With a quick glance you can easily learn someone's reputation.

A seller with a long history of good comments from satisfied buyers will have a higher level of trust and will be able to sell goods at a higher price than a seller with a poor or no reputation.

Even if a seller is selling directly to consumers she can offer a list of past clients (with their permission of course). A customer testimonial section on the seller's Web site or even a public forum where members can voice their satisfaction can help to build trust. However, none of these measures of trust are foolproof. Reputation can be falsified using shell accounts. Moreover, who is to say that a comment by a satisfied "customer" was real?

Certification by Third Parties

Many organizations offer certifications for merchants. These certifications are designed, in part, to build trust for consumers by showing that the merchant meets certain standards. Online, similar (and often the same) certifications exist. For example, organizations offering certification for online businesses include: the Better Business Bureau Online,[2] Webassured,[3] and SquareTrade.[4]

There are also specialized certification organizations that address areas such as Web security and protection of user privacy.[5]

To get certification by one of these independent groups, a seller must meet certain standards. Knowing a seller has met these standards can help build trust for buyers.

Unfortunately, even certification by a third party is not a sure sign that there is no risk. Edelman's (2006) recent empirical research suggests that organizations offering third party certification are often lax and "[their] approach gives rise to adverse selection: The sites that seek and obtain trust certifications are actually significantly less trustworthy than those that forego certification." Edelman found that certifying cites had a revoked very few certifications and related this to the financial incentives to keep sites paying for annual certification.

Thus, in order to build trust there are several steps one can take before entering into a transaction. None of these suggestions are new but there are some new twists particular to the online environment.

Even if the parties are able to build some level of trust, once the parties decide to engage in an exchange, how can they reduce risk?

REDUCING RISK DURING THE EXCHANGE

Rather than a complicated legal analysis of the exchange of goods in trade, this section will approach things from the perspective of children. We can learn a lot by watching how children interact as their world is one mostly without enforceable laws. Without an easy way to enforce "rights" children have developed their own methods to reduce risk.

The Law of the Playground: Simultaneous Exchange

If you have ever watched children engaging in a trade of prized items such as a toy, you will notice that they are often very distrusting of their "trade partners." Without any business or legal training, children have developed a fine method of overcoming this distrust. The children will face each other, toy in hand, and simultaneously grab the toy offered by their partners. Only once both sides have a firm grasp on the other's toy will they release their toy and complete the transaction.

This simultaneous exchange protects both parties to the transaction. The parties can size up the item offered in exchange and eliminate the risk of not receiving the toy in exchange since they only release their toy once they have the other firmly in their grasp.

For items such as "virtual goods" that can be exchanged simultaneously online, one can follow the rule of the playground. For example, for virtual goods in online environments such as Second Life,[6] the parties to a transaction can see exactly what is offered for exchange before clicking the "I accept button." Once both parties accept, the transaction automatically occurs.

Although this method can work for some online transactions, simultaneous exchange is normally impractical for transactions involving non-virtual goods. Moreover, part of the attraction of online transactions is the fact that you *do not* have to meet anyone in person. This means that our online parties must seek out other methods to reduce their risks.

The Second Law of the Playground: The Trusted Third Party

If children cannot or will not engage in a simultaneous exchange they will often enlist the aid of a trusted third party. A parent or elder sibling will be called upon to hold both prized toys and deliver the items to each party.

The third party is responsible for making sure each party gets the bargained for item. In legal terms this is an escrow[7] contract. Use of an escrow protects both parties since the escrow agent only releases the items upon proper receipt from both parties. *Farago v. Burke* (1933) (The court ruled that the escrow agent has a fiduciary duty to both the buyer and seller to release funds only upon performance of agreed upon obligations). Moreover, the agent *must* release the items once in proper receipt from both parties. *Moore v. Trott* (1909) (The court ruled that once the agreed upon conditions are met, the escrow agent must deliver the items held in trust). Failure to release the items subjects the escrow agent to liability. *Bruckman v. Parliament Escrow* (1987) (The court ruled that the escrow agent liable for intentional or negligent failure to perform duty to buyer or seller).

Not surprisingly, this arrangement is available for online transactions. Typically transactions with online escrow companies follow this basic pattern:

1. Buyer and seller conclude their agreement
2. Buyer sends payment to escrow company
3. Escrow company notifies seller of receipt of funds
4. Seller ships goods
5. Buyer receives and accepts or rejects goods (limited time for inspection)
6. Upon acceptance of goods (automatic at end of inspection period), the escrow company pays the buyer.[8]

Use of an escrow agent offers protections to both the buyer and the seller. For the buyer, any risk of not receiving the item or receiving the wrong item is eliminated. The escrow agent cannot release the funds until the buyer has had a chance to inspect the goods.

The seller is also protected by this arrangement. First, the escrow agent is responsible for making sure that the funds really exist before notifying the seller to ship. This eliminates the possibility of things such as a check being returned for insufficient funds.

Use of an escrow company is not free of charge. For example, escrow.com charges a minimum of $25 for any transaction and uses a sliding scale that ranges from 3.25% to 0.89% of the total transaction value.[9] For small transactions, the $25 fee is enough to render the service too expensive. However, for larger transactions, the fee is modest compared to the potential risk. For example, the escrow fee for the sale of a $7,500 item is $169, 2.25% of the sale price.

Despite these benefits, few auction based trades have made use of an escrow agent (Sorkin, 2001). Sorkin suggests that escrow use is not more widespread because of the cost and the fact that users tend to ignore the risk involved in transactions.

Unfortunately, use of an escrow company is not without its own risk. First, the company must be a *trusted* third party. A common scam involving escrow agents is where the escrow company is in reality a front for the scam artist, often the same person as the seller (Barrett, 2004).

Just finding a proper escrow company is a challenge. For example, Sorkin (2001) suggested, "there are several online escrow services, the best known of which is Tradenable (formerly i-Escrow)." Despite being the best known online escrow service during Sorkin's research in 2001, Tradenable closed its doors in December of the same year (Rao, 2001). As with any online transaction, updated research is critical for a prudent businessperson.

Multiple Exchanges

Another way to limit risk is to spread it out over multiple orders. Rather than taking all the risk in a single order, splitting it into smaller orders will help to spread the risk out. For example, if our buyer wanted to get 12 wooden statues from the Kenyan crafter, the parties could agree on three separate shipments of four statues. While this will increase the cost of shipping and insurance slightly, it helps protect both parties from a complete loss on the entire order.

This relatively simple method is attractive because it helps both the buyer and seller mitigate their risk without substantial cost.

Risks in Misunderstanding the Deal

Regardless of the form of the transaction, the parties should be sure to clearly communicate the deal. One of the problems with remote negotiations is that the parties may interpret terms and promises differently. Does "genuine ebony" mean the same thing to the Kenyan seller and foreign buyer? If shipping costs are not mentioned who pays? Who bears the risk if the item gets lost or damaged in the post?

Parties to online transactions should take care to clearly and carefully describe the terms of the deal. Many international commercial transactions rely on special terms, called Incoterms, established by the International Chamber of Commerce that clearly define the rights and duties of parties to a transaction.[10] In business to consumer transactions a consumer is not likely to understand terms such as "CIF." A better practice is to clearly state the allocation of risks in the contract.

For example, "This price includes standard shipping by air and insurance from us to your address. The customer is responsible for any custom duties or other costs." Being clear at this stage can prevent misunderstandings and will help avoid disputes.

Beware of the Payment Risks

In the event that the parties choose not to use an escrow agent, there is a risk that the payment will not reach the seller. The level and nature of the risk varies with the payment method.

Sorkin (2001) divides payment methods into traditional and online systems. In 2001, according to Sorkin, "[p]ersonal checks and money orders are the most commonly used payment mechanisms for online auction transactions."[11] However, the current trend has seen that increasingly, credit cards have become the main means of payment. Moreover, personal checks are less likely to be used in international transactions given the difficulty and cost with cashing them. This section will examine the risks and advantages of each of the main payment systems.

Personal Checks

Personal checks present a variety of risks for both parties. For the seller, personal checks, in addition to being costly and difficult to deposit, can be subject to rejection for insufficient funds if the account does not have funds to cover the payment when cashed.

Further, there is a significant delay between the time that the check arrives with the seller and the point when the seller actually receives the funds. This delay increases the risks. Another problem with the delay involves fluctuations in exchange rates. The longer the time between the sale and the final deposit of the funds, the greater the risk of the exchange rate changing.

A personal check also presents risks to the buyer. With a check, the buyer has little recourse should something be wrong with the item ordered. Once a check has been deposited there is virtually nothing the buyer can do to stop payment. For these reasons, personal checks are not an attractive method of payment.

Money Orders

For the seller, money orders offer a bit more protection since they are issued by financial institutions and not normally at risk for return due to insufficient funds. Money orders do however increase costs since the issuing institution will levy a fee. The seller is also likely to be charged a separate fee to deposit the funds into her account. In addition, the money order physically has to travel from the issuing institution to the seller. This delay results in similar exchange rate risks associated with the personal check discussed.

The buyer is similarly at risk when using money orders. Should something be wrong with the order there is virtually nothing the buyer can do to withhold payment on a money order. For these reasons, money orders are not very attractive.

Cash

It almost goes without saying that cash is a highly risky form of payment. However, despite the obvious risks, Sorkin (2001) observed, "[s]urprisingly, cash is another popular payment mechanism for online auction transactions."

The risks with cash are numerous. First, currency is frequently "lost" in mailing. Even if it is not lost there is no way to track that it was actually received by the seller. Second, counterfeit currency is a risk to the seller. Third, depending on the denomination and currency, the seller might have difficulty exchanging it. For example, older bills are often not accepted.

Credit Cards

Credit cards are increasingly becoming the payment means of choice for many online consumers. From the buyer's perspective, a credit card allows for the funds to be more quickly deposited reducing risks of changes in exchange rates. Moreover, with a credit card payment there is no risk of return for insufficient funds. Payment via credit card also removes difficulty with foreign exchange since the merchant can charge the customer in one currency and receive payment in another. Finally, a one-click credit card order has fewer steps to allow the consumer to change her mind before the sale is completed.

The credit card is not without difficulty for the seller however. First, obtaining a merchant account in order to receive credit cards can be difficult for small merchants. In addition, credit cards take a percentage of every transaction from the payment thereby increasing the cost to the seller. Finally, a buyer can dispute a charge through their credit card company and the seller will receive a chargeback until the matter is resolved. While attractive to a buyer, this uncertainty in payment makes the credit card less attractive to a seller.

From the buyer's perspective, a credit card helps reduce the risks significantly. First, many cardholder agreements give the right to the buyer to dispute charges. In these cases, the credit card company will issue a chargeback to the merchant pending resolution of the matter (Sorkin, 2001). Moreover, federal regulations in the United States give a cardholder the right to dispute charges and requires the credit card company to conduct a reasonable investigation, 12 CFR 226.13 (2006). Finally, a credit card eliminates any risk with changes in exchange rates since the transaction occurs almost instantly.

Some buyers are however reluctant to relinquish their credit card numbers online for fear of interception by nefarious parties. With the rise in awareness of identity theft, consumers are rightfully weary of releasing too much information to unknown parties online. There are ways to mitigate against this risk such as one-time use credit card numbers. These numbers are issued by the buyer's credit card company and are linked to their primary account. The number can only be used for one transaction, thereby eliminating the risk of future fraudulent charges on the same account. Credit card companies continue to develop safer methods for online transactions.

Online Payment Systems

With the expansion of online commerce there has been a parallel expansion in forms of online payment. eBay's PayPal[12] is the industry leader; however, on June 29, 2006, Google introduced a competing service, Google Checkout.[13] Typically these services stand in between a buyer and a seller and help facilitate transfer of funds. In this sense, online payment systems resemble credit card transactions and have most of the same advantages and disadvantages.

One added advantage is that although online payment companies do not serve as an escrow agent,[14] services such as PayPal have well-defined dispute mechanisms.[15] If the parties conducted their transaction under the umbrella of eBay there is the added benefit of having the auction, payment, and dispute mechanism all operated by the same corporate entity. The advantages of this will be further discussed in the third section.

Cost is another advantage associated with online payment systems. For example, for international transactions under $3,000, PayPal charges the merchant 3.9% + $0.30.[16] Google Checkout is free through December 31, 2007, thereafter the charge will be 2% + $0.20 per transaction.[17] It is also relatively easy for a merchant to establish an account, comparatively easier than getting a credit card merchant account.

The online payment system is equally attractive to buyers. The transaction happens nearly instantaneously, they are well protected in the event that they do not get the goods they bargained for, and they do not have to relinquish their credit card numbers over the Internet. With an online payment system, their personal information is protected and their credit card number is not released to the merchant.

Reducing Risk Final Comments

Risk is something that cannot be completely eliminated from any transaction. Even in the simultaneous exchange on the playground, the parties run risks such as later finding latent defects. They also face more immediate risks such as being beaten up and losing everything. In the online world there are unavoidable risks as well. However, by structuring the exchange and using proper payment systems, both buyers and sellers can limit these risks.

Despite these efforts, should a problem arise, what recourses might our seller and buyer avail themselves of in this online world? The third section discusses the various methods available for dealing with online disputes.

DEALING WITH DISPUTES

The short answer is that for the vast majority of online international transactions, if a dispute arises, the aggrieved party has already lost. By the time the party hires a lawyer, files a case, and eventually prevails in court, the party will probably have expended more than the value of the dispute. Moreover, even if the party prevails and obtains a judgment, enforcement of a judgment in the foreign jurisdiction of the other party will be prohibitively expensive if not altogether impossible. The traditional judicial system fails small and medium enterprises engaged in international transactions.

Online Dispute Resolution (ODR) offers hope and better access to justice for these parties.

There are many interpretations of the scope of ODR. This chapter will use the commonly cited American Bar Association definition:

ODR is a broad term that encompasses many forms of alternative dispute resolution (ADR) that incorporate the use of the Internet, websites, email communications, streaming media and other information technology as part of the dispute resolution process. Parties may never meet face to face when participating in ODR. Rather, they might communicate solely online.

This definition makes it clear that ODR is a wide concept contemplating a variety of methods of communication. Moreover, ODR is a flexible concept that will expand to include new forms of communication as they come into existence.

ODR can be broadly divided into three categories: online negotiation, online mediation, and online arbitration. This section will analyze these categories and evaluate them from the perspective of a small to medium enterprise.

Advantages of ODR Over Traditional ADR

ODR has many advantages over traditional ADR. First, ODR is convenient since it eliminates the need to travel great distances to meet face-to-face. It is also relatively inexpensive and generally much faster than its traditional counterparts. Moreover, most ODR methods do not require the assistance of an attorney. Finally, ODR offers an online environment already familiar to our online seller and buyer. They chose to enter into their relationship online; it only makes sense to resolve any disputes in the same environment.

Online Negotiation

At its essence, negotiation is no more than the parties discussing their dispute in an attempt to resolve it. If the parties can come to mutual understanding, they can end their dispute and perhaps continue their business relationship.

Ponte (2005) argues that face-to-face negotiation is "often a game of brinkmanship; both sides posture and make excessive demands and offers to settle...in short, a game of legal 'chicken.'" Moreover, in face-to-face negotiation, people often employ pressure tactics and other strategies that make it very stressful. Online negotiation eliminates many of the problems. For example, intimidation tactics that rely on physical presence are obviated online. Online parties are forced to address the merits of the dispute rather than rely on other tactics.

While online negotiation can be done entirely by the parties such as through an exchange of e-mail, there are two types of online negotiation that involve the help of a third "party"[18]: assisted negotiation and automated negotiation.

Assisted Negotiation

Assisted negotiation involves the use of information technology to help the parties organize their thoughts (Kaufmann-Kohler, 2004, p. 13). By way of example, Kaufmann-Kohler cites software that helps organize proposals from both sides.

Normally the assistive software is designed to help the parties identify the issues and move towards a mutually agreeable settlement. SquareTrade[19] is an example of a site offering assisted negotiation services. At SquareTrade, assisted negotiation is free of charge. If the parties cannot reach a resolution, SquareTrade offers other ODR services for a charge.

The advantage of assisted negotiation is that it is easy, free (in the case of SquareTrade), and has a very high success rate. According to Katsh and Rifkin (2001), SquareTrade direct negotiations have an 80% success rate (p. 24).

SquareTrade is closely aligned with eBay and offers a procedure to specifically address negative feedback on eBay. SquareTrade also offers a "seal program" that is similar to the trusted third party certification discussed. Essentially, SquareTrade incorporates several of the strategies to help reduce risk and increase trust between parties.

Automated Negotiation

If the parties are disputing over a single issue such as price, automated negotiation can be a useful tool. Some scholars refer to automated negotiation as "blind bidding" (Ponte & Cavenagh, 2005, p. 39). These systems allow the parties to enter their offers but do not reveal the amount to the other party. "If the offers are within a certain range, often 30 percent, of each other, the parties [automatically] agree to settle and split the difference" (Katch & Rifkin, 2001, p. 61).

In addition to being simple and low cost or free, these systems also protect the offers in the event that no settlement is reached. In other words, a party is not forced to reveal its bottom line during the negotiations. Cybersettle[20] is an example of a site offering automated negotiation services.

One limitation of automated negotiation is that it normally can handle cases with only one variable in dispute, such as price. If the parties are disputing price and an apology, the simple software cannot account for both variables.

A relative new site called SmartSettle[21] has much more sophisticated software that allows for multivariable negotiations. Essentially, SmartSettle lets the parties assign their own values to the different variables. For example, one party might value an early payment more than a higher total payment. This party would be willing to accept a lower total payment if it was made relatively quickly. SmartSettle allows these interests to be taken into account and should result in better settlements than in traditional blind bidding would allow. Since SmartSettle is relatively new, there is not enough data to draw any firm conclusions but it looks promising.

Online Mediation

Online mediation started in the United States in July 1996 (Kaufmann-Kohler & Schultz, 2004, p. 21). In the first case, an online ombuds office helped mediate a dispute between a Web site owner and a newspaper.[22] Within less than a month, the ombuds office helped the parties reach a mutually agreeable solution.

At its essence, online mediation is the use of a third party (a real person unlike assisted negotiation) to help resolve a dispute between two or more parties. Since this process necessarily involves a third party, the cost increases dramatically over the often free online negotiation process. In fact, sites such as SquareTrade offer negotiation free of charge, relying on online mediation to provide income to the company.

Mediation can be helpful since the neutral third party can listen to both sides and offer suggestions to help move the parties to settlement. In the case of SquareTrade, an eBay seller can get negative feedback removed. Given the importance of the feedback rating to parties, this can be a strong motivation to use these services.

The success rate of online mediation is difficult to assess since most resolutions are confidential (Kaufmann-Kohler & Schultz, 2004, p. 26). Kaufmann-Kohler and Schultz estimate that online mediation, at least as of 2004, "does not appear to have scaled great heights. There are over 25 providers of online mediation, but none seems very active except SquareTrade" (p. 26 *citation omitted*). As of December 2006, according to SquareTrade, it "has handled over 2 million disputes across 120 countries in 5 languages."[23] Unfortunately, SquareTrade does not break down its cases in to negotiation and mediation.

In any case, mediation can be a useful tool for resolving disputes. Given the increase in cost, it is more appropriate for larger disputes than for negotiation. The parties should try online negotiation, only if that fails should they escalate things to mediation.

Online Arbitration

The online negotiation and mediation methods result in a mutual agreement in successful cases. Arbitration is different; the parties submit their cases to a third party for a ruling. In this sense, arbitration is more hostile in that both (and in some case neither) agree with the ultimate ruling.

The process normally involves the parties submitting their cases to an arbitrator or a panel of arbitrators. The parties are required to set out both the facts and the legal basis for their arguments. This often requires the assistance of legal counsel, further adding to the costs. The arbitrators will review the filings, take evidence through videoconference or other means, and render a judgment.

The primary problem, aside from cost, is the fact that enforcement of the agreement is not assured. In the case of a mutually agreed upon resolution through negotiation or mediation, it is

Doing International Business Online for the Small and Medium Enterprise

more likely that the parties will comply with the agreement since they affirmatively agreed to it. In arbitration, the parties may disagree with the arbitrator's findings and refuse to comply with the decision. The issue of enforcement of an arbitral award is similar to enforcement of a court decision. In both cases, small or medium businesses will find that enforcement is both expensive and in many cases nearly impossible.

Ultimately, online arbitration suffers from too many of the shortcomings of traditional courts to be of much use to small and medium businesses doing international business. These businesses are advised to try to solve their disputes through negotiation or mediation.

CONCLUSION

Returning to the Kenyan seller and foreign buyer, in order for their transaction to occur, they must overcome the problems of lack of trust and high risk. To address these problems, before the transaction occurs, both parties can take steps to increase their trustworthiness. Further, once they agree to proceed with the transaction, there are steps they can take to reduce the risk to both sides.

If a problem arises, the buyer and seller can resolve their dispute efficiently and to the satisfaction of both parties through the use of online dispute resolution.

A seller should look at joining a private marketplace that offers all of these services. For example, eBay has ways to track reputation and offers good methods of communication through both asynchronous and synchronous communication methods. eBay's ownership of PayPal offers a relatively risk free method of ensuring payment for goods. Finally, eBay also has a relationship with SquareTrade, allowing sellers to avail themselves of third party certification, online negotiation, and online mediation services. This integrated approach makes online marketplaces such as eBay very attractive for merchants.

One problem that this reveals is that online justice is increasingly becoming privatized. This privatizing of justice has caused some to argue that "eBay law" is developing outside of the public legal system. Common disputes are being resolved confidentially and without oversight by the judicial branch. Without feedback over the problems, the courts and the legislature cannot react and make the necessary changes to laws.

Although the legal system has failed the small and medium enterprise engaged in online international transactions, should the private sector provide private justice? While less of a concern to the enterprises, this should be a concern for policy makers.

FUTURE RESEARCH DIRECTIONS

The Traditional Economy

This chapter has focused on traditional transactions involving the sale of goods between remote parties. Online payments and dispute resolution systems will continue to evolve to help facilitate these types of transactions. As this area is still relatively undeveloped, there will be many changes.

As a need is identified, parties will rush to provide services such as is the case with e-escrow services. Many of these services will be similar in nature to existing services. There will also be innovative methods of addressing the specific concerns with online commerce. Researchers should look for needs that need to be addressed and consider their own innovative methods of solving them.

The Virtual Economy

Although this chapter addressed transactions in the traditional economy, increasingly, trade is being done in virtual goods. As commerce expands into the virtual space, so will disputes.

For example, many companies have offices in the virtual world of Second Life. Moreover, as recently as September 2006, according to Colin Rule, eBay's Director of Dispute Resolution, the most often traded commodity on eBay consists of virtual goods. These virtual goods range from gold for online games such as World of Warcraft to real estate in other virtual worlds. Online, virtual dispute resolution will eventually come to these online worlds.

These online worlds exist in a grey area in terms of legal enforcement. Courts are reluctant to enforce contracts for virtual goods. In fact, in early 2007, eBay decided to ban the sale of virtual items from online games (Pham, 2007). eBay's announcement underscores the legal uncertainties, "We can't say definitely if it's legal or illegal."

Who is the actual owner of these virtual goods, the company providing the environment or the "citizens" themselves? How should a contract be enforced in an online world? This virtual economy and its real disputes is an area ripe for additional research.

REFERENCES

American Bar Association Task Force on E-Commerce and ADR. (2002). *Addressing disputes in electronic commerce*. Final Report and Recommendations. Retrieved December 9, 2006, from www.law.washington.edu/ABGA-eADR

Barrett, R. (2004). Take the money and run: Fake online escrow services target big-ticket buyers. *Consumer Reports*. Retrieved September 8, 2006, from http://www.consumerwebwatch.org/dynamic/e-commerce-investigation-take-the-money-and-run.cfm

Black's Law Dictionary (6th ed.). (1990). Saint Paul: West Publishing.

Chauhan, J. (2003). Online dispute resolution systems: Exploring e-commerce and e-securities. *Windsor Review of Legal and Social Issues, 15*, 99.

Edelman, B. (2006, September 6). *Adverse Selection in online "trust" certifications*. Retrieved from http://www.benedelman.org/publications/advsel-trust-draft.pdf

Epstein, L. (2001). Symposium: Alternative dispute resolution in the twenty-first century: Cyber e-mail negotiation vs. traditional negotiation: Will cyber technology supplant traditional means of settling litigation? *Tulsa Law Journal, 36*, 839.

Ewing, G. P. (2002). Technology and legal practice symposium issue: Using the Internet as a resource for alternative dispute resolution and online dispute resolution. *Syracuse Law Review, 52*, 1217.

Katsh, E., & Rifkin, J. (2001). *Online dispute resolution resolving conflicts in cyberspace*. San Francisco: Jossey-Bass.

Kaufmann-Kohler, G., & Schultz, T. (2004). *Online dispute resolution challenges for contemporary justice*. The Hague, The Netherlands: Kluwer Law International.

Lodder, A. R., & Zeleznikow, J. (2005). Article: Developing an online dispute resolution environment: Dialogue tools and negotiation support systems in a three-step model. *Harvard Negotiation Law Review, 10*, 287.

My virtual life: A journey into a place in cyberspace where thousands of people have imaginary lives. Some even make a good living. Big advertisers are taking notice. (2006, May 1). *Business Week*.

Ogunnaike, L. (2006, November 26). 'Yours truly' The e-variations. *New York Times*. Retrieved December 9, 2006, from http://www.nytimes.com/2006/11/26/fashion/26email.html?ex=1165726800&en=dcac567c9dbefa8a&ei=5070

Pham, A. (2006, February 3, 2007). eBay bans auctions of virtual treasures:

Players of online games spend big on digital loot. But the site is worried about legal issues. *Los Angeles Times*, p. Business 1.

Ponte, L., & Cavenagh, T. D, (2005). *CyberJustice online dispute resolution (ODR) for e-commerce*. Upper Saddle River, NJ: Pearson Education, Inc.

Rao, R. (2001). Tradenable reaches the end of the road. *Online reporter*. Retrieved September 2007, from LexisNexis (3183239).

Rule, C. (2002). *Online dispute resolution for business B2B, e-commerce, consumer, employment, insurance, and other commercial conflicts*. San Francisco: Jossey-Bass.

Rule, C. (2006). Comments at Center for Information Technology and Dispute Resolution Cyberweek conference Sept. 25-29, 2006. http://www.odr.info/cyberweek2006/program.php

Selis, P., Ramasastry, A., & Wright, C. S. (2002, June). Bidder beware: Toward a fraud-free marketplace—Best practices for the online auction industry. *Washington State Attorneys Office*. Retrieved December 9, 2006, from http://www.atg.wa.gov/consumer/Publications/auction_best_practices082302.doc

Shah, A. (2004). Using ADR to resolve online disputes. *Richmond Journal of Law & Technology, 10*, 25.

Sorkin, D. E. (2001). Payment methods for consumer-to-consumer online transactions. *Akron Law Review, 35*, 1.

Tusser, T. (1557). *Five hundred points of good husbandry*. Liverpool, UK: Kessinger Publishing.

Whitman, M. (2006). Keynote address. *Proceedings of eBay shareholders convention*. Audio transcript of the keynote available at: http://www.wsradio.com/internet-talk.cfm/radio/ebay-keynote-2006.htm

CASES

Bruckman v. Parliament Escrow, 190 Cal. App. 3d 1051 (Cal. Ct. App. 1987)

Farago v. Burke, 262 N.Y. 229 (N.Y. 1933)

Moore v. Trott, 156 Cal. 353 (Cal. 1909)

REGULATIONS

12 CFR 226.13 (2006)

ADDITIONAL READING

Fisher, R., & Brown, S. (1988). *Getting together building relationships as we negotiate*. New York: Penguin.

Fisher, R., & Ury, W. (1991). *Getting to yes: Negotiating agreement without giving in*. New York: Penguin.

Ury, W. (1993). *Getting past no negotiating your way from confrontation to cooperation*. New York: Bantam.

Web Resources

Center for Information Technology and Dispute Resolution, http://www.odr.info/

Center for Information Technology and Dispute Resolution has a very comprehensive listing of materials in their online library, http://www.odr.info/library.php

International Forum on Online Dispute Resolution, http://www.odr.info/liverpool/

Findlaw is an excellent site for getting general legal information. http://www.findlaw.com/

The United States Small Business Administration has very good information for small business owners; http://www.sba.gov/

ENDNOTES

[1] A "VOIP me" button is a link on a Web page that allows a user to instantly commence a voice over IP (VOIP) telephone call with the party. Skype is one such VOIP service.

[2] http://www.bbbonline.org/

[3] http://www.webassured.com/

[4] http://www.squaretrade.com/

[5] For example, TRUSTe (http://www.truste.org/) "is an independent, nonprofit enabling trust based on privacy for personal information on the Internet. We certify and monitor web site privacy and email policies, monitor practices, and resolve thousands of consumer privacy problems every year."

[6] "Second Life is a 3-D virtual world entirely built and owned by its residents." It offers an environment where people can sell virtual goods for online currency that can be exchanged for "real" currency. http://secondlife.com/

[7] "Escrow. A legal document (such as a deed), money, stock, or other property delivered by the grantor, promisor or obligor into the hands of a third person, to be held by the latter into the happening of a contingency or performance of the condition, and then by him [or her] delivered to the grantee, promisee or obligee. A system of document transfer in which a deed, bond, stock, funds, or other property is delivered to a third person to hold until all conditions in a contract for fulfilled; e.g. delivery of deed to escrow agent under installment land sale contract until full payment for land is made." Black's Law Dictionary, sixth edition, page 545, West publishing Co. 1990, Henry Campbell Black, M. A.

[8] For example see https://www.escrow.com/solutions/escrow/process.asp (visited September 8, 2006).

[9] https://www.escrow.com/support/calculator.asp (visited September 8, 2006).

[10] http://www.iccwbo.org/incoterms/id3045/index.html *Also see* http://www.iccwbo.org/incoterms/wallchart/wallchart.pdf for a handy chart depicting the differences in the terms.

[11] Sorkin cites Andy Roe, E-Payment Reluctance, AuctionWatch.com (Mar. 2, 2001), at http://www.auctionwatch.com/awdaily/features/reluctance/ (noting that over 80% of eBay sales involve payment by personal check, money order, or cashier's check); National Consumers League, supra note 2 (noting that 69% of buyers pay by check, money order, or cashier's check).

[12] http://www.paypal.com/

[13] https://checkout.google.com/

[14] For example, in PayPal's help section they specifically state that they are not an escrow agent. https://www.paypal.com/cgi-bin/webscr?cmd=_help-ext&nodeid=25355&leafid=1030&prior_transaction_id=33405&answer_id=16777216 (accessed December 9, 2006).

[15] For example, PayPal's User Agreement (November 2, 2006) states the steps necessary dispute a charge. http://www.paypal.com/cgi-bin/webscr?cmd=p/gen/ua/policy_buyer_complaint-outside (accessed December 9, 2006).

[16] PayPal Transaction Fees for Cross-Border Payments—United States, https://www.paypal.com/us/cgi-bin/webscr (accessed December 9, 2006).

[17] http://checkout.google.com/seller/fees.html (accessed December 9, 2006).

[18] The party is not a person but normally computer software.

[19] http://www.squaretrade.com

[20] http://www.cybersettle.com

[21] http://www.smartsettle.com

[22] The full case can be found at http://www.ombuds.org/narrative1.html

[23] http://www.squaretrade.com/cnt/jsp/abt/aboutus.jsp, Retrieved December 9, 2006.

Chapter XII
Consumer Protection in Cross-Border E-Commerce Markets

Shino Uenuma
South Toranomon Law Offices, Japan

ABSTRACT

Due to the development of the Internet, global e-commerce markets are growing greatly. From the viewpoint of consumers, cross-border transactions involve some difficulties in obtaining redress from problematic businesses. In e-commerce markets, consumers have also experienced other kinds of difficulty. To increase consumer protection in global e-commerce markets, various attempts have been made by the private and public sectors. This chapter gives an overview of current attempts, and considers the possibility of future methods to achieve effective consumer protection in cross-border e-commerce markets.

INTRODUCTION

The development of the Internet has made radical changes in the market, by creating an e-commerce market. It enabled users to find goods or services easily and purchase them at any time without physically going to stores. When the e-commerce market started growing,[1] problems peculiar to the e-commerce market had been already recognized (OECD, 1999[2]).

The issues in cross-border transactions have been historically discussed.[3] However, in the past discussions, these issues were discussed in the context of transactions between business to business, that is, B2B transactions.[4]

The Internet by its nature has no borders; therefore, the e-commerce market naturally grew into the global market. In consumer transactions, commonly discussed are different from those in B2B transactions, because time and money consumers can spend to resolve the issue are generally more limited than the party in B2B transactions.

This chapter will analyze and review the peculiar nature of B2C transactions in the cross-border e-commerce market.

OVERVIEW OF THE CURRENT CONDITIONS IN E-COMMERCE MARKET

The Growth of Cross-Border E-Commerce Markets

An e-commerce market is rapidly growing these days.[5] Because of the global nature of the Internet, cross-border transactions are growing as well. Accordingly, the number of complaints from consumers, related to cross-border transactions has increased. According to OCED statistics (OECD, 2006)[6], the U.S. Federal Trade Commission received 64,797 Cross-Border Complaints in 2004, and 86,390 in 2005. The statistics of the U.K. European Consumer Centre Cross Border Queries also showed the following figures:[7]

Year 2002	291
Year 2003	492
Year 2004	776
Year 2005	1887

When the market is growing, troubles in the related transactions are also increasing. Have such troubles been effectively resolved in cross-border e-commerce market?

WHAT IS PECULIAR TO CROSS-BORDER E-COMMERCE MARKETS

It is essential to review the peculiar natures of cross border e-commerce markets in order to conside how to establish effective consumer protection systems there.

Distance (Not Face to Face)

In the e-commerce market, consumers do not purchase the goods or services on the premises of the sellers. The transactions are generally made over the Internet through commercial Web sites operated by businesses. It allows consumers to just sit before their computers, click on the order buttons, and wait for the goods to be delivered. A consumer can purchase goods sold in a foreign country without personally going there.

This convenience has made the e-commerce market rapidly growing; however, it also brings problems which seldom exist in the face to face transactions. In transactions made on the premises, a purchaser has a chance to inspect a product before purchasing, and the goods or services are generally delivered on the spot in exchange for payment.

Some types of problems peculiar to the e-commerce market are related to this distant nature. One of them is the problem of delivery. According to the statistics of e-consumer complaints reported by econsumer.gov, 21% of complaints received during the period starting from January 1 through June 30, 2005, are those related to merchandise or service which was never received.[8] How to obtain redness in case of such problems from distant businesses is another peculiar type of the problems.

The Low Value of The Transactions

Another feature of the e-commerce transaction is the low value of each transaction. According to the survey conducted by DoubleClick, an average transaction value was U.S. $134.01 in 2003.[9] Another report related to the ADR Pilot Project by the Next Generation Electronic Commerce Promotion Council of Japan (ECOM) showed the value of the dispute was less than 50,000 Japanese yen (approximately U.S. $435[10]) approximately 70% of the complaints received by ECOM.[10] Even in extraordinary cases such as fraud, 45% of the total number of complaints in 2005 were the complaints in which the amount paid is lower than U.S. $500 (Federal Trade Commission, 2006[11]).

This feature limits the method a consumer can employ to obtain redress. Since the value they claim is small, consumers cannot afford or are not willing to spend a large amount of cost to solve their problems, for example, by formally filing a law suit.

Language Barriers

Third, the cross-border transactions generally involve more than one language. A consumer may purchase merchandise from the Web site written in a language which is not their mother tongue. In the ordering stage, the process is not so complicated; therefore, a consumer can handle the matters even if it is written in his/her non-mother language. However, solving problems requires much higher language skills.[12]

Differences in Legal Systems

Last, cross-border transactions necessarily involve laws and regulations of different nations. Each nation has different standards of consumer protection in its legal system.[13] The systems of dispute resolution are also different among nations. Once a dispute occurs, it often raises questions about jurisdiction, venue, governing laws, and enforcement. In a cross-border dispute, a consumer has to determine with which court and under which law, one has to file a suit. Even after one obtains a judgment, to obtain actual redress, one has to make the judgment effectively enforced against the business in question.[14]

THE CURRENT ATTEMPTS TO ESTABLISH DISPUTE RESOLUTION SYSTEMS

To handle the features of the e-commerce disputes, several attempts are currently employed to establish effective dispute resolution systems. This section provides information about the current attempts and evaluates such attempts.

Private Sector's Voluntary Attempts

Businesses have noticed that it is important to provide efficient dispute resolution systems to build consumer confidence in e-commerce. Industrial leaders recommend that internal resolution systems should be offered.[15] "Internal resolution" is not limited to be provided within each business. Instead, it is provided within in each industry, among companies in the same industry. One example of an efficient attempt is that which is provided for credit card industry.

The credit card is the most frequently used payment method in e-commerce, especially in the cross-border market.[16]

The credit card industry has its own unique dispute resolution system called the "chargeback." The chargeback system formally refers to the process by which an issuer returns the fund to the acquirer, not having direct impact on the legal obligations between merchants and cardholders. However, through compliance with the rules relating to chargeback, a cardholder, generally the consumer, can receive a refund for the disputed transactions, if a cardholder's claim satisfies the requirements.[17] In addition to mandatory card holders' protection which is provided in some nations,[18] this industrial practice is also working as consumer protection.

The major card networks also provide another protection to their cardholders called "zero liability policy," which provides a stronger protection than a mandatory one. This "zero liability policy" protection gives card holders full protection against any monetary losses due to fraudulent use of their payment cards.

The problem of this cardholder protection system is that it is not suitable for solving quality related problems with the merchandise, because the chargeback process does not directly involve a cardholder and a merchant.[19] However, in combination with an ADR system, it will work with this quality related problem.

ADR Systems

ADR is the abbreviation for alternative dispute resolution, which refers to a dispute resolution system which is provided outside, as an alternative to, the governmental judicial process. This system is provided either by a governmental body or by a private sector. It covers a variety of mechanisms and processes for dispute resolution, the most common forms are negotiation, mediation, and arbitration (OECD, 2000[20]). Because of this flexibility, ADR can adopt an appropriate system for the disputes in the e-commerce market, that is, employing technological measures.

Online dispute resolution, often referred to as ODR, is one of the such systems. ODR still does not have a solid definition; however, it is generally understood as an ADR system which is carried on through computer networks (Hozumi, K., 2005[21]).

Because it is assisted by technology, personal attendance is not required in ODR; therefore, this system seems promising in the disputes related to e-commerce to deal with its distant nature. It can save costs and also time.

In spite of its promising appearance, there are not many bodies actually providing ODR services.[22] They are Square Trade,[23] Smart Settle,[24] Cybersettle,[25] iCourthouse,[26] and Singapore Mediation Centre.[27] The number of cases handled by these bodies are not so surprisingly large. For example, Square Trade has handled 2 million cases,[28] Cybersettle has handled over 160,000,[29] iCourthouse has received over 11,000 cases,[30] and Singapore Mediation Center has received more than 1,000 disputes.[31]

In addition to the small number of the cases referred to such bodies, another ODR's weak aspect is that ODR has no legal binding effects. In a facilitated negotiation process, if either of the parties refuses participation, the process cannot proceed. In a mediation process, participation is voluntary also, and whether the proposed resolution is accepted or not is dependant on each party's intent. In an arbitration process, the arbitration decision is biding upon both parties only when there has been the parties' prior consent for such binding effect.[32]

Combinations

Combination systems are being employed in some current attempts. One of them, and seemingly the most effective one, is the combination of the Online Trustmark program and the ODR system. An online trustmark is a mark which represents a certification by a third party. The mark certifies that the party reaches a certain standard with regard to certain aspects of its practice.[33] Examples of such online trustmark programs are TRUSTe[34] and VeriSign.[35]

In the e-commerce market, it often happens that consumers are not sure whether the merchant really exists on the opposite side of the Internet, whether the merchant is involved in any fraudulent activities, or whether not a consumer can really trust the merchant. The online trustmark plays a role in certifying such reliability of online merchandise.

The Better Business Bureau (BBB)[36] provides the Reliability Seal Program through which, the BBB certifies that the business keeps the good standing of the business for 1 year or longer, that the business has established ethical standards for its commercial activities, that it has a satisfactory complaint handling record with the BBB, and that the business agrees to participate in the BBB's dispute system, at the consumer's request.[37] The trustmark which is permitted to be displayed on the Web site of business is linked to the database of the BBB, and a consumer can confirm the status of the membership of the business by clicking on the trustmark. The BBB also keeps its database available to the public on its Web site, which carries information regarding businesses, not only its members, but also non-member businesses, reported to the BBB. The information contains the number of the complaints filed against such businesses, the nature of the business, and whether such a complaint was resolved.[38]

In this combined system, the participation in the dispute resolution system is a unilaterally mandatory on the business who is a member of the program. And if a dispute is not resolved, such information is published through the BBB's database.

The statistics of the activities for the year of 2005 is as follows:[39]

- **Company report requests:** 41,456,334
- **BBB Online Seal Program confirmations:** 9,981,141
- **Complaints processed:** 781,455
  - **Through mediations and arbitrations:** 37,458
- **Complaints counseling and referrals:** 261,043

Compared to the other ODR bodies reviewed in the section on "ADR systems", this system is more widely used among consumers.

Small Claim Law Suit Systems

For businesses who do not try to voluntarily solve the disputes, consumers shall take legal actions against them to exercise their legal rights. Many nations have less formal judicial procedures for small claims than normal law suit procedures. They are generally designed to be appropriate for small claims in terms of costs and time.

Although the systems vary among nations; it is common to have a maximum limit of the amount which can be claimed at such courts. In most nations, the threshold limit is less than EUR 10,000.[40] To make systems proportional to the amount claimed, some systems are employing simplified procedures and have limited jurisdiction over the nature of the claim (i.e., such as only for monetary claims).

For example, a small claim procedure in Japan is only available for a law suit in which simple monetary claim is sought, and evidences or witnesses are limited to those which can be investigated in one day at the trial. An appeal to the appellate court is not allowed; however, if a respondent raises the objection that the disupte is solved by such procedure before commencement of the procedure, the case shall be handled in accordance with the normal court procedure.[41] Also, the small claim suit falls under the jurisdiction of a summary court where requirement that the advocate representing the party, be a licensed attorney at law in another courts, is relaxed.[42] Many countries employ simplified systems similar to those in Japan for a small claim to save costs and time to settle disputes.[43]

As reviewed in the section on "ADR systems", most disputes related to e-commerce involving consumers fall under the amount limit for these types of a small claim suit systems.

However, this system has some difficulties, and is not sufficiently efficient so far. One is that the system does not always relax the requirement of personal appearance of the parties, which is against the distant nature of the e-commerce market as mentioned in the section on "Private Sector's Voluntary Attempts". Travel expenses may easily exceed the amount of the dispute.

Another difficulty is that this system is operated by the governmental office; therefore, it is not always useful in cross border disputes. The problems related to jurisdiction still exist in the small claim suit systems as in the normal court procedures. And even a plaintiff succeeds in obtaining the judgment, then the plaintiff faces the problem of enforcement of such judgment in a foreign country.

Collective Claim Systems[44]

Some nations have a collective claim system which is a procedure for collective action lawsuits, on behalf of consumers. This system is useful to overcome small values of disputes by collecting the claims of multiple plaintiffs.

Systems vary among nations in terms of the party who can file a suit on behalf of consumers and the kind of remedy that can be sought in such systems.

For example, the United States has a class action system, where a single consumer can file a law suit seeking monetary damages on behalf of other consumers who have similar interests in the suit, without obtaining prior authorizations to do so. Many civil law countries do not have a similar collective suit system where a prior authorization is not required. In such a civil law country, for a party to file a law suit on behalf of other persons, the party has to contact each of the other plaintiffs and obtain a prior authorization. This system does not work very well in the e-commerce market due to its distant nature and lack of a method to exchange the information about who has the same interest in the law suit.

In response to this barrier, some nations have introduced other types of the collective claims where a proper consumer association may commence a representative action on behalf of consumers without identifying each individual consumer. However, one of the problems in this system is that the type of remedy is limited only to injunctive relief, and monetary damage is not covered in such a system.[45]

Problems related to the jurisdiction and enforcement of the judgment are also applicable to collective claim systems like the small claims suit systems.

THE COMMON PROBLEMS IN THE CURRENT ATTEMPTS

As reviewed in the section "The Current Attempts to Establish Dispute Resolution Systems," every current attempt has problems. This section analyzes common problems in these attempts.

Problems Among Private Sectors

How to Be Funded

One of the most serious problems to the private sectors in providing a dispute resolution system such as ODR is how to secure the funding.[46] Since the judicial procedures are funded by governments, that is, tax, they have no funding problems. However, when the dispute resolution systems are provided by a private organization, they have to consider how to secure the funding to maintain an organization and to keep providing the service.

Charging fees to the participants does not work as a funding method. The system will be ineffective if it costs more than the value of the dispute[47] and consumers generally do not want to pay fees to solve the small amount of the dispute.[48] Therefore, fee revenue alone cannot be expected to be enough to support the services.

Several ODR services were provided as part of experimental research studies funded by governmental bodies. However, these kind of experimental attempts are so unstable that they cannot be used as a long-term plan for the developing systems.[49]

Some programs are trying to solve the funding problems by imposing fees only on businesses. For example, in the BBB system, the ADR program is funded by the businesses who are members of the BBB without charging any participation fees to the consumer.[50] However, this method encounters difficulty in how to encourage businesses to participate in such programs. If a business does not see any merit in participation, then it will not be willing to pay such costs. Therefore, in this type of funding, it is essential to design the system to give businesses incentives to participate in the system.

Another type of funding method for the ADR system is the one used by the banking and insurance industry in the U.K. and Ireland which is funded through a scheme controlled by the government or independent bodies.[51] In these programs. One of them is the U.K. Financial Ombudsman Service. The program is financed by levies on the industry which is made mandatory by the regulations.[52] This method can be an option to solve the problem how to encourage businesses to participate in such programs.

Not Effective for Businesses which have no Intent to Solve the Disputes

Since the private sectors' attempt is a contractual-based dispute resolution systems, as reviewed in the above section, in order to procede with the program, consent from the parties is essential. Generally, the incentive to participate in the dispute resolution program is arising from the incentive to keep a good reputation in the market. Therefore, this system does not work with businesses that do not have any intent to solve disputes, such as those businesses intentionally involved in fraudulent activities.[53]

In the e-commerce market, many consumers have expeienced that they cannot even contact the merchant.[54] After consumers make payment, the merchant cannot be reached, or even the Web site of the business disappears.

As reviewed in the above section, if the consumer makes payment through a credit card, a charge back system may be working in some cases, such as the complaint based on no delivery of goods or services. However, where a consumer makes payment by a method other than credit card, and where other systems provided by a private sector are not working, the remaining resort for the consumer is to obtain remedy through legal authority, that is, a formal judicial process having enforcement power over the defendant.

Problems Among Public Sectors

Barriers in Different Legal Systems

As already reviewed in the above section, the systems operated by the public sectors have difficulty due to the differences among the applicable legal systems, such as jurisdictional matters, applicable law matters, and enforcement issues.

A consumer generally wants to file a law suit with a court located in one's place of residence. It is much easier than filing a suit with a court in another nation, in terms of the language, the applicable procedural law, or the ease of access the court. However, in a cross-border case, whether the court located in the plaintiff's nation has jurisdiction over the dispute or not is often unclear; therefore, a plaintiff consumer bears a risk in determining where to file a law suit.

Even if the court located in the plaintiff's place of residence has the jurisdiction over the dispute, there is another problem regarding enforcement. Since the judicial authority stems from each nation's sovereignty, a judgment made in one country cannot be automatically enforced in another country. Generally, the assets of the defendant exist in the location of the defendant, not of the plaintiff. Therefore, to obtain monetary remedy, the plaintiff has to enforce the judgment in a nation other than that where such judgment is decreed if the plaintiff filed a suit with the court located in the place of the plaintiff. Recognition of a foreign judgement by the nation where enforcement is sought is required to enforce the foreign judgment.[55]

In the public sectors, these problems cannot be promptly resolved without having some international formal treaties or agreements. On the other hand, in the private sectors, since the system can be proceeded on a contractual basis, treaties or agreements are not as significant as in the procedure in the public sectors. Enforcement is not so problematic either. A business is expected to obey the order made in the procedure carried out in the private sectors when a business desires to keep its good reputation to those markets where a private dispute resolution system has difficulties in creating benefits in participation.

THE KEY TO FACILITATE CONSUMER PROTECTION

Based on the weakness reviewed in the previous section, this section examines how to overcome such weak aspects to establish efficient dispute resolution systems.

Considerations for Private Sectors

How to Offer Incentives to Businesses

As reviewed in the previous section, funding problems can be solved by encouraging businesses to invest funds in a private organization that provides dispute resolution services. If a business believes that the participation in such a system is beneficial, it will invest the funds to participate in the dispute resolution services.[56] Combination with online trustmark programs operated by the BBB, as reviewed in the section, "The Current Attempts to Establish Dispute Resolution Systems," appears to be working to create such incentives. The success of the BBB system exists because its online trustmark program is highly recognized among consumers.[57] Without recognition from consumers, a business would not see any benefit in participation in such programs. The database system of the BBB is also playing a role in its success. Since consumers are checking the database to seek information about a business before purchasing from a business with which the consumer is not familiar, a business does not want to have bad information displayed in the database, which it will lose business opportunities. Combination with an online trustmark program and a private dispute resolution system are working in the market consumers want to have a method to check the reliability of businesses.

On the other hand, in markets where consumers generally trust online merchants, the online trustmark program is not working very well because the the particiaption in such a program does not bring any benefit to the businesses.[58] Other incentives must be created in such markets.

An ombudsman system, like the UK Financial Ombudsman Service, is another type of system which seems promising to those markets where a private dispute resolution system has difficulties in creating benefits in participation. Regulations can create solid incentives for businesses to participate in dispute resolution programs. This system can solve the funding issues and is expected to obtain recognition from consumers.[59] Imposing regulations by the government may cause objections; however, if employed only in certain industries where disputes often occur between merchants and consumers, this system may provide efficient dispute resolution, through good cooperation with governmental authorities and private sector which actually provides the dispute resolution service through flexible proceedings.

International Cooperation

International cooperation among the private sectors providing dispute resolution programs is also a promising system. The private sectors may dominate in this aspect since international cooperation among the public sectors is not easy and is slow because of the need for formal agreement. An example of this cooperation is international referral services. For example, organization "A" receives a complaint from a consumer residing in one country where the organization A exists, A organization refers the complaint to organization "B" located in another country where the business in question exists. Consumers can submit complaints within their country using their own language, and can receive the dispute resolution services through a voluntary agreement between the two organizations.

Examples of such international cooperation is Asia Trustmark Alliance singed by private ADR organizations in Japan, Korea, Singapore, and Taiwan[60] and Global Trustmark Alliance lead by the BBB.[61]

Developments of international cooperation can provide efficient dispute resolution systems for cross-border e-commerce markets.[62]

Consideration for Public Sectors

How to Get Redress for Victims of Fraudulent Activities of Businesses

As already reviewed in the previous section, the private sectors' programs do not work for businesses who have no intention of resolving the disputes. Only systems operated by the public sectors can handle these types of businesses through governmental authority with enforcement power.

As reviewed in the section on "Small Claim Law Suit Systems", a law suit undertaken by an individual is not usually effective even if it is a small claims suit. It is natural to expect that a law suit against a business who has no intention of resolving a dispute would need time and costs. The collective suit system seems more promising from this point of view; however, availability of such systems are limited. In most nations, monetary remedies cannot be sought in representative suits. Injunctive relief is important so as not to create other victims in the future, but it is not enough for the existing victims to whom monetary losses have already been incurred. Obtaining a monetary remedy is important for such existing victims.

One of the most aggressive measures to secure a monetary remedy for consumers who have suffered monetary damages is a method employed by the U.S. Federal Trade Commission (FTC).[63] The FTC can file a law suit against a business and obtain a court order for equitable monetary relief on behalf of consumers as a whole, for violations of unfair and deceptive practice provisions of the FTC Act[64] and other regulations set forth by the FTC. The legal authority to seek redress on behalf of consumers as a whole is not expressly set forth by the FTC Act; however, FTC began to construct Section 13 (b) of the FTC Act. This section authorizes the FTC to seek preliminary and permanent injunctions to remedy "any provision of law enforced by the Federal Trade Commission" thereby setting forth the FTC's authority not only to permanently bar deceptive practices, but also to impose equitable monetary relief such as restitution and rescission of contracts to remedy past violations.[65] With this tool, from April 2004 through March 2005, the FTC filed 86 actions in federal district court and obtained 81 judgments ordering the return of more than U.S. $573 million in redress to consumers.[66]

The FTC has a tool to identify fraudulent activities of businesses by accepting consumer complaints[67] and keeping their database called consumer sentimental.[68] After deciding a certain business is engaged in unfair and deceptive practices through such tools, the FTC files a law suit against the business on behalf of consumers as a whole and then will distribute the funds to victim consumers after obtaining judgment or reaching settlement.

Even foreign consumers can receive benefits from such activities by the FTC. For the period from 2000 through 2005, the FTC distributed U.S. $7.3 million to more than 100,000 consumers in 116 countries outside the United States.[69]

Considering these facts, the FTC method seems very efficient for consumers to obtain monetary remedy, and it seems to be working even for cross-border fraudulent activities. However, some unsolved questions remain in this method.

One of them is whether a governmental agency has the authority to file a claim with a foreign court as a plaintiff. Each nation shall have its own sovereignty, and a foreign government cannot directly enforce its law in the territory of another country. The FTC's filing of a law suit based on the U.S. FTC Act with a foreign court will raise this issue, an issue that was actually argued in some cases.[70]

Enforcement of the judgment in a foreign state also causes problems because many countries do not enforce U.S. court judgments obtained by governmental agencies.[71] It is generally understood that a penal or a public law shall be sought to be enforced by the sovereign alone. The FTC's action therefore can be construed as one to enforce regulatory rights and powers,[72] although the FTC stands on the position that a distinction should be drawn between government obtained judgment for fines and penalties and judgments providing monetary remedies to consumers.[73] Considering these issues, it seems that some type of an international governmental arrangement, such as a treaty or a convention is required to make this type of remedy obtained by a governmental agency more efficient for cross-border disputes.

How to distribute the funds to victim consumers might also be a problem. One of the examples is the SkyBiz.com case. The FTC filed a law suit against SkyBiz.com., Inc., which was allegedly involved in illegal international pyramid operation, and the FTC reached settlement to receive U.S $20 million to be distributed to consumers.[74] It is alleged that victim consumers are from more than 160 different countries and up to 400,000 in number. The funds are to be distributed to legitimate victim consumers. To invite consumers to submit claims, Web sites were established and are maintained in five languages.[75] The Web page opened in February 2003, and was publicized by cooperative organizations in other countries such as consumer protection governmental agencies to victim consumers in their country. The Web sites set forth the due date for submitting the claim on July 31, 2004.[76] However, the number of submitted claims was not so large, so the Web page is still inviting the submission of claims.[77]

Consumers residing outside of the U.S. seldom have opportunities to know the FTC's action, and may hardly be aware that they can obtain monetary remedy by submission of such claims. It is very important for such consumers to know such opportunities to obtain remedies to secure their right. Once the FTC collects the funds from the defendant business and the collected funds are distributed only to consumers who submitted the claim to the FTC, there will be no more assets in the business in question. Victim consumers who had no knowledge of the FTC's action and no opportunity to submit the claim, have no way to obtain monetary remedy any more.

The FTC type remedy can certainly provide the most efficient system for cross-border fraudulent cases; however, there remain problems which shall be more fully discussed.

Cooperation Among Nations

As already considered in the preivous section, issues of enforcement of a judgment in another country are one of the most significant problems with the systems provided by the public sectors.

Especially when considering the sovereignty issue, securing enforcement of the judgment in another country requires a formal international arrangement except for cases among the countries which are members of Lugano Convention of 1988[78] and Brussels I Regulation of 2001[79] in Europe. However, there are no such other comprehensive international treaties regarding enforcement. The Convention on the Recognition and Enforcement of Foreign Judgments in Civil and Commercial Matters, concluded on February 1, 1971, has only four signatory nations. In 2000, the Hague Conference on Private

International Law reported a preliminary draft of the Convention with a Jurisdiction and Foreign Judgments in Civil and Commercial Matters Section;[80] however, the finally adopted Convention covered only enforcement of judgments based on exclusive choice of court agreements in the context of a B2B relationship.[81] If the scope of the preliminary draft of the Convention was kept in the final adopted version, the jurisdiction issue could have been made clearer.

As reviewed in the previous section, disputes with the businesses having intention to solve the problems to keep their good reputation can be handled through the private sectors. They can arrange voluntary international arrangement on a contractual basis. The disputes with the businesses which cannot be expected to solve the problem at the voluntary basis should be handled through the public sectors having legal authority, which inevitably involves the sovereignty issue. Therefore, to take advantage of the public sector method, appropriate international arrangements shall be sought. If multi-national arrangements cannot be reached easily, bilateral arrangements, which will work to some extent, should be considered.

CONCLUSION

The growth of e-commerce has enabled consumers to enjoy goods and services from distant locations. The development on one side always comes together with problems on another side. In the past, consumers were seldom involved in cross-border transactions and therefore in cross-border disputes. However, after the e-commerce market became popular, the potential for suffering from a cross-border issue has become much greater.

Currently, the businesses, who recognize the value of the e-commerce market, are recommending that their industries encourage consumer confidence in the market. Effective dispute resolution systems can help the development of consumer confidence. Where the dispute resolution system can be provided on a contractual basis, and the arrangement is well organized, can be overcome. Unfortunately, the current dispute resolution systems provided by the private sectors are not greatly developed nor widely used because of their lack of funding. If businesses share their view on the importance of providing effective dispute resolution, the systems can be automatically encouraged to be developed, then, consumer protection can be realized and the market are more growing. It means both businesses and consumers can enjoy and benefit from the development of the dispute resolution system.

Regretfully, there exist businesses that are involved in fraudulent activities and not interested in solving the problems with their consumers. They are persons who are not interested in the growth of the market. For the disputes which involve these kinds of merchants, a private sector's dispute resolution system cannot be expected to work well, and the public sector should play a role in such situations. Currently, some legal procedures exist which are designed for consumers' use; however, it is not designed for consumers who are involved in cross-border disputes. To facilitate such consumers, governmental authority's effort, including international arrangement among nations, is essential.

Both private and public sectors have their own role and strong points. Good combinations between the private and public sectors is essential to establish efficient consumer protection systems in cross-border e-commerce markets.

FUTURE RESEARCH DIRECTIONS

Cross-border e-commerce markets are now growing and how to get redress for consumers in such markets are now at the trial stage.

As discussed in this chapter, ODR was considered as an effective way to resolve the problems in e-commerce markets. Although not all of them have achieved success, this method still seems to have some merits in e-commerce. Continuous observation of the existing ODR providers is desired in this field.

To solve the problems in cross-border transactions, private sectors are currently trying to arrange an international alliance because businesses understand importance of consumer protection in cross-border transactions to promote their commercial activities. How they arrange their alliance and obtain the funding for it, can also be considered as an important subject in this area.

As for public sectors, some nations have special agencies which have extensive power for consumer protection in B2C transactions. Examples are the Federal Trade Commission in the United States and Korea Consumer Protection Board in South Korea. It is necessary to conduct continuous study in their policy making, including seeking international agreements with other nations, and its enforcement activities.

REFERENCES

Federal Trade Commission. (2006). *Consumer fraud and identity theft complaint data, January—December 2005*. Federal Trade Commission.

Hozumi, K. (2005). ODR arbitratin for settlement of e-commerce disputes. *Journal of the Japanese Institute of International Business Law, 33,* 11.

OECD. (1999). *OECD guidelines for consumer protection in the context of electronic commerce.* OECD.

OECD. (2000, December 11-12). *Building trust in the online environment: Business to consumer dispute resolution*. Paper presented at the Joint Conference of the OECD, HCOPIL, ICC.

OECD. (2002). *Report on consumer protections for payment cardholders.* OECD.

OECD. (2005, April 27-28). *OECD Workshop on Consumer Dispute Resolution and Redress in the Global Marketplace*. Background report, presentation, and the reports for the workshop. OECD.

OECD. (2006). *Report on the implementation of the 2003 OECD guidelines for protecting consumers from fraudulent and deceptive commercial practices across borders.* OECD.

The Hague Conference on Private International Law. (1994). *Annotated checklist of issues to be discussed at the meeting of the Special Commission of June 1994.*

ADDITIONAL READINGS

Federal Trade Commission. (2005). *The US SAFE WEB Act: Protection consumers from spam, spyware, and fraud* (A Legislative Recommendation to Congress). Available at http://www.ftc.gov/reports/ussafeweb/USSAFEWEB.pdf

Martin, M. S. (2002). Note: Keep it online: The Hague Convention and the need for online alternative dispute resolution in international business-to-consumer e-commerce. *B.U. Int'l L.J, 20.* 125.

FTC v. Skybiz.com, Inc., 57 Fed. Appx. 374 (10th Cir. 2003).

FTC v. Skybiz.com, Inc., 102 Fed. Appx. 649 (10th Cir. 2004).

OECD. (2003, February 3). *Consumers in the online marketplace: The OCED guidelines three years later.* Committee on Consumer Policy on the Guidelines for Consumer Protection in the Context of Electronic Commerce.

"Development of Consumer Protection Policy in South Korea and Its Suggestion to Japan" (*Kankoku ni okeru Shouhisha-Seisakku no shin'ten to Nihon-heno Shisha*) by Koichi HOSOKAWA and Chong In Lee in Journal "ESP"

(February 2005), published by Cabinet Office in Japan (available in Japanese)

"How to Handle Credit Card Crimes and Troubles" (*Credit Card Hanzai Trouble Taisho-ho*) by Takayoshi SUEFUJI, (published by Minjihokenkyukai Co., Ltd.) 2003 (available in Japanese)

ENDNOTES

[1] An article titled "Tremble, everyone" published in Economist in 1997 reported the growth of electronic commerce. See http://www.economist.com/surveys/PrinterFriendly.cfm?Story_ID=596309 (last visited on November 30, 2006).

[2] In 1999, OECD published "OECD Guidelines for Consumer Protection in the Context of Electronic Commerce."

[3] The Hague Conference on Private International Law held its first meeting in 1893, and the organization was established in 1955. See http://www.hcch.net/index_en.php?act=text.display&tid=26 (last visited on November 30, 2006).

[4] When the Hague Conference on Private International Law announced in 1994, "Annotated checklist of issues to be discussed at the meeting of the Special Commission of June 1994," the checklist did not contain any reference to consumer transactions. The text is available at http://www.hcch.net/index_en.php?act=publications.details&pid=3484&dtid=35 (last visited on November 30, 2006).

"Report on the preliminary draft Convention on Jurisdiction and Foreign Judgments in Civil and Commercial Matters" announced in 2000 reflected discussion about consumer transactions. The text is available at http://www.hcch.net/index_en.php?act=publications.details&pid=3494&dtid=35 (last visited on November 30, 2006).

[5] For example, U.S. Census Bureau News reported that estimated quarterly U.S. retail E-Commerce Sales as a percent of total quarterly retail sales in the 2nd quarter of 2006 was almost 2.7%, while in the 4th quarter of 1999, it was only 0.6%. http://www.census.gov/mrts/www/data/html/06Q2.html (last visited on November 30, 2006).

[6] "Report on the implementation of the 2003 OECD guidelines for protecting consumers from fraudulent and deceptive commercial practices across borders" published by OECD in 2006.

[7] "UK European Consumer Center Cross Border Queries 2005" available at http://www.eej-net.org.uk/index/publications/other_reports/activity_apr06_cross_border_queries_2005.htm (last visited on November 30, 2006).

[8] Available at http://www.econsumer.gov/english/contentfiles/pdfs/PU15%20Jan-June%202006.pdf (last visited on November 30, 2006).

[9] Available at http://www2.cio.com/cmo/metrics/viewmetric.cfm?METRIC-791 (last visited on November 30, 2006).

[10] The summary of the ADR Pilot Project is provided in "ECOM Journal 2006" available at http://www.ecom.or.jp/en/ecomjournal/2006/ECOMJournal2006_E.pdf (last visited on November 30, 2006).

[11] "Consumer Fraud and Identity Theft Complaint Data January-December 2005" published by Federal Trade Commission in January 2006.

[12] ECOM provided a language assistance in English to Japanese consumers, to solve the problem with U.S. retailers (ECOM's ADR Pilot Project Report for the fiscal year of 2005 available in Japanese).

[13] In Eurobarometer 57.2 and Flash Eurobarometer 128: "Public opinion in Europe: Views on bsiness-to-consumer cross-border trade," November 14, 2002, shows 79% of

consumer respondents think it a very or fairly important obstacle to cross-border shopping is that they do not know what consumer protection is, provided by other EU countries law.

[14] Forty-three percent (43%) of the consumer respondents see the nationality authorities intervention on one's behalf in the other EU countries as a very important measure to increase confidence in cross-border purchases. Ibid.

[15] See "The Miami Recommendations" dated September 26, 2000, published by Global Business Dialogue on Electronic Commerce. (GBDe)

[16] According to the sentinel data for the period from January 1 through December 31, 2005, credit cards share 30% of the payment method among received complaints. For Internet related Fraud complaints, the share is up to 37%. See "Consumer Fraud and Identity Theft Complaint Data January-December 2005, published by Federal Trade Commission in January 2006.
ECOM's ADR Pilot Project Report for the fiscal year of 2005 (available in Japanese) reported that the credit cards shared 16.3% of the payment method of received complaints by ECOM, but the share is up to 51.5% among the cross-border complaints.

[17] See generally "Report on Consumer Protections for Payment Cardholders" published by OECD in June 2002.

[18] For example, in the United States, under Federal regulations, the liability of a cardholder for unauthorized use of credit cards shall be limited to USD 50 if the timely notice is given to the financial institute. If the timely notice is not given, the limit is USD 500. 12 CFR 205.6.

[19] See "Prepared Witness Testimony: MacCarthy, Mark" available at http://energycommerce.house.gov/107/hearings/05232001Hearing235/MacCarthy359.htm (last visited on November 30, 2006).

[20] See Orientation Document for Building Trust in the Online Environment: Business to Consumer Dispute Resolution (DSTI/ICCP/REG/CP(2000)1) published by OECD, 2000.

[21] See Kinbe Hozumi, "ODR Arbitratin for Settlement of e-Commerce Disputes" Journal of the Japanese Institute of International Business Law Vol.33, No.11 (2005) available in Japanese.

[22] See generally, Melissa Conley Tyler and Di Bretherton "Seventy-six and Counting: An Analysis of ODR Sites" (2003) available at http://www.odr.info/unece2003/pdf/Tyler.pdf (last visited on November 30, 2006).

[23] www.squaretrade.com. Square Trade is introduced as "eBay's preferred dispute resolution provider" (see http://pages.ebay.com/services/buyandsell/disputeres.html. last visited on November 30, 2006).

[24] http://www.smartsettle.com/

[25] http://www.cybersettle.com. The total transaction to date reported on its Web site was 166,569 as of November 30, 2006. (See http://www.cybersettle.com/info/about/factsheet.aspx).

[26] http://www.i-courthouse.com

[27] http://www.mediation.com.sg

[28] See http://www.squaretrade.com/cnt/jsp/abt/aboutus.jsp;jsessionid=tumel213c1?vhostid=daffy&stmp=squaretrade&cntid=tumel213c1 (last visited on November 30, 2006).

[29] See http://www.cybersettle.com/info/about/factsheet.aspx (last visited on November 30, 2006).

[30] The case number submitted to iCourthouse was reported to reach 11572 on its Web site as of November 30, 2006. (See http://www.i-courthouse.com/main.taf?area1_id=cases&area2_id=&start=0&page=1).

[31] See http://www.mediation.com.sg/intro.htm (last visited on November 30, 2006).

[32] See Article 2.1 of Arbitration Law of Japan.

[33] See generally, Timothy R. D. Grayson "Evolution of the online trust-mark" (2002). Available at http://timothygrayson.com/PDFs/trustevolution.pdf.pdf (last visited on November 30, 2006).

[34] http://www.truste.org/businesses/seal_programs_overview.php

[35] https://seal.verisign.com/splash?form_file=fdf/splash.fdf&dn=WWW.VERISIGN.COM&lang=en

[36] The Better Business Bureau system is a network covering the United States and Canada, it is referred to as BBB. It was founded in 1912 and is supported by more than 300,000 local business members. The umbrella organization for the BBB system is the Council of Better Business Bureau (CBBB), which is supported by its membership, national corporations, and by each BBB. BBB and CBBB are all private, non-profit organizations. See generally, the BBB official Web site available at http://www.bbb.org

[37] The requirement of the BBB Reliability Program is available at http://www.bbbonline.org/reliability/requirement.asp (last visited on November 30, 2006).

[38] The information about the report is available at http://www.bbb.org/reports.asp (last visited on November 30, 2006).

[39] 2005 Complaints & Inquiry Stats available at http://www.bbb.org/about/stat2005/intro.pdf (last visited on November 30, 2006).

[40] In 14 out of 18 nations responded to an OECD inquiry, threshold limit for a small claim court system is set forth less than EUR 10,000. "Background Report for OECD Workshop on Consumer Dispute Resolution and Redress in the Global Marketplace" published by OECD in 2005 (hereinafter "OECD Workshop 2005") at p 24.

[41] Article 368-381 in the Civil Procedure Code in Japan.

[42] Article 3 of the Judicial Scrivener Law in Japan.

[43] See "Background Report" supra. at p. 21.

[44] See generally, "Background Report for OECD Workshop 2005" and "Report for consumer collective claim systems in foreign nations" published by Japanese Cabinet Office in September 2004 (available in Japanese).

[45] For example, in Japan, the Amendment to Consumer Contract Act was enacted on May 31, 2006, which allows a certified consumer association to initiate a representative claim seeking an injunction relief against a certain business; however seeking monetary remedy is not allowed there. This Amendment will come into force on June 7, 2007.

[46] See the presentation by Steven Cole at the OECD Workshop 2005; available at http://www.oecd.org/dataoecd/23/50/34827627.pdf (last visited on November 30, 2006).

[47] At p. 8 of "Summary of Public Workshop" for Alternative Dispute Resolution for Consumer Transactions in the Borderless Online Marketplace, June 6-7, 2000, published by the Federal Trade Commission and Department of Commerce in November 2000, available at http://www.ftc.gov/bcp/altdisresolution/summary.pdf (last visited on November 30, 2006).

[48] ECOM's ADR Pilot Project Report for the fiscal year of 2005 reported regarding consumers inquiry conduced in August, 2005 (available in Japanese), 27% of the individuals who submitted complaints to ECOM answered they would not use the dispute resolution service if the fee is imposed and 38% said they would use the service only if the fee is less than JPY 1,000 (approximately U.S. $8).

[49] For example, ECOM's ADR Pilot Project starting from 2002, came to end as of March 31, 2006. Internatinal Conflict Resolution Centre which conducted feasibility study of ODR, operated by the University of Melbourne ceased its activity as of June 30, 2005.

[50] See public comment by BBB submitted to Joint Workshop on Alternative Dispute Resolution for Online Consumer Transactions, available at http://www.ftc.gov/bcp/altdisresolution/comments/underhillbbb.pdf (last visited on November 30, 2006).

[51] See p. 47 of the Transcript for Breakout Session 2 of the Joint Workshop on Alternative Dispute Resolution for Online Consumer Transactions (2000), available at http://www.ftc.gov/bcp/altdisresolution/00607bo2.pdf (last visited on November 30, 2006).

[52] See presentation by Iain Ramsay at OECD Workshop 2005, available at http://www.oecd.org/dataoecd/23/53/34827446.pdf (last visited on November 30, 2006).

[53] See p. 47 of ECOM's ADR Pilot Project Report for the fiscal year of 2005 (available in Japanese).

[54] According to the statistics of e-consumer.gov. during the period of January 1 through June 30, 2006, among e-consumer complaints, 10% of the alleged violations is that a consumer cannot contact merchant. Available at http://www.econsumer.gov/english/contentfiles/pdfs/PU15%20Jan-June%202006.pdf (last visited November 30, 2006).

[55] For example, obtaining a judgment recognizing the foreign judgment is required to enforce the foreign judgment in Japan. Article 118 of the Civil Procedure Code, and Article 24 of the Civil Enforcement Act.

[56] See GBDe's Minami Recommendations supra.

[57] According to the statistics provided in the previous section. "Combination", confirmation of the online mark reaches almost 10 million during the period of 1 year. This figure shows the high recognition of the its trustmark program among consumers. Also the Web site of the BBB provides that just under 90% of online shoppers say they would feel more confident buying from a site displaying the BBB OnLine Reliability seal, than from one that does not. See http://www.bbbonline.org/reliability/Rel_EN.asp (last visited on November 30, 2006).

[58] In Japan, some major cyber malls, such as Yahoo or Rakuten, generally requires higher standards of business practice to its tenants, than those which is required for the online trustmark program, and consumers generally trust the online merchant. The online trustmark program is not farily developed there. For example, the number of issued online trustmark provided by the Japan Chamber of Commerce and Industry is only 308 as of November 30, 2006, http://mark.cin.or.jp/ (available in Japanese), while the number of Web sites covered by the reliability seal of BBB is 31662, http://www.bbbonline.org/consumer/ (last visited on November 30, 2006).

[59] One of the reasons the ODR is less frequently used is considered lack of recognition among consumers. See Report of OECD Workshop 2005 available at http://www.oecd.org/dataoecd/43/10/35395258.pdf (last visited on November 30, 2006).

[60] See http://www.apec.org/apec/documents_reports/electronic_commerce_steering_group/2003.MedialibDownload.v1.html?url=/etc/medialib/apec_media_library/downloads/taskforce/ecsg/mtg/2003/pdf.Par.0057.File.v1.1 (last visited on November 30, 2006).

[61] http://www.globaltrustmarkalliance.org/

[62] See Draft Recommendations on Consumer Confidence by GBDe 2006, available at http://www.gbdeconference.org/summit2006/recommendations/GBDe%202006%20Reco%20CC.pdf (last visited on November 30, 2006).

[63] At p. 33 of Background Report of OECD Workshop 2005. supra.

[64] Section 5(a) of the FTC Act (15 USC 41 et seq.) provides that "unfair or deceptive acts or practices in or affecting commerce are declared unlawful" (15 USC 45 (a) (1)).

[65] See "A Brief Overview of the Federal Trade Commission's Investigative and Law Enforcement Authority" revised September 2002, available at http://www.ftc.gov/ogc/brfovrvw.htm (last visited November 30, 2006).

[66] See the presentation by Stacy Feuer at OECD Workshop 2005, available at http://www.oecd.org/dataoecd/23/19/34827910.pdf (last visited November 30, 2006) and "The FTC in 2005: Standing Up for Consumers and Competition" published by the Federal Trade Commission in April 2005.

[67] FTC Consumer Complaint Form is available at https://rn.ftc.gov/pls/dod/wsolcq$.startup?Z_ORG_CODE=PU01 (last visited on November 30, 2006).

[68] At p. 21 of "The FTC in 2005" supra.

[69] At p. 10 of the Report of OCED Workshop 2005 supra.

[70] See The United States of America v. Yamec 67 O.R. (3d) 394 (2003). The question about the FTC's authority to make a claim for damages on behalf of unnamed persons for unspecified amounts was raised in this case.

[71] At p. 6 in Prepared Statement of The Federal Trade Commission on Cross-Border Fraud before the Subcommittee on Commerce, Trade, and Consumer Protection of the House Committee on Energy and Commerce, dated September 17, 2003, citing Evans v. Citibank Limited & others, Equity Division Proceedings No.4999 of 1999 (Sup. Ct. New South Wales).

[72] The High Court of the Cook Islands sees the FTC's action as enforcement of penal code and dismissed the U.S. action. United States v. Asiatrust Limited, Plaint No. 57/1999, (4 Dec. 2001 Judgment).

[73] See Background Report for OECD Workshop 2005 supra.

[74] See the FTC's press release available at http://www.ftc.gov/opa/2004/05/skybiz.htm, http://www.ftc.gov/opa/2001/06/sky.htm, and http://www.ftc.gov/opa/2003/03/skybiz.htm (last visited on November 30, 2006).

[75] See www.skybiz-redress.com (last visited on November 30, 2006).

[76] For example, National Consumer Affairs Center of Japan announced about SkyBiz-Redress Web page on its Web site, http://www.kokusen.go.jp/soudan_now/skybiz.html (available in Japanese, last visited on November 30, 2006).

[77] As of September 21, 2007 the Web site "Skybiz-redress.com" reported that the claim process has been completed.

[78] Officially, "Convention of 16 September 1998 on jurisdiction and the enforcement of judgments in civil and commercial matters" available at http://curia.europa.eu/common/recdoc/convention/en/c-textes/lug-idx.htm (last visited on November 30, 2006).

[79] Officially, "Council Regulation (EC) No 44/2001 of 22 December 2000 on jurisdiction and the recognition and enforcement of judgments in civil and commercial matters," available at http://eur-lex.europa.eu/LexUriServ/LexUriServ.do?uri=CELEX:32001R0044:EN:HTML (last visited November 30, 2006).

[80] The text is available at http://www.hcch.net/upload/wop/jdgmpd11.pdf (last visited on November 30, 2006).

[81] The text of the Convention is available at http://www.hcch.net/index_en.php?act=conventions.text&cid=98 (last visited November 30, 2006).

Chapter XIII
Cyber Contract and Indian Law

Jibitesh Mishra
College of Engineering & Technology, India

Biswajit Tripathy
Synergy Institute of Engineering & Technology, India

ABSTRACT

The usage of cyber contracts has increased exponentially in the recent times. However, the framework for this has not been clearly defined. The jurisdiction is also a major issue. In this chapter, we have revisited various types of electronic contacts, the cyber contract in the Indian content, and made an effort to find a uniform framework for this.

INTRODUCTION

A legal contract made between parties using the cyber medium covering e-commerce, e-services, and e-governance, and so forth, to operate in an online mode, is known as a cyber contract. In India, not much attention is given towards drafting of a proper contract framework appropriate to the transaction (Vivek, S. Ed., 2005). From time to time, attempt has been made by various researchers to make a globally enforceable cyber contract.

Robert L. Percial (Renault, O., & Percival, R. L., 2004) has tried to learn from the increasing wealth of judicial decisions in both Canada and the United States, considering the creation and enforceability of electronic contracts, coupled with electronic commerce legislative direction. This has resulted in the identification of certain steps and measures that drafters of electronic and online agreements can do or avoid in order to achieve greater certainty that such electronic agreements will stand as enforceable contractual instruments. Governments are challenging fundamental legal concepts such as contracts, to develop flexible frameworks to protect traditional contract law while recognizing and expanding it to include technology's borderless capabilities and maintain integrity for all legal players like judges, lawyers, legislators, and business people (Hill, J. E., 2003). In the current scenario, the business and legal limitation revolve around paper technology, which reflects a challenge to conducting business in today's information economy. The electronic contracts with their uniqueness, create tremendous uncertainty in international legal and business environments because the law is slow to respond to new technology (Sabet, R.V., 1996). The status of law to monitor the cyber commerce is often inadequate.

BACKGROUND

An e-contract can also be in the form of a "Click to Agree" contract, commonly used with downloaded software: The user clicks an "I Agree" button on a page containing the terms of the software license before the transaction can be completed (Making Contract online, 2006, from http://smallbusiness.yahoo.com/r-article-a-2603-m-3-sc-18-making_contracts_online_electronic_signatures-i).

As per the IT Act of 2000 in India, it is the provision of legal recognition for transactions carried out by means of electronic data interchange and other means of electronic communication, commonly referred to as "electronic commerce," which involve the use of alternatives to paper-based methods of communication and storage of information, to facilitate electronic filing of documents with the government agencies and further, to amend the Indian Penal Code, the Indian Evidence Act, 1872, the Bankers' Books Evidence Act, 1891, and the Reserve Bank of India Act, 1934, and for matters connected therewith or incidental thereto (The Information Technology Act of 2000; Ministry Of Law, Justice And Company Affairs, Legislative Department, India).

TYPES OF ELECTRONIC CONTRACTS

1. "Click-Wrap," "Click-Through," or "Web-Wrap" contacts are electronic contacts that require the user to scroll through terms and conditions (or multiple Web pages on a Web site) and to expressly confirm the user's agreement to the terms and conditions by taking some action, such as clicking on a button that states "I Accept" or "I Agree" or some similar statement, prior to being able to complete the transaction. Click-Through contracts are often found in software products or on Web sites.
2. "Browse-Wrap" contracts are terms and conditions of use that to do not require the express agreement of a user. They are often located in software or are posted on a Web site and may make some statement that indicates use of the software or Web site constitutes the user's agreement to the terms. Often such terms may not have been brought to the attention of the user.
3. "Electronic Mail (e-mail)," is a method of sending an electronic message from one person to another using the Internet, it is a convenient method of time-delayed direct communication. While an e-mail may be a singular message, it also possesses the ability to form contracts. Consequently, e-mail is viewed as both a formal and informal communications medium (Allison, K. H., Grossman, M., & Rothman, R., 2001). People often regard informal e-mail arrangements and business correspondence as non-contractual events. However, courts have found telegrams "with typed signatures, letterhead and/or logos [to] provide the 'signature' necessary for a binding contract" (Hillstrom

v. Gosnay, 1980). Therefore, sending an e-mail, with or without a signature line *(an example of a signature line at the end of an email is the following: B.J. Tripathy, Dept of Computer Sc., Synergy Institute of Eng. & Tech., Dhenkanal.759001. e-mailaddress@ emailaddress.com)*, including a name and pertinent contact information, may symbolize assent to contract formation (Shattuk v. Klotzbach, 2001) (holding that an e-mail signature indicates an intentional act to which a party can be bound.

- If a court concludes that the sender intended to acknowledge contents of documents, then he or she will be bound by the terms (Allison, K. H., Grossman, M., & Rothman, R., 2001). In contrast, receipt in an electronic environment does not require that the recipient know of, open, or read the message. All it requires is that the electronic message be available for processing by the recipient's information system (with default signature lines in greater use to personalize electronic communication, perhaps senders should consider removing them to avoid any unnecessary liability or change them to reflect the non-binding nature of the communication).
- In India, import of crypto software for digital signature purposes required a license, but the procedure for procurement is not restricted. As per the IT Act of 2000 in India, the encrypted messages can decrypt by the authorized agent of the controller issuing license in India for the reasons like integrity, security of the nation, as well as the friendly relationship with the other countries (ASCL White Papers on "Cryptography Laws of Major Countries" from www.asianlaws.org/whitepapers.).

"Electronic Data Interchange (EDI)" is the computer-to-computer transmission of information used by frequently contracting commercial parties to send and receive standard forms, generally purchase orders and invoices, in a store and forward message system. It is, perhaps, the clearest example of electronic contracting through the use of an electronic agent. Parties agree on the standardized terms of the transaction (Allison, K. H., Grossman, M., & Rothman, R., 2001). Transactions including quotes and automatic responses to them are sent and received daily via a phone line between electronic agents, devoid of human involvement (Allison, K. H., Grossman, M., & Rothman, R., 2001). EDI reduces the time and complexity associated with sending and receiving large volumes of information and reducing keystroke errors (Denny, W. R., 2001). Generally, large companies can only afford EDI due to proprietary networks which must be created to support it. EDI reduces the 5 to 10% key-entry error rate and the subsequent ten-fold costs to correct it. Other benefits include faster information exchange, quicker order-to-payment cycle, and improved trade partner relationships. EDI has improved the efficiency of communication for many industries that order large quantities of stock-keeping-units (SKUs), such as food and drug retailers. Savings as early as the 1970s were estimated at U.S. $170 million). Purchase orders are one of the most common uses of EDI. For example: Big Bazar, a large retailer, uses EDI to repeatedly order large quantities of consumer goods, such as soap, for its thousands of stores. EDI enables the ordering and invoicing of these goods between computer systems. Contract offer, acceptance, and assent occur automatically (Allison, K. H., Grossman, M., & Rothman, R., 2001). EDI is a tricky method of electronic contracting because the output is in a specific technical format. Messages are coded in generally acceptable national or international forms and transmitted through a store and forward system. Since parties must agree on the standards and forms before they engage in the lengthy and expensive process of establishing direct communication, contract assent is evidenced by nature of the connections. Transaction efficiency through rapid electronic contracting has gained EDI's instantaneous communication methods international approval with the development of EDIFACT (EDI for Administration, Commerce and Transport, an international EDI standard; Allison, K.H., Grossman, M., & Rothman, R., 2001).

Electronic Signature

While the federal e-signature law makes paper unnecessary in many situations, it also gives consumers and businesses the right to continue to use paper where desired. The law provides a means for consumers who prefer paper to opt out of using electronic contracts.

Prior to obtaining a consumer's consent for electronic contracts, a business must provide a notice indicating whether paper contracts are available and informing consumers that if they give their consent to use electronic documents, they can later change their mind and request a paper agreement instead. The notice must also explain what fees or penalties might apply if the company must use paper agreements for the transaction. The notice must also indicate whether the consumer's consent applies only to the particular transaction at hand, or to a larger category of transactions between the business and the consumer, that is, whether the business has to get consent to use e-contracts/signatures for each transaction.

A business must also provide a statement outlining the hardware and software requirements to read and save the business's electronic documents. If the hardware or software requirements change, the business must notify consumers of the change and give consumers the option (penalty-free) to revoke their consent to using electronic documents.

Although the e-signature law does not force consumers to accept electronic documents from businesses, it poses a potential disadvantage for low-tech citizens by allowing businesses to collect additional fees from those who opt for paper.

Digital Signature

The definition given by the U.S. Electronic Signatures in Global and National Commerce (E Sign) Act of 2000 for "electronic signature" as an electronic sound, symbol, or process, attached to or logically associated with a contract or other record and executed or adopted by a person with the intent to sign the record. Digital signatures can be considered as a subset of electronic signatures. Digital signatures can reference the same definition used for electronic signatures.

Electronic signatures, not necessarily cryptographic, are mechanisms for identifying the originator of an electronic message in common law. It includes cable, Telex, and FAX transmission of handwritten signatures on a paper document.

A digital signature method generally defines two complementary algorithms, one for signing and the other for verification, and the output of the signing process is also called a digital signature. Not all electronic signatures are digital signatures.

A digital signature is an electronic signature that can be used to authenticate the identity of the sender of a message or the signer of a document, and possibly to ensure that the original content of the message or document that has been sent is unchanged. Digital signatures are easily transportable, cannot be imitated by someone else, and can be automatically time-stamped. The sender can repudiate later after sending the message.

Public-key digital signature (PKI) is an encryption scheme for authenticating users to sign digital information through the binding of public keys to users using techniques from the field of public-key cryptography. The public keys are typically provided by the registered certifying authority (similar to Passport authority) in certificates.

Nature of Digital Signatures

Asymmetric or public key cryptography involves two keys, one is the "private key" which only the owner knows and another is the "public key" which anyone can know. Here the advantage is only one party needs to know the private key; and that knowledge of the public key by a third party does not compromise security.

Digital signatures are subject to a form of 'spoofing' by creation of a bogus public key that purports to be that of a particular person, but is not. In order to address that risk, 'certification authorities' (CAs) are envisaged, that will certify that a public key is that of a particular person. So, a digital signature cannot be confused with a digital certificate.

Generally, keys used for digital signatures are very long series of bits, which can be represented as long series of alphanumeric characters, which are almost not feasible for individuals to remember. They must therefore be stored in a way that is convenient, portable, but secure. The most likely current technology to support such storage is a chip. The chip could be embedded in a variety of carriage-mechanisms, such as a ring, watch, or brooch. At present, the main form used is a plastic card. Any such device gives rise to security and privacy issues.

Even if the individual's biometric measure remains solely on the card carried by the individual, a considerable level of security and privacy concern exists.

How Digital Signature Works

Assume you were going to send the draft/document of a contract to your friend in another town. You want to give your friend the assurance that it was unchanged from what you sent and that it is really from you.

- **Step-1:** You copy-and-paste the contract (it's a short one!) into an e-mail note.
- **Step-2:** Using special software, you obtain a message hash (mathematical summary) of the contract.
- **Step-3:** You then use a private key that you have previously obtained from a public-private key authority to encrypt the hash.
- **Step-4:** The encrypted hash becomes your digital signature of the message. (Note that it will be different each time you send a message.)

At the other end, your friend receives the message.

- **Step-1:** To make sure it is intact and from you, your friend makes a hash of the received message.
- **Step-2:** Your friend then uses your public key to decrypt the message hash or summary.
- **Step-3:** If the hashes match, the received message is valid.

There are three common reasons/benefits for applying a digital signature to communications:

1. **Authenticity:** Public-key cryptosystems allow encryption of a message using the private key of the key holder. More typically, the message will be sent in plaintext, with the encryption of a shorter *hash* appended. By decrypting the hash with the sender's public key, and checking the result against the plaintext, the recipient can confirm that the encryption was done with the sender's private key and that the message has not been altered. This signature allows the recipient to be confident that the sender is indeed who they claim to be. Of course the recipient cannot be 100% *sure* that the sender is indeed who they claim to be, the recipient can only be *confident*—since the cryptosystem may have been broken. As in case of financial

transaction, the importance of authenticity is especially obvious. For example, suppose a bank sends instructions from its branch offices to the central office in the form (x,y) where x is the account number and y is the amount to be credited to the account. A devious customer may deposit Rs.100, observe the resulting transmission, and repeatedly retransmit (x,y), which is known as a *Replay Attack*.

2. **Integrity:** Here both parties will always wish to be confident that a message has not been altered during transmission. The encryption makes it difficult for a third party to *read* a message, but that third party may still be able to *alter* it in a useful way. This is known as the *homomorphism attack*: a popular example to illustrate this, consider the same bank as above which sends instructions from its branch offices to the central office in the form (x,y) where x is the account number and y is the amount to be credited to the account. A devious customer may deposit Rs.1000, intercept the resulting transmission, and then transmit (x,y^5).

3. **Non-repudiation:** In a cryptographic context, the word *repudiation* refers to the act of denying association with a message, that is, by claiming it was sent by a third party. The recipient of a message may insist that the sender attach a signature in order to prevent any later repudiation, since the recipient may show the message to a third party to prove its origin. The loss of control of the private key means that all digitally signed communications can still be repudiated.

A general digital signature scheme consists of three algorithms:

- A key generation algorithm
- A signing algorithm
- A verification algorithm

For example, consider the situation in which Ram sends a message to Sita and she wants to be able to prove it came from him. Ram sends his message to Sita and attaches a digital signature. The digital signature is generated using Ram's private key, and takes the form of a simple numerical value (normally represented as a string of binary digits). On receipt, Sita can then check whether the message really came from Ram by running the verification algorithm on the message, together with the signature and Ram's public key. If they match, then Sita can be confident that the message really was from Ram, because the signing algorithm is designed so that it is very difficult to forge a signature to match a given message unless one has knowledge of the private key, which Ram has kept secret.

Indian IT Act of 2000

The IT Act-2000, which passed in India with effect from October 17, 2000, includes the Semi Conductor Integrated Circuits Layout Designs Act, Copyright Act amended for Computer works.

As per the IT Act, nothing in this Act shall apply to:

a. A negotiable instrument as defined in section 13 of the Negotiable Instruments Act, 1881
b. A power-of-attorney as defined in section 1A of the Powers-of-Attorney Act, 1882
c. A trust as defined in section 3 of the Indian Trusts Act, 1882
d. A will as defined in clause *(h)* of section 2 of the Indian Succession Act, 1925 including any other testamentary disposition by whatever name called
e. Any contract for the sale or conveyance of immovable property or any interest in such property
f. Any such class of documents or transactions as may be notified by the Central Government in the Official Gazette

Cyber Contract and Indian Law

As per section 2(1)(p) of the IT Act, a "digital signature" means authentication of any electronic record by a subscriber by means of an electronic method or procedure in accordance with the provisions of section 3.

Section 3 of the IT Act reads:

1. Subject to the provisions of this section any subscriber may authenticate an electronic record by affixing his digital signature.
2. The authentication of the electronic record shall be effected by the use of asymmetric crypto system and hash function, which envelop and transform the initial electronic record into another electronic record.

Explanation: For the purposes of this sub-section, "hash function" means an algorithm mapping or translation of one sequence of bits into another, generally a smaller set known as "hash result" such that an electronic record yields the same hash result every time the algorithm is executed with the same electronic record as its input, making it computationally infeasible:

1. To derive or reconstruct the original electronic record from the hash result produced by the algorithm
2. That two electronic records can produce the same hash result using the algorithm
3. Any person by the use of a public key of the subscriber can verify the electronic record.

The private key and the public key are unique to the subscriber and constitute a functioning key pair.

On an international level, the United Nations Commission on International Trade Law (UNCITRAL), the International Chamber of Commerce (ICC), and the Organization for Economic Co-operation and Development (OECD) have released, or are working on, rules with respect to electronic authentication.

In order to be valid, the electronic signature shall meet the following requirements, at the minimum:

a. Be individual, unique, and under the exclusive control of the person to whom it belongs and who uses it
b. Have the necessary security to guarantee its integrity
c. Be unequivocally verifiable through technical means of proof, as established by law, regulations, or agreement between parties.

As per the IT Act-2000 for India:

- Electronic Documents Recognized as equivalent to written documents
- Digital Signature Recognized as equivalent to written signature
- Use of Electronic Documents and Payments in Government transactions enabled
- Violation or offence to this Act punishments indicated liabilities up-to Rupees One Crore, Imprisonment up to 10 years.

It is considered as per the IT Act-2000, a person has committed a crime if he/she, without permission of the owner or any other person who is in charge of a computer, computer system, or computer network:

1. Accesses or secures access to such computer, computer system, or computer network
2. Downloads, copies or extracts any data, computer data base, or information from such computer, computer system, or computer network including information or data held or stored in any removable storage medium
3. Introduces or causes to be introduced any computer contaminant or computer virus into any computer, computer system, or computer network

4. Damages or causes to be damaged any computer, computer system, or computer network, data, computer data base, or any other programs residing in such computer, computer system, or computer network
5. Disrupts or causes disruption of any computer, computer system, or computer network
6. Denies or causes the denial of access to any person authorized to access any computer, computer system, or computer network by any means
7. Provides any assistance to any person to facilitate access to a computer, computer system, or computer network in contravention of the provisions of this Act, rules or regulations made thereunder
8. Charges the services availed of by a person to the account of another person by tampering with or manipulating any computer, computer system, or computer network

Broadly Cyber crimes committed by Hacking/ unauthorized Access, Virus/Computer Contaminant, Denial Of Service, Fraud/Impersonation, Pornography, Tampering of Evidence, Assisting in Crimes, Credit Card Fraud. Violation to the law can by enquired by the Adjudicator in Cyber Appellate Tribunal (power as of civil court) under the Judicial process. Any person aggrieved by any decision or order of the Cyber Appellate Tribunal may file an appeal to the High Court within 60 days from the date of communication of the decision or order of the Cyber Appellate Tribunal to him on any question of fact or law arising out of such order.

The standard for the Digital Signatures to use is the Asymmetric Crypto system and one way hash, that is, Standard Crypto system and RSA encryption standards PKCS#1, 5, 7, 8, 9, 10, 12 with Standard Hash-MD5, and SHA-1.

As per the Indian IT Act-2000:

- *Hacking* as per Sec. 66: Whoever with the intent to cause or knowing that he is likely to cause wrongful loss or damage to the public or any person, destroys or deletes or alters any information residing in a computer resource or diminishes its value or utility or affects it injuriously by any means, commits hacking. And the penalty for this as whoever commits hacking shall be punished with imprisonment up to 3 years, or with fine which may extend up to two lakh rupees, or with both.
- *Virus and computer contaminants* means any set of computer instructions that are designed to modify, destroy, record, transmit data or program residing within a computer, computer system or computer network; or by any means to usurp the normal operation of the computer, computer system, or computer network.
- *Tampering* with computer source code documents as per Section 65; Whoever knowingly or intentionally either himself or through another person conceals, destroys, or alters any computer information required to be kept or maintained by law, shall be punishable with imprisonment up to 3 years, or with fine which may extend up to two lakh rupees, or with both.
- *Liability of "intermediaries"*: Intermediaries are not liable if an offence was committed without his knowledge after exercising due diligence. An Intermediary means any person who, on behalf of another person, receives, stores, or transmits electronic messages or provides any service with respect to that message. Intermediaries may include ASP s/ISPs, Web hosting companies, Database maintaining companies, Browsing Service Providers (Cyber Café), E-commerce Kiosks, Internet Education Centers, Internet Medical Counseling centers, Call Centers.

As per the IT Act-2000, the cyber crimes & penalties are:

- Penalty/damages up to Rupees One Crore
- Publishing of obscene material (10 years and/or Rupees Two lakhs)
- Tampering with Source codes/documents (3 years and/or Rupees Two lakhs)
- Misrepresentation/Suppression of material facts to Certifying Authorities (2 years and/or Rupees One lakh)
- Publishing false Digital Certificate (2 years and/or Rupees One lakh)
- Breach of Confidentiality (2 Years and/or Rupees One lakh)
- Securing/Attempting to secure access to a "Protected System" (10 years)
- Failure to cooperate with the regulatory agencies (2 years and/or Rupees One lakh).
- Failure to submit returns/information and so forth, to Controller (penalty—Rs. 5000 to 10000 per day)
- Officials to be punished for offences of companies; act to apply for offences committed outside India.

However, the first step toward laying a legal foundation for electronic commerce is to clear away the barriers to electronic commerce, and the first and most obvious barrier is found in laws that require paper (Fry, P. B., 2001).

MAIN TRUST OF THE CHAPTER

Issues, Controversies, Problems

Jurisdiction Conflict

In a real-estate related case (*Sublett v. Scott Wallin and Pillar To Post, 2004)*, a plaintiff who was living in California used a home-inspection company Web site to locate an inspector for a home in New Mexico. Later, the plaintiff found the pipes in the home's radiant heating system were defective and filed an action against both the inspector and the company that maintained the Web site. The District Court of New Mexico dismissed the motion for lack of personal jurisdiction. The court held that the company's Web site was essentially passive. The site provided information about the nearest franchisee through an interactive "Locate an Inspector" search feature. The search requested only minimal information from the plaintiff and provided marketing information on the inspector. The plaintiff initiated the transaction from California via a commercial search engine. All subsequent contact phone calls and meetings did not involve the Web site. However, in *Cody v Ward* (1997), the court found that a defendant's telephone calls and e-mail to a plaintiff were sufficient contacts to satisfy due process. In this case, the defendant communicated with potential stock investors through a computer bulletin board (Alexson, H. B., 2005).

Click-Warp Viability

Hotmail sued Van Money Pie, and the court, in issuing a preliminary injunction against Van Money Pie, commented on the likelihood of prevailing on the breech of contract of the service agreement. Although the court did not directly address the enforceability of the service agreement, the e-commerce community has viewed the decision that the courts are prepared to extend their shrink-wrap position to cover click-wrap agreements as well (Snukal).

Digital Signature

Court decisions discussing the effect and validity of digital signatures or digital signature-related legislation:

- *In re Piranha, Inc.,* 2003 WL 21468504 (N.D. Tex) (UETA does not preclude a person from contesting that he executed, adopted, or authorized an electronic signature that is purportedly his).

- *Cloud Corp. v. Hasbro* (2002), (E-SIGN does not apply retroactively to contracts formed before it took effect in 2000. Nevertheless, the statute of frauds was satisfied by the text of e-mail plus an [apparently] written notation).
- *Sea-Land Service, Inc. v. Lozen International* (2002), (Internal corporate e-mail with signature block, forwarded to a third party by another employee, was admissible over hearsay objection as a party-admission, where the statement was apparently within the scope of the author's and forwarder's employment).

Solutions and Recommendations

This is a suggestions that the format for a cyber contract should contain the following fields should be specified clearly (Mishra, J., & Tripathy, B., 2006).

There should be a clear mentioning about the "name of the parties" who are making the offer as well as the party who is accepting the offer, with detail to address the business registration. The concerned country's highest authority should recognize the registrar authority. In the case of e-mail, it is the party who is initiating the process of the contract, that is, sending the mail is the party who makes the offer and the party who receives the mail is the acceptor. In the case of EDI, as this is between the parties having frequent transaction, the sender and acceptor are those who send the information and receive the information in an approved format. There should be a clear note about the "contact person" by both of the parties, with their contact number and e-mail address.

Considerations should be separately and clearly mentioned by the offering party, including mention of the service regarding training, support, and so forth..

Both of the parties should mention their time performance for the validation of the contract.

The obligation of each party should be clearly mentioned by the party who is offering the proposal. Force Majure should be mentioned, specifying as per the domain area.

As the cyber world does not have physical boundaries, a forum should constitute taking all member countries, and a representative should be present in the respective country to take legal decision, consulting the forum to handle jurisdiction & dispute settlements, considering the contract in the future is not limited to geographical limits.

Rights should be extended to all of the citizens and organizations of the member country, with a uniform law for Intellectual property rights. This also considers the privacy of the information of the user for intermediate use. The provision for a privacy policy relating to the information of the users must be clearly defined (Mishra, J., & Tripathy, B., 2006).

The terms and conditions of the contract should be clearly mentioned by the offering party. In the domain of e-commerce, the terms and conditions should include shipping agreements, risk of loss, rejection, and return, as in a traditional sales contract. This also contains the provisions if an item is out-of-stock. In the domain of service related to the goods, the terms should contain the maintenance, training, support, and so forth, under the variation procedure (Mishra, J., & Tripathy, B., 2006).

Severability should be mentioned clearly by the software companies in case of failure of some part or clause, a standard for this should be prepared by a committee to follow. Signatures (digital) should be used by the parties during a contract formation. The offering party should mention the warranty clearly, with the terms and conditions under which it stands, or void it. Penalty should be uniform related to domain areas and should be uniformly acted upon. Measures of damage in the different domain, the possible causes, if any, should be mentioned clearly by the offering party. As the user actively or passively accesses the site, clear terms should be mentioned for the site owner and the communication should reach the destination. Liability of the site owner should be clear for the active and passive site owner.

FUTURE TRENDS

As discussed, many areas are out of bounds for cyber contract. The digital signature is still also a question mark for 100% reliability. The use of biometric parameters to use as a signature must be suggested and has a great potential in future research.

CONCLUSION

After studied, mainly on the domain area where cyber contracts are used in Indian content, several recommendations are made. In order to tackle the major jurisdiction issue, the formation of an international body such as a cyber court is required. The member countries can regulate the laws of cyber contracts. Apart from this, another major issue is the use of the digital signature and its authenticity, in the contract. Further study can be done, mainly on the authenticity of the digital signature and its use in the contract framework specific to various domain areas.

FUTURE RESEARCH DIRECTION

In the current scenario, as business through the cyber medium is growing exponentially, it is very essential to have a Uniform Frame Work for e-business. The underlying electronic contracts of various domains will be studied and an integrated model of legal security will be framed. The classifications of various e-businesses will be made and impacts of such models on those e-businesses will be seen. The issues related to the reliability of the digital signature will be studied.

REFERENCES

Alexson, H. B. (2005, October). Business alert. *Current Legal Issues For The Business Community, 4*(5). Retrieved from http://www.alexsonlaw.com/americanbusinesscounsel/

Allison, K. H., Grossman, M., & Rothman, R. (2001). *Click-wrap agreements—Enforceable contracts or wasted words?* Retrieved from http://www.keytlaw.com/Articles/clickwrap.htm

Denny, W. R. (2001). Electronic contracting in Delaware: The E-Sign Act and the uniform Electronic Transactions Act. *Delaware Law Review, 4*, 33-34.

Fry, P. B. (2001). Introduction to the uniform electronic transactions act: Principles, policies and provisions. *Idaho Law Review, 37*(237), 242.

Hill, J. E. (2003). The future of electronic contracts in international sales: Gaps and natural remedies under the United Nations Convention on Contracts for the international sale of goods. *Northwestern Journal of Technology and Intellectual Propoerty.* Retrieved from http://www.law.northwestern.edu/journals/njtip/v2/n1/1/

Mishra, J., & Tripathy, B. (2006). Cyber contract: A generalized framework, ICWA 2006, CET, BPUT, Orissa, India. *Web Engineering & Applications, Macmillan Publication* (pp. 270-278).

Renault, O., & Percival, R. L. (2004, May 19-20). *E-commerce law update: Doing business on the Net (and getting it right), creating enforceable, electronic contracts.* Paper presented at the 4th Annual IT Law Spring Training Program: Legal & Business Issues for IT Transactions. Toronto: Osgoode Hall.

Sabet, R. V. (1996). International harmonization in electronic commerce and electronic data interchange: A proposed first step toward signing on the digital dotted line. *Am. U. L. Rev., 46*(511), 513.

Vivek, S. (Ed.). (2005). *Cyber law simplified.* Tata McGraw Hill.

ADDITIONAL READING

Adam, N. R., et al. (1999). *Electronic commerce: Technical, business and legal issues.* Upper Saddle River, NJ: Prentice Hall.

Alavi, M. et al. (1992). A review of MIS research and disciplinary development. *Journal of Management Information Systems, 8*(4), 45-62.

Barki, H. et al. (1993). A keyword classification scheme for IS research literature: An update. *MIS Quarterly, 17*(2), 226-309.

Buck, S. P. (1996). Electronic commerce—Would, could and should you use current internet payment mechanism? *Internet Research, 6*(2/3), 5-18.

Cavazos, E. A. (1996). The legal risks of setting up shop in cyberspace. *Journal of Organisational computing and Electronic Commerce, 6*(1), 51-60.

Forcht, K. A., et al. (1995). Security issues and concerns with Internet. *Internet Research, 5*(3), 23-31.

Hamilton, S. (1997). E-commerce for the 21st century. *Computer, 30*(5), 44-47.

Hassler, V. et al. (1999). Digital signature management. *Internet Research, 9*(4), 262-271.

Kalakota, R., et al. (1996). *Frontiers of electronic commerce.* Reading, MA: Addison-Wesley.

Nord, J. H., et al. (1995). MIS research: Journal status and analysis. *Information & Management, 29*(1), 29-42.

Oliver, S. (1997). A model for the future of electronic commerce. *Information Management & Computer Security, 5*(5), 166-169.

Turban, E., et al. (2000). *Electronics commerce: A managerial prospective.* Upper Saddle River, NJ: Prentice Hall.

Walczak, S. (1999). A re-evaluation of information systems. *Publication Forum, 40*(1), 89-97.

Wilson, S. (1999). Digital signatures and the future of documentation. *Information Management & Computer Security, 7*(2), 83-87.

Zwass, V. (1996). Electronic commerce: Structure and issues. *International Journal of Electronic Commerce, 1*(1), 3-33.

Chapter XIV
E-Commerce and Dispute Resolution:
Jurisdiction and Applicable Law in a Dispute Arising from a Computer Information Transaction

Naoshi Takasugi
Doshisha University, Japan

ABSTRACT

When a dispute arises from e-commerce involving parties located in different nations, the parties immediately face conflict-of-laws issues such as judicial jurisdiction, applicable law, and extra-territorial effects of judgments. Taking into consideration that there is no unified conflicts law rules in the global level and, if any, the conflicts rules are usually based on the traditional international transactions, this chapter tries to discuss the dispute resolution systems suitable for e-commerce, especially for computer information transactions. As the result of the discussion, it becomes clear that further enhancement of a worldwide dispute resolution system suitable for e-commerce is desirable. In establishing a new system, the 1999 Guidelines for Consumer Protection in the context of electronic commerce, approved by the OECD, gives much inspiration. It is essential to balance between small-middle sized business entities and consumers, and between freedom and regulation.

INTRODUCTION

Along with the development and growth of information technology, electronic commerce (e-commerce), that is, transactions utilizing the Internet or cyberspace, has been increasing in number, quantity, and scale. Business-to-consumer (B2C) transactions are becoming popular these days as well as business-to-business (B2B) transactions. Besides conventional electronic commerce, in which only negotiations and conclusion of contracts are done online rather than orally or in writing, there is a type of e-commerce that is completed entirely through the implementation of a contract on the net, such as by downloading and sending software on the Internet in exchange for a payment (computer information transaction). This chapter mainly focuses on the latter form of e-commerce.

In computer information transactions, conclusion and performance of a contract can be accomplished simply by visiting foreign Web sites in an instant on the Internet and clicking, without much awareness of national borders. However, when a dispute arises from e-commerce involving parties located in different nations, the parties immediately face conflict-of-laws[1] issues such as the following. First, in case a party located in Nation A files a civil lawsuit against the other party located in Nation B, the case is not necessarily heard by a court in Nation A. Judicial jurisdiction is a problem in an international civil case. Second, even if the case is heard at a court in Nation A, the law of Nation A is not always governing. In international litigation, it is first decided which nation's law is to be applied, and the final judgment is made based on the law of the relevant nation. This is the issue of selecting the applicable law. Third, even if the party in Nation A wins the case as a result of a trial in a court in Nation A, the opponent party does not always possess assets in Nation A. How can assets located in Nation B be seized? This is the issue of recognition and enforcement of foreign judgments or extra-territorial effects of judgments.

Those problems occur not only in e-commerce but also in general disputes. However, international e-commerce business dealings have aspects different from conventional cross-border transactions, and dispute settlement systems established on the assumption of conventional international transactions are not always suitable for the new type of e-commerce. This chapter discusses issues concerning private international law regarding computer information transactions, and then examines dispute resolution systems suitable for those transactions.

B2B TRANSACTIONS AND SELF-GOVERNANCE

Take the following example as Case 1: Business entity X located in Nation A buys software from another business entity Y, which is located in Nation B, through the Internet.[3] The software turns out to have a serious flaw, and X demands that Y return the payment. In case Y in Nation B does not agree to reimbursement, X in Nation A needs to file a civil lawsuit against defendant Y.

Laws of Japan

International Jurisdiction

An agreement on international jurisdiction between the parties concerned, which designates a court in a nation other than Japan as the exclusive jurisdiction, is regarded by Japanese courts as valid when the following four requirements are fulfilled:[4] (1) Existence of such agreement is stated in writing, (2) The case at issue does not belong to Japan's exclusive jurisdiction, (3) The nation agreed by the parties has jurisdiction under that nation's law, but no mutual warranty of recognizing judgments between that nation and Japan is needed, and (4) The agreement is not excessively unreasonable or against public policy. By the same token, a jurisdiction agreement to choose a Japanese court can also be regarded as valid in principle unless it is irrational.

Japanese statutory laws have no provisions on criteria for determining cross-border jurisdiction in the absence of a jurisdiction agreement, except for a fraction of case types. Precedents[5] have said that it is appropriate to determine jurisdiction rationally, based on the philosophy of ensuring fairness among parties and proper and speedy trial proceedings, and that, basically, placing a defendant under Japanese courts is considered to satisfy such rationality when the jurisdiction provision or any other provisions of Japan's Code of Civil Procedure confer jurisdiction upon Japan. However, as precedents go, if there are any special circumstances that would produce results against the principle of ensuring fairness among parties or proper and speedy proceeding of trial, the Japanese law denies its own jurisdiction (such policies are called "the doctrine of special circumstances" or "the modified reverse inference theory").

According to the criteria shown in the precedents, jurisdiction should be given to the nation where the residence or business headquarters of the defendant is situated.[6] In addition, in a contract-related case, jurisdiction is recognized for the nation where the contractual obligation is to be performed while in a case involving an illegal act, the nation where the illegal act has occurred shall have jurisdiction, unless there are any special circumstances.[7]

In Case 1, it is impossible to recognize the Japanese jurisdiction based on the address of defendant X, which is a foreign entity. A possible ground to grant the Japanese jurisdiction is that Japan is the place where the contractual obligation is to be performed. However, there are some requirements for a nation to have jurisdiction as the place of performance obligation: the place of performance of the obligation in question is clearly stipulated in the contract, or can be interpreted from the contract unambiguously; forcing the defendant to enter an appearance in the nation does not harm predictability of the defendant or do any injustice to the defendant; proper hearings are possible in the nation because evidence is usually concentrated in the place of performance. Jurisdiction is not recognized when such requirements are not fulfilled. In Case 1, both the locations of the buyer's computer and the seller's server can be regarded as the place of performance, and a simple conclusion is usually difficult. In order to ensure the Japanese jurisdiction, it is necessary to expressly provide in the contract that the obligation is to be performed in Japan. Yet the relationship with the other party may make it difficult to stipulate that Japan is the place where the obligation is to be performed, and rather, it is more likely that Y in Nation B, who is the seller, first designates Nation B as the place of performance in the contract. In that case, it is therefore fairly difficult for the Japanese jurisdiction to be recognized by asserting the rationale of the place of performance.

Determining Governing Law

Assume that the Japanese jurisdiction has been recognized over an international case. The Japanese court then decides on a governing law in accordance with Japan's private international laws. The primary legal source for private international laws in Japan is the Act on the Application of Laws, which has entered into force from 2007.

As Case 1 involves a contract, its governing law is determined pursuant to Article 7 of the Act on the Application of Laws. In the presence of a choice-of-law agreement by the parties, the designated law is governing. In case there is no agreement on or designation of an applicable law by the parties, the law of the nation that has, from an objective viewpoint, the most significant relationship to the contract at issue would be governing.[8] However, generally speaking, a case-by-case decision on the most closely-connected nation may harm legal certainty. So, the approach to infer which nation has the closest connection based on the theory of characteristic performance is adopted.[9] According to the characteristic performance theory, the legislation of Nation B, where software supplier Y is located, would be the applicable law.

Although it is doubtful whether each nation has proper legislation concerning cross-border e-commerce, especially for a computer information transaction, it is commonly said among Japanese academics that only state legislation can be governing, and that standard practices and customs in cyberspace and codes of conduct of business associations are not directly designated or applied as the applicable law.[10]

Recognition and Enforcement of Foreign Judgments

In Case 1, even if the Japanese entity wins the lawsuit, Y's assets need to be seized abroad (in Nation B) if not existing in Japan. In that case, the judgment issued in Japan needs to be recognized in Nation B, where the assets are to be seized. Enforcement would be relatively easy if Japan had a mutual enforcement agreement with Nation B. But, at present, Japan has no such agreement. Therefore, it is necessary to study domestic laws of Nation B, when the enforcement is to be carried out, to make sure that requirements are met.

Laws of the European Union (EU)

International Jurisdiction

In the European Union (EU), Council Regulation on Jurisdiction and the Enforcement of Judgments in Civil and Commercial Matters (Brussels I Regulation)[11] determines the international jurisdiction. Yet, the rules apply only to cases that are filed with courts in the EU member states and, in principle, that involve a defendant who has domicile in an EU nation. As for complaints involving a defendant whose domicile is not in an EU nation, jurisdiction rules of the nation where the court is located apply.[12]

Article 2 of the Brussels I Regulation stipulates that jurisdiction is conferred on the nation where the defendant has its domicile. So, if the defendant is a legal person, a complaint should be filed in any of the nations where the entity has its statutory seat, central administration, or principal place of business, which are stated in Article 60. In addition to that, in a contract-related case, special jurisdiction is conferred on the nation where the obligation in question is to be performed according to Paragraph 1(a) of Article 5. At issue again, here is the place of performance of the e-commerce obligation.

In this regard, conventional e-commerce, such as goods-sales contracts and service-provision contracts, have no major problem, as the Brussels I Regulation has a provision stipulating that the place of performance of the obligation in question shall be, in the case of the sale of goods where the goods were delivered or should have been delivered, while in the case of the provision of services where the services were provided or should have been provided (Paragraph 1(b) of Article 5). Meanwhile, as for a computer information transaction as in Case 1, which is not regarded as a goods-sales contract or a service-providing contract, the place of performance needs to be decided for each case according to the basic criteria provided in Paragraph 1(a) of Article 5.[13]

Yet, a decision on the place of the performance is quite difficult. Selecting the location of the buyer's computer as the place of performance amounts to giving jurisdiction always to the nation where the plaintiff is domiciled. Conversely, regarding the nation where the seller's computer is located as the place of performance means that the seller can place a server wherever advantageous to the seller, which may lead to a situation unfair to the buyer. The Brussels I Regulation does not provide a clear-cut approach to jurisdiction, at least for e-commerce.

A means to avoid such trouble would be to insert a provision of jurisdiction agreement. According to Article 23, approved styles of jurisdiction agreement include those in writing and an oral agreement, with written evidence. Electronic communications are also regarded as equivalent to "writing." A jurisdiction agreement is considered to mean exclusive jurisdiction unless otherwise specified.[14]

Determining Governing Law

The EU member states signed the 1980 Rome Convention on the Law Applicable to Contractual Obligations,[15] which unified private international law rules concerning contracts among the EU member states. Pursuant to the Rome Convention, the applicable law is to be selected first by means of designation of parties concerned, if there is any agreement (Article 3[16]), next, in the absence of designation, the legislation of a nation that has the closest connection with the contract shall be chosen (Article 4[17]). The most closely connected nation is basically inferred to be the county of the habitual residence of the party who performs characteristic performance (the theory of characteristic performance). Characteristic performance means obligation execution that characterizes the contract, usually liabilities that are not in the form of monetary payment.

In Case 1, in the absence of a choice by the parties, the obligation to supply software is primarily considered to be the characteristic performance of the contract, and the legislation of the nation where the European entity is located is chosen as the governing law.

Recognition and Enforcement of Foreign Judgments

A judgment issued through the procedures by a court in an EU country is recognized and enforced in other EU nations as well, under the Brussels I Regulation.[18] However, enforcement in nations other than the EU member states is left up to the nation's regulations on recognition and enforcement of foreign judgments.

UCITA in the United States

In the United States (U.S.) a special integrated legislation is adopted, which took account of the uniqueness of computer information transactions: the Uniform Computer Information Transactions Act (UCITA). UCITA is just a model law and has no effect in itself within a state unless it is enacted by the state. According to the UCITA, any agreement between concerned parties on exclusive jurisdiction is valid, except it is unfair (Section 110[19]). As for governing law, self-governance of the concerned parties is approved and, in the absence of choice, in principle, the law of the place where the seller (licenser) is domiciled is applied in e-commerce.[20] A judgment issued by a U.S. state court can also be executed in other sister states in principle. However, whether a judgment given in the U.S. is enforced or not in a nation other than the U.S. depends on the nation's regulations on recognition and enforcement of foreign judgments.

Self-Governance of Business Society

As discussed so far, first, it is not always clear in which nation a lawsuit should be filed regarding B2B computer information transactions. In order for parties concerned to ensure predictability, they need to at least make a jurisdiction agreement or clearly provide the place of performance. Second, determining the governing law is up to the parties concerned. In the absence of designation, it is highly possible that the law of the place where the seller is located is applied. Third, even if a plaintiff won a lawsuit, enforcement of the judgment is not necessarily easy except for limited cases, such as across EU member nations or across the U.S. states.

All told, (a) an agreement on jurisdiction and governing laws is essential to ensure predictability for parties concerned and (b) considering the difficulty in cross-border enforcement of a judgment, it would be rather realistic for a computer information transaction contract to have an arbitration clause. Regarding arbitration, the 1958 New York Convention[21] is effective in many nations, and internationally more persuasive than court decisions. If an agreement can be made between parties concerned on forum and governing law, an agreement can also be reached on an arbitration provision. Moreover, arbitration is controlled not only by state legislation as the governing law, which raises the possibility for standard practices being applicable. Use of online arbitration also becomes an option.

B2C TRANSACTION AND CONSUMER PROTECTION

Take an example of a dispute that arises from an international computer information transaction between a consumer and a business as Case 2.

Japanese Laws

International Jurisdiction

As there is no written provision on international jurisdiction, academic opinions divide on whether a jurisdiction agreement can be recognized for consumer transactions. It is uncertain whether a jurisdiction agreement will be approved for a lawsuit.

In the absence of a jurisdiction agreement, international jurisdiction rules apply as in B2B cases. For many consumer contract cases, for example, jurisdiction of a nation where the consumer's habitual residence is located would be recognized for the sake of fairness among the parties in light of the theory of special circumstances,[22] and jurisdiction of a nation where the business is located would be denied.

Determining Governing Law

If the Japanese jurisdiction has been recognized, the governing law is determined pursuant to the Act on the Application of Laws. A new provision concerning consumer contracts has been set up in the Act as Article 11. The provision says, even if there is an agreement on applicable laws between the parties, "mandatory provisions in the law of the place of the consumer's habitual residence is also applied to issues related to the conclusion and effect of the consumer contract when the consumer expresses to the business an intention to apply specific mandatory provisions in laws of the residential nation" (paragraph 1 of Article 11). In other words, the consumer side can, in effect, choose either legislation of the agreed nation or his or her residential nation, whichever is more advantageous to the consumer. In case there is no agreement of the parties on governing laws, the legislation of the nation where the consumer resides serves as the applicable law (paragraph 2 of Article 11). Both provisions are meant to protect consumers.

Note that, however, the special provisions for consumer protection are not applicable for a case in which the business did not know the habitual residence of the consumer and had due reasons for not knowing, or the business mistakenly assumed that the other party was not a consumer at the time of sealing the consumer contract and had due reasons for the misunderstanding.

Such cases are treated in a similar way as in a B2B transaction (paragraph 6 of Article 11).

In Case 2, a consumer who has his or her primary residence in Japan can file a lawsuit with a Japanese court and mandatory provisions of Japanese laws, which are advantageous for consumers, can be applied.

Laws of the European Union

International Jurisdiction

The Brussels I Regulation also applies to international jurisdiction of B2C transaction cases, and jurisdiction is given to the nation where the consumer resides as a rule. However, the Brussels I Regulation has special provisions for consumer contracts (Article 15 et seq.[23]). A consumer can file a lawsuit in his or her domicile as long as the case matches the concept stipulated in the provisions. In Case 2, it has a significant meaning when a consumer living in an EU nation sues a business in the EU territory. Specifically, a business that operates commercial activities toward Nation A via the Internet would be subject to trials in Nation A, not only in a case involving a contract concluded in Nation A by a Nation A resident, but also a contract concluded online in Japan by a Nation A resident, because of the special provisions. The special provisions were actually drawn up by taking e-commerce into consideration as well.[24] The point is whether a business is doing commercial activities to the nation where a consumer lives.

In B2C transactions, no jurisdiction agreement is recognized, except an agreement made after a dispute arises, an agreement to bestow new jurisdiction to a consumer, and an agreement between parties located in a same nation to give jurisdiction to the nation (Article 17).

Determining Governing Laws

The Rome Convention is applied to determine governing laws. For certain B2C contracts, it is not allowed to deprive consumers of protection bestowed by the law of the consumer's residential nation (Article 5). That is, even if the parties concerned designate a third nation's legislation as the governing law, consumer protection stipulated in the law of the consumer's residential nation is guaranteed at a minimum.

The point at issue is the significance and scope of consumer contracts to which the provisions apply. In this regard, the Rome Convention, different from the Brussels I Regulation, limits the eligible contracts to those of supply goods or services and credit contracts concerning the consumer contract in question.[25] Therefore, it is possible for a computer information transaction to be construed to fall out of the scope of consumer contracts stipulated in the convention. Even on the assumption that a computer information transaction is regarded as a goods/service supply contract, the provision is still not applicable when the contract is interpreted as a contract for the supply of services where the services are to be supplied to the consumer exclusively in a country other than that in which he has his habitual residence (Paragraph 4(b) of Article 5). Moreover, as protection is provided under some conditions such as "the conclusion of the contract was preceded by a specific invitation addressed to him or by advertising, and he had taken in that country all the steps necessary on his part for the conclusion of the contract" (Paragraph 2 of Article 5), it is also an issue whether the computer information transaction fulfills those conditions. Especially in a contract completed online in a nation other than the consumer's domicile, not all the steps required for contract conclusion are performed in the consumer's residential nation, which would produce enough room for the interpretation that the contract is not eligible for consumer protection. When a transaction is not regarded as a consumer contract, as in the above cases, the principles of party autonomy is recognized by going back to the basics. However, special application of mandatory provisions of the forum or a third nation (such as the consumer protection law) may be possible for certain types of cases under the Rome Convention (Article 7[26]).

Laws of the United States

The UCITA of the U.S. recognizes party autonomy for B2C transactions, but in such a case consumers cannot be deprived of protection provided by laws of the residential place of the seller (licenser).[27] The UCITA regulation is obviously favorable for the business (software provider) concerning computer information transactions, putting the consumer at a disadvantage because the business can effectively control jurisdiction and applicable laws. The UCITA has many other provisions advantageous for business, which invites strong criticism in the U.S.

Incidentally, apart from the UCITA, U.S. state laws generally adopt the following approaches: jurisdiction is recognized for the place of business operations of the defendant (general jurisdiction based on doing business), and then, even in a case where jurisdiction is recognized, the court may refrain from exercising jurisdiction on its own discretion upon a claim by a party concerned that the forum is inappropriate (the doctrine of "Forum Non Convenience"). As for jurisdiction based on doing business in e-commerce cases, (a) for active Web sites, which allow consumers living in the venue to enter contracts or to download a file, jurisdiction is recognized based on the business activity conducted there, (b) for passive Web sites, which allow access for consumers living in the venue but provide only advertisement, jurisdiction based on business operations is denied, and (c) for Web sites positioned somewhere in between the two types, which are interactive but are not available for sealing contracts, jurisdiction is determined for each case by taking the degree of interactivity into account.[28] For a computer information transaction involving a consumer, the consumer's country of residence would have jurisdiction in principle, as long as the Web site is interactive. Then, the legislation of the forum is relatively often designated as the applicable law according to the modern conflict approach.

Consumer Protection

As discussed so far, in all of Japan, the EU, and the U.S., jurisdiction is conferred on the consumer's residential country, and legislation of the country is regarded as the governing law from a standpoint of consumer protection. Still, at issue again is how the judgments issued would internationally be valid. Especially in consumer transactions, billing amounts are generally small, and enforcement in a foreign nation may result in more expense than gain. By that token, constructing out-of-court dispute settlement systems is worth considering. Some approaches attempted in the EU and other areas are discussed for reference.

The first example is the Directive of the European Parliament and of the Council on Certain Legal Aspects of Information Society Services, in particular, Electronic Commerce, in the Internal Market (Directive on Electronic Commerce[29]) which was issued in 2000. This does not specifically concern computer information transactions, but, as a dispute settlement system, it encourages enhancing voluntary codes of conduct (Article 16) and extrajudicial dispute settlement (Article 17), and then stipulates rules regarding coordinated efforts in the member countries. It is based on the concept that drafting voluntary codes of conducts is significant in view of preventing disputes involving consumers, and that a flexible and simple scheme of extrajudicial settlement means much more than a civil lawsuit, which is not necessarily easy for consumers.

The second example is establishment of the principles applicable for out-of-court procedures, which were adopted as a means to mould extrajudicial dispute settlement procedures and related organizations into an appropriate form.[30] The principle is only a recommendation by the EU Commission and is not legally binding. However, together with networking of extrajudicial dispute settlement organizations, which will be discussed, its actual influence can be substantial.

The third example is networking of extrajudicial dispute settlement organizations. Even if extrajudicial dispute settlement organizations are tailored to the "principles," it is still difficult for consumers to obtain information on which the organization handles what kind of dispute and the body's grade of performance. Thus, all the EU member states are required to inform the EU Commission of the country's organizations that satisfy the above principles, and the information is posted on a Web site operated by the commission. As more appropriate and effective procedures to settle disputes concerning international consumer transactions, the EU Commissions proposed the European Extra-Judicial Network (EEJ-Net),[31] which links qualified extra-judicial dispute settlement bodies. Each member nation systematized national out-of-court dispute settlement organizations for the EEJ-Net to support consumers and set up a clearing house to supervise them, which are further incorporated into a network. Its pilot operation started in October 2001. Under the EEJ-Net system, consumers who have complaints about or are dissatisfied with dealings can obtain information on what kind of extrajudicial dispute settlement organizations exist in their country and which bodies are available, only by accessing the information center. Also for international consumer transaction trouble, consumers can access the information center of their own nation to obtain support and advice for filing a complaint with an out-of-court settlement organization of the nation of the business side, which is expected to compensate language differences and lack of information.

CONCLUDING REMARKS

Future courses to take for constructing international dispute settlement systems will be discussed here.

Fundamental goals have already been laid out in the Guidelines for Consumer Protection in the Context of Electronic Commerce,[32] which was approved in 1999 by the Organization for Economic Co-operation and Development (OECD) Council.

First to be mentioned is the goal of balancing business protection (predictability) and consumer protection (ensuring relief measures). For predictability, clearer procedures and rules are required. For consumer protection, easy access to procedure and legislation should be afforded to consumers.

Second is balancing facilitation of e-commerce (freedom) and ensuring reliability (regulation). To encourage e-commerce, the course would be for state governments to avoid over-regulating or interfering with B2B transactions or to leave it to standard practices of the cyberspace society and the business society. On the other hand, it is indispensable for the sake of long-term development to foster confidence of transaction participants and to make transaction rules and dispute settlement procedures more appropriate, which requires involvement of the state that has the enforcement authority.

Third, coordination and allocation between judicial and extrajudicial systems are needed. Importance of the issue is evident from the moves the EU has been making for consumer transactions, and enhancing out-of-court dispute settlement systems is strongly required.

Fourth, global coordination is undoubtedly important. Coordination and cooperation among state governments capable of compulsory execution, is indispensable for settling international business disputes.

FUTURE RESEARCH DIRECTIONS

In accordance with the above-mentioned viewpoints, further research should be done towards the following directions enhancing both judicial and extrajudicial dispute settlement system in the global dimensions.

Enhancing Conflicts Rules Applied by Courts

Although there might be no need to create comprehensive rules specifically for international e-commerce in principle, particular features of e-commerce should be taken into account of, in order to cope with disputes arising from cross-border electronic transactions:

First, jurisdiction agreement for B2B transactions and consumer protection jurisdiction for B2C transactions should be stipulated in the rules. Consumer protection jurisdiction rules are especially essential for consumers to engage in e-commerce with peace of mind. Though that may be a disadvantage for businesses in short-term and micro-scale, it would lead to more proliferation of e-commerce in long-term and macro-scale, and be an advantage for businesses and a benefit to society overall. Meanwhile, consideration should be given to small and medium-sized businesses that shall enter an appearance at a foreign court. In this regard, business entities that have taken appropriate steps should be exempt from jurisdiction to redress the balance.

Second, non-state legal norms that meet certain conditions should be allowed to directly be applied by courts as the governing law, respecting voluntary rules of cyberspace and standard practices of the business society. That would be relevant both when there is a choice-of-law agreement between parties and when a court chooses governing laws in the absence of a choice-of-law agreement. As consumer protection must be considered in consumer transactions, special provisions to protect consumers should be incorporated in the rules. Such a provision should stipulate that consumers shall not be deprived of protection bestowed by law of their habitual residence place, and that the protection covers overall transactions that fall within the scope of business activities in the nation regardless of the place of conclusion of the contract, as stipulated in the Brussels I Regulation. Once again for fairer balance, businesses that have taken appropriate steps should be exempt from application of special consumer protection provisions for fair balance.

Third, a multinational cooperation system concerning mutual recognition and enforcement of judgment should be actively structured. However, it is unlikely that such a global-scale pact covering the issues will be successfully launched soon.

Enhancing Extrajudicial Dispute Settlement System

If a court settlement is difficult, the following steps and actions should be taken to enhance extrajudicial settlement schemes, which cover electronic transaction disputes as well, mainly for consumer protection:

First, voluntary drafting of codes of conduct should be encouraged. As pointed out in the EU directive on e-commerce, voluntary codes drawn up by business organizations, expert bodies, and consumer groups are instrumental in proper and fair operation and management of e-commerce, and also lead to forming and defining voluntary rules of cyber society. State governments should introduce a system to provide incentives for drafting of voluntary action regulations.

Second, procedures and organizations for extrajudicial dispute settlement should be formalized. The principles of the EU can be referred to as a specific example. Such principles should be established on a global scale, and measures to recognize and make public entities that meet the principles should be considered.

Third, in connection with the second point, networking of out-of-court dispute settlement bodies should be actively promoted. The EEJ-Net, again from the EU, serves as a model. A central information center should be set up in each country so that a consumer with trouble can access (online access should of course be considered) the center to learn routes to relief measures. The central information center supervises the organizations recognized as satisfying the aforementioned principles and also works to construct a network with similar entities in other nations.

Finally, a mechanism to ensure enforcement of international decisions in extrajudicial dispute settlement procedures should be enhanced. A system for mutual recognition and enforcement should be built not only for arbitral awards in the strict meaning, but also for a wider range of documents concerning compromise and reconciliation made through proper out-of-court settlement procedures.

REFERENCES

Boele-Woelki, K., & Kessedjian, C. (Eds.). (1998). *Internet: Which court decides? Which law applies?* Kluwer.

ADDITIONAL READING

Basedow, J. (2000). The effects of globalization on private international law. In Basedow & Kono (Eds.), *Legal aspects of globalization—Conflict of laws, Internet, capital markets and insolvency in a global economy.* Kluwer

Beatty, M. (1999). Litigation in cyberspace: The current and future state of Internet jurisdiction. *University of Baltimore Intellectual Property Law Journal, 7,* 127.

Bogdan, M. (2006). *Concise introduction to EU private international law.* Europa Law Publishing.

Chen, X. (2004). United States and European Union approaches to Internet jurisdiction and their impact on e-commerce. *University of Pennsylvania Journal of International Economic Law, 25,* 423.

Chik, W. (2002). U.S. jurisdictional rules of adjudication over business conducted via the Internet—Guidelines and a checklist for the e-commerce merchant. *Tulane Journal of International and Comparative Law, 10,* 243.

Geist, M. (2000). E-commerce jurisdiction: the Canadian approach. *Journal of Internet Law, 4,* 9.

Gillies, L. (2006). The new legal framework for e-commerce in Europe. *European Law Review, 31,* 774.

Huntley, A. (2005). Contract law in an e-commerce age. *International Journal of Law & Information Technology, 13,* 291.

Jennings, M. (2005). Finding legal certainty for e-commerce: Traditional personal jurisdiction analysis and the scope of the zippo sliding scale. *Washburn Law Journal, 44,* 381.

Jezairian, S. (2000). Lost in the virtual mall: Is traditional personal jurisdiction analysis applicable to e-commerce cases? *Arizona Law Review, 42,* 965.

Katsh, E., et al. (2000). E-commerce, e-disputes, and e-dispute resolution: In the shadow of "eBay Law." *Ohio State Journal on Dispute Resolution, 15*(3), 705.

Kightlinger, M. (2003). A solution to the Yahoo! problem? The EC e-commerce directive as a model for international cooperation on Internet choice of law. *Michigan Journal of International Law, 24,* 719.

Nimmer, R. (2001). Principles of contract law in electronic commerce. In Fletcher, Mistelis, & Cremona (Eds.), *Foundation and perspectives of international trade law.* Sweet & Maxwell.

Pappas, C. (2002). Comparative U.S. and EU approaches to e-commerce regulation: Jurisdiction, electronic contracts, electronic signatures and taxation. *Denver Journal of International Law and Policy, 31,* 325.

Stone, P. (2006). *EU private international law: harmonisation of laws.* Elgar European Law.

Takahashi, K. (2006). A major reform of Japanese private international law. *Journal of Private International Law, 2*(2),

Symposium: Current debates in the conflict of laws: Choice of law and jurisdiction on the Internet: Choice of law for Internet transactions: The uneasy case for online consumer protection. (2005). *University of Pennsylvania Law Review, 153*, 1883.

Symposium on approaching e-commerce through uniform legislation: Understanding the Uniform Computer Information Transactions Act and the Uniform Electronic Transactions Act. (2000). *Duquesne Law Review, 38*, 205.

ENDNOTES

[1] The words of conflict-of-laws, conflicts law, or private international law are used as interchangeable terms in this chapter.

[2] *See* generally, K. Boele-Woelki and C. Kessedjian ed., *Internet: Which Court Decides? Which Law Applies?* (Kluwer, 1998). According to the "Introduction" of this book, "[t]he main question is whether the challenges created by the global information revolution to the conflicts lawyer are matters of substance or only matters of degree."

[3] In case of computer information transactions like this hypothesis, the object of the contract is software that is not goods in a strict sense. One could regard this contract as a sale contract, and the others as a license contract.

[4] Supreme Court Judgment of Nov. 28, 1975, *Minshu* Vol. 29, No. 10, p.1554.

[5] Supreme Court Judgments of Oct. 16 1981, *Minshu* Vol. 35, No, 7, p. 1224 and especially of Nov. 11, 1997, *Minshu* Vol. 51, No. 10, p. 4055.

[6] Article 4 of the Code of Civil Procedure.

[7] Articles 5 of the Code of Civil Procedure.

[8] Article 8 (1) of the Act of the Application of Laws.

[9] Article 8 (2) of the Act of the Application of Laws.

[10] Nevertheless, some academics, including this author, strongly insist that certain non-state legal norms have qualifications to be applied directly as the applicable law through Japanese Private International Law rules. These norms include at least the Unidroit Principles, the 1980 UN Convention on Contracts for the International Sale of Goods that is not entered into force in Japan, the Uniform Customs and Practice for Documentary Credits, and so forth, in the author's view. *See*, 1994 Inter-American Convention on the Law Applicable to International Contracts (Mexico Convention) adopted by the Organization of American States. The Proposed Rome I Regulation also has a similar provision. COM (2005) 650 final.

[11] OJ 16. 1. 2001, L 12/1. The Brussels I Regulation modernizes and replaces the 1968 Brussels Convention on the same matters. The Brussels Convention continues to apply in relation to Denmark, to which the Brussels I Regulation does not apply. *See* Article 1 (3) of the Regulation.

[12] Article 4 (1) of the Regulation.

[13] Paragraph 1 of Article 5 reads: "A person domiciled in a Member State may, in another Member State, be sued:
1. (a) In matters relating to a contract, in the courts for the place of performance of the obligation in question;
(b) For the purpose of this provision and unless otherwise agreed, the place of performance of the obligation in question shall be:
- In the case of the sale of goods, the place in a Member State where, under the contract, the goods were delivered or should have been delivered,

- In the case of the provision of services, the place in a Member State where, under the contract, the services were provided or should have been provided,
    (c) if subparagraph (b) does not apply then subparagraph (a) applies."

[14] Paragraphs 1 and 2 of Article 23 state as follows:
  1. "If the parties, one or more of whom is domiciled in a Member State, have agreed that a court or the courts of a Member State are to have jurisdiction to settle any disputes which have arisen or which may arise in connection with a particular legal relationship, that court or those courts shall have jurisdiction. Such jurisdiction shall be exclusive unless the parties have agreed otherwise. Such an agreement conferring jurisdiction shall be either:
      a. In writing or evidenced in writing
      b. In a form which accords with practices which the parties have established between themselves
      c. In international trade or commerce, in a form which accords with a usage of which the parties are or ought to have been aware and which in such trade or commerce is widely known to, and regularly observed by, parties to contracts of the type involved in the particular trade or commerce concerned.
  2. Any communication by electronic means which provides a durable record of the agreement shall be equivalent to "writing."

[15] The most recent consolidated text of the Convention is found in OJ 30.12.2005 C 334 p.1.

[16] Paragraph 1 of Article 3 reads: "A contract shall be governed by the law chosen by the parties. The choice must be expressed or demonstrated with reasonable certainty by the terms of the contract or the circumstances of the case. By their choice the parties can select the law applicable to the whole or a part only of the contract."

[17] Paragraphs 1 and 2 of Article 4 state as follows:
  1. "To the extent that the law applicable to the contract has not been chosen in accordance with Article 3, the contract shall be governed by the law of the country with which it is most closely connected. Nevertheless, a separable part of the contract which has a closer connection with another country may by way of exception be governed by the law of that other country.
  2. Subject to the provisions of paragraph 5 of this Article, it shall be presumed that the contract is most closely connected with the country where the party who is to effect the performance which is characteristic of the contract has, at the time of conclusion of the contract, his habitual residence, or, in the case of a body corporate or unincorporate, its central administration. However, if the contract is entered into in the course of that party's trade or profession, that country shall be the country in which the principal place of business is situated or, where under the terms of the contract the performance is to be effected through a place of business other than the principal place of business, the country in which that other place of business is situated."

[18] *See* Chapter 3 of the Regulation.

[19] Section 110 titled "CONTRACTUAL CHOICE OF FORUM" reads:

a. "The parties in their agreement may choose an exclusive judicial forum unless the choice is unreasonable and unjust.
b. A judicial forum specified in an agreement is not exclusive unless the agreement expressly so provides."

[20] Section 109 titled "CHOICE OF LAW" reads:
a. "The parties in their agreement may choose the applicable law. However, the choice is not enforceable in a consumer contract to the extent it would vary a rule that may not be varied by agreement under the law of the jurisdiction whose law would apply under subsections (b) and (c) in the absence of the agreement.
b. In the absence of an enforceable agreement on choice of law, the following rules determine which jurisdiction's law governs in all respects for purposes of contract law:
   1. An access contract or a contract providing for electronic delivery of a copy is governed by the law of the jurisdiction in which the licensor was located when the agreement was entered into.
   2. A consumer contract that requires delivery of a copy on a tangible medium is governed by the law of the jurisdiction in which the copy is or should have been delivered to the consumer.
   3. In all other cases, the contract is governed by the law of the jurisdiction having the most significant relationship to the transaction.
c. In cases governed by subsection (b), if the jurisdiction whose law governs is outside the United States, the law of that jurisdiction governs only if it provides substantially similar protections and rights to a party not located in that jurisdiction as are provided under this [Act]. Otherwise, the law of the State that has the most significant relationship to the transaction governs.
d. For purposes of this section, a party is located at its place of business if it has one place of business, at its chief executive office if it has more than one place of business, or at its place of incorporation or primary registration if it does not have a physical place of business. Otherwise, a party is located at its primary residence."

[21] New York Convention on the Recognition and Enforcement of Foreign Arbitral Awards of June 10, 1958.

[22] As to the theory of special circumstances, *see* above II 1 (1).

[23] Article 15 reads:
1. "In matters relating to a contract concluded by a person, the consumer, for a purpose which can be regarded as being outside his trade or profession, jurisdiction shall be determined by this Section, without prejudice to Article 4 and point 5 of Article 5, if:
   a. It is a contract for the sale of goods on installment credit terms; or
   b. It is a contract for a loan repayable by installments, or for any other form of credit, made to finance the sale of goods; or
   c. In all other cases, the contract has been concluded with a person who pursues commercial or professional activities in the Member State of the consumer's domicile or, by any means, directs such activities to that Member State or to several States including that Member State, and the contract falls within the scope of such activities.

2. Where a consumer enters into a contract with a party who is not domiciled in the Member State but has a branch, agency or other establishment in one of the Member States, that party shall, in disputes arising out of the operations of the branch, agency or establishment, be deemed to be domiciled in that State.
3. This Section shall not apply to a contract of transport other than a contract which, for an inclusive price, provides for a combination of travel and accommodation."

[24] See especially, Paragraph 1(c) of Article 15.

[25] Paragraph 1 of Article 5 titled "Certain consumer contracts" states as follows;
1. This Article applies to a contract the object of which is the supply of goods or services to a person ("the consumer") for a purpose which can be regarded as being outside his trade or profession, or a contract for the provision of credit for that object.

[26] Article 7 titled "Mandatory rules" reads:
1. "When applying under this Convention the law of a country, effect may be given to the mandatory rules of the law of another country with which the situation has a close connection, if and in so far as, under the law of the latter country, those rules must be applied whatever the law applicable to the contract. In considering whether to give effect to these mandatory rules, regard shall be had to their nature and purpose and to the consequences of their application or non-application.
2. Nothing in this Convention shall restrict the application of the rules of the law of the forum in a situation where they are mandatory irrespective of the law otherwise applicable to the contract."

[27] See mentioned Section 109.

[28] See for example, *Zippo Manufacturing Company v. Zippo Dot Com, Inc.*, 952 F. Supp. 1119 (W.D. Pa. 1997), which is not a consumer contract case.

[29] OJ 17.7.2000 L 178/1.

[30] COMMISSION RECOMMENDATION of 30 March 1998 on the principles applicable to the bodies responsible for out-of-court settlement of consumer disputes, OJ 17.4.98, L 115/31 and COMMISSION RECOMMENDATION of 4 April 2001 on the principles for out-of-court bodies involved in the consensual resolution of consumer disputes, OJ 19.4.2001, L 109/56. As a world-wide project, *see* the UNCITRAL Model Law on International Commercial Conciliation.

[31] Commission Working Document on the creation of an Extra-Judicial Network (EEJ-Net), SEC (2000) 405.

[32] "VI. DISPUTE RESOLUTION AND REDRESS", "A. APPLICABLE LAW AND JURISDICTION" of Part 2 of the Guidelines states as follows;
"Business-to-consumer cross-border transactions, whether carried out electronically or otherwise, are subject to the existing framework on applicable law and jurisdiction.
Electronic commerce poses challenges to this existing framework. Therefore, consideration should be given to whether the existing framework for applicable law and jurisdiction should be modified, or applied differently, to ensure effective and transparent consumer protection in the context of the continued growth of electronic commerce. In considering whether to modify the existing framework, governments should seek

to ensure that the framework provides fairness to consumers and business, facilitates electronic commerce, results in consumers having a level of protection not less than that afforded in other forms of commerce, and provides consumers with meaningful access to fair and timely dispute resolution and redress without undue cost or burden."

Chapter XV
Cross-Border Court Jurisdiction and Economic Law Application in Electronic Commerce

Takeshi Kawana
Waseda University, Japan

ABSTRACT

The purpose of this chapter is to examine international jurisdiction and choice of law for e-commerce involving economic legal issues. International jurisdiction and choice of law will be determined under private legal principles, but as e-commerce involves economic law as a law to ensure national economic stability, the court may consider economic law with both private and public legal functions. At that time there may be some conflict of law involving state economic policy, and it must be considered how to coordinate the conflict and create a universal legal structure for non-territorial cyberspace. This chapter will propose three layers of legal structure for e-commerce: the private law layer, the economic law layer, and the criminal law layer, all of which have perspectives for borderless cyberspace.

INTRODUCTION

The more international transactions have been increasing, the more international disputes have been brought to courts. International civil cases include two main preliminary issues—international court jurisdiction, in which a court should have the jurisdiction to the international case, and choice of law, in which a law should be applied to the case. For both issues, in principle, the most appropriate court and law should be chosen to settle the dispute. As the rules to decide which court and law is appropriate are different from state to state, many authors have pointed out the inconvenience that there are no unified rules internationally. However, as opposed to criminal and administrative cases, the exercises of the civil jurisdiction have rarely been protested by another state, because they belong to private legal issues.[1]

However, recent private law has reflected economic policies of a state and the number of economic laws[2] involving those policies has been increasing in many states. These statutes are competition law, financial transaction law, intellectual property law, and others. There are different views concerning which character the law has, public or private. However, originally, economic law intends to control private transactions from the viewpoints of public interests. Therefore, economic law naturally includes both public and private law functions, which should be emphasized on the basis of the position of each provision included in each statute. Of course, the dichotomy of public and private law is peculiar to continental law and not seen in common law countries. And, basically, if law is a system to ensure justice in a society, the difference between a dispute which should be settled privately and that which should be intervened publicly is relative and can not be always divided clearly. However, in order to divide the categories of public and private law for this chapter's analysis, one possible criterion can be whether it is a rule for prosecution or private lawsuit.[3]

Japanese economic laws are divided into three categories, depending on the criterion mentioned. First, laws with more public functions include antitrust law, foreign exchange and foreign trade law, and prize expression law. An offender against these laws is prosecuted according to their penalty clauses. Second, laws with more private functions, include unfair competition prevention law, consumer protection law, specific commercial transaction law, product liability law, and intellectual property law. These laws are basically quoted at civil cases though they are enacted to ensure proper economic transactions from public standpoints. Third, laws with public and private functions equally, includes financial law, for example, securities exchange law and investment law, and labor law, which have many penalty clauses as well as private contract provisions.

This section targets the second category and analyzes the characteristics concerning the decision of jurisdiction and choice of law when the economic law is applied to civil cases and the difference from the application of purely private laws. Because over-jurisdiction or biased choice of law may occur when economic law with specific state policy is applied, though in civil cases proper court and law most related to the case should be chosen for the dispute settlement as well as private autonomy being permitted. At that time, public order at the forum, such as protection of its residents and maintenance of legal order may be considered rather than impartial settlement of private transaction disputes. Then, recognition of jurisdiction is closely related to choice of economic law as applicable law at the forum because of its public character (Campbell, D., & Woodley, S., 2002[4]).

As for normal transactions, we can see many achievements in such fields as product liability or consumer protection. Then, this section focuses on international e-commerce, which is expanding in the aspects of geography and the participants. In e-commerce, by electronic tools like the Internet, everyone can deal with other people worldwide. Therefore, both service providers and customers may have a transaction with insupposable kinds of persons. For these uncertain transactions, economic law may be significant to maintain legal order and protect nationals at the forum, and it is necessary to examine how the mentioned consideration affects the decision of international jurisdiction and choice of law.

From these standpoints, the next section will examine how the U.S., Europe, and Japan deal with the cases in relationship with economic law in a normal transaction. It will mainly discuss consumer protection law, product liability law, privacy and personality law, unfair competition prevention law, and intellectual property law as applied in civil lawsuits. Then, the characters of e-commerce for decision of jurisdiction and choice of law will be indicated and next, the attempt of the U.S., Europe, and an international forum will be seen. Finally, it concludes with what roles economic law should play in international e-commerce.

COURT JURISDICTION AND ECONOMIC LAW APPLICATION IN NORMAL TRANSACTIONS

United States

In the U.S., to recognize court jurisdiction, "minimum connection" has been the most important element. There, international transaction is an extension of interstate jurisdiction, where foreseeability that a defendant will expect which court he will be brought to, must be considered under "due process" under the Constitution. Then, when the defendant intentionally uses a place in a state, the court of the state recognizes its jurisdiction on the basis of the minimum connection between him and the state.

On the other hand, choice of law is dealt with according to the rule of conflict of the law of the forum. However, the choice of law can be related to recognition of jurisdiction. Namely, when the case has a significant relationship with the state's interests to regulate certain activities, especially tort cases, the courts have recognized their jurisdiction for these viewpoints, and apply the law of the forum, which is economic law in some cases. At that time, not only minimum connection under private law but also any possible elements have been considered, and the long arm act has been applied as one of the precise examples for these cases.

However, it is not so clear what case it is that the jurisdiction is recognized and the law of the forum is chosen. For example, in product liability cases, where a U.S. national sues a foreigner in the U.S. and a foreigner sues a U.S. national in the U.S., we can see both the cases where the allegation was accepted and the cases where it was not. When jurisdiction is not recognized, the major reasons are 'forum-non-convenience', but it is not clear that the "convenience" is based purely on private legal consideration. After all, in the cases where state interests, namely, public interests are included, it depends on the connection policy of the forum, therefore, it may spoil the foreseeability for both the plaintiff and defendant.

EU

In the EU, as for the international jurisdiction, Brussels Convention on Jurisdiction and the Enforcement of Judgments in Civil and Commercial Matters[5] was concluded in 1968, and the Lugano Convention on Jurisdiction and the Enforcement of Judgments in Civil and Commercial Matters,[6] which is applied to EFTA states, was concluded in 1988. Then, after the Amsterdam Treaty came into force, the Brussels Convention was replaced by Brussels Rules[7] as secondary legislation of the Union. The directive provides unified rules to distribute jurisdiction to proper courts in the region.

According to the Brussels Rules, with regard to tort, it recognizes delict or quasi-delict the courts for the place where the harmful event occurred or may occur (Article 5, para. 3). As to the consumer contract, a consumer may bring proceedings either in the courts of the member state in which that party is domiciled or in the courts for the place where the consumer is domiciled (Article 16, para. 1). In principle, private autonomy is not permitted unless an agreement is entered into after the dispute has arisen, an agreement allows the consumer to bring proceedings in other courts, or an agreement is entered into by the consumer and the other party to the contract, both of whom are, at the time of conclusion of the contract, domiciled or habitually resident in the same member state, and which confers jurisdiction on the courts of that member state, provided that such an agreement is not contrary to the law of that member state (Article 17).

As to individual contracts of employment, an employer may be sued in the courts for the place where the employee habitually carries out his work or in the courts for the last place where he did so, or if the employee does not or did not habitually carry out his work in any one country, in the courts for the place where the business which engaged the employee is or was situated, as well as in the courts of the member state where an employer is domiciled (Article 19). As opposed, an employer may bring proceedings only in the courts of the member state in which the employee is domiciled (Article 20). Both provisions take employees' interests into consideration. Similarly to consumer contracts, private autonomy is not permitted unless an agreement on jurisdiction is entered into after the dispute has arisen, or allows the employee to bring proceedings in other courts (Article 21).

As to intellectual property, in proceedings concerned with the registration or validity, the courts of the member state in which the deposit or registration has been applied for, has taken place or is under the terms of a community instrument or an international convention deemed to have taken place, shall have exclusive jurisdiction regardless of domicile (Article 22, para. 4).

Additionally, where proceedings involving the same cause of action and between the same parties are brought in the courts of different member states, any court other than the court first seized shall of its own motion stay its proceedings until such time as the jurisdiction of the court first seized is established, and where the jurisdiction of the court first seized is established, any court other than the court first seized shall decline jurisdiction (Article 27).

As was described, the EU provides the distribution of jurisdiction in detail, so there is little room that each court can judge its jurisdiction at its discretion.

As to choice of law, Convention on the Law Applicable to Contractual Obligations Opened for Signature in Rome[8] was adopted in 1980 for contractual obligations, and with regard to non-contractual obligations, Proposal for a Regulation of the European Parliament and the Council on the Law Applicable to Non-Contractual Obligation (Rome II)[9] was submitted in 2003.

Under the proposal, as a general rule, the law applicable to a non-contractual obligation shall be the law of the country in which the damage arises or is likely to arise, irrespective of the country in which the event giving rise to the damage occurred and irrespective of the country or countries in which the indirect consequences of that event arise (Article 3, para. 1). Then, it provides special rules for product liability, unfair competition, privacy, environmental damage, and intellectual property infringement.

As to product liability, the law of the country in which the person sustaining the damage is habitually resident is applied (Article 4). But considering the forseeability of the defendant, in the case that the person claimed to be liable can show that the product was marketed in that country without his consent, the applicable law shall be that of the country in which the person claimed to be liable is habitually resident. As to unfair competition, considering the effect to the market as a whole, the law of the country where competitive relations or the collective interests of consumers are or are likely to be directly and substantially affected shall be applied (Article 5, para. 1). Where an act of unfair competition affects exclusively the interests of a specific competitor, under the general clauses of Article 3, the non-contractual obligation shall be governed by the law of that country (para. 2). As to violence of privacy and rights relating to the personality, the law shall be designated by the general clauses of Article 3, but in the case that it would be contrary to the fundamental principles of the forum as regards freedom of expression and information, the law of the forum shall be applied (Article 6, para. 1).

As to environmental damages, in principle, the law of the country in which the damage arises or is likely to arise shall be applied according to Article 3, but in the case that the person sustaining damage prefers to base his claim on the law of the country in which the event giving rise to the damage occurred, the law shall be applied (Article 7). As to intellectual property infringement, the law of the country for which protection is sought shall be applied (Article 8).

Though the recognition of jurisdiction has little room for discretion of the forum, the rules of the choice of law permits some discretion to the forum. As the first exception, the forum may choose the more closely connected law if it is clear from all the circumstances of the case (Article 3, para. 3, Article 4, and Article 5, para. 2). From the standpoints of purely private law, it is necessary to permit the forum to choose the most connected law in despite of the general rules. But, these clauses might be referred to when the forum is asked to apply certain economic law by the plaintiff in order to protect him, who lives in the forum. Second, though the law of the country in which the damage arises or is likely to arise shall be applied in general, as to privacy and rights relating to the personality, in the case that it would be contrary to the fundamental principles of the forum as regards freedom of expression and information, the law of the forum shall be applied. This just refers to contradiction to "principles," so it may be similar to "public order" at the forum, which has been recognized in traditional private international law. But it should be noted that the clause includes "freedom of information" as well as traditional freedom of expression. For, as present society has been developed with information technology, economic values and interests to regulate information, so economic law concerning information may be preferred to maintain the legal order of the forum.

It is also said with regard to environmental damage or intellectual property. As to environmental damage, the plaintiff may have a right to refer to the law of the country in which the event giving rise to the damage occurred. It comes from the thoughts particular to Europe that environmental regulations in the region should converge in higher levels uniformly.[10] Moreover, as to intellectual property, the applicable law is only the law of the country for which protection is sought while private autonomy is not permitted. It is true that the law of the country for which protection is sought is applied exclusively because intellectual property is recognized locally and the disputes involve validity of the rights as well as its damage. But, in the case of only damage, the law of the country in which the damage arises or is likely to arise may be more proper from the standpoint of purely private law. The reason why in any lawsuit the law of the country which protection is sought is chosen, is that economic policy for intellectual property will be considered.

In the EU, which has clearer rules concerning jurisdiction than the U.S., there is less possibility that the issues of jurisdiction and choice of law are considered as combined. As to choice of law, despite the mentioned concerns, it attempts to keep in reasonable balance, private law and public interests, for example, permission of freedom of choice of law except for intellectual property though it is only after their dispute arose (Article 10). However, this clear categorization as private law to decide jurisdiction and choose the applicable law may make some gap between the legislative purport of the law to be chosen and interpretation by the forum. Moreover, it is not completely denied that the forum is likely to choose its economic law in a broad sense for protection of its nationals and accomplishment of its legal purposes, because the application of mandatory rules at the forum is still not prevented (Article 12, para. 2).

Japan

As Japan has no explicit rules for international jurisdiction, the courts have depended on the order ('*Jori*'), that an international dispute should be settled in equality to the parties and with fairness and swiftness of the procedure, which is called jurisdiction-distribution doctrine.[11] Therefore, '*Jori*' concept is so vague that some other doctrines have been asserted, for example, modified-reverse-estimation doctrine, which considers local jurisdictional rules in Civil Procedural Code as the rules to distribute jurisdiction concerning the place, and makes a court deny its jurisdiction when special circumstances are recognized; modified-analogy doctrine, which analyzes and modifies domestic local jurisdictional rules, considering international aspects; interest-balance doctrine, which decides jurisdiction, considering a variety of elements in each case instead of applying local jurisdictional rules directly. However, though they have reasonable arguments individually, they can not but make a court decide its jurisdiction depending on vague standards such as "special circumstances," "analogy and modify," or "interest balance" to judge '*Jori*'. Therefore, these doctrines show no clear forseeablility in which the court might have the jurisdiction.

On the other hand, as choice of law concerning tort generally, Article 17 of the Act on General Rules of Application of Laws, enacted in 2006 provides the law of the place where the events causing the claims occurred, is applied. However, when the events that comprise the tort occurred abroad and do not constitute a tort under Japanese law, or when the injured person may not demand recovery of damages under Japanese law (Article 22) the law can not be applicable. This new act includes special clauses for consumer contract, employment contract and product liability, which will protect consumers and employees in Japan. Though there is some room to discuss what extent these rules can be applied to in the concrete cases, broad interpretation of the clauses may narrow applicability of foreign law in Japanese courts.

While Japan is under the mentioned unclear circumstances, there are few cases that have the issues concerning economic law. As to intellectual property, the law of the country for which protection is sought has been applied, which follows the present international trends. In the case where intellectual property which is registered in the foreign country may be infringed in Japan, the court dismissed the compensation claim based on locality of intellectual property rights, though the court recognized its jurisdiction.[12]

Presently, it is not clear what position the Japanese court will have in the future. Generally speaking, it is said that Japanese courts are reluctant to recognize their jurisdiction in international cases. But, when the courts is required to apply economic law to protect interests of Japanese people and firms who are entering more and more international transactions. What legal reasoning the court should deal with these kinds of economic law on? This question should be considered for the future.

DIFFERENTIAL CHARACTER IN JURISDICTION AND APPLICATION OF ECONOMIC LAW TO E-COMMERCE

As mentioned, while the decision of jurisdiction and choice of law are basically based on international private legal principles, they have not always been decided only on the principles, especially in the relationship with economic law. It is because of the dual function of economic law. In international judgments, the forum tends to consider its legal order in a broad sense, and the public function of economic law appears to emerge clearer. On the other hand, as the international civil lawsuit is a civil one, courts intend to resolve the disputes to be lodged on the private legal principles as much as possible. There are some conflicts between public and private legal functions.

Therefore, how are international jurisdiction and economic law recognized in e-commerce where the concepts of territoriality are less? In normal transactions, as a transaction and tort are made in a territory, court jurisdiction and applicable law are decided from the viewpoints of the legal connection between the territory and the act and the maintenance of legal order in international private law. However, e-commerce is dealt with in the cyberspace, which is less connected to the territory where the business should be executed, in some respects.

First is how the concepts of "territory" should be recognized. Even if the transaction is performed in cyberspace, in the case that the products and services are provided in the real world, the transaction has few differences with a normal transaction because the products and services will be used in a territory. But, in the cases that just information causes the problems in cyberspace, it is difficult to define where the information exists (Kessedjian, C., 2000[13]). Is that a terminal computer which the information was set in and uploaded from, the server which the information was uploaded to, the terminal computer which a user downloaded the information in? Considering the information and the user are connected when the user downloaded it, the place where the user downloaded the information occasionally might be the place where the damage occurred.

Second is how "the act" should be recognized. Which among the mentioned acts to distribute information is an act to "cause damage" to the victim? Especially, as recent technology enables the personal computer to search inside another computer, if it is connected with the Internet and certain software, and to download some software automatically, just setting some information in some personal computer connected with the Internet might cause damage to someone, somewhere, sometime.

Third is how the "counterpart in transaction" is recognized. In e-commerce, only if someone uploads his products or services on the Web, he can enter a transaction with anyone, anywhere in the world. Especially, if the products are just information, it is difficult to identify where the customer accesses the Web site. In case that it is related with consumer contracts or intellectual property, court jurisdiction or applicable law may be different according to the attributes of the customer.

Since e-commerce has these kinds of characters different from a normal transaction, most countries and the international forum are worried about the management. Then, the next section will see the current movement in major countries and the international forum, to deal with international court jurisdiction and choice of law.

ATTEMPT FOR INTERNATIONAL JURISDICTION AND CHOICE OF LAW TO E-COMMERCE IN THE U.S., EUROPE, AND HAGUE INTERNATIONAL PRIVATE LAW CONFERENCE

United States

In the U.S., as to international jurisdiction, the courts depend on the "minimum connection" as in the normal cases. Then, they emphasize on whether the defendant "purposely" acted in the place of the forum. Concerning the minimum connection standards to the activities on the Internet, in the 1997 Zippo case, the federal district court provided the framework with three standards; (i) the case where the defendant clearly made Internet activities at the place of the forum, (ii) the case where the defendant just enabled the users to access his information on the Internet, and (iii) the degree to the interactivity and commercial character of the activity when the case can not be identified to the above two types. In this case, though the defendant, a company which is established under California law and had no branches in Pennsylvania, provided information through the Internet to 3,000 Pennsylvanians, who are 3% of all the users. Therefore, the court recognized its jurisdiction concerning the claim of Zippo's trademark infringement [Type (i)].[14] On the other hand, in the 2003 Toys'R'Us case, where the plaintiff claimed trademark infringement, the federal court denied its jurisdiction because the defendant, which was a Spanish company, had no establishments, bank accounts, and employees in the place of the forum, and ran its Web site only in Spanish.[15]

As to copyright damage cases, in the 2002 ALS Scan Inc. case, the plaintiff who lived in Maryland, claimed compensation because the defendant, an Internet service provider, overlooked the fact that the copyright of a photograph where the plaintiff had appeared on the Web site, was infringed.[16]

Thus, the U.S. federal courts emphasize on the defendant's intent and do not recognize their jurisdiction, only because the U.S. residents just can access the Web site or have damages when they are at the place of the forum through the Internet.

However, the concept of the "purpose" is still relative. For example, in the Inset Systems Inc. case, the federal court recognized its jurisdiction only because the defendant indicated the advertisement with his toll free dial number on his Web site. In this case, the court applied the long arm act and recognized that the defendant had appeared in Connecticut and accepted more than 10,000 accesses from there.[17]

As to interstate in the U.S., the indication on the Web site or the condition of the access from the place of the forum affected the recognition of the jurisdiction. On the other hand, internationally, if it is not easy to use the Web site from the U.S. in respects of language, currency, or customer services, the courts may not readily recognize their jurisdiction. Especially, when the service provider has no establishments in the state, it must be noted that the indication on and the utilization of the Web site will be the ground for the jurisdiction.

European Union

As to international jurisdiction, in the process to make the Brussels rules, how to deal with the issues of e-commerce was discussed. In the matters relating to tort, a person domiciled in a member state may, in another member state, be sued in the courts for the place where the harmful event occurred or may occur (Article 5, para. 3). The place where the harmful event occurred includes the place where the fact that causes the harmful event occurred. However, following this interpretation, any place may be the place where the harmful event occurred, considering the Internet accessibility is expanding worldwide. But, focusing on the damage in information distribution in cyberspace, defamation cases and intellectual property infringement cases should be discussed while other cases generally include "real" product distribution, the same as a normal transaction.

A defamation case may be analogized from a publishing case. According to the precedents, as to individual damages, the court of the place where the harmful event occurred has jurisdiction under the general principle, and in the case including multiple plaintiffs, the court of the place where the publisher was established legally has jurisdiction concerning the overall damages. The precedent may be applied to Internet cases with many plaintiffs in the world.

As to individual contract of employment, the contract where the employee just provides information and products through the Internet may be recollected, but in the case that the employee does not or did not habitually carry out his work in any one country, an employer domiciled in a member state may be sued in the courts of the place where the business which engaged the employee is or was situated (Article 19, para. 2-b), so no particular difficulties may be estimated, even in Internet cases.

The provisions that were amended considering Internet cases were the clauses concerning consumer contracts. The Brussels Convention regarded as consumer contracts the cases where in the state of the consumer's domicile the conclusion of the contract was preceded by a specific invitation addressed to him or by advertising, and the consumer took in that state the steps necessary for the conclusion of the contract. The contracts include a contract for the sale of goods on installment credit terms, a contract for a loan repayable by installments, or any other form of credit made to finance the sale of goods, and any other contract for the supply of goods or a contract for the supply of services. Then, where the consumer enters into a contract with another party who is not domiciled in a contracting state but has a branch, agency, or other establishment in one of the contracting states, that party shall, in disputes arising out of the operations of the branch, agency, or establishment, be deemed to be domiciled in that state (Article 13 Item 3). However, in e-commerce, if the service provider advertises its products on the Internet somewhere in the world, he may enter a contract with a consumer in the EC and the advertisement on the Internet may be interpreted as another establishment in the contracting state.[18] Brussels rules provide that the contract has been concluded with a person who 'directs' commercial or professional activities to the member state of the consumer's domicile or to several states including that member state, and the contract falls within the scope of such activities (Article 15, para. 1-c). In the process to make the rules, the opinions that an agreement concerning the jurisdiction should be recognized under the condition that enough information must be provided, or those that the state should have jurisdiction when the activities are provided purposefully like the U.S. were argued, but the final clauses just provide "direct such activities to that member state."

As to intellectual property, though there are some issues concerning the differences between the validity of the intellectual property and infringement to the property, no actual problems will occur because the rules recognize the exclusive jurisdiction to the courts of the member state in which the deposit or registration has been applied for.

Next, as to choice of law, the Draft Rome II Rules will be examined. For unfair competition, the law of the country where competitive relations or the collective interests of consumers are or are likely to be directly and substantially affected shall be applicable (Article 5), therefore, only effect is not enough to recognize the connection. If multiple markets are affected directly and substantially, for each effect, each law of the market shall be applicable. Namely, since the effects provided under the article are considered as 'real' effects, there may be no special issues for e-commerce.

For violations of privacy and rights relating to the personality, some argued that the law of the place where the victims live should be applicable, because multiple laws may be applicable if the 2002 preparatory draft mentioning the law of the place where the violation occurred was maintained. However, it is not appropriate that the law of the place where the publication is not distributed even if the victim lives there, can be applicable. Therefore, the principle that the law of the place where the damage occurred is applicable was maintained. As to the Internet, though it is convenient that the law of the place where the victims live is applicable because the place where the damage occurred is less foreseeable, there are strict and subtle problems concerning which place is where the damage occurred on the Internet. So, with the principle that the law of the place where the damage occurred is applicable is kept, according to the individual case, more closely connected laws should be searched under Article 3, paras. 2 and 3.

As to intellectual property, as the law of the country for which protection is sought is objectively applicable, there is no room that any conflicts occur.

As mentioned, the EU has clearer rules in both jurisdiction and choice of law. However, there are possibilities that the law of the forum or the law of the third party may be applied as overriding mandatory rules (Article 12). In the case, the difference between public function involved in economic law applicable to private transaction and the traditional public order or mandatory law may be in question, but the final decision may depend on the judgment of the forum.

2001 Draft Convention on Jurisdiction and Foreign Judgments in Civil and Commercial Matters

As to international jurisdiction and recognition of foreign decisions on civil and commercial cases, considering the lack of internationally uniformed rules, with a start of the proposal by the U.S., the draft convention has been compiled for many years. Then, in October 1999, the special committee concluded the prepared draft and sent it to the diplomatic conference. But, as some delegates provided the opinions that the draft included some items which they could not agree to, in June 2001, the first diplomatic conference was held on the condition that it would adopt only the items which all the delegates would be able to achieve the consensus to. Therefore, the items including differences among the delegates were attached with most arguments of the delegates, and the interim draft of articles was concluded. The main ground that the draft was not adopted as a whole is how to deal with e-commerce, as well as the difference between common law systems and continental law systems.[19]

The first issue is a consumer contract. The 1999 draft provided basically the court of the state of the habitual residence of the consumer has the jurisdiction concerning a consumer contract (Article 7). However, in order to apply this provision, it is necessary that the conclusion of the contract on which the claim is based is related to trade or professional activities that the defendant has engaged in or directed to that state, and the consumer has taken the steps necessary for the conclusion of the contract in that state (para. 1). Especially, for Internet-related business, "in particular in soliciting business through means of publicity," it is required that the defendant has directed to that state. An agreement to jurisdiction is limited to the case that such agreement is entered into after the dispute has arisen or to the extent that it only allows the consumer to bring proceedings in another court (para. 3). These provisions are similar to the Brussels Rules of the EU. However, in e-commerce, the parties can not recognize whether the counterpart is a consumer at once. Therefore, the 2001 draft involved the condition that the provision is not applied in the case that a party proves that he has no reasonable ground that he can recognize another party is a consumer, and that he could not enter a contract with the party if he recognized it (Article 7, para. 1, proviso). Furthermore, the cases that a party proves that a consumer entered a contract outside his habitual residence and the consumer used the product or service outside his habitual residence, and the cases that a party takes reasonable measures to avoid entering a contract with a consumer, are out of the application of the Article (Article 7, paras. 2 and 3). Concerning an agreement to jurisdiction, there are the opinions that the agreement should be valid or invalid considering consumers' protection, but each involved complicated procedures and was indicated in the 2001 draft.[20]

Second, as to tort, though the 1999 draft provided the court of the place where the damage or the cause occurred (Article 10), it was argued that additional provisions should be supplemented because it is not foreseeable when, where, and how both an assailant and a victim will be involved in a problem on the Internet. It was difficult to find effective measures in the 2001 draft discussion, and the clause that the defendant avoided directing the activities to the state was adopted.

Third, as to unfair competition, Article 10, para. 2 of the 1999 draft provided that in the case that the damage came from infringement of the anti trust law, the court of the place where the damage occurred shall not have jurisdiction, but in the 2001 draft it is clearly indicated that this kind of damage is eliminated from the substantive scope in the paragraph. For the amendment, there is an argument that unfair competition cases or consumer contract cases should be noted not to be affected. Though the elimination should be recognized because of the pubic character of the anti trust law, the effect of the amendment to other economic law was concerned (Lehr, W. H., & Pupillo, L. M., 2002[21]).

Fourth, as to intellectual property, the 1999 draft provided that the courts of the state in which the deposit or registration has been applied for, have exclusive jurisdiction (Article 12). Additionally, in relation to the proceedings which have, as their object, the infringement of the intellectual property, both the clause that the courts of the state in which the deposit or registration has been applied for has exclusive jurisdiction (para. 4) and the clause that the jurisdiction of any other court under the convention or under the national law of a contracting state is not excluded (para. 5), are indicated. If political character to keep any decision concerning intellectual property is emphasized, the former provision will be more preferred. Furthermore, since copyrights are established by no formalities rule, general clause of tort shall be applied. However, as there are some differences concerning recognition of industrial values of copyrights among the states, the opinions that a state should be able to deny recognition and enforcement of foreign judgments were presented (Kumar, K., 2001[22]).

Therein, the following points are made as the issues of jurisdiction and economic law application concerning e-commerce. Namely, the convention aims to distribute court jurisdiction concerning private legal activities with private legal theories, but it lacks how to consider the effect of economic law concerning e-commerce with less territoriality. In both tort and contract breach, it is required to clarify which law is applied and which court will have jurisdiction to remove legal instability as the parties are invisible in the transaction. However, the less territoriality e-commerce has, the more the law will have a character as economic law to ensure and supplement legal stability. To be able to transact any party all over the world through the Internet is the supreme advantage and supreme risk in e-commerce. Coordinating the reasonableness in the private transaction will be achieved by private law while ensuring legal stability from the viewpoint of public interest will be achieved by public law. And the more how to reduce the legal instability is considered, the more the public law function of economic law is closed up. Then, the forum is likely to want to apply economic law with public functions to ensure legal stability in own country. In this case, the forum will set the locality of the e-commerce excessively to itself. But it is opposed to the dis-locality of e-commerce. If the unstable jurisdiction setting and choice of law expands, e-commerce might be just a local media without its global character.

CONCLUSION

As a result, at the present there are no clear rules for international jurisdiction and choice of law for international e-commerce while the e-commerce transaction is expanding rapidly. The reason is that the states reach no common recognition concerning the merit and the risks of e-commerce. Namely, while e-commerce is purely a private transaction in cyberspace, it includes high instability of broad geography and participants worldwide. The former is related to private legal function and the latter has connection with public legal function. The degree of necessity for public functions in private transactions is not accurate to the borderless world.

Here, as a conclusion, legal regulation of e-commerce will be considered from a long-term stance. The start point is grasping e-commerce as not a local market divided by each state but a single market connected in cyberspace, because territoriality of the transaction is less in cyberspace, as mentioned, and it cannot help being regarded a single market substantially. In this sense, at least concerning information distribution that is completed just online, securing its own national interests and legal order by each domestic economic law should be recognized no longer effective.

Then, how to make the rules for e-commerce as a single market is important. Here, three layers can be indicated. First, the private legal system recognizing the character of e-commerce as a private transaction space must be considered. The basic concepts of regulation are like *lex mercatoria*, eliminating territorial division. If it is normal that recognition of the parties and geography of transaction is difficult, the element of the rules for equivalent participants must be considered. In the present, when private law is "publicated," most domestic laws have public function and purely private law is extremely rare. If the conflict of publicated private laws is to be resolved, only through traditional rules of conflict of law, there will be severe clashes of law such as competition law or environmental law. In e-commerce, it is difficult to establish economic law to deal with a participant in the transaction inequivalently. As the result, considering its characteristics, and being apart from the interest of forum, a cybertribunal that deals with conflicts concerning e-commerce may be needed. As most conflicts concerning e-commerce involve real damage in a place, the concepts such as cybertribunal are now doubted by many authorities. But, like WIPO's cases concerning domain name disputes, which rise just as an issue in the cyberspace, these concepts can be constructed field by field (Ficsor, M., 2002[23]).

Then, second, if some economic law is needed in order to secure fairness and stability of e-commerce as a whole, "cyber economic law" should be considered, not individual domestic law for interests of each state. Namely, as past economic laws such as competition law were conflicted among specific states through its extraterritorial application and later, cooperation and harmonization progressed gradually, considering stability of global economy, effective legal regulation of e-commerce from the public standpoints worldwide should be considered as a rule for the market as a whole (Kleinwæchter, W., 2003[24]). Therefore, these kinds of rules must be established in some international forum where as many parties as possible can participate, including governmental representatives, NGOs and multinational corporations.

If further public function to secure the order in cyberspace is needed, as the third step, cyber criminal law can be recognized, which is developed for anti-terrorism, money laundering, and network/computer destruction (OECD, 2006[25]).

If the mentioned legal system may be estimated at all, what drives the movements forward? That is pressure of the market in e-commerce. The pressure of the market mentioned here is not just the invisible God hand and the power of the stronger market participants. Market is observed not only by participants in the market but also by a lot of states and people to be effected from the market. The actions and movements by many kinds of stakeholders affect the market and make a trend towards formation of sounder rules.

If the conflicts in e-commerce are to be resolved by distribution of jurisdiction of choice of law of one state, many fictions must be supposed to decide the territoriality of the transaction. The solution by conflict of law will be searched for a while. But then, extra jurisdiction and extra application of law of the forum may expand in the unstable cyberspace to secure individual interests of each state, the potential of e-commerce may be made narrow. Beyond such introversive and reductionism trends, it is expected that e-commerce is expanding as an innovative market in a global era.

FURTHER RESEARCH DIRECTIONS

E-commerce has been expanding rapidly and a lot of regulations of e-commerce have been introduced domestically and internationally. This chapter researched the issues in the judicial process concerning jurisdiction and choice of law. On the other hand, substantial regulatory harmonization and integration for e-commerce can be examined. Focusing on online transactions that involve no off-line dealing for the matters, the two main fields to be examined are intellectual property rights and consumer protection.

Intellectual property rights protection is important for B2B. Though intellectual property rights such as music copyrights and business secrets are significant properties for the present global business, the rights are protected country by country. Then, how to protect the rights and solve the infringement must be examined at the global level. WIPO and ITU have provided some suggestions, which should be watched to establish the appropriate international scheme.

Consumer protection is mainly for C2C as well as B2C because it is difficult to know whether the participants are B or C. Now, consumer protection issues have not only economic but criminal legal matters like fraud. These crimes, which are committed through the servers placed in a lot of countries, are invisible for the victims and authorities. The international framework which will investigate the global network is needed. As suggested at the conclusion of this chapter, the cyber law has three layers, private, economic, and criminal. Purely private legal matters will be resolved as contract issues, but many problems involve more and more economic/criminal elements to protect global business and consumers at policy bases. The above two fields will be the apex for the problems.

REFERENCES

Brussels Convention on Jurisdiction and the Enforcement of Judgments in Civil and Commercial Matters. (1972, December 12). *Official Journal*, L299/32.

Campbell, D., & Woodley, S. (2002). *E-commerce: Law and jurisdiction: The comparative law yearbook of international business: Special Issue 2002 (Comparative Law Yearbook of International Business)*. Kluwer Law International.

Convention on Jurisdiction and the Enforcement of Judgments in Civil and Commercial Matters. (1988, September 16). Presented at Lugano (88/592/EEC). *Official Journal*, L 319/9, 25/11/1988.

Convention on the Law Applicable to Contractual Obligations Opened for Signature in Rome. (1980, June 19). 80/934/EEC, *Official Journal*, L266/1, 09/10/1980.

Council Regulation (EC). (2000, December 22). Jurisdiction and the Recognition and Enforcement of Judgments in Civil and Commercial Matters. (No. 44/2001). *Official Journal*, L12/1, 16/01/2001.

Ficsor, M. (2002). *The law of copyright and the Internet: The 1996 WIPO treaties, their interpretation and implementation*. Oxford University Press.

Kessedjian, C. (2000). Commerce électronique et compétence juridictionnelle internationale, Ottawa, 28 février au 1er mar 2000, Rapport des travaux. *Conférence de la Haye de droit international privé, Exécution des jugements, Doc. Prél. No 12*.

Kleinwaechter, W. (2003). From self-governance to public-private partnership: The changing role of governments in the management of the Internet's core resources. *Loyola of Los Angels Law Review, 36*.

Kumar, K. (2001). *Cyber laws: Intellectual property and e-commerce security*. Dominant Publishers & Distributors.

Lehr, W. H., & Pupillo, L. M. (2002). *Cyber policy and economics in an internet age (topics in regulatory economics and policy)*. Springer.

OECD (2003). *Guidelines for protecting consumers from fraudulent and deceptive commercial practices across borders.*

OECD (2003). *Proposal for a regulation of the European Parliament and the Council on the law applicable to non-contractual obligations* ("ROME II"). COM (2003) 427 final, 2003/0168 (COD).

OECD (2006). *Protecting consumers from cyber fraud.* Policy Brief. OECD Observer.

ADDITIONAL READINGS

Andrea, A. (2003). Applicable law aspects of copyright infringement on the Internet: What principles should apply. *Singapore Journal of Legal Studies.*

Bailey, J. (2003). Private regulation and public policy: Toward effective restriction of Internet hate propaganda. *McGill Law Journal, 49.*

Bauchner, J. S. (2000). State sovereignty and the globalizing effects of the Internet: A case study of the privacy debate, Brook. *Journal of International Law, 26.*

Bergemann, K. L. (2002). A digital free trade zone and necessarily-regulated self-governance for electronic commerce: The World Trade Organization, international law, and classical liberalism in cyberspace. *The John Marshall Journal of Computer & Information Law, 20.*

Bigos, O. (2005). Jurisdiction over cross-border wrongs on the Internet. *International and Comparative Law Quarterly, 54.*

Borchers, P. J. (2003). Tort and contract jurisdiction via the Internet: The 'minimum contacts' test and the brussels regulation compared. *Netherlands International Law Review, 50.*

Christou, G., & Simpson, S. (2006). The Internet and public-private governance in the European Union. *Journal of Public Policy, 26.*

Cindy, C. (2004). United States and European Union approaches to Internet jurisdiction and their impact on e-commerce. *University of Pennsylvania Journal of International Economic Law, 25.*

Citron, D. K. (2007). Reservoirs of danger: The evolution of public and private law at the dawn of the information age. *Southern California Law Review, 80.*

Collins, M. (2006). *The law of defamation and the Internet.* Oxford University Press.

Coteanu, C. (2005). *Cyber consumer law and unfair trading practices: Unfair commercial practices (markets and the law).* Ashgate Publishing.

Eblen, C. C. (2004). Defining the geographic market in modern commerce: The effect of globalization and e-commerce on Tampa electric and its progeny, Baylor University. *Baylor Law Review, 56.*

Engel, C. (2006). The role of law in the governance of the Internet. *Journal International Review of Law, Computers & Technology, 20.*

Foss, M., &; Bygrave, L. A. (2000). International consumer purchases through the Internet: Jurisdictional issues pursuant to European law. *International Journal of Law and Information Technology, 8.*

Garfinkel, T. B. (1996). Jurisdiction over communication torts: Can you be pulled into another country's court system for making a defamatory statement over the Internet—A comparison of English and U.S. law. *Transnational Lawyer, 9.*

Gilden M. (2000). Jurisdiction and the Internet: The "real world" meets cyberspace. *ILSA Journal of International & Comparative Law, 7.*

Hestermeyer, H. P. (2005). Personal jurisdiction for Internet torts: Towards an international solution. *Northwestern Journal of International Law & Business, 26*.

Hopkins, S. L. (2003). Cybercrime convention: A positive beginning to a long road ahead. *Journal of High Technology Law, 2*.

Kilbey, I. (2003). Jurisdiction and choice of law clauses in Internet contracts. *International Travel Law Journal*.

Kim, J. S. (2002). Sales of securities over the Internet: Extra-territorial reach and limit of the federal securities laws in the U.S. *Korean Journal of International and Comparative Law, 30*.

Kohl, U. (2004). The rule of law, jurisdiction and the Internet. *International Journal of Law and Information Technology, 12*.

Krisch, N., & Kingsbury, B. (2006). Introduction: Global governance and global administrative law in the international legal order. *European Journal of International Law, 17*.

Leong, S. H. S., & Saw, C. L. (2007). Copyright infringement in a borderless world—Does territoriality matter? Society of composers, authors and music publishers of Canada vs. Canadian Association of Internet Providers [2004] 2 SCR 427. *International Journal Law of Information Technology, 15*.

Love, M. (2003). International jurisdiction over the Internet: A case analysis of YAHOO!, Inc. v. La Ligue contre le Racisme et L'antisemitisme. *Temple International and Comparative Law Journal, 17*.

Maggs, P. B., Soma J. T., & Sprowl, J. A. (2005). *Internet and Computer Law* (2nd ed.). American Casebook Series. West.

Marossi, A. Z. (2006). Globalization of law and electronic commerce toward a consistent international regulatory framework. In *Proceedings of the ACM International Conference* (p. 156).

Nelmark, D. (2004). Virtual property: The challenges of regulating intangible, exclusionary property interests such as domain names. *Northwestern Journal of Technology and Intellectual Property, 3*.

OECD (1999). *Guidelines for consumer protection in the context of electronic commerce*.

OECD (2002). *Best practice examples under the oecd guidelines on consumer protection in the context of electronic commerce*.

Rice, D. T. (2000). Jurisdiction in cyberspace: Which law and forum apply to securities transactions on the Internet. *University of Pennsylvania Journal of International Economic Law, 21*.

Rothman, M. S. (1999). It's a small world after all: Personal jurisdiction, the Internet and the global marketplace. *Maryland Journal of International Law and Trade, 23*.

Savin, A. (2006). Intellectual property: Economic and legal dimensions of rights and remedies. *The Economic Journal, 116*(509).

Schu, R. (1997). The applicable law to consumer contracts made over the Internet: Consumer protection through private international law. *International Journal of Law and Information Technology, 5*.

Shih, C. F., Dedrick, J., & Kraemer, K. L. (2005). Rule of law and the international diffusion of e-commerce. *Proceedings of the ACM, 48*(11).

Sidak, J. G. (2006). A consumer-welfare approach to network neutrality regulation of the Internet. *Journal of Competition Law and Economics, 2*.

Warner, R., Dinwoodie, G.., Krent, H., & Stewart, M. (2006). *E-Commerce, the Internet and the law, cases and materials (American Casebook Series)*. West Group.

Willem, J. L. C. (1998). Harmonisation of laws and the Internet. *International Business Law, 26*.

Yang, D. W., & Hoffstadt, B. M. (2006). Countering the cyber-crime threat. *American Criminal Law Review, 43*.

Zollers, F. E., Shears, P., & Hurd, S. N. (2002). Fighting Internet fraud: Old scams, old laws, new context. *Temple Environmental Law & Technology Journal, 20*.

ENDNOTES

1. As some cases which Japan is related to, the IMB-Hitachi case and Korean Air case are reminded.
2. The definition of economic law is getting vague because more economic policy introduced into private legislation. However, the element is to complement legal blank in civil law according to the demands of social harmonization with the basis of civil law, and economic law copes with the public aspect of civil society as well as the private aspects of its activities. So here is economic law defined as a law to satisfy social demands to harmonize social difficulties coming from private economic activities.
3. Some statutes have both provisions for public prosecution and private lawsuit, but extremely, these characters can be categorized by analyzing clause by clause.
4. Campbell, D. & Woodley, S. (2002), *E-Commerce: Law and Jurisdiction : The Comparative Law Yearbook of International Business : Special Issue 2002 (Comparative Law Yearbook of International Business)*, Kluwer Law International, pp. 32-39.
5. Brussels Convention on Jurisdiction and the Enforcement of Judgments in Civil and Commercial Matter, *Official Journal, L 299/32*, 31/12/1972.
6. Convention on Jurisdiction and the Enforcement of Judgments in Civil and Commercial Matters- Done at Lugano on 16 September 1988, 88/592/EEC, *Official Journal, L 319/9*, 25/11/1988.
7. Council Regulation (EC) No. 44/2001 of 22 December 2000 on Jurisdiction and recognition and Enforcement of Judgments in Civil and Commercial Matters, *Official Journal, L 12/1*, 16/01/2001.
8. Convention on the Law Applicable to Contractual Obligations Opened for Signature in Rome on 19 June 1980, 80/934/EEC, *Official Journal, L 266/1*, 09/10/1980.
9. Proposal for a Regulation of the European Parliament and the Council on the Law Applicable to Non-Contractual Obligation, COM(2003) 427 final, 2003/0168 (COD). Final regulation was adopted on 11 July, 2007. See teh law applicable to non-contractual obligations (Rome II, Official Journal, L199/40, 31/7/2007.
10. Explanatory Memorandum, attached to "Proposal," *supra* note 9, pp. 19-20.
11. Malaysian Airlines Case (Decision by the Supreme Court in October 16, 1981), *Minshu, Vol. 35*, No. 7 p. 1224.
12. "Card Reader Case", (Decision by the Supreme Court on September26, 2002), *Minshu, Vol. 56*, No. 7, p. 1551.
13. Kessedjian, C. (2000), «Commerce électronique et compétence juridictionnelle internationale, Ottawa, 28 février au 1er mar 2000, Rapport des travaux», *Conférence de la Haye de droit international privé, Exécution des jugements*, Doc. Prél. No 12, pp. 7-8.
14. Zoppo Mfg. Co.v. Zippo Dot Com, Inc., 952 F. Supp. 1119.
15. Toy"S"Rus Inc., v. Step Two S.A., 918 F. 3d 446 (3rd Cir. 2003)
16. ALS Acan, Inc., v. Digital Serv. Consultants, Inc., 293 F. 3d 707 (4th Cir. 2002).
17. Inset Systems, Inc., v. Instructions Set, Inc., 937 F. Supp. 161 (D. Conn. 1996).
18. As a contract is concluded by the agreement by the both parties, only application by the

[19] consumer on the web can create a contract, but in the case that the products or services to be provided are just information prompt payment and use are useful, so to confirm the attitudes of the applicants individually is not possible. Though there is the method to identify the attitudes by the place where the credit card for the payment was issued, it cannot define the habitual resident of the consumer.

[19] This article will examine only the Hague Private Law Conference, but there are many types of international forum which are discussing legal problems of e-commerce such as OECD and WIPO. As one example provided by another forum, OECD (2003) *Guidelines for Protecting Consumers from Fraudulent and Deceptive Commercial Practices Across Borders*.

[20] Employment contract has the same issues as consumer contract, then the conclusion was carried over in the discussion for the 2001 draft.

[21] Lehr, W. H. & Pupillo, L. M. (2002), *Cyber Policy and Economics in an Internet Age (Topics in Regulatory Economics and Policy)*, Springer, pp. 45-48.

[22] Kumar, K. (2001), *Cyber Laws; Intellectual Property and E-Commerce Security*, Dominant Publishers & Distributors, pp. 77-80.

[23] Ficsor, M. (2002), *The Law of Copyright and the Internet: The 1996 WIPO Treaties, Their Interpretation and Implementation*, Oxford University Press, pp. 88-90.

[24] Kleinwæchter, W. (2003), "From Self-Governance to Public-Private Partnership: The Changing Role of Governments in the Management of the Internet's Core Resources", *Loyola of Los Angels Law Review, Vol. 36*, pp. 1124-1125.

[25] OECD (2006), *Protecting Consumers from Cyber fraud*, Policy Brief, OECD Observer.

Compilation of References

Abdul Razak, A. (2001). The Payment and Settlement Systems in Malaysia. In Magno L. Torreja, Jr. (Ed.), *The Payment and Settlement Systems in theSEACEN Countries,* Vol. 2 (pp. 105-162). Kuala Lumpur: The SEACEN Centre.

Aguilar, J. (2000). Over the Rainbow: European and American Consumer Protection Policy and Remedy Conflicts on the Internet and a Possible Solution. *International Journal of Communications Law and Policy, 4*, 1-57.

Alboukrek, K. (2003). Adapting to a new world of E-Commerce: The need for uniform consumer protection in the international electronic marketplace. *The George Washington International Law Review, 35*(2), 425-460.

Alexson, H. B. (2005, October). Business Alert *Current Legal Issues For The Business Community, 4*(5). Retrieved from http://www.alexsonlaw.com/american-businesscounsel/

Allison, K. H., Grossman, M., & Rothman, R. (2001). *Click-wrap agreements—Enforceable contracts or wasted words?* Retrieved from http://www.keytlaw.com/Articles/clickwrap.htm

American Bar Association Task Force on E-Commerce and ADR. (2002). *Addressing disputes in electronic commerce.* Final Report and Recommendations. Retrieved December 9, 2006, from www.law.washington.edu/ABGA-eADR

APACS. (2006). *Fraud: the facts 2006.* Available at http://www.apacs.org.uk/resources_publications/documents/FraudtheFacts2006.pdf

Associated Press. (2006, September 28). *Belgian premier says SWIFT secretly supplied U.S. with bank data.* Retrieved September 30, 2006, from http://www.siliconvalley.com/mld/siliconvalley/news/editorial/15630604.htm?template

AusCERT. (2006). *Australian Computer Crime and Security Survey, 20.* Retrieved from http://www.auscert.org/au/render.html?it=2001

Australian Institute of Criminology. (2005, January). *High tech crime brief, concepts and terms, new crimes and old crimes committed in new ways.* Retrieved from http://www.aic.gov.au

Bainbridge, D. (2004). *Introduction to Computer Law* (5th ed.). Harlow, UK: Longman.

Bank for International Settlements. (2001, January). *Core principles for systemically important payment systems.*

Bank of International Settlements. (2003). *Payment and Settlement Systems in Selected Countries.* Available at http://www.bis.org/publ/cpss53.pdf

Bank of Japan. (2000). *The Importance of Information Security for Financial Institutions and Proposed Countermeasures—With a Focus on Internet-Based Financial Services.* Retrieved February 25, 2007, from http://www.boj.or.jp/en/type/release/zuiji/kako02/data/fsk0004b.pdf

Bank of Japan. (2003). *Business Continuity Planning at Financial Institutions.* Retrieved February 25, 2007, from http://www.boj.or.jp/en/type/release/zuiji/kako03/fsk0307a.htm

Bank of Japan. (2003). *Business Continuity Planning at the Bank of Japan*. Retrieved February 25, 2007, from http://www.boj.or.jp/en/type/release/zuiji/kako03/sai0309a.htm

Bank of Japan. (2003). Response *to the Disclosure Framework for Securities Settlement Systems*. Retrieved March 22, 2007, from http://www.boj.or.jp

Bank of Japan. (2005, December). *Proposal for the next-generation RTGS project of the BOJ-NET funds transfer system.*

Bank of Japan. (2006). *Framework for the next-generation RTGS project of the BOJ-NET funds transfer system.*

Bank of Japan. (2006). *Outline of the 2005 Issue of the Payment and Settlement Systems Report.*

Barrett, R. (2004). Take the money and run: Fake online escrow services target big-ticket buyers. *Consumer Reports*. Retrieved September 8, 2006, from http://www.consumerwebwatch.org/dynamic/e-commerce-investigation-take-the-money-and-run.cfm

Barrio, F. (2006). Regulación o autorregulación de los derechos del consumidor en Internet? Esa es la cuestion., Revista de Derecho, Comunicaciones y Nuevas Tecnologias, Number 2, Bogota, Colombia: GETCI

Barrio, F. (2007). The consistent inconsistency in defining cyberspace spatial boundaries, Revista Académica Facultad de Derecho de la Universidad La Salle Año IV No. 8, Mexico, pp. 83-100

Barrio, F., & Rosario, Santiago, M. O. (2007). Consumer protection, the regulation of privacy across the Atlantic and the creation of a business-friendly environment. *Script-ed*, *4*(4). Edinburgh, Scotland.

Basel Committee on Banking Supervision. (2003). *Sound Practice for the Management and Supervision of Operational Risk*. Retrieved February 25, 2007, from http://www.bis.org/publ/bcbs96.htm

Basel Committee On Banking Supervision. (2004). *International Convergence of the Capital Measurement and Capital Standards: a Revised Framework*. Retrieved February 25, 2007, from http://www.bis.org/publ/bcbs107.htm

Bech, M. L., & Hobijn, B. (2006, September). *Technology diffusion within central banking: The case of real-time gross settlement*. Federal Reserve Bank of New York Staff Reports.

Beltramini, R. (2003). Application of the unfairness doctrine to marketing communications on the Internet. *Journal of Business Ethics, 42*(4), 26-27.

Benjamin, J. (2000). *Interests in securities*. Oxford University Press.

Benjamin, J. et al. (2002). *The Law of Global Custody* (2nd ed.). London: Butterworths.

Bernasconi, C. et al. (2002). General introduction: Legal nature of interests in indirectly held securities and resulting conflict of laws analysis. In R. Potok (Ed.), *Cross border collateral: Legal risk and the conflict of laws*. London: Butterworths Lexis Nexis.

Bessembinder, H. & Venkataraman, K. (2003). Does an electronic stock exchange need an upstairs market?,*Journal of Financial Economics, 73*(1), 3-36.

Biegel, S. (2003). *Beyond our control? Confronting the limits of our legal system in the age of cyberspace*. Cambridge, USA: MIT Press.

BIS. (1990). *Report of the Committee on Interbank Netting Schemes of the central banks of the Group of ten countries (Lamfalussy Report)*. Retrieved March 22, 2007, from http://www.bis.org

BIS. (1993). *Central bank payment and settlement services with respect to cross-border and multi-currency transactions* (Noël Report). Retrieved March 22, 2007, from http://www.bis.org

BIS. (1995). *Cross-Border Securities Settlements, by Committee on Payment and Settlement Systems*. Retrieved March 22, 2007, from http://www.bis.org

BIS. (1996). *Settlement risk in foreign exchange transactions*. Retrieved March 22, 2007, from http://www.bis.org

BIS. (1998). *Reducing foreign exchange settlement risk: a progress report.* Retrieved March 22, 2007, from http://www.bis.org

BIS. (1999). *Securities lending transactions: market development and implications.* Retrieved March 22, 2007, from http://www.bis.org

BIS. (2000). *Clearing and settlement arrangements for retail payments in selected countries.* Retrieved March 22, 2007, from http://www.bis.org

BIS. (2001). *Core Principles for Systemically Important Payment Systems.* Retrieved March 22, 2007, from http://www.bis.org

BIS. (2001). *Recommendations for securities settlement systems.* Retrieved March 22, 2007, from http://www.bis.org

BIS. (2003). *A Glossary of terms used in payments and settlement systems.* Retrieved March 22, 2007, from http://www.bis.org

BIS. (2004). *Recommendations for central counterparties.* Retrieved March 22, 2007, from http://www.bis.org

Black's Law Dictionary (6th ed.). (1990). Saint Paul: West Publishing Co.

Boele-Woelki, K., & Kessedjian, C. (Eds.), (1998). *Internet: Which court decides? Which law applies?* Kluwer.

Borrus, A. (2005, November 14). Invasion of the stock hackers. *Business Week, 38,* 40.

Brenner, S. W. (1998). Cybercrime Law and Policy in the United States. In Pauline C. Reich (Ed.), *Cybercrime and security.* Oceana, a division of Oxford University Press.

Brindle, M. et al. (Eds.). (2004). *Law of bank Payments* (3rd Ed.). London: Sweet & Maxwel.

Brown, J. (2002). The Separation of Banking and Commerce. GIS for Equitable and Sustainable Communities, last modified on October 7, 2002. Available at http://www.public-gis.org/reports/sbc.html

Bruin, R. (2002). *Consumer Trust in Electronic Commerce.* London: Kluwer Law International.

Brussels Convention on Jurisdiction and the Enforcement of Judgments in Civil and Commercial Matters. (1972, December 12). *Official Journal,* L299/32.

Business Continuity Institute. (2005). *Good Practice Guidelines: A Framework for Business Continuity Management.* Retrieved February 25, 2007, from http://www.thebci.org/gpg.htm

Campbell, D., & Woodley, S. (2002). *E-Commerce: Law and Jurisdiction: The Comparative Law Yearbook of International Business: Special Issue 2002 (Comparative Law Yearbook of International Business).* Kluwer Law International.

Capie, F. (1999, November 19). Strength and weakness of the international monetary system. In *Proceedings of the Conference on Gold and the International Monetary System in a New Era* (pp. 25-26). Paris: World Gold Council.

Caprio, G.., Levine, R. E., & Barth, J. R. (2001, November). Bank Regulation and Supervision: What works best? Policy Research Working Paper 2725. The World Bank. Available at the World Bank Web site.

Chauhan, J. (2003). Online dispute resolution systems: Exploring e-commerce and e-securities. *Windsor Review of Legal and Social Issues, 15,* 99.

Cocheo, S. (1997, October). What's at stake with Unitary Thrifts? *ABA Banking Journal,* http://www.banking.com/aba/unitary_1097.asp

Collins, L. (Ed.). (2000). *Dicey & Morris on the Conflict of Laws* (13th Ed.). London: Sweet & Maxwell.

Committee of Sponsoring Organizations of the Treadway Commission (COSO). (2004). *Enterprise Risk Management—Integrated Framework—Executive Summary.* Retrieved February 25, 2007, from http://www.coso.org/Publications/ERM/COSO_ERM_ExecutiveSummary.pdf

Computerworld. (2006, October 24). *New symantec survey reveals security doubts shape Internet behavior.*

Compilation of References

Retrieved November 8, 2006, from http://www.computerworld.com.au/index.php/id;1356571409;fp;;fpid;;pf;1

Consumer Action. (2005). *Credit Cards: what you need to know.* Available at http://www.consumer-action.org/downloads/english/2005_CC_terms_en.pdf

Convention on Jurisdiction and the Enforcement of Judgments in Civil and Commercial Matters. (1988, September 16). Presented at Lugano (88/592/EEC). *Official Journal,* L 319/9, 25/11/1988.

Convention on the Law Applicable to Contractual Obligations Opened for Signature in Rome. (1980, June 19). 80/934/EEC, *Official Journal,* L266/1, 09/10/1980.

Council of Europe. (2001, November 23). Convention on Cybercrime (CETS 185). Budapest. Retrieved from http://conventions.coe.int/Treaty/en/Treaties/Html/185.htm

Council Regulation (EC). (2000, December 22). Jurisdiction and the Recognition and Enforcement of Judgments in Civil and Commercial Matters. (No. 44/2001). *Official Journal,* L12/1, 16/01/2001.

Cranston, R. (2005). *Principles of Banking Law* (2nd ed.). Oxford, UK: Oxford University Press.

Cresswell, P. et al. (Eds.). (looseleaf). *Encyclopaedia of Banking Law.* London: Butterwoths.

CREST. (2001). *The International Framework.* Retrieved March 22, 2007, from http://www.cresto.co.uk

Cronin, J. (2006, March 15). Taking on Britain's banking fraudsters. *BBC News.* Retrieved November 8, 2006, from http://news.bbc.co.uk/2/hi/business/4808830.stm

CUISPA IT Security Cooperative. (2006). *Announcements.* Retrieved October 10, 2006, from http://www.cuispa.or/announcement.php?12

Dalhuisen, J. (2004). *Dalhuisen on International Commercial, Financial and Trade Law.* Oxford: Hart Publishing.

De Leon, J. M. (2006, November 29). Anatomy of a scam. *The Frederick News-Post.* Retrieved December 1, 2006, from http://www.fredericknewspost.com\sections/printer_friendly.htm?storyid=54393&secti...

Dempsey, J., & Rubinstein, I. (2006, May/June). Lawyers and techologies: Joined at the hip? *IEEE Security and Privacy* (pp. 15-19).

Denny, W. R. (2001). *Electronic contracting in Delaware: The E-Sign Act and the uniform Electronic Transactions Act. Delaware Law Review, 4,* 33-34.

Drucker, P. F. (1999). *Management Challenges for the 21st Century.* New York: HarperCollins Publishers Inc.

Edelman, B. (2006, September 6). *Adverse Selection in online "trust" certifications.* Retrieved from http://www.benedelman.org/publications/advsel-trust-draft.pdf

Edwards, G. (2006, October 3). *U.S. banking group sees protections in Internet gambling bill.* Retrieved October 3, 2006, from http://www.smh.com.au/news/breakingnews/us-banking-group-sees-protections-in-int...

Ellinger, E. P. et al. (2002). *Modern Banking Law* (3rd ed.). Oxford: Oxford University.

Ellinger, E. P., Lomnicka, E., & Hooley, R. J. (2006). *Ellinger's Modern Banking Law* (4th ed.). Oxford, UK: Oxford University Press.

Entrust, Inc. (2006, August). *Understanding the FFIEC guidance on authentication: What you should know as the deadline approaches.* Retrieved from www.knowledgestorm.com/shared/write/collateral/WTP/12962_29300_28879_Understanding_FFIEC_Guidance.pdf?kis=1296244&KSC=1261869603

Epstein, L. (2001). Symposium: alternative dispute resolution in the twenty-first century: Cyber e-mail negotiation vs. traditional negotiation: Will cyber technology supplant traditional means of settling litigation? *Tulsa L.J., 36,* 839.

Espiner, T. (2006, June 27). *Police arrest suspected bot herders.* Retrieved December 6, 2006, from http://news.com.com/2102-7348_3-6088552.html?tag=st.util.print

Evans, D. S., & Schmalensee, R, (2005). *Paying with Plastic* (2nd ed.). Cambridge, USA: MIT Press.

Ewing, G. P. (2002). Technology and legal practice symposium issue: Using the Internet as a resource for alternative dispute resolution and online dispute resolution. *Syracuse Law Review, 52*, 1217.

Fairfield, J. (2005). Virtual property. *Boston University Law Review, 85*, 1047-1102.

FBI/CSI. (2005). *2005 Computer crime survey*. Retrieved December 6, 2006, from http://www.digitalriver.com.v2.0-ing.operations/naievigi/site/media/pdf/FBICCS2005.pdf

Federal Reserve Board (FRB). (2001). *Supervision of Large Complex Banking Organizations*. Retrieved February 25, 2007, from http://www.federalreserve.gov/pubs/bulletin/2001/0201lead.pdf

Federal Reserve Board. (2003). *Interagency Paper on Sound Practices to Strengthen the Resilience of the U.S. Financial System*. Retrieved February 25, 2007, from http://www.federalreserve.gov/boarddocs/SRLETTERS/2003/sr0309.htm

Federal Reserve Board. (2006). *Notice of Proposed Rulemaking to Implement Basel II Risk-based Capital Requirements in the United States for Large, Internationally Active Banking Organizations, Federal Reserve Release*. Retrieved February 25, 2007, from http://www.federalreserve.gov/boarddocs/press/bcreg/2006/20060330/default.htm

Federal Reserve Board. (2006). *A U.S. Perspective on Basel II Implementation, Remarks by Governor Susan Schemidt Bies*. Retrieved February 25, 2007, from http://www.federalreserve.gov/boarddocs/speeches/2006/20061130/default.htm

Federal Reserve System. (2004). The 2004 Federal Reserve Payments Study. Analysis of Noncash Payments Trends in the United States: 2000-2003.

Federal Trade Commission (1998). Privacy Online: a report to Congress. Available at http://www.ftc.gov/reports/privacy3/priv-23a.pdf

Federal Trade Commission. (2006). *Consumer Fraud and Identity Theft Complaint Data January–December 2005*, Federal Trade Commission.

FFIEC. (2006). Retrieved November 1, 2006, from www.ffiec.gov/pdf/authentication_guidance.pdf (hereinafter "Guidance")

Ficsor, M. (2002). *The Law of Copyright and the Internet: The 1996 WIPO treaties, their interpretation and implementation*. Oxford University Press.

Financial Law Board. (2000). *Interim note on legal rules relating to book-entry securities settlements*. Retrieved March 22, 2007, from http://www.flb.gr.jp.

Financial Markets Law Committee. (2004, July). *Analysis of the Need for and Nature of Legislation relating to Property interests in Indirectly Held Investment Securities, with a Statement of Principle for an Investment Securities Statute*. Retrieved March 22, 2007, from www.fmlc.org

Fletcher, I. F. (1999). *Insolvency in private international law*. Oxford: Clarendon Press.

FRBSF. (1998, July 3). *The Separation of Banking and Commerce*. Federal Reserve Bank of San Francisco (FRBSF) Economic Letter. Available at http://www.sf.frb.org/econrsrch/wklyltr/wklyltr98/el98-21.html

Fry, P. B. (2001). *Introduction to the uniform electronic transactions act: Principles, policies and provisions*. Idaho Law Review, 37(237), p. 242.

FSA. (2004). *Financial Advisory Agency No Action Letter of April 20, 2004 to Barclay Vouchers K.K*. Retrieved March 15, 2007 from http://www.fsa.go.jp/common/noact/kaitou/001/001_06b.pdf

FSA. (2004). *Financial Advisory Agency No Action Letter of July 9, 2004 to K.K. Daiichi-Bussan*. Retrieved March 15, 2007 from http://www.fsa.go.jp/common/noact/kaitou/001/001_08b.pdf

FSA. (2006). *June 2006 newsletter in English* (pp.2-3). Retrieved March 15, 2007 from http://www.fsa.go.jp/en/newsletter/2006/06a.html#01

FSA. (2007). *March 2007 newsletter in English* (pp.23-25). Retrieved March 15, 2007 from http://www.fsa.go.jp/en/newsletter/2007/02.pdf

Compilation of References

Fuchita, Y. (1999). Regulations on stock exchanges and regulations on proprietary trading system. *Jurist, 1155*, 185-191.

Fujiike, T. (2002). Public regulations on settlement services by operating companies, i.e., not financial institutions. *Kinyu-houmu-jij, 1631*, 19-26. Tokyo: Kinzai.

Geva, B. (2001). *Bank collections and payment transactions comparative study of legal aspects*. Oxford: Oxford University Press.

Geva, B. (looseleaf). *The law of electronic funds transfer*. New York: Matthew Bender.

Goode, R. (1987). Ownership and obligation in commercial transactions. *Law Quarterly Review, 103*, 433.

Goode, R. (1996). The nature and transfer of rights in dematerialised and immobilised securities. *Journal of International Banking and Financial Law, 1996*(4), 167.

Goode, R. (1998). *Proprietary Right in commercial assets: Rethinking concepts and politics*. In R. Goode (Ed), *Commercial law in the next millennium*. London: Sweet & Maxwell.

Goode, R. (1998). Security entitlements as collateral and the conflict of laws. *The Oxford Colloquium on Collateral and Conflict of Laws, Special Supplement to Journal of International Banking and Financial Law, 1998*(7), 22.

Goode, R. (2004). *Commercial law* (3rd ed.). London: LexisNexis UK,.

Goto. K. (1990). Recent court decisions and problems concerning remittance. *Kin'yu Homu Jijo, 1269*, 10-17.

Griffin, G. E. (1994). *The creature from Jekyll Island—A second look at federal reserve*. [Review in Idaho Observer, June 2003]. Westlake Village, CA: American Media (pp.133-170). Retrieved November 9, 2003, from http://proliberty.com/observer/20030603.htm

Grimmelmann, J. T. L. (2004). Virtual worlds as comparative law. *New York Law School Law Review, 47*, 147-184.

Gross, G. (2006). *Security vendor settles charges after getting hacked*. Retrieved November 20, 2006, from http://www.computerworld.com/action/article.do?command=viewArticleBasic&tax...

Hall, M. (2006, November 30). U.S. Warns That Terrorists Are Calling for Cyberattack on Banks, Brokerages. *USA Today*. Retrieved from http://infragard.net/library/us_warns.htm

Harold, K. (2006, September 6). Bill makes threat of 'Big Brother watching' very real, experts warn. *Ottawa Business Journal*. Retrieved from http://www.ottawa-businessjournal.com/329658445911597.php

Harrington, D. (2004). Consumer vulnerability on an all-IP world. *Intermedia, 32*(4), 26-27.

Hata, M. (1997). The validity of deposit claim in cases where remittance was made to different person by mistake made by the originator. *NBL, 618*, 78-83.

Hayakawa, T. (1997). Erroneous remittance and validity of deposit. *Kansai Daigaku Hogaku Ronshu, 47*(3), 449-483.

Hayashi, M. (1999). *Keiho Kakuron* (Specifics of Criminal Law). Tokyo: Tokyo Daigaku Shuppankai.

Hayek, F. (1990). *The denationalisation of money—The argument refined* (3rd ed.). London: Institute for Economic Affairs.

Hayton, D. (1994). Uncertainty of Subject-Matter of Trusts. *Law Quarterly Review, 1994*, 335.

Hayton, D. (2003). *Underhill and Hayton law relating to trusts and trustees* (16th Ed.). London: Butterworths.

Hayton, D. et al. (2002). The use of trusts in international financial transactions. *Journal of International Banking and Financial Law, 2002*(1), 23.

Helleiner, E. (2003). *The making of national money: Territorial currencies in historical perspective*. Ithaca: Cornell University Press.

Hill, J. E. (2003). The Future of Electronic Contracts in International Sales: Gaps and Natural Remedies under the United Nations Convention on Contracts for the International Sale of Goods. *Northwestern Journal of Technology and Intellectual Propoerty.* Retrieved from http://www.law.northwestern.edu/journals/njtip/v2/n1/1/

Hiramatsu, M. (2006). The urgency of protecting electronic money users: issues related to prepaid electronic payments on the internet. *Kinyu-zaisei-jijo, 2708*, 18-21. Tokyo: Kinzai.

Hiwatashi, J. (2004). Solutions on Measuring Operational Risk. In V. Subbulakshmi (Ed.), *Operational Risk—Measurement and Management* (pp.54-60). Punjagutta, Hyderabad: ICFAI University Press.

Hiwatashi, J., & Ashida, H. (2004). Operational Risk Management for Central Banks. In R. Pringle and N. Carver (Eds.), *New Horizons in Central Bank Risk Management* (pp.83-97). London: Central Banking Publications.

Honda, M. (2001). Legislation in respect of the Transfer of Financial Assets. *Minshoho Zashi 123*(6), 1.

Horrocks, D. (1991). Insolvency and the Eurobond Market. *Journal of International Banking and Financial Law, 2,* 51.

Hozumi, K. (2005). ODR Arbitratin for Settlement of e-Commerce Disputes. *Journal of the Japanese Institute of International Business Law, 33,* 11.

Ida, R. (2002). *Keiho Kakuron* (Specifics of Criminal Law). Tokyo: Kobundo.

Imakubo, K., & McAndrews, J. J. (2005, August). *Initial funding levels for the special accounts in the new BOJ-NET.* Bank of Japan Working Paper Series.

Internet Gambling Enforcement Act of 2006. Retrieved from http:www.rules.house.gov/109_2nd/text/hr/49543.portscr.pdf <accessed 12/6/06>, www.playwinningpoker.com/online/poker/legal/uigea <accessed 12/6/06>

Ito, H. (1996). Validity of ordinary savings contract relating to the remittance in cases where there are no underlying relationship of the remittance between the originator and the named recipient. *Kin'yu Shoji Hanrei, 1001,* 43-51.

Iwahara, S. (1985). Computer-aided settlement and law. *Kin'yu Ho Kenkyu* (Financial Law Research), *1,* 9-59.

Iwahara, S. (1996). Is the originator allowed to insist the third party objection against the seizure on the deposit claim of the recipient resulting from erroneous remittance? *Kin'yu Homu Jijo, 1460,* 11-16.

Iwahara, S. (2003). *Denshi Kessai To Hou* (Electronic Payments and Law in Japanese). Yuuhikaku., p. 625.

Iwahara, S. (2003). *Electronic payment and law.* Tokyo: Yuhikaku.

Iwahara, S. (2003). *Electronic payment and legislation* (p.594). Tokyo: Yuhikaku.

Iwahara, S. (2005). The ideal future of regulations on electronic money. In The First Subgroup of the Study Group on the Financial System of the Japanese Bankers Association (Zenginkyo). *E-money legislation* (pp.68-76). Tokyo: Zenginkyo.

Japanese Bankers Association. (2004). *Proposal for reorganizing fund transfer systems in Japan—Introducing a "large value settlement system" (overview).*

Japanese Bankers Association. (2006). *The Banking System in Japan.* Zenginkyo. p.161 & p. 19.

JSDA (Japan Securities Dealers Association). (2002). Development on JSDA regulations related to announcement system of quotation, etc. of proprietary trading system. *Shoken Gyoho, 615,* 6-13.

Kaizuka, K., Kousai, Y., Nonaka, I. (Eds.). (1996). *Nihon Keizai Jiten* (Dictionary of Japanese Economy in Japanese). Nihon Keizai Shinbun-sha. p. 1387.

Kanzaki, K. (2000). Abolition of no off–exchange trade rule. In Shouken Torihiki Hou Kenkyu Kai (Securities Law Study Group) (Ed..), *Kin'yu shisutemmu kaikaku to shoken torihiki seido* (pp. 145-160). (Financial System Reform and Securities Trading System). Tokyo: Nihon Shouken Keizai Kenkyujyo..

Kaspersen, H. W. K. (2006). Jurisdiction in the Cybercrime Convention. In Brenner and Koops (Eds.), *Cybercrime and jurisdiction: A global survey.* The Hague: T.M.C. Asser Press.

Katsh, E., & Rifkin, J. (2001). *Online dispute resolution resolving conflicts in cyberspace.* San Francisco: Jossey-Bass.

Kaufmann-Kohler, G., & Schultz, T. (2004). *Online dispute resolution challenges for contemporary justice.* The Hague, The Netherlands: Kluwer Law International.

Kawada, E. (1992). The issues on the validity of Deposit resulting from remittance by mistake. *Kin'yu Homu Jijo, 1324,* 4-5.

Kawada, E. (1996). The validity of deposit by an erroneous remittance by the originator. *Kin'yu Homu Jijo, 1452,* 4-5.

Kawaguchi, K. (2000). Erroneous Remittance and fraud. *Nara Hogakukai Zasshi, 13*(2), 1-34.

Kawashima, I. (2001). Electronic securities trading system and securities law (Issues on Civil & Commercial Law No. 10),.*Senshu Daigaku Hogaku Kenkyujo Kiyou, 26,* 31-73.

Kessedjian, C. (2000). «Commerce électronique et compétence juridictionnelle internationale, Ottawa, 28 février au 1er mar 2000, Rapport des travaux». *Conférence de la Haye de droit international privé, Exécution des jugements, Doc. Prél. No 12.*

Kimura, M. (2003). *Enshu Keiho* (Exercises in Criminal Law), Tokyo: Tokyo Daigaku Shuppankai.

Kinami, A. (1991). Remittance by mistake and validity of deposit. *Kin'yu Homu Jijo, 1304,* 7-10.

Kindleberger, C. P. (1981). *International Money, a Collection of Essays.* London: George Allen & Unwin Ltd.

Kinyu Chousa Kenkyu Kai (KCKK: Financial Research Study Group in Japanese). (2006, July). *Kinyu No Conglomerate Ka Tou Ni Taiou Shita Kinyu Seido No Seibi.* Creating A New Financial System. The Financial Research Study Group (Report No. 36). original is in Japanese only.

Kinyu Ho Iinkai (Financial Law Committee). (2002). Interim organizing of issues concerning the concept of "Securities Market". *Jurist, 1225,* 38-50.

Kiuchi, Y. (1989). *Financial law.* Tokyo: Seirin Shoin.

Kleinwaechter, W. (2003). From Self-Governance to Public-Private Partnership: The Changing Role of Governments in the Management of the Internet's Core Resources. *Loyola of Los Angels Law Review, 36.*

Kodaira, Y. (2006). The urgency of protecting electronic money users: Japanese government has to develop legislation in anticipation of electronic money issuer's bankruptcy. *Kinyu-zaisei-jijo, 2708,* 22-25. Tokyo: Kinzai.

Kominami, K. (2003). Report on the 29th Asian Racing Conference's Business Session on Wagering. *Japan Association for International Horse Racing Journal,* Available at http://www.jair.jrao.ne.jp/journal/v11n2/cover.html

Konishi, N. (2000). Regulations on electronic securities market–focusing on ATS (Alternative Trading System) Regulation. *Sandai Hogaku, 33*(3&4), 326-360.

Konvisser, J. B. (1997). Note: Coins, notes and bits: The case for legal tender on the Internet. *Harvard Journal of Law & Technology, 10,* 327-328,37.

Koyama, Y. (2004). *Banking law.* Tokyo: Kinzai.

KPMG. (2005). *UK Financial Sector Market-wide Exercise 2005.* Retrieved February 25, 2007, from http://continuitycentral.com/news02493.htm which links the KPMG report.

Krazit, T. (2006). *FBI nabs phishers in US, Poland; Next stop: Romania.* Retrieved December 6, 2006, from http://networks.silicon.com/webwatch/0,39024876,39163835,00.htm

Krebs, B. (2006, March 16). Hacking Made Easy. *Washington Post.* Retrieved October 15, 2006, from http://www.washingtonpost.com/wp-dyn/content/article/2006/03/16/AR20060316009...

Kubota, T. (2003). *Legal issues of Japanese funds payment systems.* Tokyo: Kokusai Syoin.

Kubota, T. (2003). *Legal issues related to fund settlement systems* (pp.179-208). Tokyo: Kokusai-shoin.

Kumar, K. (2001). *Cyber laws: Intellectual property and e-commerce security*. Dominant Publishers & Distributors.

Lai, E. (2006). Identity thieves hit customers at TD Ameritrade, E-Trade. *Computerworld*. Retrieved November 20, 2006, from http://www.computerworld.com/action/article.do?command=printArticleBasic&art...

Lam, J. (2003). *Enterprise Risk Management*. Hoboken, New Jersey: Wiley Finance.

Lastowka, F. G., & Hunter, D. (in press). The laws of the virtual worlds. *California Law Review*.

Lehr, W. H., & Pupillo, L. M. (2002). *Cyber policy and economics in an internet age (topics in regulatory economics and policy)*. Springer.

Lemley, M. A. (2002). Place and cyberspace. *California Law Review, 91*, 521-549.

Levitt, S. D., & Dubner, S. J. (2006). *Freakonomics*. London: Penguin Books.

Leyden, J. (2006, November 7). *UK credit card fraud down to GBP209.3 m. The Register*. Available at http://www.theregister.co.uk/2006/11/07/credit_card_fraud_stats/

Lloyd, I. J. (2004). *Information Technology Law* (4th ed.). Oxford: Oxford University Press.

Lodder, A. R., & Zeleznikow, J. (2005). Article: Developing an online dispute resolution environment: Dialogue tools and negotiation support systems in a three-step model. *Harvard Negotiation Law Review, 10*, 287.

Lomas, N. (2006). *Security from A to Z: Botnet*. Retrieved December 6, 2006, from http://news.com.com/2102-7355_3-6138435.html?tag=st.util.print

Macintosh, K. L. (1998). How to encourage global electronic commerce: The case for private currencies on the Internet. *Harvard Journal of Law & Technology, 11*(3), 733-796.

Macintosh, K. L. (2001, January 5). Electronic cash—More questions than answers. Proceedings of the Association of American Law Schools, Annual Meeting held in San Francisco, Section on Law and Computers.

Boston University Journal of Science and Technology Law, 7, 214-218.

Maeda, M. (1999). *Keiho Kakuron Kogi* (Lectures on Specifics of Criminal Law) (3rd ed.). Tokyo: Tokyo Daigaku Shuppankai.

Maeda, T. (1976). Furikomi (Remittance to Account). In I. Kato, R. Hayashi, & I. Kawamoto, I. (Eds.), *Ginko Torihiki Ho Koza* (Lesson on the Law for Bank Transactions): *Vol. 1*. Tokyo: Kin'yu Zaisei Jijo Kenkyukai.

Maeda, T. (1997). The case where a deposit claim against a bank was established through credit to the recipient's account resulting from mistake made by the originator. *Hanrei Jiho, 1585*, 192-200.

Maeda, Y., Kanda, H., Morishita, T., Maeda, S., & Iwahara, S. (2005). *E-money legislation*. Tokyo: Zenginkyo.

Makino, T. (2006, February 20). *Operational Risk Management Overview*. (pg. 29). Document presented at the Tokyo Round Table on Operational Risk sponsored by RMA. Retrieved March 10, 2006, from http://www.kriex.org/tokyoroundtable.asp

Makiyama, I. (1990). The case where the recipient did not acquire deposit claim where the originator designated wrong recipient. *Kin'yu Homu Jijo, 1267*, 12-19.

Makiyama, I. (1996). The validity of ordinary savings contract through remittance in cases where there was no underlying relationship for the remittance. *Kin'yu Homu Jijo, 1467*, 12-19.

Mann, F. A. (1963). *The legal aspect of money, with special reference to comparative, private and public international law* (2nd ed. reprint). Oxford: Clarendon Press.

Mann, R. J. (2006). *Charging Ahead: the growth and regulation of payment card markets*. New York: Cambridge University Press.

Manning, R. D. (2000). *Credit Card Nation: The consequences of America's addiction to credit*. New York: Basic Books.

MasterCard. *Corporate Overview*. Available at http://www.mastercard.com/us/company/en/docs/Corporate%20Overview.pdf

Matsumiya, T. (2001). Erroneous remittance and interpretation and legislation of crimes with regard to properties. *Ritsumeikan Hogaku, 278*, 999-1024.

Matsuoka, H. (1997). Validity of deposit claims resulting from remittance with error in the recipient's name. *Jurist*, (Extra edition), *113*, 73-74.

Matsuoka, H. (2003). Tangle of criminal law and civil law. *Keiho Zasshi, 43*(1), 90-102.

McIntyre, H. (2000). *How the U.S. securities industry works.* New York: The Summit Group Press.

Mentha, J. et al. (2000). Legal risks associated with acting as a global custodian—Mitigating the risks. *Journal of International Banking and Financial Law, 2000*(4), 122.

Ministry of Finance. (1997). *The first electronic money round-table conference report.* Retrieved March 15, 2007, from http://www.fsa.go.jp/p_mof/singikai/kinyusei/tosin/1a1201.htm

Ministry of Finance. (1998). *The second electronic money round-table conference report.* Retrieved March 15, 2007, from http://www.fsa.go.jp/p_mof/singikai/kinyusei/tosin/1a1202.htm

Mishra J., & Tripathy, B. (2006). Cyber contract: A generalized framework, ICWA 2006, CET, BPUT, Orissa, India. *Web Engineering & Applications, Macmillan Publication* (pp. 270-278).

Miyoshi, H. (2000). *Shoken shijo denshika no subete* (All about computerization of securities market). Tokyo: Tokyo Shoseki Kabushikigaisha.

Monetary Authority of Singapore. (2003). MAS Consultation Paper: Proposed Business Continuity Planning (BCP) Guidelines. Retrieved February 25, 2007, from http://www.mas.gov.sg/masmcm/bin/pt1Consultation-Papers_Archive.htm

Morishita, T. (2000). Legal issues in respect of international securities settlements (1). *Jyochi Hougaku Ronsyu, 44*(1), 1.

Morishita, T. (2001). Legal issues in respect of international securities settlements (2). *Jyochi Hougaku Ronsyu, 44*(3), 35.

Morishita, T. (2002). Legal issues in respect of international securities settlements (3). *Jyochi Hougaku Ronsyu, 45*(3), 149.

Mortlock, G. (1999). *An assessment of the causes of financial instability and possible policy solutions* (Occasional Papers No.30). Kuala Lumpur: The SEACEN Centre.

Moshinsky, M. (1998). Securities held thorough a securities custodian—Conflict of laws issue. The Oxford Colloquium on Collateral and Conflict of Laws. *Journal of International Banking and Financial Law, 1998* (Special Supplement 7), 18.

Mostrous, A., & Cobain, I. (2006). CIA's secret UK bank trawl may be illegal. *The Guardian*, Retrieved August 21, 2006, from http://www.guardian.co.uk/terrorism/story/0,,1854813,00.html

Mühlberger, M. (2005). Alternative trading systems: a catalyst of change in securities trading. *Deutsche Bank Research, 47*, 1-12.

Nakajima, M. (2003). *Global trends in payment systems and their implications for Japan.* Forum of International Development Studies, Nagoya University.

Nakajima, M., & Shukuwa, J. (2005). *All about payment systems* (2nd edition). (in Japanese), Toyo Keizai Inc.

Nakanishi, K. & Ogura, T. (2005). Outline of development of cabinet orders, etc. with respect to introduction of obligation of best execution under the Securities and Exchange Act. *Shoji Homu, 1726*, 31-37.

Nakazaki, T. (2007). Anti-money laundering laws of Japan. *Anti-money laundering International law and practice.* pp. [uncertain, to be published by the end of March]. London: Wiley & Sons.

Nakazaki, T. (2007). *Converting in-game currency in U.S. Dollars at "Second Life" - is this violating the investment law?* Retrieved March 15, 2007, from http://www.itmedia.co.jp/bizid/articles/0702/15/news109.html

Nakazaki, T. (2007). *Will a game contest offering big money prizes in the virtual world constitute an illegal gamble?* Retrieved March 15, 2007, from http://www.itmedia.co.jp/bizid/articles/0703/16/news046.html

Nakazaki, T. (2007). *Will real money trading be a legitimate business?* Retrieved March 15, 2007, from http://www.itmedia.co.jp/bizid/articles/0701/26/news008.html

Nikko Shoken Homubu (Ed.) (1999). Provision of definitions concerning securities, etc. *Shoji Homu, 1528*, 28-35.

Nishida, N. (2002). *Keiho Kakuron* (Specifics of Criminal Law) (2nd ed.). Tokyo: Kobundo.

Nolan, S. (2003). Freedom from contract. *Ebusinesslex.net*. Retrieved from http://www.ebusinesslex.net/front/dett_art.asp?idtes=94>

Nomura Research Institute. (2006a). *Business currency in 2010*. Tokyo: Toyo Keizai Inc.

Nomura Research Institute. (2006b). *Estimates for nine major industries in Japan for the 2005 fiscal year.* Retrieved March 15, 2007, from (http://www.nri.co.jp/english/news/2006/060816.html

OECD (2003). *Guidelines for protecting consumers from fraudulent and deceptive commercial practices across borders.*

OECD (2003). *Proposal for a Regulation of the European Parliament and the Council on the Law Applicable to Non-Contractual Obligations* ("ROME II"). COM (2003) 427 final, 2003/0168 (COD).

OECD (2006). *Protecting consumers from cyber fraud.* Policy Brief. OECD Observer.

OECD. (1999). *OECD Guidelines for Consumer Protection in the Context of Electronic Commerce.* OECD.

OECD. (2000, December 11-12). *Building Trust in the Online Environment: Business To Consumer Dispute Resolution.* Paper presented at the Joint Conference of the OECD, HCOPIL, ICC.

OECD. (2002). *Report on Consumer Protections for Payment Cardholders.* OECD.

OECD. (2006). *Report on the Cross-border enforcement of privacy laws.* Available at http://www.oecd.org/dataoecd/17/43/37558845.pdf

OECD. (2006). *Report on the implementation of the 2003 OECD guidelines for protecting consumers from fraudulent and deceptive commercial practices across borders.* OECD.

Office of Thrift Supervision. (2006, November 8). *Historical Framework For Regulation of Activities of Unitary Savings and Loan Holding Companies.* http://www.ots.treas.gov/docs/4/48035.html

Ogunnaike, L. (2006, November 26). 'Yours truly' The e-variations. *New York Times.* Retrieved December 9, 2006, from http://www.nytimes.com/2006/11/26/fashion/26email.html?ex=1165726800&en=dcac567c9dbefa8a&ei=5070

Oiaga, M. (2006). *Panda software warns of online money laundering schemes.* Retrieved October 15, 2006, from http://news.softpedia.com/news/Panda-Software-Warns-of-Online-Money-Laundering...

Osaki, S. & Kozuka, S. (2001). Electronic securities trading and issues on legal system. *Jurist, 1195*, 98-103.

Osaki, S. (1999). Electronic Communications Network (ECN). *Shihon Shijo Quarterly, 3*(2), 49-61.

Osaki, S. (2000). *Kabushiki shijo kan kyoso-NASDAQ no sekai senryaku to nihon* (Competition among stock exchanges– Global strategy of NASDAQ and Japan). Tokyo: Diamond Corp.

Osaki, S. (2001). New PTS (Proprietary Trading System) Regulation on Japan. *Shihon Shijo Quartlerly, 4*(3), 66-75.

Osaki, S. (2005). Progress in borderless transactions on securities exchanges and market regulations, In K. Egashira, & Y. Masui (Eds.), *Tokeru sakai koeru ho 3 shijo to soshiki (Market and Organization)* (Melting border and flowing out of laws No.3). (pp. 85-203). Tokyo: Tokyo Daigaku ShuppanKai.

Osaki, S. (2006). PTS for Night Trading of Stocks in Japan: Significance and Issues. *Nomura Capital Market Review, 9*(4), 16-24.

Otani, M. (1985). Illegal use of cash cards and crimes relating to properties. *Hanrei Times, 36*(12), 84-89.

OUT-LAW News. (2006, November 1). *UK banks agree to data sharing, warn on outcomes.* Retrieved November 20, 2006, from http://out-law.com/default.aspx?page=7438

OUT-LAW News. (2007, January). *Bank hit by 'biggest ever' hack.* Retrieved February 28, 2007, from http://out-law.com/deafult.aspx?page=7629

OUT-LAW News. (2007, January). *London Police can't cope with cybercrime.* 1/30/07, 2007 Archives, OUT-Law_COM.htm

Paul, L. G. (2006, August 7). Bank Thwarts Threats from Within. *eWeek.* Retreived September 19, 2006, from http://www.eweek.com/article2/0,1895, 1997957,00.asp

Pham, A. (2006, February 3, 2007). EBay bans auctions of virtual treasures: Players of online games spend big on digital loot. But the site is worried about legal issues. *Los Angeles Times,* p. Business 1.

Physorg.com. (2006). *FBI survey finds cybercrime rising.* Retrieved November 30, 2006, from http://www.physorg.com/printnews.php?newsid=10166

Physorg.com. *Fingerprint advances will fight cybercrime.* Retrieved November 30, 2006, from http://www.physorg.com/printnews.php?newsid=11171

Physorg.com. *More targeted cyber attacks likely in 2006.* Retrieved November 30, 2006, from http://www.physorg.com/printnews.php?newsid=10148

Ponte, L., & Cavenagh, T. D, (2005). *CyberJustice online dispute resolution (ODR) for e-commerce.* Upper Saddle River, New Jersey: Pearson Education, Inc.

Pullen, K. (1999). Fungible securities and insolvency. *Journal of International Banking and Financial Law, 1999*(7), 286.

Purugganan, A. A. (1998). Philippine Cybersecurity Update: Laws, Cases and other Legal Issues. In Pauline C. Reich (Ed.), *Cybercrime and Security.* Oceana Publications: Oxford University Press.

Rao, R. (2001). *Tradenable reaches the end of the road. Business and industry online reporter.*

Reed, C. et al. (2000). *Cross-border electronic banking* (2nd ed.). London: LLP.

Renault, O., & Percival, R. L (2004, May 19-20). *E-commerce law update: Doing Business on the Net (and getting it right), creating enforceable, electronic contracts.* Paper presented at the 4th Annual IT Law Spring Training Program: Legal & Business Issues for IT Transactions. Toronto: Osgoode Hall.

Rogers, J. (1996). Policy perspective on revised U.C.C. Article 8. *UCLA Law Review, 43,* 1431.

Rogers, J. (1998). Of normalcy and anomaly: Thoughts on choice of law for the indirect holding system. The Oxford Colloquium on Collateral and Conflict of Laws. *Journal of International Banking and Financial Law, 1998*(Special Supplement 7), 47.

Rule, C. (2002). *Online dispute resolution for business B2B, e-commerce, consumer, employment, insurance, and other commercial conflicts.* San Francisco: Jossey-Bass.

Rule, C. (2006). Comments at Center for Information Technology and Dispute Resolution Cyberweek conference Sept. 25-29, 2006. http://www.odr.info/cyberweek2006/program.php

Ryan, R. (1990). Taking securities over investment portfolio held in global custody. *Journal of International Banking Law, 10,* 404.

Sabet, R. V. (1996). *International harmonization in electronic commerce and electronic data interchange: A proposed first step toward signing on the digital dotted line.* AM. U. L. REV., *46*(511), p. 513.

Saeki, H., & Dogauchi, H. (2001). *Keiho to Mimpo no Taiwa* (Dialogue between criminal law and civil law). Tokyo: Yuhikaku.

Sasaki, S. (2006). *Keynote speech*. Conference for the Asian IT Standardization (CAIST), Singapore, November 2, 2006 (author's file).

Schaig, K., Kane, G., & Sorey, V. (2005). Privacy, fair information practices and the Fortune 500: The virtual reality of compliance. *The Data Base for Advances in Information Systems, 36*(1), 49-63.

Schwarcz, S. L. (2001). Indirectly held securities and intermediary risk. *Uniform Law Review, 2001/2*, 283-299.

Scott, H. S. (2004). *International finance: Law and regulation.* London: Sweet & Maxwell.

Scott, H. S., & Wellons, P. A. (1999). *International Finance: Transactions, Policy, and Regulation* (6th ed.). New York: Foundation Press.

Sealy, L. S., Hooley, R. J. A. (2003). *Commercial Law Text, Cases and Materials* (3rd Ed.). London: LexisNexis UK.

Seaman, R. (1998). *English translation of Japanese Banking Law.* (updated January 1998). http://www.japanlaw.info/banking/1981.htm

Security Breach Information Law, SB 1386. Ch. 915 (California). Retrieved from http://info.sen.ca.gov/pub/01-02/bill/sb_1351-1400/sb_1386_bill_200220926_chaptered.html

Selis, P., Ramasastry, A., & Wright, C. S. (2002, June). Bidder beware: Toward a fraud-free marketplace—Best practices for the online auction industry. *Washington State Attorneys Office.* Retrieved December 9, 2006, from http://www.atg.wa.gov/consumer/Publications/auction_best_practices082302.doc

Shah, A. (2004). Using ADR to Resolve Online Disputes. *Richmond Journal of Law & Technology, 10*, 25.

Shimizu Y. (2000). Alternative Trading System (ATS) in US and SEC regulations. *Shoken Keizai Gakkai Nenpou, 35*, 83-88.

Shimizu, Y. (1997). Proprietary Trading System (PTS) in US and competition among markets. *Shoken Keizai Kenkyu, 7*, 121-140.

Shin & Kim (2006). *Legal Update: Recent Developments in the Korean Legal Environment.* Summer 2006 (pp. 7-8).

Shinomiya, K. (1989). *Trusts Law new ed.* Tokyo: Yuhikaku.

Shiozaki, T. (1991). Seizure on deposit resulting from remittance by mistake and permissibility of the third party objection by the originator. *Kin'yu Homu Jijo, 1299*, 11-19.

Shiozaki, T. (1996). Erroneous remittance by the originator and validity of deposit contract between the recipient and the bank. *Ginko Homu 21*(523), 4-11.

Smith, G. (2000, April 3). Would global crisis make e-gold glitter? *BusinessWeek Online*, E.Biz: Perspective. Retrieved October 16, 2003, from http://www.businessweek.com/ebiz/0004/ep0403.htm

Smitherman, L. (2006). Online banking won't be so easy anymore. *Nashua Telegraph.* Retrieved October 12, 2006, from http://www.nashuatelegraph.com/apps/pbcs.dll/article?Date=20061010&Category=B

Sommer, J. (1998). A law of financial accounts: modern payment and securities transfer law. *Business Lawyer, 53*, 1181.

Sone, T. (2001) *Keiho Kakuron* (Specifics of Criminal Law) (3rd. ed.). Tokyo: Kobundo.

Sorkin, D. E. (2001). Payment Methods for Consumer-to-Consumer Online Transactions. *Akron L. Rev., 35*, 1.

Stankey, R. F. (1998). Internet payment systems: Legal issues facing businesses, consumers and payment service providers. *CommLaw Conspectus, 6*, 11-15.

Sugiura, N. (2003). Legal issues related to point-based rewards programs. *Kinyu-zaisei-jijo,.2561*, 41. Tokyo: Kinzai.

Sugiura, N., & Kataoka, Y. (2003). *Future Electronic Money and its legal infrastructure* (p.38). Retrieved March 15, 2007, from http://www.fsa.go.jp/frtc/seika/discussion/2003/20030828-2.pdf

Suzuki, M. (1991). Remittance by mistake and finding of depositor. *Hanrei Times, 42*(6), 103-106.

Takahashi, Y. (Ed.). (2003). *Article by article commentary of the Book-entry Transfer of Corporate Bonds Act.* Tokyo: Kinzai Institute for Financial Affairs.

Takahashi, Y. (Ed.). (2004). *Article by article commentary of the Book-entry Transfer of Corporate Bonds and Shares Act.* Tokyo: Kinzai Institute for Financial Affairs.

Takeuchi, T. (1999). The case where a deposit claim of the recipient is deemed to be valid through an erroneous request for remittance without an underlying relationship. *Toin Hogaku, 5*(2), 137-157.

Takizawa, M. (1993). Validity of deposit claims resulting from remittance by mistake and permissibility of the third party objection by the originator. *Jurist, 1018*, 118-121.

Taylor, M. (2001). E-tail watchdog. *CIO, 14*(9), 48.

Tennekoon, R. (1991). *The law and regulation of international finance.* London: Butterworths.

The American Law Institute, National Conference of Commissioners on Uniform State Laws, *Uniform Commercial Code, Official Text—2000, revised art 8 (1994 revision).*

The Hague Conference on Private International Law. (1994). *Annotated checklist of issues to be discussed at the meeting of the Special Commission of June 1994.*

The Register. (2006, October 16). UK.gov may allow data sharing on 40 million bank accounts. Retrieved November 20, 2006, from http://www.theregister.co.uk/2006/10/16/uk_bank_data_sharing_proposals/ Consultation paper at http://reporting.dti.gov.uk/cgi-bin/rr.cgi.http://www.dti.gov.uk/files/file34513.pdf

The Society for the Study of Securities Exchange Law. (2004). *Theory and practice in respect of paperless securities.* Tokyo: Syojihomu.

Tusser, T. (1557). *Five Hundred Points of Good Husbandry.*

Tyson-Quah, K. (1996). Cross-Boarder Securities Collateralisation Made Easy. *Journal of International Banking and Financial Law 1996*(4), 177.

U.S. Department of Justice. (2003). *Operation cyber sweep, Justice Department announced 'operation cyber sweep' targeting online economic fraud.* Retrieved November 20, 2003, from http://www.fbi.gov/dojpressrel/pressrel03/cyber112003.htm and http://www.fbi.gov/cyber/cysweep1.htm

UK Financial Services Authority. (2002). *FSA Working Paper on Business Continuity Management.* Retrieved February 25, 2007, from http://www.fsa.gov.uk/Pages/Library/Communication/PR/2002/045.shtml

UK Financial Services Authority. (2005). *Business Continuity Management: A Staff Guide.* Retrieved on February 25, 2007, from http://www.fsa.gov.uk/pages/Information/pdf/incident.pdf

UK Law Commission Report. (1995). *Fiduciary Duties and Regulatory Rules.* (Report No 236.). London: HMSO.

UK Law Commission Report. (1995). *Fiduciary Duties and Regulatory Rules* (Report No. 236). London: HMSO.

Umeda, A. (2006, April). *Ginkou To Shougyou No One-Way Kisei Ni Tsuite (Regarding "One-way" regulation of banking and commerce in Japanese).* Mizuho Research Institute. p. 18.

UNIDROIT. (2003). *The Position Paper of The UNIDROIT Study Group on Harmonised Substantive Rules Regarding Indirectly Held Securities.* Retrieved March 22, 2007, from http://www.unidroit.org

UNIDROIT. (2004). *Preliminary Draft Convention on Harmonised Substantive Rules regarding Securities Held with an Intermediary: Explanatory Notes.* Retrieved March 22, 2007, from http://www.unidroit.org

United Press International. (2006). *Japan Police struggle against cybercrime.* Retrieved November 30, 2006, from http://www.physorg.com/printnews.php?newsid=11178

Vaz, S. (2003). Internet and personal data protection. *Ebusinesslex.net.* Retrieved from http://wwwebusinesslex.net/front/dett_art.asp?idtes=94>

Virtual World, Real Money. (May 1, 2006). *Business Week.*

Visa Corporation. *Visa facts*. Available at http://www.usa.visa.com/download/about_visa/press_resources/company_profile/visa_facts.pdf

Vivek, S. (Ed.), (2005). *Cyber law simplified*. Tata McGraw Hill.

Vroegop, J. (1990), The role of correspondent banks in direct funds transfers. *Lloyd's Maritime and Commercial Law Quarterly*.

Waddell, D. (2006, June 7). *Internet wagering becomes a felony in Washington State*. Retrieved December 6, 2006, from http://info.detnews.com/casino/newdetails.cfm?column=waddell&myrec=251

Waddell, D. (2006, October 11). *Congress passes Unlawful Internet Gambling Enforcement Act of 2006*. Retrieved December 6, 2006, from http://info.detnews.com/casino/newdetails.cfm?column=waddell&myrec=262

Watanabe, T. (2006, July). *Ginkou No Gyoumu Han-i Kisei Ni Tsuite (On Regulations of the Scope of Bank Business Activities in Japanese)*. Kinyu. pp. 3-11.

Weinberg, J. (2006). *Everyone's a winner: Regulation, not prohibiting, Internet gambling*. 35 S.W. U.L. Rev.293, 2006.

Weismann, M. F. Miquelon (2006). International Cybercrime: Recent Developments in the Law. In Ralph D. Clifford (Ed.), *Cybercrime: The investigation, prosecution and defense of a computer-related crime*. (2nd Ed.). North Carolina: Carolina Academic Press.

Whitman, M. (2006). Keynote address. *Proceedings of eBay shareholders convention*. Audio transcript of the keynote available at: http://www.wsradio.com/internet-talk.cfm/radio/ebay-keynote-2006.htm

Wilkinson, S. (2002, October 22). British Credit Cards hit by US sanctions. *Cuba Si*, available at http://www.cuba-solidarity.org/cubasi_article.asp?ArticleID=13

Wood, P. (1995). *Comparative law of security and guarantees*. London: Sweet & Maxwell.

Working Group on Information Technology Innovations and Financial Systems under the Sectional Committee on Financial System of the Financial System Council of the Financial Services Agency. (2006). *The chairman memorandum "Issues facing the development of new electronic payment services."* Retrieved March 15, 2007, from www.fsa.go.jp/news/newsj/17/20060426-5/01.pdf

World Bank. (2000, 2003). *Bank Regulation and Supervision: Finance and Private Sector Research*. http://www.worldbank.org

Wu, T. (2003). When code isn't law. *Virginia Law Review, 89*, 101-170.

Yamada, R. (2003). *Private international law (*2nd ed.). Tokyo: Yuhikaku.

Yanaga, M. (2006). PTS regulations in European countries. *Shoji Homu, 1781*, 4-19.

Yoshino, I. (2001). Current situation and issues concerning establishment of Proprietary Trading System (PTS) in Japan. *Gekkan Shihon Shijo, 188*, 57-70.

Yoshioka, S. (1997). Erroneous remittance without its underlying relationship and validity of deposit. *Ginko Homu 2*,(529), 38-46.

Yukizawa, K. (2004). Obligation of best execution in the Securities and Exchange Act. *Shoji Homu, 1709*, 4-23.

ZDnet. (2006). *Zombies try to blend in with the crowd* Retrieved November 29, 2006, from http://news.zdnet.com/2102-1009_22-6127304.html

ZDNETINDIA. (2006). *'Logic bomb' backfires on insider hacker*. Retrieved December 14, 2006, from http://www.zdnetindia.com/print.html?iElementId=164631

Zeller, T., Jr. (2006, February 27). Cyberthieves Silently Copy Your Passwords as You Type. *The New York Times*. Retrieved June 29, 2006, from http://www.nytimes.com/2006/02/27/technology/27hack.html?ei=5088&en=b794....

About the Contributors

Takashi Kubota was educated at the University of Tokyo, obtaining a bachelor's degree (1990) and a master's degree (1993), earned a master's degree (1996) at Harvard University, and at Osaka University, obtaining a PhD (2002). He worked for the Bank of Japan from 1990 to 1998 as a legal expert, taught international business law at Nagoya National University from 1998 to 2004 as an associate professor, and is currently a professor of law at Waseda Law School, Waseda University, Japan, where he teaches international financial law, IT law, and so forth. His recent studies include payment, electronic commerce and international financial systems, funds and securities payment laws, cybermalls and online auctions, and the Basel 2.

* * *

Fernando Barrio is the E. Desmond Lee visiting professor in Global Awareness at Webster University in Saint Louis, MO, USA, and senior lecturer in Business Law at the London Metropolitan University Business School, where he also directs the MA in E-business Regulation. He has carried out undergraduate studies in International Relations and Law in Argentina, postgraduate studies in Education and Law in the U.K., and it holds a MA and a PhD in International Cooperation from Nagoya University. He has held positions in the government of the Rio Negro Province, in Piatigorsky Lawyers, and in the University of Belgrano, all in Argentina, and currently consults for governments, NGO and international organizations in IT and IP legal and policy issues. He is a member of the editorial board of several academic journals and is also a member of the Society for Computers and Law of the U.K., the Latin American Studies Association, the International Law Association, the International Political Science Association, the British Association of Law Teachers, and the Society for Legal Scholars of the U.K.

Sam Edwards is an attorney licensed in California, Guam, the Northern Mariana Islands, and Yap State, Federated States of Micronesia. He obtained his BA in biology and public policy from Pomona College in 1991, his JD from Northwestern School of Law of Lewis & Clark College in 1995, and his LLM from Nagoya University in 2001. Edwards taught law and negotiation at Nagoya University in Japan since his graduation until 2007. In Fall 2007, he joined the Faculty, Green Mountain College in Vermont (USA), as an associate professor. He currently teaches international environmental law and negotiation related topics. His areas of research are diverse and include: online dispute resolution, negotiation, legal ethics, and international trade in endangered species.

About the Contributors

Tomonori Fujiike is an attorney at law in Japan. He has been principally involved in the fields of financial, commercial, and corporate transactions with coverage of regulatory affairs in Hori & Partners. In particular, he has engaged in payment and settlement systems, such as debit cards, electronic funds transfers, and electronic bill payment systems. He chairs the legal committee of the Japan Electronic Payment Promotion Organization. He graduated from Chuo University in Japan and obtained a LLM from the University of London in the U.K. He has published several papers in Japanese law journals, such as *The Legal Review with regard to Payment Systems operated by Business Firms other than Financial Institutions*.

Junji Hiwatashi was educated at Hitotsubashi University with a BA and at Northwestern University with an MA, both in economics. His career started at the Bank of Japan in 1980. He was seconded to the International Monetary Fund mainly as desk economist of Ethiopia during 1988-1991 and was a spokesman of the Bank of Japan for foreign media during 1991-1993. Then he worked for the Bank Examination and Surveillance Department of the Bank as an examining officer during 1993-2004. During that period, he was seconded to the Federal Reserve Board and the Reserve Bank of Chicago. During 2004-2006, he was a visiting professor of Hiroshima University, teaching both graduate and undergraduate levels. Now he is a director of the Department of Financial System and Bank Examination and teaches at the graduate school of Saitama University. He wrote several books including those on risk management, published in England and India, and wrote many papers including those on operational risk management.

Takeshi Kawana is a researcher at Waseda University Corporate Law and Society, Japan. He is also a research fellow at the Financial Service Agency of Japanese Government. He has taught international law and legal studies at Kokugakuin University and Yokohama Harbor Polytechnic College. He has studied international law, international economic law, and international financial law. His main fields of research are international financial stability and law, Asian financial markets and regional legal framework, international integration of stock exchanges, and international e-commerce and economic law. His recent published articles are "International Legal Framework for Sovereign Debt Restructuring among Multiple Creditors," International Economic Law, No.15 (2006); "Financial Cooperation in Asia and Japanese Law, with Particular Reference to the Development of Asian Bond Markets," International Corporate Rescue, Vol.3, Issue 3 (2006); "Legal Regulations on Multinational Financial Institutions—in Quest of a New Mode of Jurisdiction over Multinational Enterprises," Waseda University Graduate School Law Review, No.110 and 111 (2004).

Evelyn Lim Meow Hoong (ACIS, MAICSA) was educated at the University of Malaya and she obtained her Bachelor of Jurisprudence (External) in 2001. She further obtained her Masters of Arts in International Development in 2005 from the Nagoya University. She has been an associate member of the Malaysian Institute of Chartered Secretaries and Administrators since 2005. She has worked in the commercial banking business for 2 years in remittance and trade finance departments (1991-1993); and in correspondent banking business for 5 years (1997-2002) where she specializes in advising on U.S. dollar trade financing and U.S. dollar funds transfers.

Jibitesh Mishra (mishrajibitesh@gmail.com) was educated at Utkal University, obtaining his master's degree in computer application (1991) and a PhD in computer science (2001). He worked for

About the Contributors

many universities in the capacity of IT faculty both in India and abroad. His research interests are fractal graphics, multimedia computing, Web engineering, and e-commerce. He is currently heading the Department of Information Technology in the constituent college of the Technical University of the State of Orissa in India.

Masashi Nakajima is a professor of the International School of Economics and Business Administration, Reitaku University. He has a long career at the Bank of Japan (BOJ). At the BOJ, he conducted a number of researches about payment systems and securities settlement systems (SSSs). On accumulation of the researches, he published two books (both in Japanese), namely *All about Payment Systems* (2000 and 2nd edition in 2005) and *All about SSSs* (2002). These two books cover wide-ranging payment systems issues and are highly regarded and widely read in business circles and academia. He also had working experience as a member of the Secretariat for the Committee on Payment and Settlement Systems (CPSS) of the Bank for International Settlements (BIS) in 2003-2005 and as director of the Research Department of the Center for Financial Industry Information Systems (FISC) in 1999-2001.

Takashi Nakazaki is an associate at Anderson Mori & Tomotsune (http://www.andersonmoritomotsune.com/en/lawyer/02/prof/0245.html), with broad experience in the areas of financial regulations, securities transactions, business dispute resolution, intellectual property (copyright law), and cyber law. More specifically, Mr. Nakazaki has experience concerning disputes over various technologies including cross-border online transactions, real estate online auctions, electronic banking, digital currency, computer software for medical devices, genetic engineering, open source software, and file sharing software. He has also been involved with a wide range of matters dealing with the liquidation of real estate and bonds. Nakazaki earned a Bachelor of Laws degree from Tokyo University, Faculty of Law in 1998 and was admitted to practice in Japan.

Pauline C. Reich is an American lawyer and a professor at Waseda University School of Law. During her sabbatical year (2000-2001), she was a visiting scholar conducting research on cyberlaw, e-commerce, and use of the Internet for legal research at Boalt Hall School of Law at the University of California, Berkeley, Santa Clara University School of Law, the Australasian Legal Research Institute (AUSTLII), a joint program of the University of New South Wales Law Faculty and the University of Technology Sydney Law Faculty, and the International Labor Organization (ILO) International Labor Institute in Geneva, Switzerland. In addition, she visited the University of Haifa Law Faculty and cyberlawyers in Israel and attended cyberlaw and e-commerce courses at Stanford Law School. During the same period, she participated in an online conference at the United Nations Headquarters in Geneva to a workshop in Tokyo for participants from developing countries throughout Asia, on the topic of the Legal Infrastructure of the Internet for the purpose of policy planning.

Naoshi Takasugi was educated at the Osaka University Graduate School of Law, from which he obtained a Master of Law degree (1989). He is currently a professor of law at Doshisha University in Kyoto, Japan, where he teaches private international law, international business law, and international civil procedure law. He is in a position of an expert mediator appointed by the court as well as a council board member of some academies including the Academy for International Business Transactions and the Japanese Association of International Economic Law.

Motoaki Tazawa is a Japanese lawyer and a professor of law at Meijo University, teaching company law, financial & securities law, and international business law. He worked for the Bank of Tokyo and the Bank of Japan as a legal expert, and obtained a LLB from Tokyo University, MBA, LLM, and PhD degrees from Tsukuba University. During his sabbatical two years, he was a visiting scholar conducting research on e-finance and securities regulation at Harvard Law School and Institute for Advanced Legal Studies of University of London.

Biswajit Tripathy (biswajit69@gmail.com) was educated in at Utkal University, obtaining a BTech (1991) and an MTech at FM University (2007). He is currently working as faculty in the Dept. of Computer Science and Engineering, Synergy Institute of Engineering & Technology, Dhenkanal, 759 001(India). He has a total of 15 years experience both in software industries and teaching, in the field of computer science. His areas of interest are software engineering, e-commerce, and network security.

Shino Uenuma obtained a Bachelor of Law degree at the University of Tokyo (1991) and a LLM at Washington University in St. Louis (2004). She was admitted to practice law in Japan (1997) and in New York State (2006). She did her internship at Perkins Coie in Seattle (2004), the Federal Trade Commission, and the Council of the Better Business Bureau (2005). She is currently working at South Toranomon Law Offices, and her main practice fields are intellectual property, IT, international business law, and children's right.

Masao Yanaga is a professor of law and accounting and head of the business law course of the Graduate School of Business Sciences, University of Tsukuba. He is a member of the Business Accounting Deliberation Council, the Financial Services Agency/ Small and Medium Enterprise Policy Council, the Small and Medium Enterprise Agency/ Financial System Council, the Financial Services Agency, and was a member of the Company Law Modernization Subcommittee, Legislative Council, Ministry of Justice/Advisory Committee on Energy and Natural Resources, Natural Resources and Energy Agency. He is a non-voting member of the Science Council of Japan as well. He has written more than 400 articles and notes, 50 contributions to books, and 20 books, including *Legal Aspect of Fair Value Accounting* (Nihon Hyoronsha, 1996), *Legal Aspect of Accounting for Derivatives* (Chuo Keizaisha, 1998), *Limiting Auditors' Civil Liability* (Yuhikaku, 2000) and *Auditors' Independence in Appearance* (Shoji Homu, 2002), as well as *Commentaries on Enforcement Regulation for Company Law and Company Account Regulation* (Shoji Homu, 2006 and 2007).

Index

A

alternative trading system (ATS) 67

B

B2B transactions 240
  self-governance of business society 243
B2C transactions 244
  consumer protection 246
bank for international settlements (BIS) 109
Basel II 39
botnets 15

C

commodity based digital currency (CBDC) 169
  legal concept of money 169
  supervisory and regulatory control 173
computer crime 2
cross-border e-commerce markets 210–226
  consumer protection 210–226
    key to facilitating it 217–220
  court jurisdiction
    application of economic law 260
    European Union 257
    Japan 259
    United States 257
  current conditions in e-commerce market 211
  dispute resolution systems 212
  problems among private sectors 215
  problems among public sectors 216
cross-border e-commere markets
  court jurisdiction 255
cybercrime 2–33
  council of Europe convention on 6
  financial institutions affected 7
  forms of 13
    identity theft 13
    phishing 13
  law enforcement needs 17
  surveys assessing the extent of 3–5
cyber risk management 40
  five step framework 42–47
cybersecurity 2–33
  surveys assessing the extent of 3–5

D

designated-time net settlement (DTNS) system 112
digital
  currency 168–181
  signature 230
    nature of 231

E

e-crime 2
e-money, e-payments 12
electronic
  communications network (ECN) 67
  contracts 228
    Indian IT Act of 2000 232
  money 144
    definition 145
    existing regulations on 147–154
    its classification 146
  signature 230
enterprise risk management
  ERM framework 38
evolution of enterprise risk management 37

G

global card payments 128–141
  jurisdiction, privacy, and data protection in 133–138
  participants and technology 130
global electronic currencies (GEC) 170

H

hybrid system 114
  examples of 114
  situation in Japan 115

I

integrated system 115
  large value transfer system (LVTS) 115
  Paris integrated system (PIS) in France 116
international business online 195–209
  dealing with disputes 202
    alternative dispute resolution (ADR) 202
    online dispute resolution (ODR) 202
  problems inhibiting online transactions 196
    building trust 196
  reducing the risk during the exchange 198
    payment risks 200
  small and medium enterprises 195–209
Internet crime 2

K

keylogging software 14

M

mistakes in remittance to account viii–x, 182–194
  doctrine 185
  former lower courts decisions 184
  reasoning 184

N

next-generation RTGS (RTGS-XG) project 117
  and the global trend 121
  benefits 122
  implementation timetable 120

O

on-line securities firms 9

P

payment systems vi–x, 88–108
price discovery and execution 72
privacy issues 17
proprietary trading system (PTS) 67–87
  definition of 71
  guidelines for 74
  prospects of 79

R

real-time gross settlement (RTGS) system 112
  adoption of 113
  in Germany 116
  merits 112

S

securities settlement systems vi–x, 88–108
  cross-border risk 96
  desirable securities systems analysis 98
  examination of risks and legal issues 89
    in England 90
      funds systems 92
      securities systems 92
    in Japan 90
      funds systems 93
      securities systems 93
separation policy of banking and commerce 53–66
  banks entering into commerce 58
  comparison of the U.S. and Japan 61
  in Japan 56

Index

    current law 57
  international trends 62
  in the U.S. 55
    regulators' concerns 56

T

trojan horses 15